Technological Innovation in Retail Finance

Routledge International Studies in Business History

Series editors: Ray Stokes and Matthias Kipping

Technological Innovation in Retail Finance

International Historical Perspectives

Edited by
Bernardo Bátiz-Lazo,
J. Carles Maixé-Altés
and Paul Thomes

Routledge
Taylor & Francis Group
New York London

First published 2011
by Routledge
711 Third Avenue, New York, NY 10017

Simultaneously published in the UK
by Routledge
2 Park Square, Milton Park, Abingdon, Oxon OX14 4RN

Routledge is an imprint of the Taylor & Francis Group, an informa business

First printed in paperback 2012

Typeset in Sabon by IBT Global.

Library of Congress Cataloging-in-Publication Data
Technological innovation in retail finance : international historical perspectives / edited
by Bernardo Bátiz-Lazo, J. Carles Maixé-Altés, and Paul Thomes.
    p. cm. — (Routledge international studies in business history ; 20)
    Includes bibliographical references and index.
    1. Banks and banking—Technological innovations—Europe.   2. Banks and banking—
Technological innovations—United States.   3. Banks and banking—Technological
innovations—North America.   4. Financial services industry—Technological innovations—
Europe.   5. Financial services industry—Technological innovations—United States.
6. Financial services industry—Technological innovations—North America.   I. Batiz-Lazo,
Bernardo.   II. Maixé Altés, Joan Carles.   III. Thomes, Paul.
    HG2974.T433 2011
    332.1094—dc22
    2010019693

ISBN13: 978-0-415-88067-1 (hbk)
ISBN13: 978-0-203-83942-3 (ebk)
ISBN13: 978-0-415-65436-4 (pbk)

Contents

PART V
Wrapping Up and Grand Conclusion

Figures

Tables

Acknowledgements

We would like to thank the generosity of RWTH Aachen University, Institut d'études politiques de Bordeaux together with GRETHA research centre at Bordeaux University, and the University of Leicester School of Management for sponsoring our meetings. We also appreciate the support and encouragement of Matthias Kipping and Ray Stokes as editors of the series and Stacy Noto and Laura Stearns at Routledge in helping to bring the manuscript to light.

In addition, Ian Martin would like to thank all the interviewees who kindly invited him into their homes and gave up their time to share their memories. His thanks also to all the archivists who provided a warm welcome and expert assistance; in particular, Nicholas Webb and Maria Sienkiewicz at Barclays Group Archives.

Joakim Appelquist would like to acknowledge valuable comments provided by the participants in the Workshop on IT in Shaping Work Processes and Organizations at Copenhagen Business School (June 2009), and in the session on Automation and Mechanization of Financial Services at the XVth World Economic History Congress (August 2009, Utrecht).

Gustavo del Angel would like to thank Rubén Aguilar Monteverde and Agustín Legorreta Chauvet for all the long and pleasant conversations on banking. Bernardo Bátiz-Lazo's wisdom was priceless to develop this research. José Antonio Bátiz-Vazquez provided useful insights to the archival sources. Joan Carles Maixé-Altés's, Alan Booth's, and Paul Thomes's comments on his chapter were very valuable.

Alan Booth and Mark Billings thank Nigel Hardman of Alliance and Leicester plc (now part of Grupo Santander) for his assistance with Giro's records and for his insights into its history, and the archivists at the Royal Mail Archive for enormous help, including making available uncatalogued material. In addition Alan would like to thank the British Academy for support in undertaking research for his project, the (then) Arts and Humanities Research Board for financing, and the University of Exeter for granting study leave.

Martha Poon wishes to express acknowledgements to Steven Epstein, Philip Scranton, Josh Witford, Brian Rajski, Zsuzanna Vargha, and the editors for their thoughtful assistance in the preparation of this chapter. The research reported here was supported by the National Science Foundation (SES-0451139). This chapter was drafted while in residence at the Hagley Museum and Library (Wilmington, Delaware) on a summer grant-in-aid.

David Stearns would like to thank all those who graciously gave of their time to educate him on the Visa payment system, especially Tom Cleveland, Walt Conway, Win Derman, Frank Fojtik, Scott Harrison, Tom Honey, Roger Peirce, Bill Powar, Chuck Russell, Ron Schmidt, and B. Ray Traweek. Special thanks must also be extended to Ingrid Kollmann, the coordinator of Visa's unofficial alumni network, who connected him with many of the key participants.

Juan Pablo-Pardo Guerra would like to thank Bernardo Bátiz-Lazo and J. Carles Maixé-Altés for their comments and suggestions on previous versions of his chapter. His project was supported by the CONACYT Postgraduate Fellowship number 192297.

Part I
Introduction

1 In Digital We Trust

The Computerization of Retail Finance in Western Europe and North America

Bernardo Bátiz-Lazo, J. Carles Maixé-Altés, and Paul Thomes

THE MAKING OF THE DIGITAL BANK

This volume offers a new and original approach to the study of technological change in retail finance. It offers a massive research base reflecting
not only the breadth of contributor interests, but also a unity of purpose
that comes from several workshops and comments on each other's work.
The contribution of this volume is particularly novel in that no comparable
titles investigate how computers have transformed the internal workings
of financial service organizations in different competitive environments.
Indeed, much has been said about the effects of computer technology in
banking and other financial services but with the exception of contemporary case studies for the UK, documented by Fincham et al. (1994) and the
longitudinal Anglo–U.S. comparison study by Booth (2007), the current
'state of the art' in the study of the computerization of financial services
from an historical perspective is overwhelmingly focused on developments
in the U.S.: the path-breaking studies of Chandler (2001) and Chandler
and Cortada (2000) are of a general nature and do not offer case studies
of individual organizations. Yates (2005) investigates the insurance market
and Cortada (2006) offers evidence on information and telecommunication
technologies (ICT) in retail banking.

Whereas the majority of contributions to this volume reflect European
experience, other countries are not neglected. Hence, contributions to this
book confirm the need to consider the histories of computer use within
the broader contexts of nations, industries, and societies (e.g. Yates 1989,
2005). This as early computers were purchased, configured, and applied not
by isolated individuals but by large organizations. But every country has its
own story of computer use and adoption as it cannot be assumed that adoption of similar hardware in two nations implies that both countries would
make similar use of computer technology or experience equivalent results.

Without a doubt, the continuity in the evolution of ICT infrastructure
noted by Chandler and Cortada (2000: 263) populates the competitive

environments of North America and highly industrialized European nations. Indeed, there is evidence of networks of innovation spreading across the Atlantic dating to early modern capitalism (e.g. Meyer 2006) whereas, more recently, there was intense exchange of ideas around the introduction of computer technology between U.S. and British financial intermediaries (see further Bátiz-Lazo and Wardley 2007). However, we cannot brush aside other competitive environments, although marginal to the construction of that continuity, where individual organizations were also successful in assimilating new technology to, first, speed up internal operations and, second, reconstruct and intensify the flow of information within and across organizations. Considering organizational characteristics and sources of competitive success of the firms populating both the inside and outside of the construction of Chandler and Cortada's continuity, the research documented in this book offers to enhance our understanding of the links between technological change and competitive advantage while avoiding the rationalization of success often associated with a 'Whig' interpretation of history.

Our proposal overcomes the usual bias towards the so-called 'Atlantic continuity' in the understanding of technological change related to applications of ICT by offering a number of sources of distinctiveness, namely:

- It documents developments in the U.S. side by side with stand-alone and comparative case studies from different parts of the world, specifically Mexico and Europe (Britain, France, Germany, the Netherlands, Spain, and Sweden).
- It addresses the variety of financial institutions that populated the markets for retail finance.
- It envisions technological change in banking as a long-term process of evolution, with the changes resulting from the two world wars acting as accelerators to that process.
- It articulates an interdisciplinary approach to the study of technological change in banking.
- It develops recurrent themes. These emerged as authors debated their ideas at length in four forums convened specifically for that purpose (namely, Aachen in 2007, Bordeaux in 2008, and Leicester and Utrecht in 2009).

In this edited volume we highlight the relative importance of European actors in the globalization of technological change by comparing cases in different competitive environments. Specifically, the UK (Bátiz-Lazo and Maixé-Altés; Booth and Billings; Martin; Pardo-Guerra); France (Bonin); Germany (Thomes); the Netherlands (Mooij); Spain (Bátiz-Lazo and Maixé-Altés); and Sweden (Appelquist). Developments in Europe sit side by side with those in Mexico (del Angel) and the U.S. (Poon; Stearns).

In many countries the commercial or clearing bank was traditionally the organizational form with the largest share of the market for retail deposits. It was also common that the latter had a monopoly in managing payment systems. The combination of regulatory change and technological innovation during the 1980s resulted in the geographic, product market, and customer group diversification of participants in retail banking (see, among others, Ballarín 1985; Bátiz-Lazo and Wood 1999; Canals 1997; Hoschka 1993). Diversification effectively meant that a large number of intermediaries accepting low-value, high-volume deposits increased the services offered to individuals, households, and small and medium-sized enterprises (SME). However, throughout the 1980s and 1990s, deposit-taking remained the most important factor in maintaining an established customer base in retail banking (Bátiz-Lazo and Wood 2003; Gardener and Molyneux 1990: 93; Walter 1997). Moreover, it is possible to speculate that in the absence of ICT applications, financial intermediaries would offer a limited range of services whereas the intensity of competition in retail banking would be quite different.

But however important ICT applications have been to the delivery of competitive and organizational change in banking, systematic studies which have examined the specific role of ICT in shaping business practices and organizations have been few and far between. Surprisingly, detailed documentation and analysis of the role of automation and information processes within financial intermediaries as well as the role of bankers in shaping technology has been largely neglected. This edited volume directly addresses the processes of mechanization and computerization of retail banks throughout the twentieth century (Bonin; Martin; Appelquist; del Angel; Thomes) while articulating an international comparison.

We reject the view that considers commercial/clearing banks the only organizational form worth studying. This is because before and after regulatory change, in many nations the retail financial market was populated by, among others, savings banks (Thomes; Bátiz-Lazo and Maixé-Altés), mutual banks (Mooij), State-owned banks (Booth and Billings). All these competed directly with clearing/commercial banks in the market for low-value, high-volume deposits and sat side by side with a host of non-banking intermediaries (Stearns; Pardo-Guerra) as well as suppliers of industry-specific hardware and software (Poon). However, these other financial intermediaries often had a less diversified portfolio and/or focused on different market segments than commercial banks.

Other common characteristics of this edited volume are noting retail financial intermediaries' response to regulatory change and new technology and their common assumption of a rather deterministic nature of technological change in banking. On the whole, this assumption is often expressed in the form of new technology having been developed independently of the strategies of financial intermediaries. However, there is increasing evidence to the contrary in the form of systematic studies documenting episodes throughout the twentieth century in which financial intermediaries were not just reacting but actively shaping the development of general purpose and industry-specific applications (Bátiz-Lazo and Reid 2010; Campbell-Kelly 1992, 1998; McKenney and Fisher 1993; McKenney 1995; McKenney, Mason, and Copeland 1997; Yates 2005).

We therefore reject ideas which are synonymous to disruptive innovation. We articulate the process of evolution, first, by mapping the introduction of mechanical, electromechanical, and digital (including computer) technologies. Second, we identify the aspirations and realities of technological change in retail finance. A wide range of actors lived within and outside the participant organizational forms mentioned earlier (such as managers, operations and methods, accountants in financial intermediaries, engineers at manufacturers, politicians, and regulators). These actors and clusters contributed to the shaping of new applications. The intensity of their involvement varied through time but so did individuals' and individual cluster's expectations of what new technology could deliver. These aspirations were shaped by a process of trial and error associated with greater use and familiarity with new applications as well as changes in the wider environment and in the strategic priorities of individuals and clusters.

This book documents detailed evidence that financial intermediaries were significant actors in the design, use, and diffusion of new technology. We explore the business, economic, and social dimensions of technological change within participants of retail financial markets offering a long-term view of the process that led to the adoption of computers and computer applications. We thereby demonstrate how these processes had a major role in the shaping and developing of administrative processes, procedures, and organizational capabilities in banking organizations. We show when and how technological change altered the competitive intensity in the markets for retail finance. As a result, we are uniquely positioned to evaluate the scope and consequences of these phenomena in an international context.

We achieve all these results by:

- discussing the diffusion of mechanical and digital technology across different organizational forms that populate retail financial services (namely, commercial/clearing banks, savings banks, co-operative banks, and postal banks)
- comparing developments in the same organizational form across different competitive environments
- analysing the interaction of financial services organizations and manufacturers of ICT in the creation, use, and diffusion of new hardware (e.g. tabulators, mechanical accounting machines, automated teller machines, mainframe computers, credit cards, and point-of-sale terminals) as well as software applications (e.g. the creation and use of credit scoring algorithms)

- querying the impact of mechanical, electromechanical, and computer applications on the management of banks, non-banks, non-financial intermediaries, and their interactions with retail customers
- critically exploring the sometimes complex relationship between globalization, national goals for the development of strategic industries, technological innovation (particularly computer applications), and the development of internal management control systems

Addressing these themes draws out issues regarding the relative importance of institutional setting, staff, and gender; the process of technological innovation and change; the use of general purpose technology to reduce scale disadvantages and contest bank markets; the supply of capital as a differential factor on the extent and pace of mechanization and computerization; the reshaping of existing processes, procedures, and control systems (with particular attention to the accounting function); division of labour; and the role of the State.

Accordingly and given the variable intensity of technological change in the retail financial sector, some contributions focus on individual organizations, others on changes in the competitive process, and others at the collaboration between several organizations. Some cases provide an overview over an extended period of time whereas others are interested in specific activities taking place in a rather narrow time-span.

Although the majority of contributions fall under the umbrella of business history, this approach is not exclusive. Contributions and contributors embody different branches of learning and specifically economic history, the history of technology, the sociology of finance, and economic geography. Different analytical approaches sit side by side in a respectful dialogue around the central theme.

To conclude, the scarcity of contributions on the theme of innovation in financial services and the fact that we offer an international comparative study suggests that this research monograph proposes a new area of study. This novelty is not solely thematic. The contributions in this co-authored volume build upon questions and multiple source material usually expected in business history (e.g. surviving company documents, contemporary publications, oral histories, official reports, trade journals, etc.). But at the same time, we extend the range of questions and materials that have dominated other studies of this type as reflected in accommodating studies from other research traditions as well as the use of alternative sources such as interpreting political memoirs, design blueprints, images, and many others. As a result we offer a solid research base, consistent academic quality across the breadth of contribution interests, and unity of purpose. The publication of these contributions under a single title offers innovative scholarship, thematic unity, organization, and a debate that runs across chapters.

THE COMPUTERIZATION OF RETAIL FINANCE
IN WESTERN EUROPE AND NORTH AMERICA

Considering the effects of technological change in diverse organizational forms in multiple banking systems is the backbone of this edited volume. This diversity is reflected in the three-part structure of the book, representing what we consider the most significant organizational forms active in retail bank markets across nations, namely, commercial/clearing banks, other deposit-taking institutions, and non-financial intermediaries.

Part II is entitled "Digitalizing Commercial Banks". Hubert Bonin begins with Chapter 2. Evidence from French banks is the basis to argue that much of the recent work done by industrial economists on the history of the banking establishment is mostly limited to the last three decades of the twentieth century and leaves much to be desired regarding the process by which these heavy-footed, staid banks turned into the sleek "firms" of today. To fill this lacuna, Bonin believes, we need to delve into what may be called a "prehistory" of the banking establishment and its managerial practices. We will examine how the banking establishment grew from being a rather informal structure, which used administrative tools and accounting practices dating back to the fifteenth through the eighteenth centuries, to the highly "organized" edifice we see today. "Streamlining" was the keyword which instigated and determined this progression towards an entirely new type of service economy—from being "informal", if not downright "disorganized", to very much "formalized" and "streamlined". The entire process was kick-started when banks suddenly realized that they could no longer keep track of the extent of the risks they were running. The identifying, understanding, and coming to terms with this became the cornerstone of their business. It made for the rapid adoption of "industrial" methods and the establishment of a true "service organization". The introduction of mechanical accounting machines formed only part of the entire streamlining process.

Chapter 3 is by Ian Martin, who looks at the first British computer centre. In this chapter he traces the life of this building starting with its official opening on 4 July 1961 and ending with its protracted closure a decade later. From its initial status as the most advanced bank bookkeeping system in the world serving as a highly visible symbol of the bank's technological power, to a final repurposing of its grandiose reception as a distribution point for pre- and post-decimalisation output, the building's various meanings are revealed. Making use of written, oral, and visual sources, Martin explores the centre's spatial characteristics, its relation to the distributed structure of the branch, and its place as a first dedicated working home for a newly emerging computing subculture. A blend of multiple perspectives internally from the top down and bottom up, and externally from customer and competitor, provide a detailed analysis that uncovers the part played by the first computer centre in the British banking automation race.

In Chapter 4, Joakim Appelquist investigates the relation between the implementation of ICT applications and organizational change in the Swedish banking industry from 1975 to 2003. The analytical framework focuses on the complementary nature between major trends in the organization of work and general developments in computer technology during the last forty years. To structure the analysis, a deskilling/reskilling hypothesis is formulated and discussed. The analysis identifies three techno-organizational stages and refutes the hypothesis as the level of skills of employees in Sweden continues to increase during the entire period of study. This is a result of a combination of technical investments, strategy decisions, and labour relations.

In Chapter 5, Gustavo del Angel documents the computerization of commercial banks and the building of an automated payments system in Mexico between 1965 and 1990. Adoption of computers in Mexican banking began in 1965, opening a route of continuous technological change in the industry. The central argument of this chapter is that computerization of retail operations and data processing responded to the massification of bank services and that this technological platform allowed building an automated payments system in that country. On the one hand, the massification of services (in particular savings and checking accounts and the introduction of credit cards) required computer applications that gave greater speed and precision to established procedures. On the other hand, the integration of different fragmented systems resulted in the creation of a national automated payments system towards the end of the period under study. The chapter also shows how computerization required redesigning various operational methods and how banks used adoption of computers as an emblem of modernization. However, it is unclear how the implementation of computer technology represented a strategy to reduce operational costs of banks. The chapter centres on the experiences of the two largest Mexican banks, Bancomer (today part of BBVA group) and Banamex (today part of Citigroup).

Chapter 6 is the first instalment of Part III, "Digitalizing State, Mutual, and Savings Banks". In this chapter Paul Thomes tackles the German savings banks. He investigates the development path of mechanization and digitalization which began around 1900. The analysis includes an outline of the German banking system. It embeds the case study of savings banks in their wider socio-economic and business as well as political contexts. It addresses commercial and technological issues. The two world wars played an important role for different reasons. The 1950s and 1960s saw the complete restructuring of individual organizations. This included the adoption of the most modern equipment—mostly of U.S. origin. Another important incentive for the computerization of savings banks was a need to respond to rising costs associated with servicing their large numbers of retail customers, shortages in the labour market, the introduction of cashless (direct to account) payments, as well as a private giro banking system in the early 1960s. Although "[n]obody had a master plan" (Cortada 2008), a specific German IT path in banking developed with the savings banks—as intermediaries of the 'common people'—spearheading the move to digitalization.

In Chapter 7, Bernardo Bátiz-Lazo and J. Carles Maixé-Altés dwell on organizational changes associated with the automation of non-bank financial intermediaries (namely, savings banks) in the UK while making a running comparison with developments in Spain. This international comparison helps to ascertain the evolution of the same organizational form in two distinct competitive environments. Changes in regulation and technological developments (particularly applications of information technology) are said to be responsible for enhancing the competitiveness of retail finance. Archival research on the evolution of savings banks helps to demonstrate how, prior to competitive changes taking place, participants in bank markets had to develop capabilities to compete. Moreover, they had to assess the response of collaborative agreements to opportunities opened by technological change (in particular to resolve apparent scale disadvantages to contest bank markets). Of particular interest are choices made between applications of computer technology to redefine the relation between head office and retail branches as well as between staff at retail branches and customers.

In Chapter 8, Alan Booth and Mark Billings investigate the early years of Britain's National Giro, which opened for business in 1968. The Giro's establishment and development is placed within the wider political, social, and economic context, addressing commercial and technological issues at a time when techno-nationalist and wider macro-management concerns were far stronger than at the present time. The Giro was established to operate a national payments system, making use of the post office branch network. It provided an alternative to the traditional cheque-clearing system operated by the major commercial banks, which British governments in the 1960s regarded as uncompetitive and inefficient hoarders of labour and constant threats to government attempts to control inflation. Booth and Billings add to the growing literature examining the role played by technology in financial institutions and extend existing scholarship by examining this unusual business organization: the Giro was established as a State-owned financial institution, rare in Britain, and it was designed to function from the outset on a computerized basis, a key element in the government's techno-nationalist stance (promoting Harold Wilson's "white heat of the scientific revolution"), which sought to nurture the British computer industry against U.S. competition.

In Chapter 9, Joke Mooij presents an overview of how mechanization and automation affected Rabobank's financial services in the period from 1945 to 2000. Rabobank is a broad financial services provider based on co-operative principles. Its roots lie in local co-operative farmers' credit banks, which were founded at the end of the nineteenth century, and in the two central banks of 1898. The co-operative organizational structure, whereby the autonomous local banks are members of the central organization, gives Rabobank a unique vitality and has distinguished it from other banks from the very beginning.

Chapter 10 opens up the fourth part of the book, "Socio-Historical Aspects of Digitalization". Here Juan Pablo Pardo-Guerra documents the technological history of the London Stock Exchange between c. 1955 and 1990. By exploring the development of the Stock Exchange's market information systems, this chapter presents a vivid case study of the introduction of digital technologies in financial institutions. In analysing the Stock Exchange's development efforts, this chapter addresses an important lesson on technological change in finance. In particular, it demonstrates that technological change was not the result of the passive use of digital technologies in increasing economic efficiencies. Rather, change resulted from a process of organizational learning and co-adaptation associated to the implementation, maintenance, and updating of market technologies in relation to pre-existing organizational imperatives that included providing equality of access to the membership of the Stock Exchange.

In Chapter 11 Martha Poon deals with the emergence of commercial credit scoring. The "scorecard" was introduced in the late 1950s through the commercial initiatives of Fair, Isaac and Company Incorporated. In its most general description, the scorecard is an algorithmic tool that allows credit managers to associate risk with individual consumers. What is remarkable is that the original techniques for credit scoring emerged out of a manual underwriting, prior to the utilization of computers and electronic infrastructures in business. The chapter shows how the early convergence of statistical approaches with manual practices demanded that order be put to raw materials through a series of physically demanding and materially intensive tasks. It suggests that to understand the innovation of risk management systems it is important to trace how risk management tools have grown, gradually, out of past managerial environments, through the intervention of external and often commercial actors.

David Stearns examines in detail the origins of the electronic payment systems known today as Visa in Chapter 12. Specifically, he describes how the system initially formed, how it became widely adopted, and how it transitioned from mostly paper-based to fully electronic processing. Along the way, he points out ways in which the technologies that make the system function were shaped by the system's social dynamics, and the ways in which those technologies then began to reshape those social relations in return.

In the final chapter Lars Heide compares conclusions and observations from the preceding chapters and suggests their implications for the study of ICT in business organizations. First, based upon the stories in the preceding chapters, he summarizes the role of financial intermediaries, regulation, and technology in the computerization of retail finance across Western

Europe and North America. He considers the computerization strategies applied and their impact on intermediaries and their customers. Second, he discusses how this narrative fits into the general bureaucratization of Western Europe and North America and addresses the impact of computerization of retail banking on other businesses. This section of the chapter is based upon published literature and major inspirations are JoAnne Yates and Robbie Guerriero Wilson. Third, he discusses the impact of the emergence of computerized mathematical models on financial intermediaries and their customers. Here the point of departure is Donald McKenzie, Trevor Pinch, and Richard Swedberg.

Finally, in what follows you will find that we have prepared notes and source citations for each chapter. These detail primary and secondary material. There is also a list of secondary references in the final part, which only includes published sources to facilitate locating full information.

Part II
Digitalizing Commercial Banks

2 From Prehistory to the History of Computers in Banking

Mechanization of Data Processing and Accounting Methods in French Banks, circa 1930–1950

Hubert Bonin

INTRODUCTION

Recent research by industrial economists on the history of banking is increasingly focused on the last three decades of the twentieth century. This body of work leaves much to be said regarding the process by which these heavy-footed, staid organizations turned into the "sleek" firms of today. To fill this lacuna, we need to delve into what may be called a "prehistory" of banking and its managerial practices. This chapter aims to assess how banks grew from being a rather informal structure which employed administrative tools and accounting practices dating back to the fifteenth through the eighteenth centuries, to the highly "organized" edifice we see today. "Streamlining" was the keyword which instigated and determined this progression towards an entirely new type of service economy—from being "informal", if not downright "disorganized", to very much "formalized" and "streamlined".

The process was kick-started when managers of banks realized that they could no longer keep track of the extent of the risks they were running. The requirements for identifying, understanding, and controlling what otherwise is the cornerstone of their business made for the rapid adoption of "industrial" methods and the establishment of a true "service organization".

The introduction of mechanical accounting machines formed only part of the entire streamlining process which swept over banks from the early 1920s to the late 1950s. Standardisation, elimination of duplicates, carbon copies and redundant services, setting up of control mechanisms, and the introduction of automation for writing and bookkeeping (Hodder 1934) were all used to usher a new era of "information technology" in the banking sector. This happened after a rather lengthy period of maturation in other geographies and sectors (e.g. Yates 2005). The growth of the volume of bills of exchange or of documentary credit forms, on one side, and the development of order forms and bookkeeping linked with private banking and operations on the Stock Exchange on the other side, converged with the development of accounting books within big banking organizations to fuel plans to rationalise data management and to introduce mechanization or proto-computing.

Growing union militancy and labour issues added to the travails of the bankers: a massive increase in the workforce (to 22,000 in 1929 at the leading deposit bank, Société générale), rising inflation, and labour demands swelled administrative expenses alarmingly. Labour strikes took place in the mid-1920s. These were initiated by female employees involved in manual processes at data processing units who demanded stable jobs instead of day-to-day paid auxiliary ones (Booth 2008; Lowe 1987; Wardley 2006).

What at the time seemed the best way of reducing the workforce was streamlining work processes while introducing automated machines (see also Appelquist in this volume). At the same time, just as in the industrial and public sectors, administrative and technical managers began to gain in importance. Although junior, middle, and senior managerial personnel assigned to "retail banking" remained preponderant, the balance of power gradually began to shift towards the people who managed the new "service organizations". These "new kids on the block" began to form influential networks and wield ever-greater power at the core of the big banking houses. They began their climb to power in the 1920s under the banner of modernization (see Appelquist in this volume for a similar process in Sweden). They continued to gain importance and stature during the struggle to shore up declining profits in the crisis years of the 1930s. The dust had hardly settled when they were given a further boost as top managers of banks turned to them in order to find solutions that would keep pace with the exponential growth of operations in the 1950s.

The story of mechanization and automating of accounting processes in banking also sheds light on the spread of technological innovations at the national as well as the European levels. Technological progress within the banking community thus affords pertinent insights into the forces and agents which progressed alongside theirs for the whole economy (Carmille 1938).

The first step was taken when several banking houses began a rapid process of mechanization in the 1920s and the subsequent installation of large accounting machines in the 1930s (for further details, see Bonin 2004). This had obvious repercussions on the reorganization of the "work space": these machines needed floor-space. According to need, banks acquired either small or medium-sized accommodation (sometimes even entire buildings) near their Paris headquarters. These dwellings housed tens, if not hundreds, of the new machines. Some of them, like the *Crédit commercial de France* (CCF), located the machines in cellars.

Meanwhile, another technological revolution was knocking at the gates, namely, the punched-card accounting machines. In their heydays during the 1940s and 1950s, they would dominate the work space like nothing else had done before them. They represented the apex of electromechanical technology and also heralded its demise, because improving their operation led to the dawn of the age of electronics and computerized management information systems. The main issue for this transformation was reducing data capture tasks relating to the transfer of basic information in paper documents (such as financial figures and account numbers), while at the same time, keeping reliable and standardised trails of data throughout the process. This allowed each step of the data capturing process (whether at the local branch, the regional or national specialised division at the head-quarters, the administrative centre, or computing centre) to be able to check data against originating documents and, later on, to transform this data into new information.

But the electromechanical machines did not surrender easily. Not without a proper shake-up of the system where the two technologies intersected. Once again the entire organization and work space (buildings as well as the geography) had to be reshuffled in accordance with the new data transmission networks created by this technological "revolution". Finally, a third stage followed with the advent of computers and our modern-day electronic equipment, which were pioneered in France by IBM and Bull in the 1950s and 1960s.

We intend, therefore, to establish bridges between the general history of technical innovation in banking and the building of firm organization, which gained momentum in the 1900s and accelerated during the interwar period. We shall insist on the precocity of some forms of "industrialization" of big services companies, and how "models" of practice were taught and transferred across Western Europe. A first section will gauge the need of rationalizing and reorganizing banking firms; a second one will tell about the move towards the mechanization of accounting tasks; a third one will analyse the organizational effects of the use of accounting machines; and the assessment of some kind of technological apex will be fourthly determined. We used printed documents, either banking magazines or firms' internal publications and adverts. Surviving documents in banks' archives were helpful to tell about their investments and modernization, within a global project of the history of banking organizations and firms. All these enabled us to deepen insights into the automation process of French banks, and to go beyond the mere social history of employees.[1]

---

1. For further details, see Bonin (1988). This text was presented at the first seminar on the history of information technology held at Grenoble. Since then, extensive studies (in collaboration with the *Conservatoire national des arts et métiers—centre Science, technologie & société*) have been carried on dealing with the evolution of information technology at the turn of the 1960s, for example, Mounier-Kühn (1989). Béatrice Touchelay has dealt with accounting and computing in state organizations in Touchelay (2005, 2008a, 2008b) and Touchelay and Verheyde (2009). Meanwhile, the history of commercial data processing in the years 1920–1960 has been ably dealt with by Heide (2004, 1994).

THE PREHISTORY OF COMPUTING IN BANKS

The second modern banking revolution took place between the 1850s and the 1960s. It was characterised by a change in the scale of banking activities. The expansion of banking firms reached a ceiling with the saturation of its administrative organization to process millions of paper-based transaction documents such as bills, slips, and cheques. Managers began to discuss the way to tackle such an issue: rapidly, experiences were shared on a European scale, which contributed to the comparison of the equipment conceived by new firms specializing in managing data processing systems. As in every "revolution", the demand by users of systems and machines was met by solutions supplied by engineers.

The European Community Experience in Mechanical Engineering

During the course of World War I there emerged a European, or rather, due to the strong presence in Europe of U.S.-based companies such as Remington Rand[2] and IBM,[3] a transatlantic technological community. These companies quickly established commercial survey networks. However, the adoption of innovative technologies was more due to a pan-European network of specialists actively involved in the banking sector. These reorganizers, or "streamliners", met regularly at conferences and meetings in which information flowed freely. The advertisements issued by the machine manufacturers demonstrated the innovations: these specialists could then discuss among themselves the best ways of incorporating the new machines into their organizations and the changes to be implemented in the work process. In fact, mechanization by itself would hardly have worked had it not been accompanied and supported by a reorganization of data processing methods, a streamlining of the data flow, and a standardisation in the presenta-

---

2. Remington Typewriter (established in 1876) fused with the Rand Kardex group in 1927. The Rank Kardex group was itself created in 1925 when the Rand Ledger Company (established in 1876) fused with the American Kardex Company (established in 1915), which specialised in loose-leaf ledgers. Remington Rand then bought over other companies such as the Dalton Adding Machine Calculators (established in 1902) and the Powers Accounting & Tabulation Machines Company of New York (established in 1913) to form a conglomerate, which then became large enough to challenge IBM and its European sister concerns. See Cortada (1993).

3. Computing Tabulating Recording, created in 1911 by the merger of several firms, became IBM in 1924, after having devised a tabulating and printing machine which competed against the Powers models (Belden and Beldena 1962). Since 1922 in Germany, IBM used its sister company, *Deutsche Hollerith Maschinen Gesellschaft mit begrentser Haftung* or Dehomag. The process began with the inventions of Herman Hollerith, who built the first punched-card statistical machine in 1884; he then went on to launch the Tabulating Machine Company in 1896 (Austrian 1982).

tion of such data. The vocabulary used in manufacturing (and introduced by Taylorisation, Fordism, and the streamlining of the work process movement) found an echo in the banking world, just as it did throughout the service sector and amongst accounting professionals.

It appears that these new technologies were initially implemented in Germany. Their development was favoured by the quality of precision engineering attained in that country as well as the size of its banking market (see further Thomes in this volume). Office automation spread in Germany either by means of a technology transfer from the U.S. or as a result of local innovations. Thus, Powers machines made major inroads into German banks (*Diskonto, Dresdner-,* and *ReichsBank*) in the 1920s, while Bull cornered the market in Darmstädter. These enterprises gained a large body of experience which then proved to be a rich breeding ground for their European colleagues. There was, for example, in the late 1920s the publication of *La « rationalisation » des banques en Allemagne* (*The "Streamlining" of German Banks*) by Montréer (1928) and a lecture, in Paris, by Rambow (1930), a director of *Dresdner Bank*. This lecture was accompanied by the projection of a documentary film on the mechanized services of this German bank and, during 1930, was also screened at Nancy, Lille, Lyons, and Marseille. Thus, during 1930, the secret functioning of this range of calculating machines was revealed throughout the four corners of France.[4]

French managers, in turn, increased the number of visits abroad in order to evaluate the possibilities offered by streamlining and mechanization. Thus, in May 1923, two executives of CCF made a trip to *Rotterdamsche Bankvereiniging* in Amsterdam:

> in order to better acquaint themselves with the new systems which had been implemented in its accounting division and which consisted of a large number of ingenious machines which could handle large numbers of book-keeping vouchers and even correspondence with great rapidity. This system allowed it to reduce the number of its employees by a third, from 1,500 to 1,000, even though the workload had increased a little. At the same time, accounting errors, which stood at 1.5 per cent to 2 per cent in the old system, fell to 1 per cent.[5]

Numerous foreign visits were sponsored by the Bankers' Association (*Union syndicale des banquiers*). The first took place in October 1930, with a visit to two banks: *Banque de Bruxelles* on the ninth and *Dresdner Bank* in Berlin on the tenth. A second trip was made between 12 and 17 October 1931 with a visit to Brussels (*Banque de Bruxelles, Société générale de Belgique,* and *Caisse générale de reports et de dépôts*), and then on to Amsterdam (*Nederlandsche Handel* and *Incasso-Bank*) before

---

4. *Banque* journal, December 1930, p. 853.
5. Record of proceedings of board of directors of CCF, 25 May 1923.

a final stop was made to banks in London (Midland Bank and Westminster Foreign Bank). Thus, during the 1920s and 1930s, a whole network of technological innovators and streamliners sprang up across Europe and helped form a body of "bank engineers".

The Rise of the French Streamliners

The contacts formed throughout the rest of Europe and the work of manufacturers of machinery stimulated Parisian bankers. An automation committee was formed within the Permanent Committee on Banking Organization which led bankers into discussing the management of operating costs. Regular discussions were held regarding technological progress and the practicability of new techniques. This facilitated the transfer of new technologies and the sharing of the lessons learned from the first trials in reorganization and mechanization. Alfred Pose, a director of *Sogénal*, a bank in Alsace which was the subsidiary of *Société générale* in Strasbourg, became one of the French specialists of the scientific organization of work in banks and was one of the promoters of the ideas of Henri Fayol, an engineer with novel ideas regarding the reorganization of business. The scientific organization of work fever, though, had caught on almost everywhere and encouraged specialists to envisage ever more efficient ways of reorganizing the service sector. Such specialists, like Marius Dujardin, who began with the shares service in *Crédit lyonnais* in the 1920s, were pioneers. Similarly, in January 1927, *Société générale* recruited Joseph Boyé, an "in-house engineer" who, up until June 1934, was put in charge of "mechanical and electrical installations in the central buildings" and who oversaw the implementation of the machines.[6]

In a more general fashion, the magazine *Banque*, whose editor was close to the big Paris banks, turned into an instrument for the popularisation of techniques dealing with the streamlining and mechanization of banking between 1928 and 1931. "Streamlining specialists", who conducted courses in special schools oriented towards the training of employees who wanted to climb the corporate ladder, also contributed and shared their experiences within *Banque*'s pages (Pineau 1928; Berthau 1928).[7] The review's director and editor-in-chief even went on a series of lectures throughout the country: through December 1928 to January 1929 he spoke in thirteen towns on "streamlining and banks" to underline the importance and usefulness of "calculating and accounting machines", which, in those days, consisted of punching and tabulating machines and sorters. *Banque* also organized a significant event under the heading "Bank and Stock-Exchange Week", which brought together bank officials, technicians, and streamlining specialists under the aegis of a "Banking Organization Congress". This was held for the first time in September 1928, with a second congress following in October 1929.

6. The company's automation service was launched in 1931.
7. Pineau was general controller of Renauld, a bank.

At these first two congresses, the mechanization and reorganization of banks became a central theme, with the presentation of numerous case studies, three lectures on the German, Belgian, and American experiences, and numerous presentations. The third congress, in October 1930, was marked by the participation of many big banking houses (*Banque de France, Comptoir national d'escompte de Paris, Banque nationale de crédit, Banque de l'union parisienne*). The fifth congress, held in 1932, was divided into two parts: after a conference in Paris on 22 and 23 October, with a "[s]alon of new accounting machines and organisational material", the participants travelled to a centre of such innovations, Mulhouse in Alsace, where they visited a major branch of the Sogénal.[8] Throughout the first half of the 1930s, the monthly *Banque* journal continued its efforts to encourage the mechanization and streamlining of the banking system (Géry 1932) and, as in the Anglo-Saxon countries, even published or godfathered a series of books on this technical subject, which collected its articles and inquiries within the very divisions of banks dedicated to mechanization, rationalization, and "reorganization".

Ads and Technical Culture: The Dispatching of the U.S. Model

Adverts published in technical journals, business magazines (for instance, *L'Organisation*),[9] and industry publications (mainly Banque) help to understand how French managers could have been convinced to adopt the "U.S. model" of data processing. This was the case in automotive manufacturing, the pioneering breakthroughs achieved by U.S. scientists and engineers (Medwick and Mahoney 1988). Moreover the "advance" of U.S. firms in "business machines" (typing or data processing; see Wootton and Kemmerer 2007) encouraged a competitive spirit among French bankers who were prone to foster such equipment to face the growth of their administrative organization. It is important to remember that as was the case for U.S. companies such as DuPont and General Motors, by this point in time several French banks had become "big (service) business" too.

Marketing campaigns strengthened the brand image of U.S. companies and also cemented the legitimacy of the managers who had to convince the direction of the usefulness of such costly investments (see further Appelquist in this volume). Adverts and pre-marketing campaigns insisted not only on the technical nature of individual devices, but also on the very fact that they contributed directly to solving a key issue, that is, how to send customers account documents regularly while keeping them accurate and up to date. The internal life of banking organizations was thus not solely at

---

8. "Report of the *Congrès d'organisation bancaire*, 27 October 1932", *Banque*, December 1932, 843–55.

9. CNOF, *Revue mensuelle de l'organisation*, 1927–1968.

stake: bankers' relationship with clients was involved (see further Poon and Stearns in this volume; Bátiz-Lazo 2009; Bátiz-Lazo and Wood 2002).

Globally the technical revolution of the accounting and bookkeeping electromechanization resulted from a combination of internal demands for rationalization and cost savings (which were met by consultants in services and suppliers in technology); from the influence of foreign actors (i.e. U.S. and Belgo-German influences); and through annual connections within the banking community of interests and permanent transfers of "models" (see further Bátiz-Lazo and Maixé-Altés in this volume). No strict "national" approaches prevailed, processes of imitation and transfer were completed, and an interaction between local and international "progress" fostered momentum, all of which caused the banking professional journals to promote technical "modernity" in the name of "rationalization".

THE COMING OF AGE OF A STREAMLINED AND AUTOMATED BANKING SYSTEM (FROM THE SECOND HALF OF THE 1930S TO THE YEARS 1940–1950)

Whereas accounting machines and streamlined filing systems began to appear as early as the 1920s, the entire movement was given an added fillip by the introduction of the electronic accounting machine. The slump in revenue caused by the economic crisis of the 1930s helped to reinvigorate the streamlining process that had begun in the post-war years (Omnès 2003) and greatly helped in cutting costs both at the centre and at the network of retail bank branches in the periphery. Moreover, the tendency towards centralization caused by the crash that took place in the first half of the 1930s also contributed to this process of standardization and streamlining—especially within the stronger banking houses which had a greater capacity for self-finance (Bonin 2000): *Banque nationale pour le commerce et l'industrie* (BNCI) took over several mid-size to medium-large regional banks, *Crédit du Nord* absorbed the large *Banque générale du Nord*, and the *Crédit industriel & commercial* (CIC) group increased the number of its regional banks. When CCF took over the massive *Banque de Mulhouse* in 1929, it started a process of rationalization and of introduction:

> We have sent Pajot, the chief accountant at our Lafayette branch [the largest of the group, at Paris] to study the accounting system at the Mulhouse branch so that we can have the daily situational reports and monthly evaluations, just as we do with the other branches of our bank.[10]

---

10. Minutes of the meeting of CCF's board of directors held on 7 March 1929.

From Kernels of Experimentation to Industrialization

In a sense, the banking sector turned out to be of major importance in the growth of the electromechanical industry, especially in a country which had some catching up to do vis-à-vis some other developed countries such as Germany and the United States. In 1931, Germany accounted for seven hundred of the eighteen hundred accounting machines installed in Europe; Great Britain had five hundred whereas France had only 210, just ahead of the Netherlands, which had 180, but far in advance of Switzerland (eighty) and Belgium (thirty-five).[11] Let us not forget, for example, that Georges Vieillard, who introduced the Bull brand to France in 1932–1933, had previously served as a consultant engineer to *Banque d'Alsace-Lorraine*. In fact, *Banque d'Alsace-Lorraine* and *Sogénal* (another major banking house from the Alsace-Lorraine region) served as the link for the transfer of electromechanical accounting technology from Germany to France.

By the early 1930s, a whole new industry had taken shape—banks, with twenty-three units, and insurance companies[12] with fifty, accounted for a full third of the 268 electromechanical office equipment installed in France up until March 1933.[13] Several other firms also got into the fray and helped in the revival of Bull France (a sister concern of the Norwegian company which had branches all over Northern Europe) and the emergence of the subsidiary of Remington Rand Powers Corporation. In France, the British Powers company (established in 1913) set up *Société anonyme des machines à statistiques* (SAMAS or Samas) in September 1922 as the distributor for its Powers range of office equipment imported from its British factory at Croydon.[14] It quickly found for itself some solid clients in *Banque de France* and several insurance firms. Then, when it registered itself as a French corporation in 1935, it was also patronized by *Société générale*.[15] Similarly, the young Bull corporation found several new clients when it turned into a French company in 1932–1933. These patriotic firms included insurance companies such as *La Paix* and *Assurances générales*, as well as the (small)

---

11. Source: the Bull archives, via the good offices of Olivier Darrieulat. See also Daumas (1996).

12. Life insurance companies needed powerful calculators to devise their actuarial tables. See further Campbell-Kelly (1992); Yates (1993, 2005).

13. Source: Bull archives, via the good offices of O. Darrieulat.

14. The Powers machines distributed by SAMAS were manufactured in Cincinnati, Ohio, and Croydon (south London), England. See further Heide (2009: 192–94).

15. The group of French investors who transformed SAMAS into a full-fledged French company brought in 75 per cent of the capital, while the agent of *Société générale*, Henri Poirier, took over as the chairman of the board. SAMAS was the sole distributor of the Powers range of equipment manufactured by American and English companies. In fact, its managing director was an Englishman, Arthur Impey. This information has been culled from Darrieulat (1992).

bank *Laydernier.*[16] These were all clear signs that the French business community preferred dealing with French companies regarding the modernization and automation of office equipment rather than having them imported from the United States (as was done by the Powers company between 1924 and 1933; see Darrieulat 1992). At the same time, care was taken to ensure that this did not create any monopolies which could be exploited by either U.S. firms (especially IBM; see Rodgers 1971 and Vernay 1989) or British and German factories.

The Appearance of Electromechanical Tabulators in the Second Half of the 1930s

The introduction of the innovative punched-card system (first used in the weaving industry by the Jacquard looms) greatly helped in the mechanization of the banking industry. The first wave of electromechanical tabulators began entering service at the turn of the 1930s, with some fifty machines sold every year. Still, it took several more years of constant refinement for them to achieve a modicum of reliability. It was only in the second half of that decade that these new machines were finally made reliable enough for the serious business of banking (for the British case, see Bátiz-Lazo and Wardley 2007).

At the heart of the system was the "printing tabulator" perfected in the United States by the Powers corporation (in 1917) and by the Computing Tabulating Recording Company, which later turned into IBM in 1924. This tabulator could add and edit subtotals, automatically collate and string together various operations, punch result cards, and also print letters and forms with its built-in alphanumeric printer. Banks used these machines primarily for keeping track of cash flows and securities.

Their biggest advantage lay in the fact that data needed to be entered only once, thus avoiding all the pitfalls and errors associated with duplication, not to mention the wasted time and money. Data entry error reduction had assumed vital importance with the massive increase in the client base due to larger networks and the entry of small and medium-sized enterprizes and the middle class (itself growing rapidly; see further Poon in this volume). Every time that there was an account activity, the entry worksheet was required to be sent to the customer account and placed in the right "position" so that it could be adjusted forthwith—thus avoiding errors which were extremely costly to repair *a posteriori*, not to mention the damage done to the bank's brand image. In the case of securities, the statement

---

16. It was the paper manufacturer Aussedat-Calliès who took the initiative and formed a group of his personal contacts to invest in Bull, which was then in some difficulty. They had not failed to notice that Bull could open for them a huge "captive market" for punched cards—in which Aussedat would soon specialise in. The group formed by Vieillard bought over 40 per cent of Bull's capital.

of accounts had to be derived and the applicable scales calculated (every quarter) for the closing off of an interest account.

All these jobs, which the banks took upon themselves during the interwar years, necessitated an ever-greater dependence on these electromechanical accounting machines. Although the punched-card data was still entered twice—the second time to check that the two entries matched by superimposing the two cards—automatic sorting and collating machines quickly arranged the bookkeeping vouchers in any order required. "The sorting machines can arrange cards at the rate of 650 per minute, while the tabulators can print a hundred lines of a hundred characters each in the same time."[17] In their final avatar, these tabulators and calculators could input data, carry out extensive and complicated calculations, and print results in various formats. They achieved their speed by using electromagnetism instead of cumbrous mechanics as this eliminated the force of inertia of moving parts and the wear and tear which plague all machinery. Of course, this was prior to the advent the transistor—not to mention the vacuum tube—and the electronic revolution. The tabulators were soon joined by specialized machines which did just one part of the work, as and when required: calculators, card reproducers, etc. *Crédit lyonnais* ordered its first machines in 1934. The first punched-card machine (a *Hollerith*) was installed on 10 September 1937 at its *Comptabilité-Titres* (Securities Accounts Department): "Every investment security was represented by a punched card containing the client account number, a code representing the amount and the quantity held."[18] By 1939 these machines handled the accounts of some 1.5 million of the French banks' clientele.

THE CENTRALIZATION OF THESE OPERATIONS WITHIN "ACCOUNTS DEPARTMENTS" AND, LATER, AS INDEPENDENT SERVICES

Service Centres in Paris

Increasing demand for and dependence on mechanization took a toll on banks' organizational structure. Banks were forced to rethink their resource allocation strategies and streamline the usage of the accounting

---

17. Chief of the Electro-Mechanical Accounting department, *Les banques et le machinisme. La mécanisation dans les grands établissements financiers à succursales multiples*, typed note, April 1952, Historical Archives of *Société générale* (original file H56).

18. Jacques Vanrenterghem (general inspection of *Crédit lyonnais*), "Les premiers ordinateurs au Crédit Lyonnais", paper presented to the second seminar on The History of Information Technology in France, Paris, CNAM, April 1990 (historical archives of *Crédit lyonnais*).

equipment. Consequently, Paris and its suburbs saw the mushrooming of "non-accounting" branch offices which passed on data processing jobs to the head office (which housed the machines).

For example, in 1931, *Société générale* brought together all the data processing work of its Paris branches in a single building in which its "centralized accounts department" processed all the accounts created by the bank's branches in and around Paris. The larger departments at its central headquarters were equipped with heavy-duty accounting machines capable of crunching through the enormous quantities of data generated. A gaggle of these large machines were installed by *Société générale* to serve its Accounts Portfolio department in its new administrative offices, the Édouard VII building, not far from its headquarters. Other machines for maintaining securities records, the movement of securities, general accounts (for the monthly and annual statements), and coupons were grouped together in its ultra-modern Trocadéro building.

On a smaller scale, but no less successfully, *Caisse centrale des Banques populaires* used electromechanical means and standardized processing methods to manage the accounts (managing available funds, clearings in the Paris region, etc.) for an entire group of decentralized banks. In 1937, it replaced its *Elliot-Fischers* with some *Burroughs Moon* and other statistical machines (Dottelongue and Malaval 1996). Many mid-sized banks also followed suit: in 1934, *Crédit nantais* centralised the accounting operations of all its branches by using *Multiplex* and [*Burroughs*] *Moon* machines.

A Dual System of Account Maintenance

The development and spread of these electromechanical machines raised a new problem: should they be installed at the periphery of the bank's network, at every branch office, or should they be centralized into massive data processing hubs which would take care of all the bank's accounting operations?

In the beginning, the entry of these electromechanical machines in the larger, Parisian deposit banks followed a subtle though persistent trend: data preparation and entry was done at every teller window. This decentralizing of operations meant that each branch was required to treat a substantial part of the data with the help of specialized, relatively light-weight accounting machines:

> *Société générale* adopted the "spot accounting" system which was also used by the majority of Anglo-Saxon banks. In this system, every branch used and maintained its own accounting position with the help of these electro-mechanical machines. It thus avoided the duplicating of positional and accounting reports traditional to French banks.[19]

---

19. Maurice Lorain, *Réformes et méthodes modernes de travail dans les banques*, lecture on 23 June 1952, Paris, Les Cours de droit, 1952, p. 13.

Apart from an abortive attempt at transferring the data processing onto electro-accounting machines in 1934–1939, this "spot position" system was maintained by *Société générale* till the early 1950s. This system substituted the punched-card machines for accounting machines (especially the *Ellis* type), which seemed better suited for the maintenance of "client accounts" because it was more important to be able to keep track of these accounts on a ready, day-to-day basis. This balance between modernity (accounting machines) and tradition (no shift towards electromechanization) can be explained by the working hours prevalent in France. In contrast to banks in Belgium, French banks closed very early in the afternoons and night work was avoided (as opposed to Germany after 1929). This made it very difficult for the delayed relaying of data to a central data processing hub after the closure of teller windows. No wonder then that the "spot position" system was adopted right from the beginning in 1926 when the *Société générale* embarked upon its mechanization drive. Every branch entered data in duplicate, with one copy staying at the window and the other sent to the central headquarters for the general accounts, trial balances, and audits. This traditional duplication of individual accounts, with one kept "on the spot" and the other sent for "accounting" also added to security.

> This required that accounting machines be installed close to the teller windows so that reports could be generated rapidly and the position of an account known at any given point of time and tallied with the reports generated by the worksheet.[20]

Société générale, which had always taken special care of its internal audits after the problems and setbacks it had experienced in the 1880s, found major advantages in this process of mechanization:

> Spot accounting replaces the daily checking of account entries and monthly reconciliations—a tedious process and always delayed—with two statements of accounts of the same client, one kept at the Post and the other sent to the auditing service. This greatly helped to expedite the monthly balance sheets and the dispatching of account statements to our clients [. .]. There is no doubt that our improved operating ratio is to a large extent due to this spot accounting method.[21]

This in spite of certain lacunae in the error checking process—shortfalls which the bank was well aware of:

> The four major problems are: 1) the impossibility of getting the exact position of an account at all times due to the fact that entries are dealt

---

20. *Les banques et le machinisme*, 1952.
21. Ibid.

with in series, at the end of the day, sometimes even the next day. 2) The amount of time taken before errors in the balance sheet [*erreurs de soldes*] are corrected (in case of cancellations and drawings) [*reprises et tirages*]. Both machines and machine operators can make mistakes. Machine operators can be confused by write-backs while the machines can simply malfunction. Generally, the adjustments are made by adding the figures at the bottom of the page for checking the last balance, that is to say, in the course of the month for the finished files and at the month-end for the current entries. Till then the errors could well remain undetected. 3) The difficulty in identifying allocation errors committed by hitting the number and name of the client read off the voucher and not off the account file as instructed. Errors of this nature, which can have grave consequences, can only be identified by a separate (non-automatic) examination of every account card (ex: a Thompson inserted among all the Thomases). 4) Finally, the unavoidable risk of losing an account card. Duplicates cannot be made except through impractically long researches into worksheet entries.[22]

In several banks, it was only the bigger branches which had this equipment. At *Société nancéienne*, for example, the internal reorganization of 1935 made a clear distinction between its different "branches": "accounting centres" of the "regional operations group" were separated from the non-accounting "branch offices". *Société générale* also had many non-accounting branch offices.

THE STRATEGY FOR CENTRALIZATION: MOVING TOWARDS ELECTROMECHANIZED ACCOUNTING SERVICE CENTRES

A second, major development in the banking industry was initiated by engineers and think-tanks who wanted to apply some of the revolutionary managerial concepts regarding streamlining and the division and specialization of work to the service and banking sectors (which were labelled a "Fordian or Taylorist system" by Boyer and Freyseenet 2002; see also Freyssenet 2000). One of the first to take the plunge was BNCI, a large, Parisian bank which, since its inception in 1932, was compelled to be aggressive and constantly innovative in order to survive amid the three well-established banking houses of the country. It began by stripping its branch offices of all the equipment which had been installed[23] from as early as 1930 and instead establishing, over the next two decades, seven regional "service centres"

---

22. Ibid.
23. Belonging to BNCI or to its predecessor, *Banque nationale de crédit*, which folded in 1931 (see Bonin 2002).

(Angers, Avignon, Bordeaux, Lille, Lyon, Nancy, etc.) endowed with a bank of electromechanical accounting machines, which processed all the data generated by the growing network of its branch offices. The process, which began in the mid-1930s and continued until the mid-1950s, proved to be an excellent, albeit ambitious, investment policy. It allowed the bank to keep pace with the rapid growth of its network and to buy out several of its regional competitors—before it merged with *Comptoir national d'escompte de Paris* (CNEP) in 1966 to form BNP (see Torres 2000).

> Completely independently of the local organization [of the regional network], a centre was established at Bordeaux which centralized the account-keeping and portfolios of all the branch offices in the Garonne basin, Aude, Charente and the Western Pyrenées. Due to this reorganization, the account-keeping has improved greatly at Bordeaux.[24]

The decision to create this administrative and technological hub at Bordeaux was made in 1934. At first, it was housed with its branch office in the avenue Chapeau-Rouge, on the second and third floors. In 1948–1949, it was shifted to a modern building on the Argonne Avenue and several new *Gamma Bulls* were installed. In 1972, it was finally shifted to Mérignac-Arlac, where it assumed its final shape of a major data processing centre.[25] These centres were not "service factories"—the Bordeaux centre, for example, counted only about a dozen employees in 1934–1936, many of whom were office equipment operators deployed from Toulouse or Bayonne.

Meanwhile, *Crédit lyonnais* also realized the advantages of such an arrangement and began to reorganize, streamline, and centralize its data processing infrastructure. In 1930 it opened a series of large, electromechanical accounting centres for processing securities and vouchers. The whole process took several years and it was only in the 1950s that its eight provincial hubs (Bordeaux, Lille, Reims, Rouen, etc.) went fully operational and a ninth one was installed in North Africa. In many banking houses which chose to centralize their operations, almost all of the accounting was completed at these hubs in the evenings and the latest client account "positions" sent back the next morning to the branch offices (as was the case in Germany and Belgium). But *Crédit lyonnais* chose, like *Société générale*, to implement a dual system in which the branch offices were left to derive the day-to-day balances of their clients with the help of specialized accounting machines.

---

24. Inspection report of *Banque de France*'s Bordeaux branch, 25 May 1936. Historical archives of *Banque de France* in Paris.

25. Testimony gathered from former workers of the centre, as part of an inquiry into the oral history carried out under the aegis of *La Mémoire de Bordeaux*, 1996.

Each bank chose its own investment strategy, depending upon its budget allocation projects and the rate at which it wanted to proceed with its programme of modernization, especially in regard to the risks it might have to face concerning the efficiency and reliability of its accounting operations. In stark contrast to the industrial sector, which had navigated long in the choppy seas of ever-changing technology and evolved a great knack for contingency planning, banks had to build from scratch and painfully gather a capital of experience in implementing projects which required a comprehensive reorganization of work and remodelling the mode of work itself.

THE APEX OF A TECHNOLOGICAL
AND PROCESSING SYSTEM

Following the economic recession of the 1930s and stagnation during the Second World War, there was an urgency to restart growth in France during the *Libération* and *Reconstruction* years (1944–1950; see Bonin 1997). Banks could embrace growth thanks to investments in processing methods and equipment centres during the 1930s. But retaking growth in the volume of operations while broadening the number of customers led to a deadlock: despite fresh investments in "classical" machines, a saturation point seemed to have been reached because managers and machines were unable to cope with the growth of data.

The Overwhelming Success of the Electromechanical
Accounting Machines (At the Turn of the 1960s)

As mentioned, the *Reconstruction* and accelerated economic growth of the 1950s witnessed an increasing customer base (although the middle class still accounted for most of the banks' business). For example, the number of checking accounts in *Société générale* went up from 441,000 in 1931 to 738,000 in 1962. In fact, bank network density began increasing even before the advent of the banking laws of the second half of the 1960s because banks had begun transforming many of their non-permanent teller windows into full-fledged branches as early as the 1950s.

There was also a transformation in the regional counters of *Crédit agricole mutual*. Until then they had been mainly concerned with handing out discounted loans and in the 1950s they began to sport the first teller windows and accepting savings deposits.

Even before the advent of the "bank of the masses", the system seemed to have reached a point of saturation regarding data processing:

> The number of cheques presented by *Crédit lyonnais* to the clearing house at Paris went up from 3,840,000 in 1946 to 8,000,000 in 1953 and 16,700,000 in 1962 [. . .]. The total number of bills for discount

or for collection which numbered some 8,370,000 in 1946, went up to 30,000,000 in 1962.[26]

The apparent saturation led to a greater dependence on a wider and more systematic use of electromechanical accounting machines (Hammer 1958). Whereas the increasing business volume justified these investments, there was much to be done behind the scenes: the entire system for circulating and processing data had to be restructured, technical service departments revamped, and even the location and layout of the buildings annexed to the main offices considered. The latter would transform into mini-service factories and house the electromechanical machines which over time would be capable of handling massive amounts of punched cards: just the securities section of *Société générale* occupied more than a thousand square metres of floor space!

Ultimately, punched-card machines were adopted by all banks, small and big, which used them for a wide variety of jobs: "In 1955, *Crédit industriel d'Alsace-Lorraine* introduced punched card machines for keeping track of client accounts and cash in hand",[27] which remained in service until 1964. In 1948, the Central Teller of the people's banks installed a set of IBM 801 punched-card machines operated by twelve mechanics. In December 1950, it added the first three IBM Proof 803 machines to be imported into Europe. The 803 had thirty-two counters instead of the twenty-four in the 801s and were used, among other things, to compute the "balance". They were also more reliable and could, while processing and clearing the bills, verify, allocate (the cards fell into boxes by category), ticket-date endorsements, debit accounts, issue release notes, and pay-in slips, etc. Other machines too were added, especially statistical machines for calculating interest ladders for demand accounts. In 1955, the payroll and the equity departments were also mechanized.

At *Crédit lyonnais*, there was no question that punched-card machines had come to stay. It equipped and mechanized its various departments in quick succession: the [securities/equity] accounts section at its central headquarters had the machines before World War II, its department for the maintenance of current accounts at its Paris and Lyon branches in 1947–1948, the cash account at its central headquarters in 1948, its stock market section in 1949–1950, the department for the collection of commercial instruments at Paris in 1954, and soon after, its department of foreign services.[28] After an initial spurt during which the voucher processing and general accounting departments were given these punched-card machines,

---

26. Centenary publication of *Crédit lyonnais*, 1963, p. 230.

27. *Note sur les méthodes de travail bancaire*, *Crédit industriel d'Alsace-Lorraine*, 1930s, historical archives of CIAL.

28. Vanrentergem, "Les premiers ordinateurs". For a comparison with the growth of an English bank, see Booth (2004).

Société générale suspended further mechanization. Then, after a technological feasibility study conducted in 1947, the process was resumed and
"a progressive mechanization of all the departments"[29] took place in 1948–
1950. Subsequently, "the securities accounting, employee wages, business
accounts, clearing and foreign exchanges" [30] were also mechanized, as was
the equities department in 1955 (see Pardo-Guerra in this volume). As for
BNCI, it built for itself a vast administrative setup to handle all the data
processing for its Parisian network and corporate headquarters. Situated at
its *Annexe Barbès* on the Rue de la Nation, it soon took on all the trappings
of a full-fledged "service factory".

The electromechanical devices thus allowed banks to successfully meet
the challenges associated with an explosive growth by increasing productivity, improving the operating ratio, and providing the possibility of better checks and controls. But the most important advantage was improved
relations with customers—clients could now get their transaction notices
and statements of accounts much earlier (the very next morning for stock
market transactions, for example). Moreover, these reports were now also
more error free and reliable. One must not forget that, after all, the main
work of a banker, even when dealing with a large corporation, is essentially
a "service"-oriented job, based on personal relationships.

The Limits of the Electromechanical Accounting System

These electromechanical accounting machines helped optimize the banking
system and played a significant role in assisting the French banking establishment to cope with growth and, during periods of economic recession,
significantly reduce operating costs. Still, these accounting machines had
their limits. In the first place, a big part of the work could not be ported to
these machines because the volumes involved were too small. In such cases,
the work continued to be done by the older accounting machines, which,
being slower, hindered overall productivity. Apart from that, as these electromechanical machines did not have a "memory" as yet to store data,
they required feeding with punched cards for every run. Consequently,
they came into their own only when the job involved sufficiently large
volumes. Frequently changing jobs meant changing the plugboard, reca-
librating the print heads, going through a trial run to verify the process,
etc.—which required precious "human resources". Also, "this mechanized
process was slow due to the inertia of the moving parts themselves and the
necessity of having to make several passes on these machines for sorting the
cards".[31] A final point about these day-to-day obstacles to the implementation of thorough mechanization processes: the transfer of data required

---

29. Centenary publication of *Société générale*, Paris, 1964.
30. Ibid.
31. Centenary publication of *Crédit lyonnais*, 1963.

a physical/manual operation because no switching connections were yet available; carbon papers, huge volumes of punched cards, then later on, records, had thus to be handled. This situation remained unchanged until the 1960s–1970s.

There was another major problem: the use of these electromechanical machines required a complete restructuring of the bank's data processing infrastructure. The accounts department had to be completely reorganized. So much so that it gave rise to an entirely new branch of activity—service organization counselling. The organization of the internal services, the circulation of bookkeeping vouchers, the implementation of hierarchical "command" and "control" networks—all had to be dealt with within an impossibly short span of fifteen years.

> The running of these machines, the design and construction of the plug boards, planning the modalities of the job (the layout of the cards and printouts) can only be done by trained people—and that training, especially for the more delicate jobs, takes time. (Hammer 1958: 51)

Consequently, new technicians had to be hired and trained, which, in a sense, went against the normal practice of reducing personnel during the economic crunch of the 1930s. Even otherwise, data entry proved a costly affair because the gang-punching machines and verifiers "were hugely manpower intensive"[32] (see Poon in this volume for further details).

There were also other, unexpected technical problems: the machines were very susceptible to any change in the environment. A variation in the ambient temperature or humidity could disrupt their delicate electromagnets and cause unforeseeable malfunctions. Although manufacturers were quick to identify these issues and produce more robust components, there was yet another, more intractable problem: nobody had anticipated the volume of work and the consequent heavy usage. This took a heavy toll on the moving parts and the machines lasted only a few years, which meant that depreciation accounts had to be introduced and provisions made for added replacement expenses.

For example, a study by *Société générale* on its electromechanical machines remarked: "These machines, which had seen extensive usage these last few years, were the worst hit."[33] Repairs and maintenance visits by service technicians increased but often the degradation was beyond repair:

> This department has thirty-nine *Ellis* machines, some of which have been very heavily used right from the beginning. They are now in a

---

32. *Les banques et le machinisme*, 1952.

33. *Compte rendu sur l'état du matériel* Ellis *du groupe Kleber* [*Report on the Condition of the Ellis Brand of Equipment at the Kleber Group*], Conservation des titres, December 1934, historical archives of *Société générale*.

very bad shape and almost impossible to repair. We are trying our best, but the entire balance of the mechanism has been thrown off kilter because the core components have been replaced by pieces of inferior quality [. . .]. Of the thirty-nine *Ellis* in this department, twenty-three were installed in 1922 and 1923.[34]

Whereas this streamlining and mechanizing of the day-to-day bank work came of age in the years 1940 to 1960, there were still many smaller establishments which still used typewriting machines. These machines were used extensively in branch offices and in the growing number of mutual and co-operative banks, such as the *Crédit agricole mutuel*. In all these branch offices and regional or central data entry centres,[35] carbon paper was used to make simultaneous multiple copies—one copy was retained at the entry point while the others circulated within the bank. One of the most widely used was the Kalamazoo[36] system, which became popular in many accounts departments even outside the banking establishment. Still, the main difficulty lay in maintaining consistency in data entry.

Actually, the very principle of a centralized organization was found to have inherent managerial dilemmas. Gradually, negative economies of scale emerged with the advent of problematic corporate relations, the Taylorian unwieldiness and the heavy financial drain imposed by the constant maintenance required:

[a] centrally administered accounts department requires the coming together of a large number of people and consequently, of the delicate and difficult task of handling this personnel, of administering and trying to make the most of a constantly shifting and morphing asset. It imposes an extensive division of work and a clear and rigorous arrangement of diverse elements. The whole makes for a burdensome system which, though full of potential, is also extremely resource hungry in terms of maintenance and supervision. Well set up, the system can produce astounding results. But today, in its role as a centralizing element of banking administration, it has reached an extreme point—testing the limits of administrative flexibility, manoeuvrability and the system's capability of rapid adaptation to the constantly changing circumstances and economic conditions. To go further, that is, to have

---

34. Ibid.

35. The main ledger records data on multiple, detachable sheets—one for the centralised audit and the other for entry into the normal workflow. "The detachable sheet and the carbon paper have turned into indispensable tools of accounting" (Degos 1998: 99–100).

36. The Kalamazoo Company was established in the United States in 1904 to promote the system of loose-leaf ledgers. It was bought over by the Remington Typewriter Company in the 1920s. It spread its business in France through an autonomous sister concern.

fewer and larger data processing centres would tip the balance towards an inept gigantism, a system which would be bogged down by its own bulk, an impotent and paralysed monstrosity which, due to its sheer size—and there lies the greatest danger—go beyond the surveillance capabilities of even the best managers.[37]

Technically speaking, machine processing centres at banks had already begun, from as early as the 1940s, to understand their limits in terms of speed, the volume of documents they could process and economies of scale. The improvements, if any, were merely quantitative and one had to wait for the computer revolution before any real progress was made. (Meuleau 1992: 270)

And this revolution took place in the mid-1950s to overcome the quantitative, technological, human, and organizational bottlenecks of the "electromechanical accounting systems". The IBM 604 and 650 and the Bull Gamma 3 electronic calculators opened doors to new technological steps.

CONCLUSION

The growing use of tabulators, accounting machines, and, later, of the electromechanical data processors greatly improved productivity and helped banks overcome the various difficulties they faced in the first half of the twentieth century. One of the first advantages was that it allowed a reduction in labour during the economic crisis of the 1930s. Then when business picked up towards the end of the 1930s and really zoomed upwards at the turn of the 1950s, these devices significantly helped to improve the cost-revenue ratio. Having said that, it must also be noted that this course of mechanization never did run smooth; it was constrained at every step by recurring financial considerations. There were no one-time massive investments. Even in the bigger banks, the use of accounting machines and the streamlining of data entry and data processing work took years to gain full acceptance (from the mid-1920s to the beginning of the 1950s). Even in the 1960s, many accounts continued to be processed manually, often with the aid of some astonishing feats of mental calculation, although carbon papers and typewriters did make the task of duplication at least much easier.

Similarly, the electromechanical revolution also took time to take a hold. The first wave began in the second half of the 1930s, a second, bigger one came in 1947–1952, and the final, generalized flood swamped over the banking industry in the 1960s. There is no doubt that business-oriented managers had been able to make it amply clear to the engineers,

---

37. De Hochepied, executive officer of BNCI, conference of 25 May 1944, quoted by Meuleau (1992: 270).

reorganizers, and innovators that budgetary constraints were not to be tri-fled with. At the same time, we must also understand that, truly speaking, almost all these machines were, more or less, "experimental". They still required many trials and adjustments before they could attain some degree of reliability—and the market was trying them out in their hundreds, with-out any recourse to the data available to the computers of today.

What really mattered in the long term was that banks had been forced to make radical changes (overhauling their data processing methods, their organization, and even their physical infrastructure) in order to meet the economic challenges of the first half of the twentieth century, by an increas-ing dependence on mechanization and automation. In turn, this led to another key issue: managing the errors generated by these machines—the data entry errors, the risk of mixing up or reversing punched cards, data lost in the course of transferring it to a data processing centre, etc.

A strong case can be built around the economic advantages of standard-izing data processing methods, not to mention the added benefits of having better customer relationships because these new machines and methods helped greatly in speeding up the processing of client requests and generat-ing account statements. This last was especially true for the "most attractive clients"—those with savings to invest—it was they who benefited the most by the mechanization of the stock market and securities operations (see fur-ther Pardo-Guerra in this volume). In fact, brokerage and the administra-tion of assets were the foundation and the chief commercial activities of the big banks before the coming of the bank of the masses: at this step of mod-ernization, large service organizations had definitely adopted innovation in equipment and data processing and transformed themselves into technolog-ical crucibles and innovative organizations (Harianto and Pennings 1988; Pennings 1992; Pennings and Harianto 1992). But, in the 1960s, only the back office organizations had been involved in such a proto-computing rev-olution; huge disparities still differentiated banking institutions along with the intensity and the rhythm of mechanization; and numerous employees were used to hand processing in regional and mutual banks till the 1960s, which were realms of carbon-sheets documents. The revolution of commu-nication systems had to be complemented (see Yates 1989).

3 Britain's First Computer Centre for Banking
What Did This Building Do?

Ian Martin

INTRODUCTION

In 1950s Britain, the high-street banks were on the verge of a crisis. Across London and other major cities, the busiest branches were struggling to find space for the staff and accounting machinery required to cope with an escalating demand for banking services. Not only was there a lack of space in which to work, the banks also had to contend with a shrinking labour pool. The clerks performing the routine and often boring task of customer accounting were put under increasing pressure as they struggled to cope with weekly and monthly bookkeeping peaks. Bank costs in the form of overtime payments, and for recruitment and training, were in danger of spiralling out of control. The banks saw a way of averting this impending crisis, however, with the commercial arrival of large-scale electronic computing technology.[1]

Requiring much more space than was available in all but the biggest offices, and capable of handling the combined bookkeeping work of several of a bank's busiest branches, the computer demanded a new space of its own. To accommodate the computer's demands and make efficient use of its capabilities required the production of a new business space: the bank computer centre. For the first time in Britain, there was now a large-scale dislocation of customer accounting from its traditional confines of the individual bank branch to new collective computer centres.[2]

---

1. The Barclays press release for the opening of its computer centre cited "an ever increasing volume of work, presenting problems of overcrowding of Bank premises and staffing difficulties, particularly in London" as the impending crisis the introduction of the computer was averting. Barclays Bank Ltd., "Barclays Bank Limited No. 1 Computer Centre Press Release" [courtesy of Jim McClymont], 3 July 1961. See also Travers (1965: 4–5). For a succinct analysis of relations between banking, office automation and computing, see Booth (2007: 117–40, 141–54).

2. British banks, with the exception of the Bank of Scotland considered later, did not make use of tabulating machines to perform centralised branch accounting.

The first of the British banks to open a computer centre, in the summer of 1961, was Barclays. Barclays not only declared its building a British first, but claimed that its configuration of primarily British computer and telecommunications technology was the most advanced in the world.[3] The issue of "firsts" and pride in technological prowess are worthy of some attention, but there are more compelling reasons for business historians interested in technological change to concern themselves with the history of this building and others like it.

Sociologist of science, Thomas Gieryn, considers the importance of buildings in "What Buildings Do". His spatial analysis of Cornell's Bio-technology Building as "a site for people and organizations to define themselves and pursue their goals but also one where those meanings and purposes get structured and constrained" regards buildings as sitting conceptually somewhere between agency and structure. He sees them as both an outcome of agency and its constraint as he steers a course between Giddens and Bourdieu, seeking conceptual help from the litera-ture on the social construction of technological systems on his way. At one extreme, he reads Giddens as privileging agency with buildings as no more than what people do with them, at the other he has Bourdieu as privileging structure with buildings a constraint on social practice. Buildings, he concludes, like other technological artefacts, lie somewhere in between. They are the outcome of social practices while simultane-ously their structuring structures (Gieryn 2002).[4]

A renewed interest in spatiality more generally has taken the form of a well-documented "spatial turn" across a variety of academic disciplines (e.g. Warf and Arias 2008). In business history there has been some consideration of the applicability of spatial theory at the national (macro) and regional (meso) levels typically employed by economic geographers (Scranton 1996). But a micro-level analysis has the potential to offer business history some-thing different. It can provide an exploration of the changing role of one place as it shapes a business, its employees, and its customers, and as they in turn shape it. The focus in this chapter on one innovative place—the first bank computer centre—and the following of its various meanings allows for an in-depth contextual analysis of a socio-technical system in business use. Furthermore, a spatial focus on the micro rather than the macro reinforces the role of human agency in technology adoption and use, and avoids the spectre of technological determinism that haunts some business histories.[5]

---

3. Barclays Bank Ltd., "Barclays Bank Limited No. 1 Computer Centre Press Release", 3 July 1961, 1.

4. In addition to Gieryn's work, the role of buildings and place in the mutual shaping of science and scientists has been explored in edited volumes such as Smith, Agar, and Schmidt (1998) and Galison and Thompson (1999).

5. For a global history of technology in use that serves as welcome corrective to a prevalence of histories focused on technological innovation, see Edgerton (2006).

What follows is an examination of one British bank and its first computer centre, and the meanings that the production of this space conveyed over time. I show how as a meeting place for aesthetic and techno-scientific discourses the centre was a projection of modernity for the bank against a backdrop of 250 years of banking tradition. I emphasize the importance of the spectacle that was the centre's opening ceremony, and highlight elements of the building's design and the technology within that were instrumental in projecting this new business identity. I continue by exploring the relationship between the new centre and the traditional distributed structure of the branch, and the building's effect on those who worked within its walls and those who worked without. I examine the tensions between the new and the old and Barclays' attempts to manage the perceptions of its customers towards what was a new home for their accounts. I consider the building's significance and validate Barclays' claim as the first British bank to open such a centre, despite claims to the contrary from some quarters. I end by broaching the issue of the centre's slated closure only three years after its opening and chart its continued use up until its eventual closure. Ultimately, when considering the first British computer centre for banking, what I offer, like Gieryn, is an answer to a straightforward question: what did this building do?

CEREMONY BY DESIGN

On Tuesday 4 July 1961 Barclays opened its No. 1 Computer Centre at 154 Drummond Street, London, NW1,[6] an event that it later asserted was the opening of "Britain's first computer centre for banking".[7] As the first British bank to officially open a building of this kind Barclays hailed it as a landmark in British banking automation. Inside was an orchestration of British computing and telecommunications technologies, but Barclays hailed the building as more than just a British first. It declared its computer centre as the hub of "the most advanced bank book-keeping system in the world".[8]

Misa (1994: 115–41) contends that macro-level studies of technological change are prone to technological determinism whereas micro-level studies are more likely to emphasize the societal forces at work.

6. "The Computer Centre Opens", *Spread Eagle*, 1961, 252. The day of opening was most likely chosen as a Tuesday rather than a Monday because the first day of the week was always an especially busy day due to the requirement to process work carried over from Saturday opening (David Parsons, interview with author, Manchester, 7 August 2008).

7. Barclays Group Archives (hereafter BGA), *Barclays Fact Sheet: Principal Events*, 2.

8. Barclays Bank Ltd., "Barclays Bank Limited No. 1 Computer Centre Press Release", 3 July 1961, 1.

At a grand ceremony in the centre's reception, Anthony William Tuke, nearing the end of his twelve-year chairmanship, made a speech intended to maximize his bank's achievements. Emphasizing the progress Barclays had made during his stewardship, he paused to reflect on the bank's former position as technological laggard in the 1930s. Then, as a wave of mechanization came in the shape of ledger posting and accounting machines, Barclays only adopted these technologies as an act of "sheer self-defence".[9] Tuke impressed upon his audience that during his time in charge, however, Barclays had leapt from its trailing position of laggard to assume a leading role in the application of "electronic methods" to banking.[10] By the end of the 1950s not only had Barclays, under A.W. Tuke, become Britain's biggest bank (Ackrill and Hannah 2001: 153), it had also taken a first step in realizing its ambitions to the status of technological innovator by becoming the first British bank to place an order for a computer in August 1959. Barclays ordered an Emidec 1100 computer from British manufacturers EMI Electronics Limited at a cost of £125,000.[11]

Tuke tempered his opening speech rhetoric somewhat by sketching out the cautious and careful work underpinning Barclays' turnaround from laggard to technological innovator.[12] This work was led by two of Tuke's senior managers, John Cowen and Donald Travers. Both men had taken leading positions on the Electronics Sub-Committee set up in 1955 by the Committee of London Clearing Bankers (CLCB). Cowen, a general manager and Barclays board member, was its chair, and Travers, a general manager's assistant and head of Barclays' mechanization, was its secretary.

---

9. Quote taken from "The Computer Centre Opens", *Spread Eagle*, 1961, 252. The term *clearing banks* is a contemporary one used to denote those banks that specialised in cheque clearing as opposed to the savings banks that predominantly accepted savings deposits.

10. 'Electronic methods' was a term in general use that referred in particular to the use of electronic computers. A number of articles in the 1950s hypothesized as to how computers could be applied to banking. See, for example, Davies (1953) and Goldring (1953a, 1953b, 1953c).

11. Emidec was capitalized as EMIDEC by various actors. I use EMI's original form of the name here as recorded in EMI Electronics Ltd., "Emidec Computer News 1", c. 1960. The order for the Emidec is recorded in BGA, "Board Minutes", 30 July 1959. This figure of £125,000 was probably the cost of the Emidec and its tape peripherals; it's unlikely this figure included the cost of teleprocessing equipment and teleprinters, etc., that made up the whole data processing system. Others, such as the Royal Bank of Scotland and Williams Deacons, record a figure of £150,000 for Barclays Emidec purchase; see Royal Bank of Scotland Group Archive (hereafter RBSGA)/WD/366/2, "Computer and Sorter Readers Ordered by the Banks", 14 September 1961; and RBSGA/RB/3146, "Computer and Sorter Readers Ordered by the Banks", 1962.

12. The official history of Barclays Bank sketches Tuke as a cautious and conservative man in his later years, Ackrill and Hannah (2001: 123).

In 1955 the CLCB had tasked Cowen as the chair of the Electronics Sub-Committee to:

> promote discussion and research on developments in the field of mechanization with particular reference to electronics in so far as they may be applicable to banking practice, and on the impact of such developments on staffing problems.[13]

The Electronics Sub-Committee formed a focused three-man working party to research the possibilities of bringing electronic computing to British banking. Membership of this working party was important in establishing those banks that would become early computing pioneers. Donald Travers, Barclays' head of mechanization, was one of the three. From 1955 the banks, now collectively under Barclays' leadership as well as individually, met at home and abroad with a number of existing and would-be electronic computer manufacturers and users in order to discuss their common and specific requirements. Over the next few years British clearing banks began experimenting with centralised bookkeeping, using tabulators and computers alongside their existing mechanized distributed branch accounting operations. When satisfied that in principle centralised electronic computer accounting appeared the best solution to the growing crisis of staff and space shortages in the London area, Barclays was the first British branch to place an order for its own computer in 1959.

In his opening speech Tuke downplayed any strategic motive behind Barclays' privileged leading role in these developments, and with a wink credited simple good fortune. Barclays certainly left nothing to chance on the day of the computer centre's opening. Everything about the centre's opening was carefully managed for maximum effect. After the chairman's speech the Postmaster General, the Right Hon. Reginald Bevins MP, was invited to ceremoniously open the new centre. He did so not by cutting a ribbon with scissors in the traditional manner, but instead by "cutting an invisible ray with his hand".[14] When his hand passed through the invisible beam the lights in the centre were automatically brought to life and the centre was declared officially open. For the invited guests watching, this futuristic act was an apt conclusion to a ceremony that had radiated Barclays' newfound modernity. Behind the scenes, however, more traditional methods were still on hand. One of the computer centre staff was carefully watching as the MP's hand passed through the beam

---

13. RBSGA/WES/1177/62, John D. Cowen, "Report of the Electronics Sub-Committee to the Chief Executive Officers", 9 May 1958.
14. "The Computer Centre Opens", *Spread Eagle*, 1961, 252.

and was ready to throw a power switch in case the centre didn't light up automatically.[15]

The very presence of the Postmaster General was a significant reflection of Barclays' technological attitude. The Postmaster General was the ministerial position responsible for the General Post Office (GPO), the organization in control of all communications technology that took place outside the walls of any building in Great Britain. Barclays' computer centre was as much a showpiece for telecommunications as it was for computing technology; Barclays had worked with the GPO to link the centre to local branches via a network of GPO lines that brought together a complete data processing system.

Barclays also knew that the ceremony itself was just a beginning. A suitably large and impressive reception area anticipated a stream of visitors, including many representatives from the other banks, for years to come. After the opening ceremony the first of these visitors was led on a tour around the computer centre building where elements of this new

Figure 3.1   The Postmaster General cuts the invisible beam to officially open the centre, 1961.

15. Davey-Thomas, interview with author, Penzance, 15 October 2008.

data processing system were fully operational but also clearly intended for public display. Almost embarrassed by some of the indulgences made to visitors in the building's design, the bank's chairman concluded by pointing towards a simpler design for future computer centres. The name given to the centre spoke to the bank's competitors as it looked towards its own future; from the outset Barclays called this the No. 1 Computer Centre.[16]

The new computer centre was an old furniture showroom with a large and adaptable ground-floor interior space and a West End location that was conveniently close to some of Barclays' biggest and busiest branches and their business customers headquartered nearby.[17] The bank district that encompassed this area, Pall Mall, was second in importance only to neighbouring Lombard Street district that was home to Barclays' head office. In addition to the increasing volume of business putting pressure on existing resources at Pall Mall branches, the district's progressive managerial attitudes were also an important contributor in determining which of the two districts would be home to the first computer centre. Whereas Lombard Street was steeped in tradition—Barclays could trace its roots back to 1690 and a goldsmith's shop there—Pall Mall's directors were renowned for their forward thinking and were not averse to risk.[18]

With location fixed, the bank's in-house architect set about repurposing the 24,600 sq ft. ground floor space building to cater for the specific environmental needs of a large-scale computer and constructing a first home for its new workforce. There was a broader overriding requirement though; the architect also had to meet the political needs of Barclays' management. As a result, incorporated into the building's interior design were a number of features not related to the requirements of the bank's computer or staff, but that ensured that "allowance had been made in the layout of the centre for the reception of a steady flow

---

16. "The Computer Centre Opens", *Spread Eagle*, 1961, 254.

17. There were rumours that the building was a former car showroom (see David Parsons, interview with author, Manchester, 7 August 2008; and Barry Matthews, interview with author, Bollington, 3 October 2008). But records in Camden Local Archives indicate that the premises previously belonged to Oetzmann and Co. House Furnishings, a long-established furniture and piano retailer. Barclays was in the habit of acquiring property from bankrupt customers and this is possibly the manner in which they acquired the lease for this building (Jean Perkin, telephone interview with author, 21 July 2008).

18. Barclays had its central head office at 54 Lombard Street, but maintained a devolved Local Head Office (LHO) structure operating at a level below. Each LHO oversaw a number of branches grouped by district, inherited from acquired banks (Eric Chilton, interview with author, Wilmslow, 9 October 2008; Ackrill and Hannah 2001: 130).

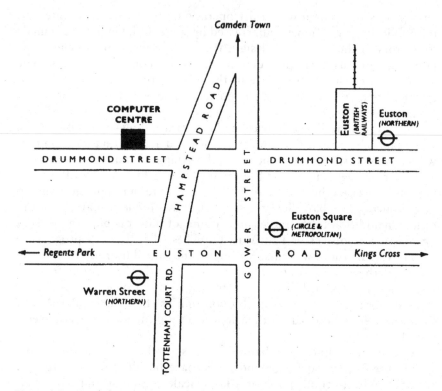

Figure 3.2   Card showing location of No. 1 Computer Centre, 1961.

of visitors".[19] Barclays designed its first computer centre as a site for public display as it demonstrated its position as technological innovator amongst the British clearing banks. In purposefully courting publicity with its Emidec installation in London, Barclays was following a tradition of computers and public display started by IBM with its Selective Sequence Electronic Calculator (SSEC) installation in 1948 in New York (Campbell-Kelly and Aspray 1996: 115).

In the building's interior design the computer's specific requirements were catered for in terms of power and temperature, humidity, and dust control. A large diesel generator was in place to cope with failures or fluctuations in power supply and thirty-three air-conditioning units on the roof were installed to dissipate heat output from the machinery to

19. "The Computer Centre Opens", *Spread Eagle*, 1961, 253–54. A classic work on technological structures built to achieve a specific social effect is Langdon Winner's "Do Artifacts have Politics", in Winner (1988: 26–38). The story may be apocryphal, see the rebuttals in Joerges (1999) and Woolgar and Cooper (1999).

stabilize temperature and humidity levels.[20] But these primary concessions to the computing equipment, like the hand on the switch that provided a backup for the opening ceremony's invisible ray, remained out of sight. Cables and ducts that brought power and air were hidden behind false floors and ceilings. On show were indicators that the building's function was about much more than simply meeting the computer's environmental needs; it also had to function as a suitably impressive "first of its kind" building for a bank wishing to demonstrate its technological prowess.

The opening ceremony took place in the building's cavernous reception area, a massive space framed by white walls, a black granite floor, and a white ceiling supported by simple unadorned large columns. This was the building's primary gesture to public display. Stretching along the length of one wall was a one-hundred-foot, three-dimensional showpiece mural. The reception area (Figure 3.3) embodied modernist architectural concepts that were in sharp contrast to traditional classical bank architecture that symbolized stability, tradition, trustworthiness, and security.[21] Even by the standards of the most recently built branches, the computer centre was a thoroughly modern and even futuristic building.[22]

COMPUTING AND TELECOMMUNICATIONS

After the opening ceremony, the building's first visitors were led from the reception area to a specially designed viewing room enclosed by floor-to-ceiling glass walls that provided "an uninterrupted view of the computer and its auxiliary equipment".[23] To the right and on show inside the first of these rooms was Barclays' own Emidec computer, installed

---

20. Barclays Bank Ltd., "Barclays Bank Limited No. 1 Computer Centre Press Release", 3 July 1961; Jim McClymont, interview with author, Bethersden, 4 September 2008; David Parsons, interview with author, Manchester, 7 August 2008.

21. Modern architecture had established itself in Britain by the middle of the 1950s, but banks were typically conservative in their approach to architectural change. Bank branches typically projected an image of strength and stability in order to engender customer trust. For an introduction to modern architecture in post-war Britain, see Bullock (2002). On changing styles in bank architecture, see Nisbet, Tucker, and Wagg (1990) and de Wit (1991: 450–52). For more recent work on the relationship between form and function in finance, see McGoun (2004: 1085–1107).

22. Barry Matthews, interview with author, Bollington, 3 October 2008; David Parsons, interview with author, Manchester, 7 August 2008; David Bound, e-mail message to author, 19 September 2008.

23. Personal Archive of Jim McClymont, Barclays Bank Ltd., "Barclays Bank Limited No. 1 Computer Centre Press Release", 3 July 1961, 7.

Figure 3.3   The spacious reception area as viewed from the entrance to the centre.

and fully operational.[24] The Emidec 1100 was the first British all-transistor computer and as such regarded as an important first in a class of computers that was termed the "second generation" of computers.[25] Using less power, producing less heat, occupying a smaller footprint, and more reliable than its valve-based counterparts, the fully transistorized computer presented an opportunity to make a clear break from the computing past. In timing its formal use of computers in banking with the commercial arrival of the transistor, Barclays was associating itself with the new.[26]

---

24. Barry Matthews, interview with author, Bollington, 3 October 2008.

25. *Second generation* was a contemporary term—see "The Computer Centre Opens", *Spread Eagle*, 1961, 253—used to differentiate computers built using transistors from their vacuum-tube-based counterparts. Computers would later be categorized as first-, second-, or third-generation machines according to the incorporation of successive innovations from the electronics industry: (a) vacuum tubes, (b) transistors, and (c) integrated circuits (Campbell-Kelly and Aspray 1996: 222).

26. The transistor had been invented in 1946 by William Shockley but it was ten years before it became widely available in commercial devices (Campbell-Kelly

On their fact-finding visits to the United States, Barclays' representatives on the CLCB Electronics Sub-Committee, Cowen and Travers, had been impressed by the innovative partnership between the Bank of America and the Stanford Research Institute.[27] The resulting Electronic Recording Machine—Accounting (ERMA) specification was built by General Electric and unveiled by Bank of America at the end of September 1955 (Fisher and McKenney 1993: 55). Barclays had not been involved in the design of the Emidec in any way approaching the level that the Bank of America was with ERMA—from 1956 EMI had been working closely with the British Motor Corporation[28]—but Barclays let everyone know that it had ordered the Emidec 1100 whilst it was still in the blueprint stage.[29] Barclays was proud of its foresight and in the technological capabilities of its chosen machine. It hailed the Emidec as "the world's first fully transistorized and magnetic core machine linked to magnetic tapes" (Travers 1965: 11).

The Emidec 1100 was a machine built with business rather than scientific applications in mind, and this was something Barclays was keen to stress in order to differentiate itself from its competitors.[30] EMI ambitiously marketed its medium-sized 1100 model as a central system component with the potential for integrating hitherto separate tasks within an organisation.[31] This marketing neatly tapped into requirements of the business world that were markedly different from the scientific requirements that earlier computing efforts had predominantly been focused upon.[32] Later, Donald Travers reflected on the beginnings of the widespread commercialization of computing and had this to say:

> The role of the equipment manufacturer was changing. He was no longer selling a computer. He was selling the capabilities of a system, with the computer only one machine in an equipment configuration at the data processing centre that would contain also punched card readers, magnetic tape units and high-speed printers; and a system which would provide also for the preparation of input data at branches, the transfer

---

and Aspray 1996: 226).

27. John D. Cowen and Donald S. Travers, "Electronics Sub-Committee Visit to the United States", September–November 1957. For more on ERMA, see Fisher and McKenney (1993: 44–57).

28. EMI Electronics Ltd., "Emidec Computer News 1", c. 1960, 3.

29. "The Computer Centre Opens", *Spread Eagle*, 1961, 253.

30. Davey-Thomas, interview with author, Penzance, 15 October 2008; EMI Electronics Ltd., "Emidec Computer News 1", c. 1960, 4.

31. EMI Electronics Ltd., "Emidec Computer News 1", c. 1960, 5.

32. The LEO is an early British business computing exception here. See Ferry (2003).

of data to the centre and the feedback of management and accounting control information. (Travers 1965: 11)[33]

Barclays portrayed its computer as the leader in an orchestration of technology from a number of predominantly British manufacturers. The Emidec was connected to Ferranti FR 300 photo-electric paper tape readers, Creed 3000 paper tape punches and Ampex magnetic tape drives, which all served as input and output devices and were also housed in this first computer room.[34] Barclays had colour coded the different units in the computer room according to their purpose and these colours were used to help describe to the visitors in the viewing room how each operated as part of the data processing whole. On the day of the opening ceremony visitors were directors at Barclays' board and local levels, afterwards they were managers and other representatives from Barclays and other banks and businesses. All were invited inside to gaze comfortably from the insulated viewing room upon the flashing lights of the computer, the busy peripherals, and the smooth efficiency of the machine attendants operating within.

As part of the complete visitor experience, guests were given a glossy pamphlet entitled *Barclays Bank Limited: Our First Computer* that emphasized some of the less visible aspects of the new computer system. Through the leaflet Barclays extolled the efficiency of the new computing system in terms of its storage capacity and the speed at which it could deal with information compared to a traditional branch-based bookkeeping system. The leaflet even suggested the new computer system was capable of simple decision making such as that done in a branch. The leaflet listed the input/output and processing capabilities of the computer system thus:

> **It can store a lot of information:** the entries on 9000 full ledger sheets can be stored on 1 reel of magnetic tape, 3600 feet long. **It can read information from paper tape very quickly:** nearly 700 entries in 1 minute. **It can sort information very quickly:** 1000 entries can be sorted in 45 seconds. **It can perform arithmetic very quickly:**

---

33. Note the shifting use of language later to data processing centre rather than computer centre; even back in 1961 language to describe the centre was fluid, visitors were issued leaflets that referred to the computer centre as the 'Data Processing Centre'; see BGA/B262, Barclays Bank Ltd., "Barclays Bank Limited: Our First Computer", 1961. Whereas the official press release described the new building as a 'Computer Centre', see Personal Archive of Jim McClymont, Barclays Bank Ltd., "Barclays Bank Limited No. 1 Computer Centre Press Release", 3 July 1961.

34. Barclays Bank Ltd., "Barclays Bank Limited No. 1 Computer Centre Press Release", 3 July 1961; Barclays Bank Ltd., "Operator's Manual No. 1 Computer Centre" [courtesy of Barry Matthews], c. 1965; David Parsons, interview with author, Manchester, 7 August 2008.

a credit can be added to a balance in 140 millionths of a second. **It can make simple decisions:** answering the question, 'Does the balance exceed the limit?' takes 410 millionths of a second. **It can punch out paper tape very quickly:** a statement sheet of 28 entries is produced in 4½ seconds.[35]

A second computer room, a mirror image of the first, was purposely empty on opening day. The room's emptiness allowed Barclays to make another statement about its technological future. Visitors were informed that this space was reserved for a second Emidec that Barclays would order from EMI later that year. Barclays needed two machines because it knew from its experimental work that the throughput of one Emidec system operated by a single shift would be about forty thousand accounts with approximately sixteen thousand update entries per day.[36] That equated to the number of accounts held by twelve large, busy West End branches. Barclays envisaged automating a larger number of branches when it designed its first computer centre, and there was talk of a "take-on" target set for Donald Travers's team at the No. 1 Computer Centre of fifty London branches.[37] Although its branch network in England and Wales at the time numbered over 2,240 branches,[38] Barclays limited its first automation efforts to a comparatively small number of branches in London. The bulk of its business took place in Britain's financial capital, and in the 1960s it was here that the pressure on banking staff and space was most acutely felt (McRae and Cairncross 1973: 1).

Past the two computer rooms and right at the back of the building were the communications bays that connected the centre to twelve Barclays branches initially. There were twenty-four GPO lines in total allowing for simultaneous input and output from and to each branch. Barclays had cast the operation of its own electronic computer system as an important British banking first, but with the communications bays it pressed home its real achievement. Here it portrayed the Emidec computer system as but one part of a sophisticated data processing system that linked branch and computer centre together by telecommunications. Twenty-four GPO lines and teleprinters allowed branch entries to be input remotely to the computer centre and statement and ledger output back to the branch simultaneously. There was nothing so old-fashioned as the movement of vouchers and paper between branch and centre. *The Banker* described this system connecting two separate

---

35. BGA/B262, Barclays Bank Ltd., "Barclays Bank Limited: Our First Computer", June 1961 [emboldened in original].

36. Ibid.

37. Jim McClymont, interview with author, Bethersden, 4 September 2008.

38. The figure for 1960 is given as 2,240 rising to 2,428 in 1965 in Ackrill and Hannah (2001: 399).

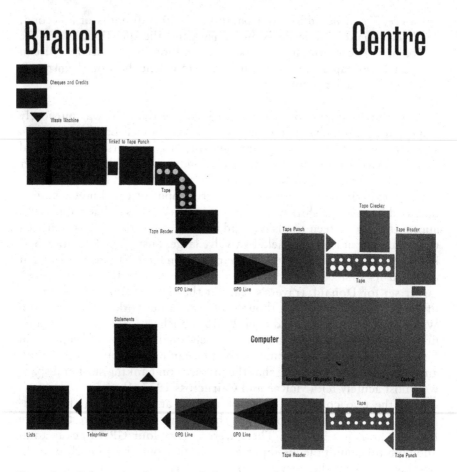

Figure 3.4   Information flow through the system of branches and centre connected by GPO lines, 1961.

places as a world first.[39] Figure 3.4 shows the system connecting branch to computer centre indicating the direction of information flow over the GPO lines. Technology and records located in the branch are to the left in the figure and those at the centre to the right.

THE ICE MACHINE

Barclays had one last trump card to play with the technology it placed inside its computer centre. Up until this moment Barclays had only been

___

39. *The Banker*, August 1961, 521.

able associate itself with the prestige of technology by proxy, but now, in a tangible example of a consumer turned producer (Oudshoorn and Pinch 2005), it had installed a piece of equipment in the centre that had been wholly conceived, designed, and prototyped by members of its own staff. This was the Input Checking Equipment, or ICE machine. Barclays drew special attention to this technology in its press release:

> At intervals the punched paper-tape is transmitted over the teleprinter lines to the Centre, where a duplicate tape is automatically produced. Before these tapes are passed to the computer they are checked electronically to detect very occasional punching or transmission errors. The computer would in fact find these errors itself, but by disposing of these errors in advance the introduction of this input checking equipment (ICE) allows the computer to operate at its greatest efficiency. ICE was designed by a member of the Bank's staff, as there was no equipment on the market, or under development, which would perform this checking function, and considerable interest has been aroused in the data processing field by this machine.[40]

The ICE machine performed a simple but important function. From public opening at 10 a.m. until after closing at 3 p.m. each branch connected to the centre would punch out five-channel paper tape that contained the day's debits and credits to be applied to customer accounts. These transactions would be transmitted in batches of fifty or a hundred across the GPO line to the computer centre where they would be reproduced as paper tape input for the Emidec. In the early 1960s these lines were expensive but for small distances just affordable to big business and fairly reliable. A standard speed data transmission of ten characters per second gave typical line error rates of one in ten thousand for the bank's bookkeeping entries. No matter how low the error rate was, however, Barclays had to ensure that none of these errors could ever reach a customer's account.[41] So Barclays took a belt and braces approach to tackling the issue of line errors. The standard Baudot-type code used by the GPO had its roots in the transmission of text for telegrams. Line errors causing dropped bits for these alphabetic characters were noticeable and not a major cause for concern, but errors in the numbers that were the foundations of the bank's business could have catastrophic consequences. It wasn't just line errors that Barclays had to guard against in this new data processing system; errors could also be introduced at source in the branch through miskeying of input or by the paper tape perforator machines in the transmitting branch or at the receiving centre. It was in fact these input mistakes and punching errors that caused far

---

40. Barclays Bank Ltd., "Barclays Bank Limited No. 1 Computer Centre Press Release", 3 July 1961.

41. For further details, see Travers (1965: 13).

more problems than the line errors.[42] Consequently, Barclays replaced the GPO's standard five-bit Baudot code with its own four-bit plus parity code that allowed a parity check to be performed for each transmitted credit or debit. In addition, it trailed each batch of transactions with a total for reconciliation purposes.

With parity code and reconciliation totals now in place thought had to be given to the most efficient way of checking these at the centre. The programmes on the Emidec had been written so that they checked that the sum of the transactions matched the batch total, but detecting errors as part of the branch update programme created an unacceptable delay for both branch and centre. Updating the accounts for each branch could not take place until after the branch had closed for business at 3 p.m. While an error would be picked up as part of this update, it would cause the whole update programme to stop while the source of the error was determined and the branch retransmitted some of its entries. Ideally what was needed was a way of checking the branch entries as and when they arrived during the day.

The Emidec was needed during the daytime for testing and training so another checking solution that did not involve the Emidec was required. With nothing suitable available on the market, this was a problem in need of a bespoke solution. Two members of Barclays' staff at the computer centre, Davey-Thomas and Doug Pearce, met the challenge by designing and building a device for checking the transmitted paper tape. Both men, like many of the early bankers recruited into computing, were keen hobbyists with interests in amateur radio and electronics consolidated during a period of national service. Having the requisite technical skills and understanding that what was required was really a simple parity checker, the two men built an initial working prototype of the ICE machine using mechanical relays. The prototype machine was slow but it proved their concept. Barclays then partnered with a small electronics firm, RDL, to bring a transistorized version into production. These transistorized ICE machines were demonstrated in place and fully functional on the centre's opening day.[43]

Something that the visitors' attention was not drawn to was Barclays' often more low-tech solution to error correction.[44] As batches of entries were received during the day they would then be read in and validated by the ICE machines. If a machine detected a parity error it would stop and mark the tape highlighting the error. It was then an operator's job to

---

42. Ibid.
43. Davey-Thomas, interview with author, Penzance, 15 October 2008; Personal Archive of Jim McClymont, Barclays Bank Ltd., "Barclays Bank Limited No. 1 Computer Centre Press Release", 3 July 1961.
44. The co-existence of the high-tech alongside the low-tech is a point well made by Edgerton (2006: chap. 2).

perform the necessary error correction. Sometimes this involved a retransmission from the branch, but usually it was no more than a case of the operator flicking the tape to dislodge a stubborn chad left behind from an incomplete perforator punch.[45]

WORK AT THE COMPUTER CENTRE

The tour of the centre was a show of computer and telecommunications strength, but it was also a demonstration of its controlled operation. In the transparent computer rooms visitors had been able to see the computer operators working within and hear their work explained in relation to the machines they were tending. The tour now involved communicating to visitors the role of Barclays' programmers whose mental labours were made visible in the form of flow charts and machine code on display. The programmers' rooms contained exhibits of the "extremely detailed instructions" that its specially trained staff had been responsible for preparing. This display served two purposes. It was not only to communicate to visitors what this new breed of banking staff, the programmer, did, it was also to dispel any notion of the Emidec being an "electronic brain" doing the thinking all of its own accord. Barclays stressed that impressive though its chosen technology was, there was no danger of it making decisions on customer accounts of its own accord. It could only do what the programmers told it do, and visitors were reminded that Barclays programmers, like its computer operators, were all bank clerks first and foremost who knew the business of banking. It was only atop a solid set of banking foundations that specialist programmer and operator training from EMI had been built.[46]

The centre's first programmers and operators were those bank employees that had experimented with centralised accounting in the 1950s under Travers. During the centre's first years of operation the team expanded drawing in staff from Barclays' branch network that had shown a particular aptitude for working with machines. These were the clerks who worked in the back office of a branch or machine room. The most senior of these back office clerks was the Officer in Charge of Mechanization (OC Mech), and although the machine room was predominantly staffed by women, the OC Mech in charge was sometimes a man. It was from this pool of male OC Mechs that many of the centre's first computing workers were drawn.[47]

---

45. Davey-Thomas, interview with author, Penzance, 15 October 2008.

46. Barclays Bank Ltd., "Barclays Bank Limited No. 1 Computer Centre Press Release", 3 July 1961.

47. Many of those interviewed who worked at the early computer centres had held the position of OC Mech. Some examples are: David Parsons, interview with author, Manchester, 7 October 2001; Stan Gray, interview with author, Haslington, 22 July

Prospective programmers and operators were often approached informally and in the main were more than happy to move to the centre from
the branch, some even relocating to London, because they saw the move as
an opportunity and a new challenge. In any case many of those approached
didn't fit comfortably within the rigid confines of the branch and some were
even self-described "trouble-makers".[48] As an alternative to them becoming
increasingly demotivated or leaving the bank, they were redeployed instead
to the No. 1 Computer Centre. Once there they experienced a welcome
liberation of sorts and the subculture of the branch machine room was
amplified in the bigger surroundings of the computer centre.

The programmers and operators were in the main young men, although
initially a significant proportion were also women, between the ages of
twenty and twenty-five.[49] From the outset computing and youth were seen
as going hand in hand. A thirty-one-year-old interviewed for the job of
programmer, and, although accepted, was considered significantly older
than the accepted norm.[50] The first computer operators and programmers
underwent a three-week training course at EMI's factory at Hayes, Middlesex, and then worked on the Emidec at Hayes prior to its delivery to
the centre. By the live date they had built up considerable experience of
the machine.[51]

The centre's programmers and operators became part of the ongoing visitor experience. On a regular basis important visitors, including representatives from other banks, would be met in the impressive reception area by
the head of Barclays' mechanization, Donald Travers, who would pause on
the way to the computer rooms by the door of one of the white-ceilinged,
white-walled offices. He would quietly open the door and point inside the
programmers' room, whispering to the visiting crowd, "These are our programmers." Later, as the visits became embedded in the weekly life of the
centre, one of these programmers would adopt the role of computer centre
tour guide.[52]

As well as two rooms to house the programmers (senior and junior),
other internal work spaces included the assistant manager's office, maintenance workrooms, a lecture room for on-site training, an office for the

2008; Gerry Jarvis, interview with author, Macclesfield, 26 September 2008; David
Prior, telephone interview with author, 15 September 2008.

48. BGA/725/30, Jim McClymont interview with Nicholas Webb, 16 August
2001.

49. RBSGA/WD/366/2, "Report on a Visit to Barclays No. 1 Computer Centre', Management of Williams Deacons bank, 7 February 1962. These were young
white British men.

50. Stan Gray, interview with author, Haslington, 22 July 2008.

51. Ken Cannell, telephone interview with author, 29 September 2008; Jim
McClymont, interview with author, Bethersden, 4 September 2008.

52. David Parsons, interview with author, Manchester, 7 August 2008.

on-site EMI engineers, and a mock-up of a typical branch.[53] Whilst Barclays' architect had allocated space for the practical, these rooms all lay off the main central space that was the building's reception area, and it was this reception area that dominated the building's interior design. The programmers affectionately named the reception "The Elephant House" and "Stonehenge", two names that reflected the relative size of the reception area compared to their own working space and its primary function as a meeting place for groups of gawking visitors that made it akin to the entrance of a tourist attraction.[54] The repurposed building was far from ideal as a working computer centre. The showroom's relatively low ceiling height meant that the introduction of false floors and ceilings to conceal cabling and ducts resulted in a building that felt rather cramped in those spaces outside of reception.[55] The needs of the staff working at the centre and the building's long-term future came second to the initial impact Barclays wanted to make.[56]

In its first year, with one Emidec serving a handful of local branches, there was a chief programmer, two other programmers, and four computer operators working at the centre. Although there appeared to be a clear division of labour indicated by these job roles, in practice the centre provided a fairly informal working environment compared to the rigid hierarchy of the branch. There was a great deal of camaraderie amongst the workers in this new environment and although there were designated job roles in practice, "everybody tended to do a bit of everything".[57]

Overseeing all of the work at the centre were a manager and controller who were both former chief clerks drawn from branches. The chief clerk was a position of authority below that of branch manager who overlooked the operations of the cashiers. The chief clerk from the first branch, Cavendish Square, had been made controller of the computer centre.[58] The manager and his deputy, the controller, oversaw the operations and programming that took place at the centre, but without the strict hierarchy that characterised working life in a branch. The absence of customers, weekly visits aside, made for a more relaxed attitude with everyone on first-name terms.

---

53. "The Computer Centre Opens", *Spread Eagle*, 1961, 254.

54. Jim McClymont, interview with author, Bethersden, 4 September 2008. David Bound, e-mail message to author, 19 September 2008.

55. Jim McClymont, interview with author, Bethersden, 4 September 2008; Jean Perkin, telephone interview with author, 21 July 2008; Davey-Thomas, interview with author, Penzance, 15 October 2008.

56. The importance of the initial statement a building has to make over its practical long-term use is not uncommon in architecture. See Brand (1995) for discussion of workable alternatives.

57. Jim McClymont, interview with author, Bethersden, 4 September 2008.

58. RBSGA/WD/366/2, "Report on a Visit to Barclays No. 1 Computer Centre", Management of Williams Deacons bank, 7 February 1962.

In addition to the computing team there was a small team of communications staff, almost entirely made up of women, responsible for ensuring receipt of the paper tapes in the centre and then carefully winding them and placing them onto spikes. The centre also required a receptionist to front the large reception area and a number of maintenance staff. The Barclays workers at the centre were augmented by on-site EMI engineers who were there to deal with machine failures, which although frequent by today's standards, were dealt with swiftly "99 per cent of the time".[59]

Initially work at the centre was organized into a single daytime shift—nine to five on weekdays and nine to one on Saturdays.[60] This time structure was inherited from the branches; like working time in the branches these hours were only indicative. The expectation in branches was that clerks left work only when all of that day's work had been balanced. Branch staff had long been used to unpredictable finish times that could play havoc with domestic arrangements.[61] The branches may have closed to the public at 3:30 p.m., but there was much work once the doors had closed and a 5 p.m. finish was seldom guaranteed. This branch culture of staying behind until everything had reconciled was easily translated into a culture in the computer centre where it was expected you stayed until all processing had been completed. Flexibility at the centre was very important as the workers came to grips with a new system. Youth was also an advantage. Hours were typically longer than those worked in the branches and although overtime was paid, the primary working incentive in this new environment was a newfound freedom. Staff at the computer centre were not only used to working late, but some also positively thrived on it, using out of hours unpaid working time in which to refine and develop new programmes for the Emidec at the centre.[62]

Even though there was an increased autonomy and a more meritocratic feel to work at the centre, there were still important elements of the inherited branch culture that persisted. They may have been specially trained by and working alongside computer specialists from EMI but this first batch of Barclays computer operators and programmers were all paid a standard bank clerk's wage. This inherited pay structure held strong until the middle of the 1960s. Up until this time their assignment to the computer centre was seen as a temporary one with it "envisaged that they [would] remain at the centre for three years after which they [would] be returned to normal

59. Ron Lewis, telephone interview with author, 28 July 2008.

60. RBSGA/WD/366/2, "Report on a Visit to Barclays No. 1 Computer Centre", Management of Williams Deacons bank, 7 February 1962.

61. Brian Hull, interview with author, Wilmslow, 21 October 2008.

62. David Parsons, interview with author, Manchester, 7 August 2008; Stan Gray, interview with author, Haslington, 22 July 2008. The use of out of hours computing time to develop new programs is part of the computing subculture explored in Levy (2001).

banking duties".[63] A move to the computer centre was viewed as a temporary secondment, with the centre's programmers, operators, controllers, and managers expected to resume their career in banking once the automation work had been completed.

WORK IN THE BRANCH

The first Barclays branch to be served by the No. 1 Computer Centre was nearby Cavendish Square. Because it was the very first branch to be automated, normal bookkeeping operations had been run in parallel with computer accounting for a few months prior to the centre's live date. On 4 July 1961, however, the ledgers in the branch were updated no more and the sole authoritative source for customers' current accounts became the magnetic tapes held at the centre. This was the date when the first Barclays branch *lost* its independence. Month by month more branches were cautiously "taken on" by the centre, one at a time, with Bond Street and Marble Arch following Cavendish Square.[64] By February 1962 the centre had taken on a total of five branches.[65]

As part of the take on process each branch would appoint a member of staff to act as a liaison officer—with the biggest branches appointing two—and it was his or her job to act as the primary point of contact between mechanization department's take on team and the branch staff. This was a key role instrumental in managing the change in the branch as a result of the switch to automation. A liaison officer experienced in the automation process would often move from branch to branch to oversee the necessary account personalization, introduction of new technology, and the change in branch procedures required before computer accounting could take place.[66]

Perhaps the most significant of these changes was the need now for cheque and paying in slip personalization and account numbering in the branch. Prior to automation, branch staff had kept paper and card records sorted by customer name, and chequebooks were a generic standard format personalized only by the customer adding his or her signature. Bank clerks became skilled at recognizing customer accounts by these signatures alone. However, the introduction of computer bookkeeping meant that

---

63. RBSGA/WD/366/2, "Report on a Visit to Barclays No. 1 Computer Centre", Management of Williams Deacons bank, 7 February 1962.

64. David Parsons, interview with author, 7 August 2008; Ian Russell, telephone interview with author, 5 August 2008.

65. RBSGA/WD/366/2, "Report on a Visit to Barclays No. 1 Computer Centre", Management of Williams Deacons bank, 7 February 1962, has the Emidec processing five branches' (fifteen thousand) accounts at the start of February 1962: RBSGA/WD/266/2.

66. Ron Lewis, telephone interview with author, 28 July 2008; Ian Russell telephone interview with author, 5 August 2008.

each account now had to have a unique identifier in the form of a number. A team within the mechanization department had the job of visiting the branch prior to perform the necessary account personalization.[67]

The new computerized and centralised accounting system was sold to branch managers as a way of releasing space and time in branches so that their staff could enjoy better working conditions and provide a better service to customers. In the machine room space was freed as the ledger/statement posting machines were replaced with an NCR 3208 waste machine modified to add a paper tape punch and a Creed 6S/6M paper tape reader to transmit entries via GPO line to the computer centre (see Figure 3.4), but space was also consumed in the branch as a result of computer automation. The requirement for personalized accounts meant that space was required within the branch to hold a library of personalized cheques. A move to centralise this storage and send new chequebooks to customers by post was made later.[68] The branch also required a teleprinter in order to receive reports from the centre for checking purposes and on which to print customer statements and the copies they retained in the branch in place of ledgers.[69] It was the biggest branches, some having upwards of ten accounting machines, that realized the greatest net gains in space.

The increased capacity of the centralised system meant that more business could be taken on in an existing branch without additional machines or staff in the branch. The computer offered a new flexibility that could meet the growth in demand for banking services in the 1960s. As one manager from a competitor bank observed on a visit to Barclays No. 1 Computer Centre:

> This [. . .] point was proved by one branch which obtained a new group of some 50 active accounts which under the conventional system would have meant an additional posting machine and perhaps extra staff at the branch. In fact the additional work was hardly noticed at the branch and was not significant to the computer.[70]

As the automation programme progressed Barclays' head office was keen to stress to branch managers with branches planned for inclusion that they would always remain in control of their customer accounts. Head office

---

67. Neil Savigear, telephone interview with author, 21 July 2008.
68. BGA/80/2827, "The Automation Programme".
69. Press publicity pack, Jim McClymont, Personal Archive. The NCR machines were modified at a cost of £3,000 to add a paper tape punch that punched out account number, transaction type, and reference number as a by-product of each transaction: RBSGA/WD/366/2, "Report on a Visit to Barclays No. 1 Computer Centre", Management of Williams Deacons bank, 7 February 1962.
70. RBSGA/WD/366/2, "Report on a Visit to Barclays No. 1 Computer Centre", Management of Williams Deacons bank, 7 February 1962.

circulars were sent out to branch managers to set an appropriate tone for the introduction of the new computerized system. One circular stressed that a preservation of the power relationship between the branch and the computer centre was central to the bank's automation strategy:

> [I]t is cardinal to all our thinking that the branch is the master and the computer centre the servant. So, as ways and means of improving customer services or the service to branches begin to be seen, the computer system will be subjected to O. & M. [organization and methods] scrutiny just as our conventional services and systems have been and are being.
>
> The branch manager continues to be responsible for *all* decision making; and the management team at the [computer] centre will never be without a man who has had experience in branch management. [. . .] [W]e shall be surprised and disappointed if greater distances should impair the excellent team spirit which exists today between staff at computer branches and at our No. 1 Centre.[71]

At first the branch manager was firmly master and computer centre servant as the following example of statement production illustrates. In the branches overdrawn balances had always been represented in red and this was a feature branch managers were adamant should remain in place when a branch was automated. The high-speed Anelex printers at the centre could not make use of a black/red ribbon whereas the teleprinters in the branch could. Consequently, statement production was initially carried out via teleprinters in the branches (Figure 3.4). Although this was slower than printing at the centre, it did preserve an existing structure and also allowed Barclays to further extol the virtues of its advanced telecommunications system where no paper at all passed between branch and centre. However, over time existing structures formed around the branch were replaced with new ones created from the centre. Sometime before April 1963 printing was moved in-house to the computer centre as the teleprinters struggled to keep pace with statement volume and branch managers and their customers were finally persuaded to accept DR next to an overdrawn balance in place of red print.[72]

There were ramifications for the branch in terms of space and the power base presided over by the branch manager, but what was the impact of the emergence of the computer centre on the branch staff themselves? After all, the introduction of computers was seen as a solution to a staffing crisis

---

71. BGA/80/2827, A.H. Foley, "The Automation Program", 2 December 1965, 10 [italics in original].

72. David Prior started work at the No. 1 Computer Centre in April 1963 and printing was then being done at the centre (David Prior, interview with author, 15 September 2008).

and the computer promised to handle work previously done by Barclays staff. When this was first mooted the banking unions had been worried that the introduction of computers would mean staff redundancies. Back in 1956 the unions had signposted their intentions to resist the introduction of computers if they were to displace staff and they sought assurance that those staff affected would be retrained and deployed elsewhere. The back-office routine work that computers were to replace was largely done by women, and an enlightened National Union of Bank Employees (NUBE) was also at this time pressing for equal pay between men and women in banking at a time when the pay gap was widening.[73] Union fears proved to be premature as the 1960s saw a boom in the business of banking. The Payment of Wages Act of 1960 began to have a real impact by the first quarter of 1963 when a section of the act authorizing payment of wages by cheque came into force.[74] An account with a clearing bank was the easiest way of cashing a cheque. British banks were busier as a result as a larger proportion of the population required banking services and the number of branches to supply these services increased. Although the introduction of computerized and centralised bookkeeping allowed a single branch to cope with a greater number of customers it did not alter the way the banks served their customers. The high-street branch was the means by which banks did business with their customers, and in order to reach more of the population in a wider geographic area banks had to open more branches.

Peak workloads at the start of the week and end of the month were particularly difficult to manage though and computerized bookkeeping smoothed out these peaks and allowed existing staff to better cope with existing volumes of work. The introduction of computers was seen as "relieving the pressure on existing staff".[75] The staff in the branch still had plenty of work to do serving increasing numbers of customers and there were still many manual processes to perform. The computer centre didn't handle all the accounting functions within a branch. To begin with account processing was limited to the current, loan, and personal loan accounts.[76] It is not difficult to see why those working in the branch were not unduly worried by the introduction of a computer; most saw it as an aside as much

73. *Guardian*, "Automation in Banking Union Not Obstructive", 15 May 1956.

74. In an article looking at the impending enactment of an order of the Wages Act, the *Guardian* examines the impact on bank opening hours as more working people require banking services at a time when opening hours were 9 a.m. to 3:30 p.m. Monday to Friday and 9 a.m. to noon on a Saturday. See K. Fleet, "Banks May Alter Hours—Wage Cheques Pose Problems", *Guardian*, 15 January 1963.

75. Barclays Bank Ltd., "Barclays Bank Limited No. 1 Computer Centre Press Release", 3 July 1961.

76. RBSGA/WD/366/2, "Report on a Visit to Barclays No. 1 Computer Centre", Management of Williams Deacons bank, 7 February 1962.

of the work in the branches carried on as before.[77] In its first few years the computer and the computer centre was seen as an adjunct to bank business, and despite the chairman's claims from the top, those working in automated branches below saw it as ancillary rather than revolutionary. Branches that were automated were certainly freed of some work but lots of other work carried on the same and there was an increasing number of customers to serve.

MANAGING CUSTOMER PERCEPTIONS

The introduction of new technologies and working practices in the branch as a result of computer centre automation took place in the back office. A customer looking around the banking hall of his or her branch on a routine visit to cash a cheque would have noticed no change in the arrangement of branch space, but this is not to say that customers did not experience change. The cheque itself was the site for a series of changes that directly affected the customer served by an automated branch. The inclusion of Magnetic Ink Character Recognition (MICR) characters for branch sort code and account number in the E13-B font at the bottom of cheques now bearing their pre-printed name was something to which customers had to become accustomed. This "personalization" of cheques by the bank was regarded by some customers as representing a depersonalization of their relationship with the bank.[78]

Changes to cheque format, layout, and use were visible changes; customers also experienced change regarding their statements. Both the look of the statement and the nature of statement ordering changed. Previously a customer would be able to visit his or her branch and request a statement that could be produced on demand. With the move to centralised accounting the flexibility of on-demand statement production was lost. Customers were now required to give the branch twenty-four hours notice when they required a statement. This was to allow the request to reach the computer centre from the branch and the completion of batch processing with the resulting customer statement being sent back to the teleprinter in the branch for printing the following morning.[79] Centralised production for both the initial remote and the later local printing of statements meant a

---

77. BGA/725/25, Sue Hargreaves, interview with Barclays Group Archives, 14 August 2001; Jean Perkin, telephone interview with author, 21 July 2008.

78. Brooks (1965: 20) expresses general concerns regarding depersonalization, and more specifically that the requirement for customers to include the account number on a credit slip is "apt to create in the customer's mind that he [*sic*] is merely a number."

79. RBSGA/WD/366/2, "Report on a Visit to Barclays No. 1 Computer Centre", Management of Williams Deacons bank, 7 February 1962, states that "branches get their statements (non-narrative) between about 10 and 11 each day."

change for customers too. The days and dates of weekly and monthly statements were moved to meet the computer centre's requirements rather than
those of the customer.

In an attempt to carefully manage customer perceptions of automation Barclays issued each customer that would be affected with a specially
commissioned leaflet entitled *Our First Computer*.[80] In this first district,
the prestigious Pall Mall, customers were mainly important businesses,
and it was paramount to Barclays that it avoided alienating or even losing
this important customer base. It had to sell the change to them and it did
so by presenting automation at the computer centre as the only practical
and sensible solution to the growing cost of providing a branch banking
service. The key advantage of electronic bookkeeping by computer was
stressed as a reduction in spiralling costs associated with staff, premises,
paperwork, and equipment. The response to the question "why a computer?" was because without a computer "it might well be that in a few
years time we should be unable to provide you with an adequate banking
service at a cost which you could reasonably be expected to pay". Barclays pressed home in its direct customer communications and a number
of newspaper and magazine advertisements that computers would contain
and reduce the cost of banking and also allow branch staff to provide a
more personal service.[81]

As part of a wider discourse, anthropomorphic representations of
computers were a common way of explaining computers that those unfamiliar with them could understand. The "electronic brain" had been a
powerful, if misleading, early metaphor used by the popular press to
convey the electronic computer concept to a wider public audience (Lean
2008: 184–85; Martin 1993: 120–33). In a number of advertisements
in business magazines and newspapers Barclays now recast its computer
not as a giant brain that could do thinking of its own accord, but as a
"workhorse" that took away the drudgery of accounting from branch
staff now freed up to provide a service that was "proportionately more
efficient".[82]

The comic writer H.F. Ellis articulated his response to computer
bookkeeping in a humorous polemic, "Give Me Back My Ledger", first
published in *Punch* in March 1962 and republished later that year in Barclays' staff publication, *Spread Eagle*. The article entertained its readers,
but it also reawakened the importance of trust in a relationship between
customer and bank, potentially undermined by automation efforts. Ellis

---

80. BGA/B262, Barclays Bank Ltd., "Barclays Bank Limited: Our First Computer", June, 1961.

81. Ibid.

82. For example, see *Economist*, "Miss Wolveridge Is Now Handling 40,000
Accounts", display advertising, 8 July 1961, and *Economist*, "Our Computer Has
a Twin", display advertising, 5 January 1963.

criticised the bank and the computer for the negative impacts associated with its seemingly simultaneous visibility and invisibility. The addition of account numbers to the bottom of customer cheques he saw as a constant visible reminder that a computer was now in control of a customer's account. This increased visibility of the computer's presence was an irritant, but the growing invisibility of customer accounts was a bigger issue, evoking both practical and emotional concerns. Using magnetic tapes to store customer accounts was seen as a long way away from the easy readability of the branch ledger. Whilst computer media such as punched cards and paper tape were touchable with the holes representing account entries clearly visible, information on magnetic tape was both untouchable and invisible. With the ability to read this new medium now resting firmly with the computer, customer trust now had to be placed in machine as well as man (Ellis 1962).[83]

Furthermore, the creation of a special centre to house the computer served to elevate its status, and holding customer account information within the centre's walls removed the account from the long-established trust and security of the branch. In spite of efforts by the bank to explain to customers how the links between branch and computer centre would work, the presence of a number of devices involved in establishing these links brought to mind more opportunities for failure or even the possibility of random numbers being generated like those from ERNIE.[84] The computer centre and its contents were now seen as especially vulnerable to attack, with imaginings of "the hooded representatives of a rival bank stealing into the Centre at dead of night with an enormous magnet and in an instant utterly demolishing all the records. Or they might feed false information to the computer, turning all my pluses to minuses and vice versa" (Ellis 1962: 432).

Perhaps fanciful, and not wholly representative, the article does provide a useful articulation of the broader issues concerning customer trust, security, accountability, and personal service that Barclays needed to address as it moved from the self-contained production unit of the branch into a distributed model of accounting that connected branch to computer centre. The banks were certainly aware that prominent vocal minorities like these could be disruptive and they sought not "to dismiss any criticisms of our system in a cavalier way" but instead to address customer concerns in order to remove resistance to the changes introduced by automation (Brooks 1965: 21). Barclays had also made contingency arrangements should a giant magnet or any other threat endanger

---

83. Ellis (1962) was reprinted in *Spread Eagle*, vol. 37, 144–45.

84. ERNIE is the Electronic Random Number Indicator Equipment. It was developed by the GPO and in 1957 quickly established itself as part of British popular culture when it was first used to randomly draw the month's winning premium bonds.

operations at the No. 1 Computer Centre. It had an agreement with British European Airways (BEA) at London Airport to use its Emidec 1100 in the event of an emergency.[85]

THE FIRST COMPUTER CENTRE AND THE OTHER BANKS

Barclays undoubtedly went to great lengths to make a powerful statement when it opened its first computer centre, but is its claim of the first computer centre for banking in Britain valid? And, furthermore, how did the opening of the first computer centre for banking relate to the automation efforts of the other British banks at the time?

The other clearing banks that made up the "Big Five"—Lloyds, the Westminster, the Midland, and the National Provincial—were only a matter of months behind Barclays, with Lloyds the closest follower; Lloyds opened its computer centre in the West End of London in September 1961.[86] However, it was another smaller English bank, Martins, which gave Barclays the closest run for its money. Martins, was much smaller than Barclays with only six hundred branches to Barclays's 2,240. Despite its smaller size, like Barclays it had also been represented on the three-man CLCB's Electronics Sub-Committee working party. Like Barclays, this placed Martins in somewhat of a privileged position, and at the start of 1960 Martins became the first British bank to successfully process the accounting and statement production of one its branches with an electronic computer. It did this at Ferranti's London Computer Centre and shortly after placed an order for its own Pegasus II to be installed at its Liverpool head office.[87] Martins could have had the first British computer centre for banking if it were not for a three-month delay as a result of a strike by Ferranti's subcontractors. As it was, Martins officially opened its computer centre a month later than Barclays on 18 August 1961.[88]

---

85. John Prouse, "Memories from John Prouse", http://www.iansmith.myzen.co.uk/emidec/emihme.htm (accessed 10 March 2009). It was not unusual for one company to borrow time on another's computer. This could be temporarily to cover peaks in workload or in a testing phase prior to delivery, or as in this case in event of machine failure. London Airport was known as Heathrow after 1966. BEA's Emidec 1100 there was used for "processing revenue data and other Head Office accounting work" ("Precision in Airline Management", *Flight*, 14 August 1959, 23).

86. *The Banker*, "Computer Banking a Survey: Action by the Clearing and Scottish Banks", August 1961, 497.

87. "Enter Pegasus", *Martins Bank Magazine*, Spring 1960, 12.

88. BGA/25/1202, Martins Bank Limited Head Office, "Announcement by Martins Bank Limited", 18 August 1961; Edna Devaynes, interview with author, Birkdale, 1 August 2008.

Barclays had also considered the Ferranti Pegasus alongside the AEI 1010 as one of two credible alternatives to the Emidec 1100 on its computer shortlist of three. Whilst there was a strong argument that favoured the Emidec because of its technical merits, including the technical and political importance of having an all transistorized machine, the final decision to go with the Emidec was made because EMI banked with Barclays.[89] This wasn't an unusual scenario; a bank preferring to do business with its customers was common practice. The Midland did the same when it ordered a KDP 10 from English Electric; English Electric banked with the Midland, they shared a board member, and the *KDP* was manufactured locally in Kidsgrove.[90] There isn't the space to do a detailed treatment of all the British clearing banks here, so instead I continue to "follow the actors" and summarize the position as seen through the eyes of one of the other clearing banks.[91]

Table 3.1, produced by Manchester-based Williams Deacons Bank two months after the opening of Barclays No. 1 Computer Centre, illustrates Barclays' leading position in relation to the rest of the "Big Five" and to some other smaller but innovative British banks. At this point it was only Barclays and Martins that were operational with computers purchased and installed on their own premises. Lloyds would open its computer centre in the West End of London with an IBM 350 installation later that month, followed by the Westminster, who eventually chose IBM, too, but a 1401 model. The rest of the "Big Five" set up computer centres of their own soon after.

The table also indicates that the Bank of Scotland was due to install an IBM 1401 by the end of 1961. This warrants further attention because some historians have claimed that the Bank of Scotland, not Barclays, was the first British bank to open a computer centre. The source of these claims appears to be Richard Saville's, *Bank of Scotland: A History, 1695–1995*, which states that the Bank of Scotland installed an IBM 1401 computer in 1959.[92] Saville does not disclose his

---

89. BGA/80/850, Barclays Bank Ltd., "Directors' Inspection of Advances", 3. EMI had its account with Barclays in Hayes, Middlesex, which was the location of EMI headquarters. There were strong rumours that the final decision came down in favour of EMI because it was a bank customer (David Parsons, interview with author, Manchester, 7 August 2008).

90. See Booth (2004: 285; 2007: 146). Reference in the first of these sources is made to a KDP 8—a machine that did not exist: there *was* a KDP 10 that was upgraded and rebadged in 1964 to the KDF 8. The second Booth source has the order as a KDF 8, but in 1961 the order would have been for a KDP 10. See Table 3.1 from a primary source later in the text.

91. One of the earliest uses of the term "follow the actors" is in Law and Callon (1988: 284).

92. For the claim that the Bank of Scotland installed an IBM 1401 in 1959, see Saville (1996: 805).

Table 3.1   Computers and Sorter Readers Ordered by the Clearing and Scottish Banks, 1961

Bank	Type of Computer	Price	Remarks
Barclays	Emidec 1100	£150,000	Installed in London. To process 40,000 accounts. Operational.
Coutts	Univac S.S. 80 STEP	£80,000	To be installed in spring 1962.
District	-	-	Hiring time on a Ferranti Pegasus.
Lloyds	3 IBM RAMAC	£350,000	To be installed at Cox & King's Branch, London, to process 30,000 accounts.
Martins	Ferranti Pegasus II	-	Installed in Liverpool to process 30,000 accounts. Operational.
Midland	English Electric KDP 10	£250,000	To be installed in West End of London to process 100,000 accounts.
National Provincial	Ferranti Orion	£200,000	To be installed at end of 1962. To process 150,000 accounts.
Westminster	IBM 1401Ferranti Pegasus	£100,000?	
Bank of Scotland	IBM 1401	£100,000	To be installed in Edinburgh by the end of this year.

Source: RBS/WD/366/2, "Computers", in "Computers and Sorter Readers Ordered by the Banks", Group Electronics File, Williams Deacons Bank.

source, but my archival work has revealed a number of sources indicating that it was not an IBM computer that Bank of Scotland installed in its pioneering Edinburgh accounting centre in 1959, but an IBM 420 tabulator. The Bank of Scotland was unique amongst the British banks in using punched-card technology to automate the branch accounting of several branches, and this acted as an intermediate step between the move from distributed mechanized accounting to centralised computerisation. It did this two years before the first of the other British banks made the leap to computerization. However, it wasn't until the end of 1961 that the Bank of Scotland made its final step and replaced its IBM

420 tabulator with an IBM 1401 computer.[93] Barclays was, therefore, the first British bank to open a *computer* centre in July 1961.

EXPANSION AND CLOSURE

In 1963 with a second Emidec in operation and statement printing moved from the branch-based teleprinters to the Anelex line printers at the centre, Drummond Street began operating a double-shift system. Two shifts of six operators and one programmer worked from 8 a.m. until 4 p.m. and then 4 p.m. until midnight or until all the evening's printing had finished.[94] Operators not only managed the printing of the statements, but also guillotined and packed them up to be delivered to the branches the next morning. In times of need, when printing carried on well past midnight, computer operators would even go as far as delivering the statements to any branches they went past on their way home in the morning after a night shift.[95]

Working a double-shift system allowed the two Emidecs to more than double their estimated workload capacities. In 1964 the No. 1 Computer Centre reached its rumoured automation target of fifty branches.[96] There was now a total of forty-eight staff members working at the centre and eleven of these were communications "girls" working during the day to deal with incoming paper tape transmissions across fifty GPO lines.[97] Take-on had been cautious but the pace was steadily increased, targeting in order those London branches in the Pall Mall and London Eastern districts where the shortage of staff and the pressure on existing premises was the greatest.[98] That year Barclays estimated it had saved 142 branch staff as a result of the new computer system

---

93. The following sources all confirm that Bank of Scotland was operating an IBM 420 tabulator from 1959 till the end of 1961 when it was then replaced with an IBM 1401 computer: RBS/WD/366/2, "Computers" in "Computers and Sorter Readers Ordered by the Banks", Group Electronics File, Williams Deacons Bank; *The Banker*, "Computer Banking—A Survey: B—Action by the Clearing and Scottish Banks", August 1961, 497; Halifax Bank of Scotland Group Archives (hereafter HBOSGA) /2001/039 Box 53, folder 12—SII/32/C/1, "Historical Review"; HBOSGA/2008/029/2, "Maida V. Gillespie Personal Training Notes", 3 November 1958. In addition, the log-book for the IBM 1401, not catalogued at HBOSGA, begins on 23 November 1961.

94. BGA/80/2827, A.H. Foley, "The Automation Program", 14 August 1964, 5; Brian Hull, interview with author, Wilmslow, 21 October 2008.

95. David Bound, interview with Janet Sykes, Gloucester, 19 October 1990.

96. BGA/80/2827, A.H. Foley, "The Automation Program", 14 August 1964, 9, lists a total of fifty-four branches taken on by the No. 1 Computer Centre at this point.

97. BGA/80/2827, A.H. Foley, "Greater London Computer Centre", 14 August 1964, 7.

98. Barclays Bank Ltd., "Barclays Bank Limited No. 1 Computer Centre Press Release", 3 July 1961.

and parallel developments in the automation of cheque clearing.[99] But a look at wider staffing figures shows that this figure of 142 was insignificant in comparison to the rise in the number of branches and staff over the same period. The fifty automated branches represented just over 2 per cent of Barclays' branches nationwide and Barclays' employee headcount rose steadily from 24,951 in 1960 to 33,240 in 1965.[100] The business of banking grew steadily and those staff shortages in London at the beginning of the sixties were still prevalent at its end. In spite of computer centre automation, all through the sixties branch staff continued to be drafted in from the provinces to the capital in order to provide relief.[101]

As the workload of the centre and its staff expanded so too did the attractions it was able to offer. Computer centre guests were now treated to computer-generated music. A young programmer, David Parsons, who had initially programmed the Emidec so that it would print out a history of the No. 1 Computer Centre, now wrote a programme that made novel use of the speaker built into the machine's operator control panel. EMI had originally provided this speaker to enable audible monitoring of a programme's progress and for sounding alerts on successful programme end or abnormal termination. An enterprising Parsons, following a growing tradition of computer-generated music stretching back in Britain to 1951 and the University of Manchester's Ferranti Mark 1 computer,[102] made use of the speaker to have the Emidec play a selection of carols to visitors at Christmas time. His programme proved so popular that it was even featured on BBC radio.[103]

In August of 1964, with Barclays head office at Lombard Street attracted to the prestige of having its own computer centre and plans afoot for a third much bigger centre to serve the whole of London, the decision was made to close down the No. 1 Computer Centre at Drummond Street. The building was now judged to have served its purpose for Barclays and left its mark. Those initial concessions made in the building's design for visitors and prestige were now reclassed as "difficulties in continuing to use Drummond Street premises as a Computer Centre".[104] However, it would be another

99. BGA/80/2827, A.H. Foley, "Greater London Computer Centre", 14 August 1964, 9.

100. Between 1960 and 1965 the number of Barclays branches increased from 2,240 to 2,428 and its staff from 24,951 to 33,240. Figures taken from Ackrill and Hannah (2001: 399).

101. Paul Reckin and Jeff Metcalfe, interview with author, Goostrey, 10 November 2008.

102. Hally (2005: 100–101); BBC, "'Oldest' Computer Music Unveiled', 17 June 2008, http://news.bbc.co.uk/1/hi/technology/7458479.stm (accessed 10 March 2009).

103. Jean Perkin, telephone interview with author, 21 July 2008; David Parsons, telephone interview with author, 21 July 2008. The speaker's function was derived from "EMIDEC 1100 Computer", http://www.emidec.org.uk/, (accessed 10 March 2009).

104. BGA/80/2827, A.H. Foley, "Greater London Computer Centre", 14 August 1964, 4.

six years before the lights were turned off and the technologies and people within stopped performing useful work. The centre's twin Emidecs eventually processed the branch, accounting for fifty-eight branches and approximately two hundred thousand accounts.[105] After 1967 these branches were gradually transferred to the Barclays new Greater London Computer Centre built nearby in an old piano factory on Tottenham Court Road,[106] but the No. 1 Computer Centre was still operational even as the sixties turned into the seventies. New programmes were being written for the twin Emidecs as late as 1969.[107]

However, at the beginning of the 1970s the centre finally did close. On a Wednesday afternoon, 10 February 1971, every branch in Britain had shut its doors, not to reopen until the following Monday morning. Over the following weekend the No. 1 Computer Centre's grand reception area was reconfigured and put to use for one last time as a distribution point for the pre- and post-decimalisation output produced by Barclays' remaining operational London computer centres numbered 2, 3, and 4. The reception's granite floor was marked out and on it was laid a million statements and ledgers ready for collection by a newly decimalised branch network.[108] For one last time the computer centre's space was the site of a break from tradition as a pounds, shillings, and pence past was replaced by a decimal future.

After decimalisation on 15 February 1971 the centre gradually fell into disuse and Barclays eventually sold the lease in 1974 to BC Facilities Ltd., a provider of banking services owned by the Hong Kong Shanghai Banking Corporation (HSBC). HSBC reused the building in 1981 as a computer centre for its British Bank of the Middle East and then again in 1984 as a computer centre for the Hong Kong and Shanghai Bank. There lie other chapters in the building's life as a bank computer centre.[109]

---

105. BGA/80/2827, A H. Foley, "The Automation Program", 2 December 1965, 1, lists fifty-eight branches; BGA 80/2827, a year previously, A.H. Foley, "Greater London Computer Centre", 14 August 1964, 3, lists fifty-four branches and 180,000 accounts.

106. Frederick Deane, telephone interview with author, 17 July 2008; Jean Perkin, telephone interview with author, 21 July 2008.

107. Barry Matthews, interview with author, Bollington, 3 October 2008.

108. John Evans, interview with author, Congleton, 22 July 2008. The figure of a million is taken from David Bound, interview with Janet Sykes, Gloucester, 19 October 1990.

109. BGA/80/632, "Schedule of Title Deeds"; *Post Office London Directories*. The building was subsequently demolished and the site redeveloped as the UK headquarters for computer consultants Logica. Logica have recently vacated the premises and NHS Camden have moved in to house a new GP-led health centre on its ground floor, "First New GP Practice in Camden for a Decade Given the Go Ahead", http://www.camden.nhs.uk/GPGoahead (accessed 10 March 2009).

CONCLUSIONS

Buildings can easily be taken for granted as they soon become part and parcel of business infrastructure. Throughout the 1960s computers were also increasingly becoming one of the basic structures of big business. Instead of allowing the first British computer centre for banking and its computers to fade into the background, this chapter has kept it firmly in the foreground in order to offer insight into the multiple meanings attached to a unique technological place. These were meanings that over time proved more adaptable than the walls of the building itself, and were more than just connected to the computer centre; they were instrumental in its construction.

For the executives of the board, the computer centre was purposefully designed as a site of public display intended to maximize the bank's status as technological innovator. It symbolized and conveyed a set of ideas and ideals as they purposefully set about realizing a vision of modernity for the bank that had the computer at its centre against a backdrop of hundreds of years of branch banking tradition. As Barclays' senior managers used the computer centre to forge a new organizational identity, so the building was a formative structure for a new breed of bank clerks turned computer specialists who themselves were busy carving out new occupational identities. But the architectural concessions made to ensure the building was a practical working home for computer programmers, operators, and ancillary staff always remained secondary to its primary purpose as a first-of-its-kind showpiece building for the bank. Ultimately this hierarchical arrangement of internal space was the building's downfall as succeeding computer centres were designed with less consideration for visitors and more consideration for computers and computing staff.

This spatial analysis of a single building has provided a fine-grained history that stands on its own, but one that can also act as a complement, and sometime corrective, to other business histories that encompass this period. The micro and the macro are both useful lenses for examining technological change. Computer centres and other technological places provide new analytical possibilities that can throw new light on issues of structure, labour, identity, power, and control. Reconstructing the micro-world of a computer centre presents certain challenges, however, which can only be successfully met by drawing upon oral and visual sources in addition to written sources. Much of the detail in this chapter has been gleaned from interviews, personal notes, photographs, and keepsakes that are underrepresented in many business archives. These are valuable sources that need to be sought out and preserved.

4 Technical and Organizational Change in Swedish Banking, 1975–2003

Joakim Appelquist

... a man honoured for fifty years of service to a Virginia bank [...] was asked at the party the bank gave to celebrate him what he thought had been "the most important thing, the most important change that you have seen in banking in this half century of service". The man paused for a few minutes, finally got up before the microphone, and said, "Air Conditioning." (Mayer 1997, quoting a man in 1973)

If the same question in the preceding quote was posed to an employee retiring in 2008 the answer would most likely come instantly and be: "Computers". The reason is that information technology has been used to transform the role of the banker and his customer relations over and over again during the last fifty years. This chapter will use the Swedish case to highlight some of these changes.[1]

PURPOSE AND DATA

The purpose of this chapter is to investigate the relation between the implementation of information and telecommunication technology (ICT) and organizational change in the Swedish banking industry from 1975 to 2003.

The rationale for beginning this study in the mid-1970s is the fact that this was the time when the major Swedish banks made massive investments in computer technology and it was diffused to all their branches. The decision to choose 1975 as the starting point has more practical grounds because the data set which is used to investigate the organizational changes covers the period 1975–2003. However, because the interaction between technological and organizational change is complex and characterised by time lags, data, especially regarding the development of computer technology, outside of the period 1975–2003, will also be used in the analysis. Following are some comments regarding the empirical data used in this chapter.

---

1. This chapter is based on Appelquist (2005), which is a doctoral dissertation published in Swedish.

Despite the information-intensive character of banking industries and the crucial role that ICT has played to increase productivity in the sector, no coherent description of the technological development of Swedish banks is currently available. In order to construct and analyse this development annual reports and education material published by the banks themselves, as well as business history literature, scientific papers, and reports from agencies and industry organizations have been used. In order to match the aggregate organizational data described in the following, the material has been used to construct a general picture of the technical development and not to give detailed descriptions of different banks. Hence, it might be considered a problem that records from only nine banks are included.[2] However, this is not the case due to the highly oligopolistic nature of the Swedish banking sector with the market share of the four largest banks, which are all included in the study, fluctuating between 81.9 per cent and 87.7 per cent in the period 1975–2003 (Appelquist 2005: 79).

To complement the qualitative analysis, industry data from Statistics Sweden, the Swedish national statistics office, have been used. Machine capital stocks are the indicator, which is being used as a proxy to study the scale and timing of ICT investments. The reason why machine capital stocks are used is because computers are virtually the only machinery equipment used in this information-intensive industry. It should be noted that the data does not only include banks, but the whole NIS class 8100, which is banks and other financial institutions. This should not be seen as too much of a problem because the Swedish banks and their subsidiaries are important actors in virtually every niche of the financial sector.[3]

Unfortunately, no consistent time series of machine capital stocks are available for the period after 1995 due to a major revision of the national accounts. Both the definition of investment and the constant price calculation methods have changed. The revisions were so substantial that no linking of the series is possible. But in order to perform a long-term analysis of the machine capital stock an extrapolation of the series has been done for the period after 1995. This was done making the value of 1995 a base year and using the annual change in the revised machine capital stock for

---

2. All of these banks were involved in mergers and acquisitions and at the end of the studied period only four remain. They are, in order of size, in 2003: Svenska Handelsbanken, Skandinaviska Enskilda Banken, Föreningssparbanken, and Nordea. The banks included in the study are: Föreningsbankernas bank, Föreningsbanken AB, Föreningssparbanken, Götabanken (GOTA bank), Nordbanken, PK-banken, Skandinaviska Enskilda banken, Sparbanken Sverige, and Svenska Handelsbanken 1978–2003.

3. Available numbers from the 1980s indicate a market share for the banks of around 60 per cent of the balance sheet total of the institutional market; *SOU 1988:29*, 158.

NIS 65, i.e. the bank and the financial sector in the new national accounts system, to get an estimated series.

The organizational development of the Swedish banking sector was studied using wage statistics jointly produced by *Bankinstitutens arbetsgivarorganisation* (the Employers' Association of the Swedish Banking Institutions) and *Finansförbundet* (the Financial Sector Union of Sweden). The data set includes information on every employee working more than fifteen hours a week on average each year.

What makes this material so valuable for a study on organizational development is the fact that every employee is classified according to a hierarchical scale, based on work content, responsibility, managerial assignment, et cetera. This makes it possible to investigate changes in the complexity of work and skill requirements of bank employees. The classification system also includes an indicator of the type of work that each employee performs, such as marketing, teller, accounting, et cetera, as well as the educational level of all employees, but these indicators will only be used sparsely. It should be noted that the data set is an industry aggregate, i.e. it is not possible to know what bank a certain employee is working for. One major change in the scope of the material is that part-time workers working more than fifteen hours a week were included in the data set from 1983 onwards.

The hierarchical classification of the bank employees uses an eight graded scale. Level 8 represents the most routine-based positions with the lowest skill requirements, whereas level 1 is reserved for the CEO and a small number of other top managers. Level 1 is not included in the data set. Following are short descriptions of level 8 to 2 based on the manual that was worked out to aid the work of classifying employees according to the BNT system (*Befattningsnomenklatur för tjänstemän* [position taxonomy for employees]) and a similar system, TNS (*Tjänstenyckel för statistik* [statistical position classification]) that replaced BNT in 1995. The change was not entirely semantical and comments regarding the interpretations of data after the revision will be made continuously in this chapter.

Level 8. Descriptions stress the unskilled nature of the work tasks. A reoccurring phrase is: "The work is performed according to detailed instructions". In connection with the change of classification system in 1995, level 8 was removed from the data set.

Level 7. This contains occupations that are slightly more qualified than level 8, but still routine work. The work is said to be carried out "according to instructions".

Level 6. Positions at this level require greater skills and come with some responsibilities, even managerial assignments. Work is carried out "according to general instructions".

Level 5. There are no reoccurring phrases that describe the work carried out at level 5, which in itself is an indication of greater complexity. Working in larger projects and with bigger clients, as well as responsibility to carry out non-routine tasks and managerial assignments, are examples of the nature of work of level 5 positions.

Level 4. The complex and independent character of these positions is highlighted through the use of verbs such as planning, analysing, developing, and designing in the descriptions. Managerial assignments are increasingly stressed.

Level 3. The same words as for level 4 are used, but the biggest difference is that the managerial responsibilities are larger as the number of subordinates increases.

Level 2. The descriptions on this level only state the number of subordinates that different types of managers are responsible for.

TECHNICAL AND ORGANIZATIONAL CHANGE—A HYPOTHESIS

The analysis of the interaction between the development of computer technology and organizational change from the mid-1970s is especially interesting because both variables change fundamentally during the period of study. Computer technology evolves from hierarchical mainframe systems to PC-based LANs connected to the Internet. Organizations go from Tayloristic bureaucracies to post-Tayloristic entities characterised by flattened management structures, outsourcing, etc. This section investigates the general development of these variables and focuses on their impact on labour relations and skill requirements. The discussion ends with a formulation of a hypothesis of the relationship and changes of these variables during the period of study.

The introduction, diffusion, and development of ICT since the 1960s, and the way it has interacted with the transformation of organization of work, provide a good illustration to the concept of complementarity. If we focus on the organizational factor a major transformation has occurred from a Tayloristic hegemony to a post-Tayloristic mode of organization.

Taylorism, or Scientific Management, is often cited as one of the defining characteristics of the second industrial revolution, and it retained its position as the dominating mode of organization during the first three quarters of the twentieth century. The most cited characteristics of the Tayloristic mode of organization are:[4]

1. division of labour
2. clear distinction between managerial and production work
3. focus on control

---

4. See Taylor (1911). See also Littler (1978: 188–89) for a similar description of Taylorism.

The implementation of the Tayloristic mode of organization made it possible to use less skilled workers and still achieve sharp rises in productivity. However, the downside was more routine-based production work and a growing lack of understanding of the work process and the end-product, i.e. alienation (Braverman 1974: chaps. 5 and 6).

The Tayloristic mode of organization reached its peak during the golden years of the 1950s and the 1960s. But in connection with reoccurring economic crises and sluggish growth rates in many Western countries during the 1970s and 1980s, Taylorism was called into question. Intensified business cycle fluctuations and shorter product cycles due to rapid changes in customer demand made companies search for a more adaptive way of organizing. Japan was initially a source of inspiration because the Japanese economy seemed immune to the economic problems. Many labels, such as "post-industrial organization", "post-Fordist", and "New Work System", have been used for the emerging mode of organization that gradually replaced the Tayloristic principles (Boynton and Milazzo 1996; Cappelli and Rogovsky 1994; Winter and Taylor 2001). Even though the literature paints a much more diverse picture than in the case of defining the Tayloristic mode of organization, some characteristics of the new, emerging mode are cited frequently.

1. *"Blurry" boundaries of companies* due to increased company interactions. Partly inspired by Lean Production and Business Processing Reengineering (BPR), thinking of the 1980s and 1990s, many firms downsized their operations by outsourcing a lot of non-core activities. Efforts to reduce cost and ensure flexibility also induced companies to use Just-in-Time systems, which led to increasing interaction with supplier firms (Davenport and Short 1990; Powell 2001; Womack, Daniel, and Roos 1990).
2. *Increased use of temporary workers* in order to cope with fluctuating demand (Tilly 1991: 10–12; Castells 1996).
3. *Increased scope of job descriptions for the permanent workforce.* A third strategy to enhance organizational adaptability was to enhance the number of tasks that each employee was expected to be able to carry out. Job rotation and team organizations are examples of organizational innovations used to achieve a more multi-skilled permanent workforce. The up-skilling of the workforce was paralleled by a decentralisation of responsibility as the number of middle managers decreased. The result was a movement towards more *flat organizations* (Smith 1997; Murphy 2002: 8–9).

In order to highlight the break with the dominating Tayloristic organizational model, this study uses post-Taylorism as the label of the mode of organization that is gradually implemented from the 1970s onwards.

Mainframe computers started to be used commercially at the end of the 1950s and the diffusion picked up pace during the 1960s.[5] Among the first industries to make use of the innovation were insurance companies, airlines, and banks (Yates 2005; Campbell-Kelly 2003; Bátiz-Lazo and Wood 2002). For the purpose of this chapter two features of computer technology are of special interest:

1. *Hierarchical technical system.* The technical design of mainframes was distinctly hierarchical with programmers and operators at the top level with full control of the work process and pace.
2. *Batch systems.* The first generation of mainframe computers did not have the calculative capacity to facilitate a database structure with constant update of information. Instead, computers were used to do batch processing resulting in paper transcripts that were used until new data and new calculations were carried out.

The continuous hardware development increased the calculative capacity, and during the 1970s so-called "dumb terminals" were introduced, which increased access to data. However, the hierarchical structure was preserved because the terminals only could be used to punch in and view data.

The commercial success of the mainframe computers during the 1960s should come as no surprise, the reason being the obvious complementarity with the existing Tayloristic mode of organization (Boynton and Milazzo 1996). Firstly, there were similarities in the hierarchical structure in both the technical and organizational models as the mainframes led to a centralisation of a number of tasks, such as programming and analysis of the registered data. The result was a complete automation or transformation of administrative work into highly routine-based tasks. Secondly, the mainframes opened up new ways for control, both through the increased possibilities of monitoring the working pace of each worker and through the design of the work process.

The interaction between the technical and organizational variables was expected to lead to outcomes previously experienced by industrial workers and parts of the white-collar workforce, i.e. increased productivity at the expense of decreased variation and increased alienation, as well as a risk of unemployment in case of complete automation of certain tasks.[6]

---

5. Unless otherwise stated the description of the technical aspects of the first phase of computer technology is based on Ceruzzi (2003).

6. In the case of Sweden, the fear of rising unemployment and deskilling of work attracted lots of attention. As a result, the State and the unions initiated investigations and other actions in order to alleviate expected negative consequences of

In the beginning of the 1970s a new innovation, which was to revolutionize the development of computer technology, was introduced: the microprocessor.[7] At first microprocessors were used to rapidly increase the capacity of mainframes as well as reducing their price.

More important was the introduction of personal computers during the 1970s. This innovation led to a decentralisation of the calculative capacity from the top level of mainframe computers to each terminal/PC. When these high-performing PCs (clients) were connected to servers and created Local Area Networks during the 1980s, a new network like technical structure emerged. The server was the central node in the networks and served as a communication centre used to store and access data, send e-mail, distribute software, and enable common use of hardware, such as printers. In the late 1990s the Local Area Networks gradually started to link up to each other, creating a rapidly expanding Internet. Some researchers argue that the introduction of the Internet constitutes such a profound change that it must be seen as the start of a third phase of computer technology (Castells 1996). However, the effects of the Internet with regard to organization of work are hard to analyse at this stage; hence, for the purpose of this study, the development will be treated as part of the second phase of the development of computer technology.

The qualitative changes of computer technology during the second phase described earlier were well in line with the organizational transformation to a post-Tayloristic mode of organization. Firstly, "blurring of company borders" was aided by interorganizational exchange of information via linked company-specific LANs, and later through the use of Internet-based solutions (Dewett and Jones 2001: 333–5). Secondly, cheaper technology providing access to large amounts of information facilitated productive use of low-skilled temporary workers (Autor, Levy, and Murnane 2002). Thirdly, and most relevant for the current study, the introduction of client-server networks showed clear complementarity with the increased scope of job descriptions of the permanent workforce. Improved tools for communication made the delegation of responsibilities easier, and improved access to information was a precondition if employees were to perform increasingly complex tasks (Malone and Rockart 1992: 637–38; Hunter et al. 2001). The combination of the improved flow of information and increasing demands on the workforce led to changes in the skill structure of the labour demand of companies, which were increasingly seeking employees with the ability to *collect,*

---

the increased use of computers; *SOU 1974:10,* chap. 4; *SOU 1984:20,* chaps. 3–6; *SOU 1984:51,* chap. 5.

7. The technical description of the second phase of computer technology is based on Ceruzzi (2003); Campbell-Kelly (2003); and Watkins (1998).

systemize, analyse, and communicate information. Consequently, the interrelated organizational and technical changes are expected to result in an increased share of high-skilled workers in the permanent workforce. This is the result of three factors:

1. The more potent technical structure facilitated accelerated automation, which decreased the demand for low-skilled temporary workers.
2. There was an increased complexity of work when middle managers were laid off and their tasks were delegated to the remaining employees in more flat organizations.
3. There is a changed character of work as more and more workers are engaged in the production of information products using information as the main input (Castells 1996).

One way to sum up the organizational and technical development and their interaction is a hypothesis where the introduction of mainframe computers during the end of the Tayloristic era is expected to result in a deskilling of the workforce. This development is then reversed as the gradual introduction of client-server networks and a more post-Tayloristic mode of organization changes the skill requirements, resulting in a reskilling, at least of the permanent workforce (Zuboff 1988). A graphic depiction of the hypothesis, which will be used in the analysis of the Swedish banking sector, is presented in Figure 4.1.

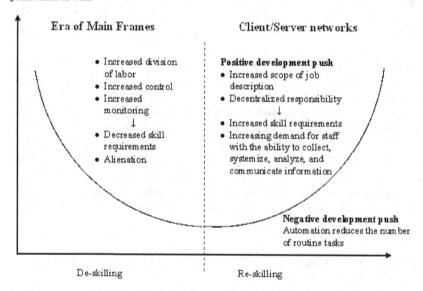

Figure 4.1   Graphical depiction of the deskilling/reskilling hypothesis.

STAGE ONE: ONLINE TERMINAL SYSTEMS
AND ABSENCE OF DESKILLING (1975–1985)

As mentioned before, banks were pioneers when it came to using computer technology and the Swedish banks were no exceptions. As early as in 1959, Skandinaviska Banken invested in its first mainframe computer and Svenska Handelsbanken and Sparbankernas Bank made the same decision two years later.[8] These computers were used to solve the very time-consuming task of calculating interest on savings accounts. This problem was accentuated because of the increasing numbers of transactions as more and more people got direct payroll payments and started to have current accounts alongside savings accounts (Börnfors 1996). With the help of computers these calculations were made regularly, but it was still a matter of batch-processing and large numbers of workers were employed to enter data into the systems using punched cards.[9] Details of these kinds of work processes in an American context are described and analysed in the chapter by Martha Poon in this volume.

The number of transactions continued to increase during the 1960s. In the beginning of the 1970s three of the major banks, Skandinaviska Enskilda Banken, Svenska Handelsbanken, and Sparbankernas Bank, respectively, initiated the development of new computer systems. The aim was to have online terminal systems that updated information in the central computer at the same time a service was carried out by a teller in a bank office. Skandinaviska Enskilda Banken was the first bank to install a real online system in 1972 and was fully operational in 1975. Sparbankernas Bank and Svenska Handelsbanken followed suit in 1972 and 1974, but only went for simulated online systems, which updated transactions made at other offices in the same bank with a twenty-four-hour delay. The reason for this solution was the high cost of online teleprocessing. The systems also included inquiry terminals, which were used to access information. Even though these systems were considered to be highly advanced at the time it should be noted that they were paper based, i.e. no monitors were used and the entering of data was guided by indicator lamps. Also note that the diffusion of the online terminal systems was a time-consuming process and it was not until 1980 that all branches of the major banks in Sweden had access to the new systems.[10]

---

8. SE-banken, "Annual Report", 9; Handelsbanken, *ADB i Handelsbanken*; Körberg (1987).

9. *ADB för bankmän*.

10. The descriptions of the development of computer technology in the Swedish banks are based on the following sources: Hedberg (1976); Skandinaviska Enskilda Banken's annual reports for 1975 and 1976; Abrahamsson and Grönstedt (1985: 9–14); Handelsbanken, *ADB i Handelsbanken*, 6–7; Bergström (1996: 24–29); Rannemo (1987: 130–34); Spadab, *Banking System for the 80's*, 13.

The rationale for installing the systems was entirely labour-saving via automation of existing tasks, especially volume transactions (Hedberg 1976).[11] The data shows no evidence of efforts to use the online terminal systems as an instrument to develop new financial services. Some accounts of the effects of the new systems are available.

Firstly, the goal of reaching higher productivity seems to have been fulfilled. Skandinaviska Enskilda Banken reports a 20 per cent increase in the workload between 1976 and 1980 at the same time as the number of staff was reduced by 8 per cent. Secondly, there were reports of increased monotony as work became more routine based. Thirdly, and very interestingly, there were also reports about initial dissolving of the sharp borders between front and back office work as the tellers got access to more information, as well as tools to answer questions and carry out services that previously only could be handled by back office personnel (Hedberg 1976; Löwstedt 1989). However, it should be noted that the accessible information was very restricted and that the technical structure was essentially hierarchical.

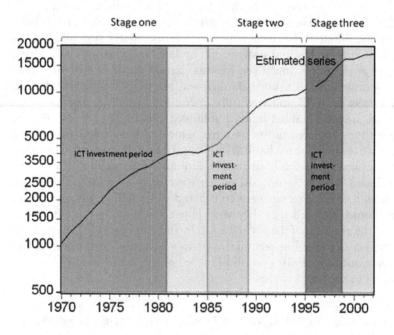

Figure 4.2 Machine capital stock in banks and other financial institutions, 1970–2002.

---

11. Bátiz-Lazo and Wood (2002) come to the same conclusion for banks in other countries during the same time period.

The timing of the investments in the online terminal systems based on the qualitative accounts is also supported by official statistics of machine capital stocks. As can be seen in Figure 4.2 there is a rapid increase in the machine capital stock in banks and other financial institutions from 1970, which ends in 1981 with the completion of the terminal projects in the smaller banks.

Turning to the organizational changes associated with the introduction of the online terminal systems, Figure 4.3 shows an increase in the aggregate number of employees from approximately thirty-one thousand in 1975 to forty-four thousand in 1985. However, more than half of this increase consisted of part-time workers, which means the rise in full-time equivalents is substantially lower. This rather modest increase in aggregate employment is well in line with the general economic development of Sweden with moderate growth during the second half of the 1970s and the beginning of the 1980s. It is only after the massive devaluation of the Swedish krona in 1982 that economic growth and the growth of full-time employees pick up pace.

Using the deskilling/reskilling hypothesis, the expected outcome of the introduction of the mainframe-based online terminal systems in Swedish banks during the 1970s would be a general trend towards deskilling. However, the data used in this study does not support the hypothesis. On the contrary, using the hierarchy indicator included in the wage statistics and calculating the average hierarchical level in the Swedish banking sector,

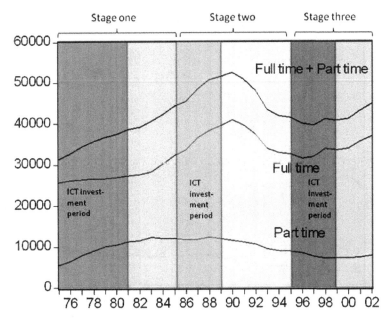

Figure 4.3   Total number of employees in the Swedish banking sector, 1975–2002.

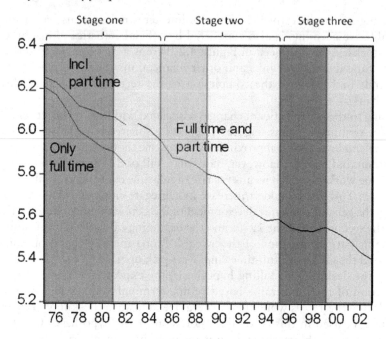

Figure 4.4   Average hierarchical level in Swedish banks, 1975–2003.

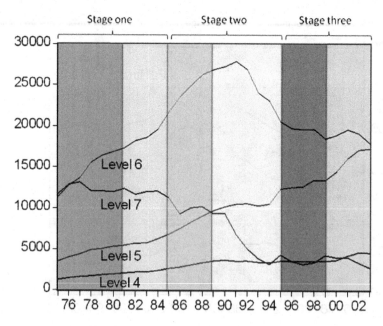

Figure 4.5   Number of employees in hierarchical levels 4 to 7, 1975–2003.

there is a continuous decrease indicating an increasing complexity of work instead of the expected deskilling trend (Figure 4.4).

Consequently, neither the detailed analysis of the number of employees in the different hierarchical levels in Figure 4.5 nor the shares of the total number of employees in Figure 4.6 show the expected patterns. Level 7 shows a fairly stable number of employees around twelve thousand whereas level 8 decreases from just above sixteen hundred to below eight hundred between 1975 and 1985. The diminishing shares for levels 7 and 8 and the rise in the average hierarchical level is driven by a rapid increase in the number of level 6, as well as a steady, but slower, growth of levels 4 and 5. How can the absence of a deskilling phase be explained?

As was pointed out earlier, the main drivers of the increased skill level during 1975–1985 were changes in the lower end of the hierarchical scale, mainly an increase of employees in level 6. This could be the result of an increased complexity in each task that was performed. Another possibility is that it is not the work tasks *per se* that have become more complex, but that the composition of *different work tasks* changed the work content that each employee was to perform in such a way that the *position* became more complex. This explanation is supported by

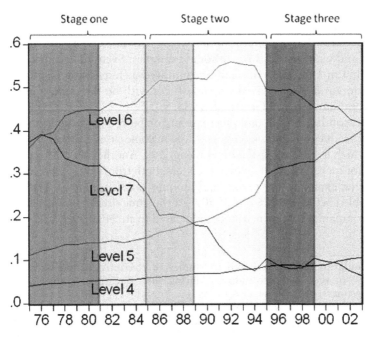

Figure 4.6 Hierarchical levels as shares of total employment in Swedish banks, 1975–2003.

studies of the effects of the introduction of the online terminal systems.[12] A higher degree of routine tasks are reported, but at the same time traditional divisions of labour were challenged and new workflows introduced. One example was the move of the task of entering data from centralised units to the bank offices. Another was the combination of customer contacts and a minor increase in access to information via inquiry terminals, which shifted some tasks from back office to front office (Börnfors 1996: 106–9; Hedberg 1976; Löwstedt 1989).[13] During 1975–1985 the technical development brought about a routinization of work tasks, but simultaneously there was an organizational response where new, more skill-demanding positions were created consisting of more tasks.

The only organizational response in line with the hypothesis is the rapid increase in the number and share of part-time employees between 1975 and 1983. The installation of the online terminals during the first wave of investments was expected to lead to increasing division of labour and more routine work, which, in turn, made it possible and profitable to employ low-skilled workers on a part-time basis.

STAGE TWO: FUNCTIONAL INTEGRATION, SELF-SERVICE, AND PERSONAL BANKERS (1985–1995)

Beginning with the technical development, it should be noted that as the implementation of the first online terminal systems proceeded new specific computer-based systems were installed in the Swedish banks. Terminals systems for transferring international payments via SWIFT, stock trading systems, and word processors are some examples. Svenska Handelsbanken reports that in 1985 the bank had one hundred different systems that were in operation at different divisions and offices with no integration between them (Abrahamsson and Grönstedt 1985: 9–12).

One reason behind the rapid increase in computer-based support systems was the introduction of minicomputers, and in some cases even personal computers, which led to decreasing investment costs. Another was the increasing demand for more advanced financial services, both from private and company clients. One example is that the total amount saved in mutual funds more than doubled between 1986 and 1990.[14] At the same time the number of people and companies that owned stocks increased from 945,000 to 1,724,000.[15]

---

12. Similar results were found in studies of the introduction of computer technology in the insurance industry during the same time; *Datoriseringen i försäkringsbranschen*, 59–64.

13. See also Skandinaviska Enskilda Banken, "Annual Report", 1987.

14. *Fondbolagens förening*, website www.fondbolagen.se (accessed 9 December 2008).

15. SOS, *Bankaktiebolagen, Fondkommisionerna, Fondbörsen och VPC 1975–1988*; SCB, *Statistisk årsbok 1989–2004*.

This development was also stimulated from the supply side as the banks made changes in their strategies to expand revenue-generating operations outside of the traditional savings and loans business.[16] An important prerequisite for these changes was, in turn, the rapid deregulation of the previously heavily regulated Swedish financial markets during the second half of the 1980s.

The fragmented technical situation became unmanageable in the mid-1980s and all of the studied banks made heavy investments in terminal systems that integrated many of the features of the existing specific systems. The new systems, once installed, consisted of online terminals with screens. They were not PC based, but terminals connected to a central computer with a relational database structure, which greatly improved the access to information and tools to sort and process it. Overviews of customer engagements, word processing, support systems for tax calculations, and credit scoring are mentioned in the available descriptions of the systems. As in the case of the first stage, Skandinaviska Enskilda Banken and Svenska Handelsbanken were in the forefront of the technical development and the other major banks followed within a few years.[17]

During the replacement of the internal terminal systems, the banks also made large investments in self-service, mainly through the enlargement of the network of automated teller machines (ATMs). The first Swedish ATM was installed as early as in 1972, but the diffusion picked up pace during the second stage with the number of ATMs increasing from 1,126 to 2,221 between 1983 and 1991.[18] Automation through the involvement of the customers in the production of financial services was enhanced further with the introduction of telebanking in the late 1980s and the beginning of the 1990s.[19]

The new internal systems and the investments in self-service by the Swedish banks constituted essential parts of the new strategies that were implemented in the mid-1980s. Less time spent on routine transactions freed resources that could be used for financial advice and to sell new, and more profitable, financial services. Götabanken was a pioneer when it came to implementing a more "selling-oriented" strategy. As early as 1984, they opened a bank office without a traditional front desk in which the tellers were replaced by "personal bankers".[20]

---

16. Skandinaviska Enskilda Banken's annual reports for 1983, 1987, and 1988; PK-banken, "Annual Report", 1985.

17. SE-banken (1985a) *Kort om data*; SE-banken, *SE Framåt—Information om S-E-bankens nya System*; Abrahamsson and Grönstedt (1985); Handelsbanken's annual reports for 1989 and 1991.

18. Stymne (1989: 35); Riksbanken Statistisk årsbok.

19. Skandinaviska Enskilda Banken, "Annual Report", 1990; Handelsbanken, "Annual Report", 1991; Nordbanken, "Annual Report", 1990; Föreningsbanken, "Annual Report", 1992.

20. Götabanken's annual reports for 1983 and 1984.

In parallel to the first stage, the timing and magnitude of the ICT investments derived from the qualitative accounts are to a large extent substantiated by the data on machine capital stocks presented in Figure 4.2.

Regarding the organizational changes, the total number of employees in the Swedish banking sector, presented in Figure 4.3, continued to rise during the first half of the second stage. This was followed by a rapid decline from 1990 to a level just above forty thousand in 1995. The development with an increase during the 1980s followed by a decrease in the beginning of the 1990s has been observed in many OECD countries (see contributions in Regini, Kitay, and Baethge 1999). However, the decrease in Sweden was steeper due to the combined financial and structural crises that hit the Swedish economy in the beginning of the 1990s. The combination of a rapid deregulation of the financial markets and the devaluation of the Swedish krona in 1982 lead to a booming economy and a rapid increase in the lending of the banks. For instance, between 1985 and 1990 the total stocks of loans from financial institutes doubled in constant prices. As the economy slowed down many financial institutes, including all major banks, experienced massive credit losses to the extent that the State was required to guarantee the depositors money in order to restore confidence for the entire financial system. The credit losses of the six major banks varied between 9.5 and 37.3 per cent of each bank's total loans (Larsson and Sjögren 1995; Lybeck 1994; Wallander 1994).[21]

The organizational effects of the ICT investments of the second stage, as they are demonstrated in the hierarchical data presented in Figures 4.5 and 4.6, were more in line with expectations even though they came to be highly influenced by the massive banking crisis in the beginning of the 1990s.

The deregulation of the financial markets and strategic changes led to a decrease in the number of employees in levels 7 and 8. However, as can be observed in Figure 4.5, the decrease was concentrated to the period 1984–1986 and was then temporarily hampered as a result of the increasing business volumes during the economic boom in the second half of the 1980s. The increased focus on selling new financial services also lead to a 28 per cent increase in the number of employees on level 6, ending at twenty-eight thousand employees in 1991. Personal bankers focusing on private clients are, for example, generally found in level 6.[22] At the same time there is a steady increase in level 5. One interpretation of the organizational data for the second half of the 1980s could be that Swedish banks chose relationship banking strategies when other international actors went for low-cost strategies (see further Regini, Kitay, and Baethge 1999).

---

21. A more extensive description of the Swedish banking crisis in English is available in Sandal (2004).

22. Information provided by Per Schönning, responsible for the production of wage statistics at Bankinstitutens Arbetsgivarorganisation.

The transformation of the Swedish banks from places of transactions to "financial supermarkets" continued during the banking crisis. Once again the least qualified workers on levels 7 and 8 found themselves on the negative side of the creative destruction process and were the ones laid off. Between 1990 and 1994 the number of employees on level 7 decreased from nine thousand to just over three thousand. This is interpreted as a combined effect of the continued strategic focus on sales of complex financial services and automation via the expansion of the ATM network and telebanking. A new feature of the organizational development was the rapid decrease in the number of level 6 employees. However, note that the drop was in line with the decrease in the aggregate number of employees, leaving the share of level 6 employees in the banking sector fairly stable.

Even though the expansion of the number of employees in level 5 was temporarily stopped during the crisis years its share, and hence the importance in the organizations, increased as levels 6 to 8 decreased. Detailed analyses combing the hierarchical data and available information on the work content of each employee shows that the increased qualifications of bank employees were especially marked for front office personnel (Appelquist 2005: chap. 5).

In regarding the aspect of interaction between the technical and organizational development it is important to stress that the implementation of the new integrated terminal systems constituted an essential tool for the new seller-oriented strategies, and that, in turn, increased the demand for employees with the ability to collect, systemize, analyse, and communicate information.

STAGE THREE: PERSONAL COMPUTERS, INTERNET BANKING, AND SPECIALISATION (1995–2003)

Soon after the integrated terminal systems were implemented in the Swedish banks the development of new PC-based systems was initiated. The first record of a PC-based internal system is from 1992 when Nordbanken replaced their old terminal system.[23] The three other major banks made the transition a couple of years later and the data indicates that it was completed in 1999.[24] The studied material contains a few accounts of the nature of these systems and from them the changes towards a more seller-oriented strategy becomes clear.

All of the studied banks develop sales support systems for advising customers. In the most detailed description of such a system from Skandinaviska Enskilda Banken in 1998, it is reported that the staff has access to complete overviews of customer engagements, as well as programmed

23. Nordbanken, "Annual Report", 1996.

24. Handelsbanken's annual reports for 1996 and 1999; Skandinaviska Enskilda Banken, "Annual Report", 1998; Körberg (1987: 291–98).

sequences that aid in the performance of a number of services, such as approving a loan. The account also states that every task at a bank office now requires the use of a computer.[25]

However, the most important technical innovation during the third stage was undoubtedly the introduction of Internet banking, resulting in a substantial automation of bank services. The first bank to introduce this new mode of distribution of financial services in 1995 was a regional savings bank, Sparbanken Finn. The large banks followed suit in 1996 and 1997 and the result was a rapid increase in the number of users from 13,700 in 1997 to over 5.2 million in 2003.[26] The share of Internet payments increased from 5 per cent in 1997 to 30 per cent of all payments in 2003, which indicates a real diffusion rather than just an automatic enrolment of customers to a new service (Rietz 2003: 42–46).

Another important source of automation was the increasing number of electronic payments via point-of-sale (POS) terminals, which reduces the costs of handling cash and cheques. Internationally, Sweden was a late adopter of this technology, but caught up rapidly. As late as in 1988 only 702 POS terminals were installed nationwide. However, this number increased rapidly and in 2003 the number was 108,055. At the same time the number of transactions increased from two million a year to 542 million.[27]

The end result of these massive investments in information technology and strategic changes towards self-services was a situation where the customers themselves performed most of the routine transactions. However, the introduction of Internet banking has also provided the customers full, and easy, access to information concerning their financial status, which was previously only readily available for bank officials. These changes can be summarized by stating that the modern bank basically has two roles.

1. providing and developing efficient ICT solutions that customers themselves use to perform routine transactions
2. acting as financial specialists providing advice and complex financial services to private and company clients

The development can be seen as an example of blurred company borders, which was one of the characteristics of the post-Taylorist mode of organization. But in this case, the blurring occurs between the bank and its customers and not between companies.

Partly as a result of the increased access to information, the average customer started to demand more qualified advice than before (Jungerhem

25. Skandinaviska Enskilda Banken, "Annual Report", 1998.
26. Marquardt (2000) and statistics from Svenska Bankföreningen.
27. *Riksbanken Statistisk årsbok 1988–1999; Den svenska finansmarknaden 2004.*

2000). A somewhat crude but illustrative measure of this qualitative change in demand is the quota between revenues generated by commissions and fees, on one hand, and the net interest on the other. From having fluctuated between 0.2 and 0.4 the share of commission and fees of net interest increased rapidly after 1995, reaching a peak just before the burst of the dotcom bubble in the year 2000 with 0.86.[28]

The response from the Swedish banks to this challenge was a move towards organizations populated by more specialised employees. The reason was that the demand for more complex financial services could not be satisfied by using the "personal bankers" of the second stage because they had a broad but shallow knowledge of a large part of the bank's service portfolio and were mainly focused on selling. From the third stage onwards the demand had to be met by employees with deeper knowledge in more specialised fields forming teams consisting of different competencies (see also Jungerhem 2000: 246–54). One indicator of this development is the increasing number of employees in each bank office from just below sixteen in 1995 to over twenty-two in 2002.[29] The increasing complexity and diversity in demand requires a wider range of specialists, and, hence, more staff, despite the fact the increasing number of services available through Internet banking reduces the need for the customers to visit a bank office.

The wage statistics also support the conclusion of a move towards more specialisation. From 1994 the share of employees on level 6 decreases, ending at a share of just over 40 per cent in 2003. At the same time, the share and number of employees in level 5, with position descriptions well in line with the new kind of demand for financial services, increases rapidly, especially after Internet banking was fully implemented in 1999 (Figures 4.5 and 4.6).

The specialisation argument was also supported by the 74 per cent increase of employees with a university degree between 1995 and 2003. As a result over ten thousand employees had a university degree in the Swedish banks in 2003, making it the second most common educational level. Hence, one important strategy to meet a more complex and diverse demand has been to employ people with more advanced degrees.[30]

The increase of more specialised employees might seem to go against the defining characteristics of the post-Tayloristic mode of organization, mainly the increased scope of job descriptions and multi-skilling. However, it should be remembered that the increased demand for specialist knowledge in defined areas did not replace but was added to other skill requirements, such as the ability to handle extensive amounts of information and being

---

28. SOS Bankaktiebolagen, Fondkommisionerna, Fondbörsen och VPC 1975–1987; SOS Sparbankerna 1975–1987; Föreningsbankerna 1975–1987; SOS Bankerna 1988–1994; SOS Finansiella företag 1995–2003.
29. *SCB Statistisk Årsbok 1975–2002; Wages for Bank Officials 1975–2002.*
30. *Wages for Bank Officials 1975–2003.*

able to interact with customers and co-workers. For instance, a combined analysis of hierarchical and work content data shows that the average hierarchical level of people in front desk positions decreased from 5.6 in 1996 to just over 5.4 in 2003. At the same time the average hierarchical level of back office staff decreased with less than 0.1 to 5.7. Hence, the increase in qualifications was more rapid among employees that were required to handle customers.[31]

The sources from the Swedish banks mainly used to study the technical development also provide a number of indications of a specialist turn. One example, which actually preceded the introduction of Internet banking, was Skandinaviska Enskilda banken's decision to centralise their trading operations from the local offices to a small number of selected offices with specialist competencies.[32] Another example was Föreningssparbanken's decision to change strategy from a "financial supermarket" to a "multi-specialist" approach, implying a change from aiming at being able to deliver any type of financial service to striving to become a market leader in each of the niches that the bank was active in.[33]

CONCLUSIONS

The purpose of this chapter was to investigate the relation between the implementation of ICT and organizational change in the Swedish banking industry from 1975 to 2003. Departing from an analytical framework focusing on the complementary nature between major trends in the organization of work and general changes of computer technology during the last forty years, a deskilling/reskilling hypothesis was formulated. Three techno-organizational stages were identified.

Stage One 1975–1985

The major Swedish banks invested heavily in mainframe-based online terminal systems during the first stage. Contrary to expectations, this hierarchical technical structure did not induce a process of deskilling of the workforce during the following years, even though the data showed an increased number of routine-based tasks being introduced. The reason that a deskilling of the workforce was avoided was the decision to simultaneously change work processes in a way that led to the creation of new, more qualified positions in which a greater number of tasks were performed by each employee.

---

31. Föreningssparbankens's annual reports for 1997 and 1998.
32. Skandinaviska Enskilda Banken, "Annual Report", 1992.
33. Föreningssparbankens, "Annual Report", 2000.

Stage Two 1985–1995

The ICT investments in the banking sector during the second stage were directed towards the introduction of new terminal systems, which gave employees better access to information and information processing tools. The other major technical investment was the rapid expansion of the network of ATMs. The ICT investments supported the strategic change in the Swedish banks, where the focus on self-services was a way to reduce the employees needed for routine transactions. Moreover, these investments enabled an increase in the number of personal bankers selling more complex financial services, which in turn generated greater revenues. As expected, the organizational effect of these changes was an increase in the skill structure of employees in the Swedish banks. This process was intensified during the banking crisis in the beginning of the 1990s, as positions with lower skill requirements were the ones being made redundant.

Stage Three 1995–2003

The introduction of Internet banking during the last stage of the study resulted in an increased focus on self-services. At the same time, the introduction of internal systems consisting of personal computers further increased the employee's access to structured information and sophisticated information process tools, such as sales support systems. The organizational changes during the last years of the study were characterised by a move towards specialisation among employees. The term *specialisation* was introduced to stress the fact that the banks went from employing personnel with a broad but shallow understanding of the products supplied by the banks to demanding expert knowledge in more narrowly defined areas. The reasons were the increased use of Internet banking and the rise in the number of services offered through them, as well as the increased demand for more qualified financial services. Indicators of a development towards increased specialisation included the increase in the share of employees in positions requiring high skills, and the fast growing numbers of employees with a university education.

5 Computerization of Commercial Banks and the Building of an Automated Payments System in Mexico, 1965–1990

Gustavo A. del Angel Mobarak

INTRODUCTION

In 2008, the Mexican banking system processed 494.85 million cheques and made 1,278 million transactions in the 31,966 automated teller machines in the country.[1] Regardless of the conditions of inclusion and access to financial services available to the Mexican population, this is a functional and relatively extensive payment system. Nevertheless, it was not a system created overnight; in fact, developing this kind of infrastructure in a developing country covering two million square kilometres whose geography imposes high costs, as well as poorly developed lines of communication, required time to consolidate. The existence of this system can be explained by a cumulative process whereby, throughout the twentieth century, the main private banks developed an infrastructure platform that serves the users of financial services through branches, which, from 1965 onward, have undergone a continuous process of computerization of operations.

This chapter looks into the history behind the adoption of information technology, particularly the process of computerization, by the Mexican banking system. The main argument of this chapter is that computerization not only led commercial banking in Mexico to automate its operations with the resulting gains in efficiency, but also eventually created a service network. This argument is contained in four points. Firstly, the adoption of computers went hand in hand with the massification of banking services available under the system in order to meet the need for processing huge quantities of documents. Secondly, the development of new services that allowed the incorporation of technology was an incentive to expand its introduction to different areas of banking activity. Thirdly, that the gradual development of a technological and service platform throughout Mexico was what enabled the formation of the current system of payments that we enjoy today. Lastly, the combination of

---

1. Information from the Banco de México.

regionalized operation of large banks and the state of information technology and telecommunications, together with the crises faced by the banking system between 1982 and 1997, caused these systems to remain fragmented for a long time, and that interconnectivity within the banking industry arrived somewhat late.

The main objective of this chapter is to demonstrate the importance of history in explaining the current state of a system in which several organizations participate. The weight of history, in terms of the evolutionary and cumulative development of events, is even more important when looking at infrastructure. In the course of time, decisions in adoption of information technology combine with other events in the banking industry to shape a pattern of development of the industry. A network of infrastructure like the present-day Mexican system of payments exhibits path-dependent characteristics that need to be explained with history.

This chapter focuses on the two main banks that have dominated the Mexican banking industry since the middle of the twentieth century: Banamex (established in 1884) and Bancomer (established in 1932). In terms of industry assets, together Banamex, Bancomer, and Bancomer's system of affiliate banks represented over 50 per cent of all commercial banking assets in the country. Over the fifty years to 2009, these financial intermediaries had, on average, more than 70 per cent of the industry's customer service centres (branches and, later on, automated teller machines or ATMs). The story in this chapter begins with the adoption of second-generation computers in 1965, considers technological developments during their nationalization in 1982, and ends with the process of reprivatization of the banking industry in 1990.

The research in this chapter was undertaken by consulting surviving internal records from both banks. These were stored at Archivo Histórico Banamex (Banamex Historical Archive), the Acervo Histórico Documental de Banco de México (Historical Documental Archive of the Bank of Mexico), the country's central bank, and the Archivos Económicos de la Biblioteca Miguel Lerdo de Tejada de la Secretaría de Hacienda y Crédito Público (Economic Archives at the Miguel Lerdo de Tejada Library of the Ministry of Finance).[2] In addition, interviews were conducted with top management executives from both banks.

The rest of this chapter is divided into five sections. The first section briefly explains the historical evolution of Mexican banking over the period being studied in order to provide a context for the research into the adoption of technology. The second section looks at the process of massification of bank transactions that gave rise to the adoption of technology. Section

---

2. Henceforward the following will be used to identify these sources: Archivo Banamex, Archivo Banco de México, and Archivos Económicos SHCP, respectively.

three explains the first steps toward adopting information technology, as well as the first computers that were adopted by the two largest banks. Section four describes the characteristics of the computerization process that these two banks underwent until 1990, in particular the motivation behind carrying out technological change gradually, the fragmentation of systems according to region and by process-products, as well as the attempts to unite the systems. Section five is a kind of epilogue that explains the nature of the process of interconnectivity within the banking industry, a consequence, not necessarily a direct one, of its past history.

THE CONTEXT OF MEXICAN COMMERCIAL BANKING

Throughout its history the Mexican financial system has essentially been made up of commercial banking entities. The banking industry's presence in Mexico came relatively late. A national banking system did not take shape until the second half of the nineteenth century (Marichal 1997). This banking system, whose activities were based partly on issuing paper money, collapsed during the Mexican revolution of 1910. Few banks survived this period. The Mexican financial system was revived through a process of reconstruction which took place between 1924 and 1941; this process involved the creation of new entities and a modern institutional framework (Anaya 2002; del Angel 2006; Turrent 2000).

Throughout the period of 1940 to 1982, Mexican banking was characterised by outstanding sustained growth and healthy operational performance. This coincided with a period of high economic growth, as well as a strong demographic explosion, and a process of urbanization of the country. Some of the main banks, such as the Banco de Londres, México y Sudamérica (1864), and Banamex (1884), had been created in the second half of the nineteenth century. However, there was a wave of creation of new and sizeable institutions like Bancomer (1932) and its network of affiliated regional banks, Banco Mexicano (1932) and the Banco Comercial Mexicano (1934). In addition to banking institutions, a number of non-bank intermediaries emerged, primarily *financieras* (non-bank intermediaries) and *hipotecarias* (mortgage institutions). The government established a central bank, Banco de México, in 1925, and introduced development banking institutions in the subsequent years.

The financial penetration of the Mexican banking industry in the economy, measured as the Bank Assets/GDP ratio, experienced sustained growth from the fifties until the seventies (from 15 per cent in 1957 to 35 per cent in 1972). This was the longest period of sustained growth of the banking system in the history of Mexico; however, when this is compared to other economies that were similar to Mexico's at that time, penetration of the financial system was less dynamic than in those economies, and much less than in industrialized countries (del Angel 2002, 2007).

An important aspect of the growth of banking during those years was the monetization of family savings through the massification of financial services. More than just massifying credit, the banks began to provide large groups of the population with access to savings accounts. This included the previously unprecedented step of providing access to the financial system through savings and checking accounts to people that previously did not have any bank account; however, it was limited to people living in urban settings and belonging to the uppers layers of income and to the emerging urban middle class. In order to massify these accounts, the larger banks found it necessary to invest heavily in customer service centres, namely, a national system of branches.

The Banking Law of 1941 established a separation between the different intermediaries according to the operations they were authorized to perform. This was similar to the Glass-Steagall Law of 1933 in the United States. But in practice, over these years the Mexican financial system went through a process of gradual consolidation. Commercial banking developed links with other intermediaries, mainly with *financieras* (non-bank intermediaries), which were the second most important intermediaries, as well as with other specialised intermediaries, such as mortgage institutions. Links were proprietary as well as operational. Over the years, commercial banking gradually consolidated with non-bank intermediaries and mortgage specialists (del Angel 2007).

In 1975, full-service banking (*banca multiple*) was authorized in the banking law. Banks could now merge with the intermediaries with which they had maintained joint operations. Banks sought to provide universal banking services, a level of integration they were unable to achieve with the exception of services of subscription to stock market instruments and insurance. The formation of full-service banking required banks to transform their systems and redesign their operations (del Angel 2007).

In 1982, at the start of the Latin American foreign debt crisis, the government nationalized the banking industry almost in its entirety. By changing the structure of corporate governance within the banking sector, the nationalization of the banking industry modified the conduct and performance that it had had previously. This had significant implications for the operations of commercial banks (del Angel 2002, 2007). In December 1989, the reprivatization of the banking industry was announced. This process took place between 1990 and 1992. The Mexican banking industry then went through a severe economic and financial crisis between 1995 and 1998. As a result of this and the overall process of globalization, all but one of the previously nationalized Mexican commercial banks either collapsed or were acquired by global financial intermediaries (Murillo 2005).

In this context, even though the number and type of commercial banks that make up the banking system has varied over the years, it has consistently been a concentrated industry where the four major banks account for a high percentage of all banking activity. During the greater part of the twentieth century, two banks have dominated the Mexican banking market: Banamex and Bancomer.

Since it was established in 1884 as Banco Nacional de México, Banamex aimed to deploy a nationwide network of retail branches. During its first thirty years, as a note-issuing bank Banamex was responsible for certain government banking functions. Nevertheless, the bank retained a broad portfolio of private customers in agriculture and commerce. Later, Banamex moved into financing long-term industrial developments, combined with a strong retail banking component (Marichal 1997).

Bancomer was established in 1932 as Banco de Comercio. Very early on it was able to expand considerably and rapidly; it became one of the largest in the country in terms of assets and branches. In Mexico City, the bank opened a larger number of branches than its competitors. To expand at the national level, Bancomer followed a strategy of associating with businesses interests to form banks that operated regionally. These regional banks formed a network of independent entities which were relatively united by an assortment of operations with the bank's head office. In 1977, this alliance was brought together into a single entity to constitute a full-service bank (del Angel 2007; Bátiz-Lazo and del Angel 2003). The national expansion of Bancomer's network of branches and regional banks overshadowed Banamex's. In 1945 Bancomer had only fifty-one branches nationwide, expanding to 288 branches in 1960, whereas Banamex had 136 branches that year. Later Banamex caught up with its competitor and in 1983 it had 734 branches, still lower than the 759 national branches of Bancomer (del Angel 2007).

In terms of market share, Banamex, Bancomer, and Bancomer together with its network of affiliate regional banks held approximately 50 per cent of total assets in the industry. Not only did Banamex and Bancomer hold a significant percentage of total assets in the banking industry, but as a result of their regional expansion, they became the financial intermediaries with the largest number of retail customers. This process was accentuated through the massification of services attained after the adoption of information technology.

GROWTH OF TRANSACTIONS IN AN ENVIRONMENT OF HIGH TRANSACTION COSTS

Computerization of transactional services by Mexican banks resulted from the need to find alternatives to process massive numbers of paper-based transactions. The massification of services initially resulted from the growth of transactions on the liability side of the banks' balance sheet (as opposed to fee-income-generating activities), namely, checking and savings accounts. This was also due to the growing transactionality in these accounts, in other words, greater use of cheques to make payments at different banking entities, letters of credit, as well as deposits and transfers (within the same bank—as interoperability developed rather late). Shortly after, credit cards took on greater importance within banking services as both income generators for the banks and access to credit by retail customers.

The growth in bank transactions during the twentieth century was associated with two phenomena. One, on the side of demand, was an expanding demography in Mexico which made it easy to include new customers in the financial system. The second, on the supply side, was the expansion of the banking industry that aimed to capture the expanding market that resulted from demographics of the country.

Between 1940 and 1990, the population of Mexico grew exponentially and went from being a predominantly rural country to being a largely urban one. In 1940, the population of the country was 19.6 million of which it is estimated that 80 per cent lived in rural areas. In 1990, the population of the country stood at 81.2 million, four times greater, of which it is estimated that 28 per cent lived in rural areas. The growth of urban centres facilitated the incorporation of customers into the banking system. However, there were limits to the process of bancarization. The geographical barriers of the country, in particular the inaccessibility of many locations, as well as income, education, and cultural restrictions slowed down expansion of the system.

Table 5.1 summarizes how the expansion of the banking industry led to an increase in the number of transactions. In the first place, the table shows the total number of checking accounts, and checking accounts as a proportion of the population. Secondly, it shows the total number of savings accounts, and savings accounts as a proportion of the population. The growth then was significant, and it is worth noting the accelerated rate from 1965 onward. Savings accounts grew from 1.3 per cent of the population in 1955 to 35.5 per cent in 1980, suggesting that an increasing proportion of the population was using bank services.

Table 5.1 Growth of Current and Savings Accounts in Mexico, 1955–1980

Year	Checking Accounts	Checking Accounts/Total Population	Savings Accounts	Savings Accounts/ Total Population
1955	247,640	0.008	386,851	0.013
1960	512,188	0.015	1,431,163	0.041
1965	691,341	0.017	4,396,013	0.106
1970	1,085,411	0.023	10,009,845	0.208
1975	1,377,623	0.024	15,913,018	0.277
1980	2,090,595	0.031	23,707,135	0.355

Source: Statistical Records at Archivo Banco de México.

Figure 5.1 shows a reconstruction of the historical statistics of the number of documents that passed through the national system of clearing houses. This is the most palpable evidence of the massification of the volume of transactions and documents that banks handle, and therefore of the need to adopt technology to deal with the large number of transactions. Despite this overall growth trend, the rate accelerated from 1963 onward, when the chart exhibits a steeper slope. The expansion of the banking system is also reflected in this sustained growth in the number of transactions. Prior to 1950, banks handled less than twenty million documents each year in clearing houses; by 1980, this number had grown to more than one hundred million. In order to be able to handle this growing volume, the system of clearing houses also grew in terms of the number of houses at different locations around the country.

Further evidence of the massification of transactions was the introduction of the bank credit card in 1968. Adopting information technology to process data was strongly associated with the growth of the credit card market, given that in addition to a high volume of retail transactions, it also implied the eventual use of ATMs. Figure 5.2 shows the growth in the number of Banamex cardholders from 1970 onward; between that year and 1982 cardholder growth was fivefold, reaching more than a million users by 1981.

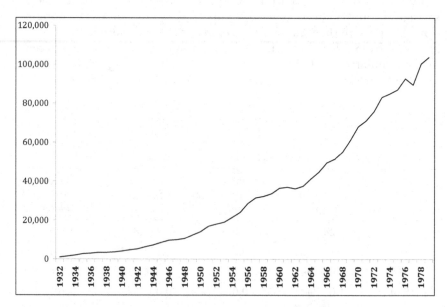

Figure 5.1   National system of clearing houses, 1932–1979.

Note: Number of processed documents, in thousands.

Source: Data from statistical records at Archivo Banco de México.

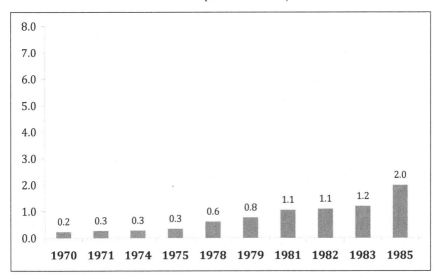

Figure 5.2 Number of credit cards issued by Banamex, 1970–1990.
Note: Numbers in millions.
Source: Data extracted from Banamex Annual Reports at Archivo Banamex.

THE FIRST STEPS TOWARD THE ADOPTION
OF INFORMATION TECHNOLOGY

As had been the case in Europe (explained in other chapters in this volume), the mechanization of the Mexican banking system started before the arrival of computer technology. However, as had been the case in Europe, this process emphasized the use of accounting machines and office equipment (Bátiz-Lazo and Wood 2002; Bátiz-Lazo and Wardley 2007).

"Mechanization" (or "automation" as it was called back then) began in 1943 with the incorporation of punched-card equipment in Banamex. Later, Bancomer also incorporated punched-card equipment.[3] This type of technology was generally based on single recording equipment. By the end of the 1940s, both banks were already using punched cards in certain checking and savings account transactions, as well as in some credit processes. However, no detailed records of these devices have been found. Whereas the use of punched-card technology represented a transition toward the use of more sophisticated technology, this equipment seems to have co-existed for a number of years in parallel with more "modern" devices such as computers that were being incorporated into day-to-day operations.

3. Interviews: Agustín Legorreta Chauvet (Mexico City, 10 and 25 March 2009), Carlos Aguilar Villalobos (Mexico City, 25 August 2006).

However, there was an innovative use of other equipment to transfer and exchange information. The first electronic devices that Mexican banks used to transfer information were wireless radio transmitters. In November 1935 Banamex installed a radio transmitting station in its corporate head offices and receivers in its Mexico City branches. By the early 1940s, both Banamex and Bancomer had radio transmitters to keep in contact with their branches throughout the country (and in the case of Bancomer, with the network of affiliated regional banks). Radio transmitters were an alternative to the relatively low penetration and high cost of telegraph and telephone services. By 1955, Banamex had forty-two radio transmitters throughout its Mexico City branches and a further thirty-six in branches located elsewhere around the country. This facilitated communication to confirm information and authorize transactions. At first, the control station was located in the bank's corporate head offices. Later, in 1957, a microwave radio transmitter with FM was built in San José de los Cedros, in the western hills surrounding the Mexico City valley. The new location enabled better communication among the branches in the valley. The success of these transmitters merited them being mentioned in the bank's annual report, which described a significant reduction in operational costs by enabling the reduction of the number of telephone calls made between branches and headquarters.[4]

Another type of technology that Mexican banks embraced and which made them stand out among other companies in Mexico and banks abroad was the use of private telephone networks, and, in the case of Bancomer, a system for sending documents through pneumatic tubes. This use of technologies was highlighted to coincide with the opening of Bancomer's new corporate head office building in 1964. In celebrating this development both the press and bank reports emphasized the technological infrastructure: the internal mail system was based on a pneumatic tube system one kilometre in length, which used compressed air to distribute documents within the building. Also highlighted was the introduction of a telephone communication system that was based on a Siemens EMD automated switchboard system, which included an automatic instrument panel with a capacity of one hundred direct lines and 820 extensions. Also installed in the building were a radio transmitter and Telex machine.[5]

The configuration of these systems was interesting as it reflected continuity in development and use of technology, that is, the pneumatic tube, a nineteenth-century apparatus, and its combination with electromechanical devices. However, this configuration was solely used for the specific task of transmitting and exchanging information. These machines were not used for administration and processing information; the transmitters allowed

---

4. Banamex's annual reports for 1953–1957 at Archivo Banamex.

5. Bancomer, "Annual Report", 1963; *Excélsior*, 28 April 1964, folio 003201-Banco de Comercio, at Archivos Económicos SHCP.

faster and more efficient communication but did not bring about significant changes in administrative processes and routines or in the way information was stored and coded.

Mexico's first computers were installed for academic and governmental use. The very first was an IBM 650 installed at the Universidad Nacional Autónoma de México or UNAM (National University) in 1958 (Cantarell and González 2002). Other state and private universities soon followed while deploying mainframe equipment. For instance, the Instituto Politecnico Nacional (National Polytechnic Institute) installed an IBM-790 in 1964 (Cantarell and González 2002). But it was not until 1965, when computer technology was used at UNAM to address administrative applications, that an IBM 1440 hosted payroll and mechanized the accounting function.[6] By the mid-1960s other large machines had been installed within the federal government such as an IBM 704 at the Instituto Mexicano del Seguro Social (Mexican Social Security Institution) and two CDC 604s at the Finance Ministry to centralise the payroll of all federal government employees.

Large banks had also started to adopt mainframe computers for similar purposes: Banco Nacional de México (Banamex) installed a General Electric 415 in 1965; Banco de Comercio installed an IBM 1440 in 1964, immediately followed by an IBM 360 in 1965; Banco Comercial Mexicano an IBM 360 in 1966; and Banco de Londres y México an undisclosed machine in 1967.[7]

There is little doubt that computerization by the banks responded to the increase in the number of transactions at counters of retail branches. Banamex and Bancomer went ahead with this process in tandem. This suggested that neither wanted to be left behind by its main competitor, not just in terms of adopting new technology, but also in projecting an image of modernity (see Ian Martin in this volume).

As mentioned, Banamex installed General Electric 415 in 1965 to host accounting and cheque applications. The computer followed the establishment of a "Departamento de Automatización" (Department of Automation) in 1964, which had a mandate for planning and installing systems along the lines of what operations and methods departments had done at European banks (Booth 2004). Banamex chose Bull, a French company, as its supplier because it offered greater proximity with the customer.[8] The agreement with Bull Mexico was signed by the local manager of the

---

6. See "History of Computing in Mexico", http://cocomc10.pereanet.com/html/coco_in_mexico.html (accessed March 15, 2008); and "50 años de la computación en México", http://www.cs.cinvestav.mx/SemanaComputoCINVESTAV/Computo.html (accessed March 15, 2008).

7. "El Banco Comercial Mexicano, S.A., adquiere un sistema electronico de proceso de datos IBM 360", *Excelsior*, 1 August 1966, at Archivos Económicos SHCP; Trueblood (1990: 84).

8. Interview: Agustín Legorreta Chauvet. This despite the fact that NCR, IBM, and Honeywell were also in Mexico at the time; NCR was in operation in

company, Michael Jalabert, and the CEO and the upper management of the bank in a ceremony to which the press were invited.

The GE 415 equipment was manufactured in Angers, France, and was technology that banks in other parts of the world were already using. Banamex's equipment took up one hundred square metres and had a memory capacity of sixteen KB; it had been acquired in 1964 by the company Bull Mexico. The machine had six magnetic tape units, punched-card puncher, reading device, printer, and high-speed sorter.[9]

An internal estimate for 1966 calculated that the processing of accounting transactions and balances took forty-nine hours each month with the new computer system. This compared to an estimated 740 hours required with the punched-card system.[10] From then on it was apparent that the incorporation of computers into the bank was an irreversible fact.[11] By 1968, the GE 415 dealt with all checking and saving account transactions of the sixty-five branches within the Mexico City metropolitan area, those of the Securities Department, and credit card transactions throughout the entire country. It also helped to consolidate general accounting of the bank.

Given the expectations of continuing growth in the adoption of computers the "Bancomático" unit was created in 1966. This was a new building located in Mexico City to house "electronic computers" and complementary devices for data processing.[12] This computer centre aimed to be both a centralised location for equipment and to centralise certain transactions. But the latter forced the bank to redesign its administrative processes.

It was not long before the "Bancomatico" unit housed additional equipment: in November 1967, the bank acquired a GE 425, which was also manufactured in France, and in 1969 a computer with magnetic disk began operation.[13]

The introduction of the bank credit card in Mexico sped up the incorporation of computer systems in banks. Banamex was the first bank in the country, and in Latin America, to introduce a bank credit card on 15 January 1968 when it launched Banc-O-Mático, later known as Bancomático (see also Stern, in this volume).

---

the country before 1910, and perhaps some of the punching-card systems used by banks were IBM.

9. Banamex, "Annual Report", 1965, 15, at Archivo Banamex; *Excélsior*, 8 October 1964, folio D04231, at Archivos Económicos SHCP.

10. Banamex, "Annual Report", 1966, 15, at Archivo Banamex.

11. Interview: Agustín Legorreta Chauvet.

12. Banamex, "Annual Report", 1966, 15, at Archivo Banamex.

13. Banamex, "Annual Report", 1967, 15, at Archivo Banamex; *El Universal*, 26 November 1967, folio D04231, at Archivos Económicos SHCP. Does not mention which piece of equipment was the magnetic disk computer.

Planning for the computer infrastructure to support the launch of the credit card was undertaken throughout 1967.[14] A proprietary software system was developed to operate Bancomático. Developing the application internally responded to a combination of compatibility issues, the high asking price of readymade software by other financial institutions (such as Chase, Citi, and Bank of America), and to the desire to use in-house programming capacity to create a system tailored to meet its own needs.[15]

In 1968, Banamex also began to expand its computerization outside Mexico City with the installation in the city of Guadalajara, the second largest city in terms of population, of an electronic processing centre that housed a GE 115. This machine was dedicated to the processing of checking and savings accounts for the ten retail branches in that city (Banamex 2004: 101).

In parallel developments, Bancomer had also begun planning to adopt computer equipment as far back as 1964. In 1965 it deployed an IBM 1440 computer, followed immediately by an IBM 360. Bancomer chose IBM, which had been established in Mexico since 1927, based on a consultant report by Cresap, McCormick & Paget (Cantarell and González 2002). The IBM 1440 was introduced to handle mortgages and, therefore, was installed in *Hipotecaria* Bancomer, the mortgage subsidiary of the bank. The IBM 360 was used by the accounting and transaction record systems. It also carried out the first electronic processing of consumer loans.[16]

The arrival of the computer system required a purpose-built dwelling to house the new equipment. Called the "Data Processing Centre", it allowed Bancomer and its regional affiliates to operate a single, centralised computer centre.[17] Through this centre, Bancomer sought to redesign its operations around technology; Bancomer adopted what was considered an image of modernity and began to use the marketing slogan "El Banco de Ideas Modernas" ("The bank with modern ideas") in 1965 (del Angel 2007).

The increased number of transactions carried out in Bancomer and its regional affiliates soon meant that the capacity of existing computer equipment was insufficient to such an extent that in 1968 Bancomer installed a second IBM 360–30 computer with the capacity for sixty thousand memory positions.[18] A year later, the bank acquired a third computer, a new 360–30 comprised of six disk units, a punched-card reader, and a printer. In that

---

14. *Banamex, Memoria, 1882–1988*, t. II, p. 92, at Archivo Banamex; *Noticiero Banamex*, 2 January 1968, headline; and Banamex, "Annual Report", 1967, 19, at Archivo Banamex. The public announcement on the appearance of Ban-O-Mático was made on 7 April 1967; *Excélsior*, 8 April 1967, folio D04231, at Archivos Económicos SHCP.

15. Interview: Agustín Legorreta Chauvet.

16. Bancomer, "Annual Report", 1965.

17. Ibid.

18. Bancomer, "Annual Report", 1968.

same year, Bancomer incorporated in the computer system the operations of *Financiera* Bancomer, the non-bank subsidiary.[19]

Bancomer faced a major challenge to expanding the use of its computer systems in regions of the country outside Mexico City. The Bancomer network of affiliated banks was a loose amalgamation of regional banks and, therefore, integration of information and operations was not as fully assimilated as it would have been under a single organization. This led to the adoption of new technology outside Mexico City that would focus only on certain operations, such as cheque, deposits, and administrative controls, where affiliate banks saw quick payoff/were particularly interested/ something else.

There is no fully documented history of the automation of other large and medium-sized commercial banks in Mexico. Nevertheless, newspaper accounts and interviews suggest that the rest of the industry followed in the footsteps of Banamex and Bancomer. For instance, Banco Mexicano, the fourth largest bank in the country, followed its competitors immediately and in 1965 acquired thirteen Sensitronic machines from Borroughs to handle the clearing of checking accounts (Cantarell and González 2002).

REMOTE DATA PROCESSING CENTRES, REGIONALIZATION, AND THE CREATION OF INFORMATION NETWORKS

During the decades of the 1960s and 1970s, the expansion of the technological infrastructure of the Mexican banking industry was characterised by two elements. The first was the mechanization of an increasing number of administrative processes. This also went hand in hand with the creation of new products and services. The second was taking computerization to a regional level in order to deal with the need for the mass processing of information.

The introduction of new computer equipment gathered momentum when management within the banking industry discovered that technology paved the way for the development of new products aimed at large, mass markets.[20] Previously, banks had faced restrictions to operating them, at least in an efficient way. This undoubtedly contributed to the creation of a paradigm in Mexican banking which went from intermediaries that specialised in large customers (an elite, strictly speaking) or whose specialisation focused on its proprietary groups, to a large market where banks began to compete to offer services that went far beyond checking and savings accounts. These products began to take on greater importance in the balance sheets of banks and, therefore, in their income as well.

---

19. Bancomer, "Annual Report", 1969.
20. Interview: Agustín Legorreta Chauvet.

A characteristic example of this was the introduction and growth of the credit card. However, the first specific credit process that was automated was the mortgage loans portfolio. At the time it mainly consisted of commercial properties and to a lesser extent mortgages for private dwellings of individuals. Computer systems were permitted to begin massive mortgage operations. The systems also facilitated the administrative operations of subsidiaries that handled specific services, such as in the case of *Financiadora de Ventas* (a subsidiary for leasing operations) and *Fondo Impulsor de la Construcción* (a subsidiary for industrial mortgages), both from Banamex, and the Bancomer mortgage subsidiary.

Ever since computers were first introduced during the sixties they have been used to process different products, and little by little, specialised systems for specific processes were developed. The development of systems for specific processes was undertaken in conjunction with technology companies. As was the case in the U.S. and Europe, the main computer manufacturers (Bull, IBM, National Cash Register, and Burroughs) were attracted to commercial banks and pushed for them to adopt new equipment. But development of software and adoption of new machines were collaborative undertakings between banks and manufacturers.[21] Banks had to educate their own technicians internally with training from the companies. This was because bank employees possessed the detailed knowledge of the operation that would be converted into an automated process.[22]

Incorporating information technology into these processes in Mexico frequently involved the practice of "copycatting". The largest banks were constantly observing what was happening in the rest of the world and, together with technology companies, developed versions or "local adaptations" to meet their needs, which were partial or less sophisticated adaptations.[23]

Providing technological solutions to operations across the country was a much more complicated undertaking. As has already been explained, technological infrastructure was first installed at purpose-built locations within corporate head offices. This infrastructure was later introduced to branches and connected to corporate head offices, or to regional centres developed for this purpose; in other words, terminals in branches would be connected to a regional head office (via the telephone network and microwave technology). The adoption of technology at a regional level began with the most important economic centres, but a number of additional factors came into play before other regions could be incorporated.

---

21. Ibid.
22. Interview: Agustín Legorreta Chauvet. In his testimony, he explained: "[a]dditionally there was a self-selection among those who were interested in participating in the process of technological change; people who were eager to innovate. In this sense, the generational change that took place in many banks by the early seventies facilitated the adoption of new technologies".
23. Interview: Agustín Legorreta Chauvet.

At the time, Banamex had divided their country operations into seven regions which were determined according to accessibility (in other words, the fastest way of arriving at a collection of branches scattered across different locations). In the case of Bancomer, up until 1977 it conducted regional operations through its system of affiliate banks which had branches in each region. After the merger of these affiliate banks, Bancomer continued this pre-merge regional division. The regional division of operations implied a number of significant restrictions for both banks.

The different regions were strongly defined by Mexico's geography and the lack of transportation routes to move between them. In addition, communication infrastructure, primarily the telephone, varied wildly among regions. This represented a barrier to introducing technology in some regions, as well as to integrating the operations of different regions. This caused the regional centres belonging to Banamex and Bancomer to essentially turn into self-contained administrative units, a virtual "viceroyalty" at times as they were subject to the whim of the local regional manager rather than guidelines from headquarters in Mexico City.

Furthermore, there were variations in business culture between each geographic region in Mexico. This was probably more evident during the construction of an integrated, national market for goods and services. Evidently different business cultures within the same nation were reflected in the organizational culture of the bank. Some branches and regional head offices were very receptive to new technology. But the majority rejected new technology and it took a great deal of effort from the central headquarters to bring regional offices to adopt new processes supported by computer technology.[24]

One of the reasons for rejecting technology was the fear that machines would replace employees in the workplace. But in the majority of cases there were two main underlying factors. One was undoubtedly cultural, given that the new automated processes were seen as "intervention from head office", meaning, "from the central corporate headquarters", and "from Mexico City, the nation's central region" where the corporate head offices of the banks and the central government of the country were both located. The other had a clear economic incentive given that increasing automation of operations enabled better control of branch expenses, which included entertainment expenses of managers and regional directors, and allowed tighter auditing of operations and potential irregularities and moral hazard problems.[25]

Consequently, the introduction of technology was not homogenous over the different regional divisions for the large banks. In addition, the

---

24. Interviews: Agustín Legorreta Chauvet, Rubén Aguilar Monteverde (Mexico City, 31 March 2009), Carlos Aguilar Villalobos.
25. Interview: Agustín Legorreta Chauvet.

state of technology during the middle of the 1960s until the end of the 1970s did not allow complete integration of regional systems, much less provide for interconnectivity. The office responsible for carrying out implementation was "Methods, Systems and Organization".[26]

On the other hand, up until the 1990s various methods for carrying out transactions co-existed: one manual and the other a combination of manual and computerized processes. The cheque system was an example. In many cases a manual record was even made of transactions carried out using computers. At the same time, there were some systems that still employed punched-card machines in conjunction with other technologies. Despite their endurance, punched-card systems were gradually substituted by more modern computers mainly due to their high maintenance cost.

BANAMEX: DIGITALIZING REGIONAL PROCESSES FROM CENTRAL HEADQUARTERS

An example of regional computerization at Banamex that covered several products took place in 1970: the savings accounts of twenty-five branches of the Veracruz (region in the Gulf of Mexico) were centralised in electronic equipment, and in Guadalajara, personal loans and the acquisition of durable consumer goods for the twelve offices in that region.[27] In that same year, recording machines which directly registered data entries on magnetic tape were installed in the regional offices, paving the way for the partial replacement of traditional punched-card systems.[28] In 1970, there were twenty-six systems aimed at supporting services and internal information.

In 1972, Banamex established an "On Line" link based on remote data processing between authorization centres in Mexico and Guadalajara, and equipment in the electronic data processing centre, which would allow "[. . . d]irect and instantaneous consultation of the files handled by the computer thereby notably speeding up service".[29] Remote data processing was introduced to the savings system in seventy-four branches

---

26. Ibid.

27. In 1971, centralising stations were set up in the regional offices of Puebla, Hermosillo, and Veracruz, whereas savings account transactions at the León regional offices were integrated into the electronic equipment at the Guadalajara regional offices; Banamex, "Annual Report", 1970, 32, and 1971, 19, at Archivo Banamex.

28. Punched cards had already reached volumes of 28 million punched cards per year, which represented a high cost for the bank; Banamex, "Annual Report", 1970, 32–33, at Archivo Banamex.

29. Banamex, "Annual Report", 1972, 32 and 40, at Archivo Banamex.

in Mexico City; in addition, *centros de autorización* (authorization centres) were created to provide authorization services for credit cards and cheques.[30] Furthermore, it was expected that this technology would eventually be integrated with branch accounting.

Remote data processing systems allowed Banamex carry out an innovation that was without precedent in the market, namely, the launching in 1972 of the first ATM in the country: "[. . .] a new service called 'Cajero Permanente Bancomático' [Bancomático full-time automatic teller], through the installation of electronic machines at different branches in the metropolitan area whose purpose is to dispense cash to customers 24 hours a day, including Sundays and public holidays, which marks a new concept of banking service".[31] The fist of these machines was deployed in a branch in a suburb in the northern part of Mexico City (named Satelite). This was important as at the time this was the main commuter urbanization for middle-class customers within the metropolitan area of Mexico City. The deployment was followed by adverts in all of the large circulation "broadsheet" newspapers, hence giving national impact to the development.

The ATMs seem to have been manufactured in the U.S. by Diebold and were auctioned by a credit card with a magnetic stripe at the back (as debit card withdrawals were introduced until the late 1980s). The system had at its heart an IBM 370/145 which allowed "online" authorization for credit card withdrawals at ATMs.[32] The new machine, however, was not as much a result of a strategy to increase cash distribution (as ATM numbers remained but a handful until the 1980s) as much as supporting the growth in credit card transactions.

Due to the lack of compatibility between the different systems, in 1973 a strategy began to unify the systems. To achieve this, a new computer centre was created in a building adjacent to the Bancomático Centre, which housed a Burroughs B6700 computer.[33] The building was considered "[. . . t]he most important private electronic centre in Latin America [. . .] built taking into consideration automation's need for growth over the next ten years".[34] But the real possibilities for integrating different applications into a single platform would be years in the making.

By the end of 1974, there were 365 terminals installed in branches and divisions in the Mexico City area connected to the computer centre via telephone lines.[35] Also in 1974, Banamex installed an "Electronic Information

---

30. Ibid.
31. Banamex, "Annual Report", 1972, 32, at Archivo Banamex.
32. *Imagen Magazine*, June 2004, at Archivo Banamex.
33. Banamex, "Annual Report", 1973, 37–40, at Archivo Banamex.
34. Banamex, "Annual Report", 1973, 46–47, at Archivo Banamex.
35. In the case of savings accounts, these terminals allowed the bankbooks of account holders to be updated with the interest earned at any time; it also allowed them to make a deposit or withdrawal from their account. In the case of credit

Processing Centre" in Monterrey, the third largest city and an industrial powerhouse in the country, while the bank expanded the one operating in the Guadalajara regional head office. At that time, Guadalajara, the second largest city, had twenty-four remote data processing terminals to handle savings services throughout its retail branches.[36] In 1974, there were 403 remote data processing terminals throughout the country, growing to 508 in 1975.[37]

However, not all of them were wired directly to Mexico City. In 1975, an Information Processing Centre was opened in the north-eastern city of Hermosillo, resulting in the automation of four out of the seven regional centres into which the bank had been divided.[38] Automation of all regions did not arrive until 1981, which provided automation for the operations of each and every branch in Mexico.

Back then, Banamex recognized that the time would come when it would have to integrate customer information in a single database.[39] Therefore, steps were taken to integrate systems that were somehow hampered by the regional division of bank operations and limited by the current state of international technology, as well as by the cost of telecommunications within the country. In 1980, a mechanism for communicating between computers was begun by linking Tandem equipment with the Burroughs B6700 mainframe (which was later substituted in 1981 with a B7800 mainframe).[40]

In 1982, despite the expropriation of the banking system and the onset of the debt crisis and macroeconomic instability that followed, Banamex was able to maintain a certain level of continuity in its automation process, as well as in the integration of its systems. It is likely that this process would have occurred much faster if it hadn't been for the economic crisis that the country was undergoing. Although Banamex in the early years was a pioneer in the integration of information technology into bank operations, it also faced strong competition from its rival Bancomer, which was eventually overtaken in terms of the size of its network. However, during the 1980s, under government control, Bancomer, like the majority of Mexican banks, slowed the introduction of technology whereas Banamex opted to

---

cards, it allowed the balance to be updated automatically when customers took out cash advances in branches. See Banamex, "Annual Report", 1974, 28, at Archivo Banamex.

36. Ibid.

37. Banamex, "Annual Report", 1975, 28, at Archivo Banamex.

38. Ibid.

39. Interviews: Manuel Medina Mora Escalante (Mexico City, 26 May 2009), Agustín Legorreta Chauvet.

40. In 1981, the bank incorporated into the Society for Worldwide Interbank Financial Telecommunication (SWIFT) the international funds transfer system network (which also had a Burroughs machine at its main hub in Europe).

continue with this strategy.[41] This allowed it to recover its leadership in the market which it had lost to its rival.

In respect to compatibility, in 1982 Banamex interconnected eight electronic processing centres in a private data transmission network, which was the largest in Mexico as late as 2008, allowing it to link 2,048 terminals in 396 branches for "online" operation, and one thousand ATMs.[42] In 1983, it began to replace equipment in regional computer centres in order to expand its operational capacity and achieve network compatibility.[43]

The integration of systems in Banamex was achieved in 1984 with an internal communications network: ten interconnected computer centres, 357 branches, and forty internal operation departments with four thousand terminals. Of these, fifty-five branches had access to the network through nearby offices. During 1984, approximately 265 million transactions were processed by Banamex's computer centres and communications network.[44] With this new platform, Banamex launched new products and services in 1984[45]: a telephone service to assist corporate clientele to manage funds and a service for making inquiries and transfers with the telephone as the means of communication. In July 1985, the "Audiomático" modality was launched, which allowed customers to carry out bank transactions and inquiries directly with a central computer through a Touch-Tone mini-terminal.

It was estimated that the average transaction cost per teller was 170 pesos, but over the telephone speaking to an operator was the equivalent of ninety pesos and employing the technology used by the "Audiomático" service, thirty pesos, less than one-fifth.[46]

Communication technology was over the telephone, which was gradually being replaced by microwave systems. Later, in 1986, Banamex began communicating through the "Morelos" satellite system. In order to capture the satellite signal the bank acquired seven ground stations, a master ground station located in Mexico City and six more for the Regional Information Service Centres.[47] In 1987, the first stage of the plan for using the Morelos Satellite System was complete with nineteen ground stations at different locations around the country. Irrespective of the fact that satellite communication made it possible to transfer data and create entirely digital networks, it was somewhat emblematic that the first national satellite system was being used by one of the country's most powerful private organizations.

---

41. Interviews: Jesús Silva-Herzog Flores (Mexico City, 1 September 2005), Fernando Solana Morales (Mexico City, 2 April 2009).

42. Banamex, "Annual Report", 1982, 16–17, at Archivo Banamex.

43. Banamex, Annual Report, 1983, p. 29, at Archivo Banamex.

44. Banamex, "Annual Report", 1984, 26, at Archivo Banamex.

45. Banamex, "Annual Report", 1984, 27, at Archivo Banamex.

46. *Banamex, Memoria, 1882–1988*, t. II, 132–33; National Bank of Mexico, "Minutes of the Board of Directors", 1985, typed version, at Archivo Banamex.

47. Banamex, "Annual Report", 1986, 34–35, at Archivo Banamex.

In 1987, the financial system took another important leap forward. Banamex began installation of an automated system to operate reception services for payments to third parties. This was the first step toward setting up the system of payments as we know it today. When this system was introduced: "[. . . i]n addition to reducing processing by the customer, it simplifies operational load and reduces branch costs and at the same time opens up new avenues for transferring payments."[48] By the end of the year, approximately 45 per cent of all payments made through Banamex's retail branches in the metropolitan area were carried out automatically. In December, a service for "payments to third parties" was introduced which allowed corporate users to transfer payments to their suppliers, affiliates, and executives.[49]

By 1990, prior to its reprivatization, Banamex was interconnected to a digital voice and data network. However, despite the fact that Banamex led the industry in this area, several processes were still fragmented regionally and there were also discrepancies at a number of stages in the processing of various products. In addition, there were stages in processing that were verified manually. These problems were more serious and widespread among other companies in the banking industry. Following the reprivatization, Banamex sought to make another technological leap forward but the 1995 crisis slowed this process.

BANCOMER: INTEGRATING A FEDERATION OF BANKS

During the first few years of the computerization process, *Banco de Comercio* and its network of regional affiliates behaved relatively conservatively, as a follower rather than innovator in the adoption of technology. However, toward the end of the 1960s and during the 1970s it managed to overtake Banamex in terms of adoption of information technology in the financial services market in several areas. The first important leap forward was the development of an audible response system, SPAC, which was designed in 1969 and provided by Siemens and IBM, that began operation in February 1971.[50]

At the beginning of the 1970s *Banco de Comercio* announced itself as the only institution in Latin America that had Audible Response System technology. The newspapers announced: "Only *Banco de Comercio* Has the Service of the 'Computer that Talks'".[51] It was an IBM 360–40, which

---

48. Banamex, "Annual Report", 1987, 22, at Archivo Banamex.

49. This was through the service *Banca en su Empresa* (in-company banking); Banamex, "Annual Report", 22, at Archivo Banamex.

50. Bancomer's annual reports for 1969–1971.

51. *El Universal*, 18 June 1971, folio 003201-Banco de Comercio, at Archivos Económicos SHCP.

operated a Siemens telephone system in the eighty-three metropolitan offices.[52] The computer would automatically read the balance and gave a voiced response if the document was authorized or not.[53]

In order to continue efforts to automate the operations of affiliate banks, a pilot test was held in *Banco de Comercio* Morelos by installing systems for cheques, remittances, and fixed assets.[54] The first steps to expand this service to affiliate banks in the rest of Mexico were taken in 1972 when a SPAC Terminal was installed in the *Banco de Comercio* Head Office for Guerrero (a state in southern Mexico).[55] This system, which was operated by a remote data processing system using microwaves, was later taken to affiliate banks in other states.[56]

Bank reports described the infrastructure in those years:

> [. . .] *Banco de Comercio*, S.A. has established an automated system for handling savings account transactions by means of remote data processing and computers, and has all but completed work on installing similar systems in the *Banco de Comercio* in Monterrey and *Banco de Comercio* Morelos. Furthermore, we will soon be able to handle by computer the processing of securities transactions made by *Financiera* Bancomer and *Hipotecaria* Bancomer customers directly in *Banco de Comercio* branches in the metropolitan area.[57]

And:

> [. . . a] new data system was installed which has replaced punched cards; a second 370/145 computer was purchased to replace the 360/40 due to the fast growth in the volume of our transactions and the expansion of adaptable systems; the remote data processing network was interconnected with the Central Computer Centre in Mexico City and our affiliate, *Banco de Comercio* Monterrey, as well as all its branches; an Automated Computerized Payment System was added, which operates in all *Banco de Comercio* Mexico City branches, to process cash advances made using our Bancomer Cards and manage the securities transactions of our affiliates, *Financiera* and *Hipotecaria* Bancomer.[58]

---

52. Ibid.
53. Interview: Carlos Aguilar; *El Universal*, 18 June 1971, folio 003201-Banco de Comercio, at Archivos Económicos SHCP.
54. Bancomer, "Annual Report", 1971.
55. Bancomer, "Annual Report", 1973.
56. *El Universal*, 4 February 1972, folio 003201-Banco de Comercio, at Archivos Económicos SHCP.
57. Bancomer, "Annual Report", 1973.
58. Bancomer, "Annual Report", 1974.

In 1973, a third 370/145 computer was installed with the capacity "to absorb the growing volume of transactions and be able to assimilate the number of transactions expected over the next two years".[59] In 1975, the IBM 360–40 computer was replaced with an IBM 370–145 and a data processing system was installed to replace the punched-card system. *Banco de Comercio* in Monterrey, as well as all its branches, was connected to the remote data processing network of the computer centre located in Mexico City.[60]

One of the limitations to systems integration was that the *Banco de Comercio* System was a network of banks. With the inclusion of full-service banking in 1977, in which the thirty-seven banks and non-bank affiliates that formed part of the system merged to become a single company called Bancomer, interconnection was an essential step. In 1978, "12 mini-computers were placed in a number of towns around the country to process checking, savings, collections and payroll account transactions".[61] The year closed with forty-five computers in forty-three locations around the country. That year, Bancomer also automated dollar savings account and statutory bank reserve transactions, as well as registration of furniture and equipment.

The most important step forward was the start of a national "online" system.[62] Amongst the results of these actions was the installation of an online cheque system. Automated systems were also installed in the trust and stock market business areas, and this process was extended to internal banking.[63] In 1980, "On-line Systems for Dollar Savings and Checking Accounts" were installed throughout the entire metropolitan area, "complementing the operations in national currency already offered and continuing with the advances in Regional Centres".[64]

When Bancomer opened its new corporate head offices in 1980, "Centro Bancomer", the building centralised the bank's technological infrastructure. The testimonies state: "[T]he 145 and 370–148 computers are located underground. [. . .] The latter cost 600 million pesos and thanks to this machine Bancomer now has an 'on-line' system consisting of screens—not unlike television—which in four seconds show all the requested information about any customer in the Distrito Federal or the rest of the country" (Espinosa Yglesias 2000: 128). The press stated: "Both computers are housed at a uniform temperature of 18 degrees. In addition, there are 40 electronic devices each the size of a small desk

---

59. Bancomer, "Annual Report", 1975.

60. *Excélsior*, 9 May 1975, folio 003201-Banco de Comercio, at Archivos Económicos SHCP.

61. Bancomer, "Annual Report", 1978.

62. Ibid.

63. Bancomer, "Annual Report", 1979.

64. Bancomer, "Annual Report", 1980.

which are peripheral to the computers. These use lasers to read and print 20 thousand lines per minute in order to generate hundreds of thousands of statements for checking accounts, credit cards ad securities investments, etc."[65] Bancomer's investment in technology began to slow after the expropriation of the banking industry in 1982. This was partly due to the severity of the crisis the country was experiencing, but was also the result of Bancomer's strategy, which was more conservative than that of its main competitor. Although Bancomer had to maintain a complete platform of systems, as it was one of the two largest banks in Mexico, its investment in technology fell behind that of its main competitor. Bancomer, not unlike its main rival, would find new impetus following reprivatization in 1992, which was also affected by the 1995 crisis.

EPILOGUE: TOWARDS INTRA-INDUSTRY CONNECTIVITY

This chapter explained the patterns of development of computerization of the operations of Mexican banks. The cases of Banamex and Bancomer are representative to explain how a major portion of the Mexican banking system digitalized its operations, creating a platform of financial services, which explains today's system of payments in Mexico.

This chapter covers the early integration of the systems of the different banks in Mexico. The technological legacy of Mexican banks at the beginning of the 1990s included systems that were not integrated; information about the customer, the product, and its clients was fragmented at the regional level. The lack of an interconnected system complicated dialogue between the different business areas of a single bank, and interconnection between banks was unthinkable. From the 1980s onward, the "regionalized" structure vanished as operations became more and more integrated.[66] Other notable factors were the effect of high costs and the poor performance of the telecommunications industry in Mexico, which from the 1980s onward made unprecedented advances in the world.

The discussion on interbank connectivity, and even the way in which banks should develop this interconnection within their own systems, matured. For a long period of time, a transfer between two different banks or even between accounts from the same bank but from different regions took time. This time lapse during which the bank retained the money brought returns that discouraged the process for eventual interconnection, at least between institutions. Ever since the 1960s,

---

65. *Excélsior*, 14 August 1980, folio 003201-Banco de Comercio, at Archivos Económicos SHCP.

66. Interviews: Enrique Grapa (Mexico City, 10 May 2009), Augusto Escalante (Mexico City, 10 May 2009).

this dilemma has aroused much debate within the largest banks in the country.[67]

The other discussion on this issue within the industry, particularly within Banamex, centred around the decision of whether large banks—which had made substantial investments in systems—should allow other banks—competitors that did not have the same information and communications infrastructure—to use their platforms (namely, the ATM networks). This would "make the cake bigger for everyone", but seemed very difficult for bankers to accept unanimously.[68] Credit card systems are another well-documented example of this dilemma (see Evans and Schmalensee 1999). During the 1970s three card platforms emerged: Carnet-Prosa, Bancomer, and Banamex.

The first step toward the integration of internal banking systems had to be taken, which was an idea that had been taking shape within the Mexican financial industry since the end of the 1980s. A technological renovation was needed. This proposal was introduced until the privatization of the banking industry, which sped up the process in response to market pressures.

During the 1970s and 1980s, one of the most important milestones had been the introduction of systems that operated in real time, *online*. Progress over that period was enormous ever since the integration of systems and, later, interconnection and electronic banking. Two concrete examples of the integration of systems refer to the use of ATMs to carry out multiple transactions with a customer's account and the ability to cash a cheque at any branch, regardless of where it was issued. The national cheque became a reality in the country in 1993. The expansion of the services offered in ATMs also happened gradually. Electronic banking was not inaugurated until the end of the decade when Banamex introduced its Internet Portal in 1999.

The most significant advance in respect to interconnection did not happen until 1997 when Banamex, Bancomer, and the Red system chose to sign an agreement to unite the three ATM networks. With these efforts to consolidate the system of payments, the private banking industry would build a public asset with their own funds.

The national system of payments became stronger over the first decade of the twenty-first century. However, this would have been impossible without a long history of investment and creation of banking services and technological platforms.

---

67. Interview: Augusto Escalante.
68. Ibid.

Part III

Digitalizing State, Mutual, and Savings Banks

6 Is There an ICT Path in the German Savings Banking Industry?
Circa 1900–1970s

Paul Thomes

INTRODUCTION, MOTIVATION, AND THESES

Today's banking is one of the most intensive users of applications of information technology (IT). However, as the contributions to this volume suggest, the innovational change that led to that state has not yet been documented in detail. Exceptions prove the rule, though. There is Cortada (2006), an interesting U.S.-based attempt to explain change, which stimulated this chapter. There is also Bátiz-Lazo and Wood (2002). The latter did not only try to sum up research in IT innovations in the UK banking industry, seen here as a benchmark, it also delivers a systematic analysis of the development, covering a chronological classification combined with a systematic segregation in front office and back office activities, respectively of product and service innovations. But this chapter is mainly driven by Bátiz-Lazo (1998), the author's own studies around the German savings banks, and, of course, U.S. and British literature, mainly dating from the 1990s.

On the one hand, German banking historians, unlike their Anglo-Saxon colleagues, have yet to deal systematically with questions of automation and mechanization (including the role of IT applications). This lacuna extends to include the process of technological change through a comparative approach contrasting the experiences within different organizational forms that co-exist in German retail markets, such as commercial banks, mutual banks, and savings banks—all acting as universal providers and direct competitors (Pohl, Schulz, and Rudolph 2005: 316ff.; Mura 1995: 135–38).

On the other hand, the analysis of IT innovations seems essential for the understanding of modern banking practices: applications of IT are perceived to have helped bring about organizational changes. But these applications also altered customer relations profoundly. At the same time, these applications were a precondition for the integration of almost all individuals into the financial system. As late as 1970, cash was the only medium of payment for about half of the adult population in many developed countries/societies; at the same time, working-class individuals had a simple interest savings account and some hire purchase credit. There were regulatory changes, ending the post-war era, across Western Europe and North America associated with new products and services. These combined with mass business (for a developing country, see del Angel also in this volume). As the majority of individuals gained access to banking services (and unfettered access to credit), the automation of financial intermediaries increasingly required the computer industry to offer technical solutions in a reciprocal process. So rather than offering an isolated view of technical developments, this chapter aims to explain the economic, social, and political context of the adoption of IT innovations. As a result, it deals with the forerunners and emergence of computer-based banking up to the 1970s, when computing in German banks reached the front office and, for instance, automated teller machines (ATMs) opened a new dimension in customer relations (see further Bátiz-Lazo 2009).

The purpose of such a holistic comparison is to reconstruct the processes of innovation and decision making, which will enable us to analyze whether there is an individual "path dependence" in German IT banking (see David 1985). We also want to determine whether there are variations within the three main groups of participants in German retail deposit markets (namely, co-operative banks, savings banks, commercial banks), and if so, why. As a result, this chapter will articulate an international comparison when considering whether the "British IT path", suggested by Bátiz-Lazo and Wood (2002), fits in with German trends (see Cortada 1996: 146, 161). A common link here might be the hardware, which has been, especially after 1945, dominated by U.S. companies such as IBM. A strong indicator that there might be variations is the quite late spreading of Giro transactions in the UK, which might be a consequence of different business cultures, the UK maintaining a cheque culture, and Germany having a Giro payment culture (Böhle and Arbussà 1999: 53; Wissenschaftsförderung 1995b: 19–34).

In what follows, the second section outlines the main similarities and differences in the provision of retail financial services by co-operative, savings, and commercial banks. The third section documents and analyzes the process of computerization, discussing "massification" of retail bank markets and arguments for and against a specific German path dependence. The German savings banks will be identified as first-movers in the process of mechanization and computerization (see Bonin and Mooij in this volume). Two intermediaries will serve as exemplary references. One is Kreissparkasse Saarbrücken (DSB), a district savings bank, which in 1961 was the first German intermediary to attempt a move towards full electronic data processing (Mura 1995: 144; Thomes 2008: passim). Developments at DSB's local competitor, Stadtsparkasse Saarbrücken (CSB), a city savings bank, will be explored as a way to portray developments in the savings banks "movement" as a whole. Evidence for these stories is composed of board minutes (BM), business reports (AR), and public information.

The final section aims at generalizing the results in a comparative international view.

OUTLINE OF THE GERMAN FINANCIAL SECTOR: UNIVERSAL BANKING AS THE "NORM"

At the beginning of the twentieth century, the German banking sector showed a clear structure that differed significantly from those of other countries (Cortada 2006: 39ff.). Three groups had developed during the nineteenth century which offered more or less the same products and services but whose business models differed, especially in their corporate governance (Ashauer 2005: 22–41, 87–124).

1. The savings banks—as the biggest group concerning market share (for details see the following)—have their roots in the late eighteenth century (see also Bátiz-Lazo and Maixé-Altés in this volume). To date, they are predominantly local, limiting their scope to a city or a district with local authorities as stakeholders. Their business model is that of non-profit institutions that direct their attention towards social welfare (their surplus financing public and cultural activities for that city or district).

From their beginning, alongside the collection of small-scale and liquid deposits, most of these savings banks developed an independent lending business. Soon they became the most important regional credit institutions, providing personal and mortgage loans as well as public financing by direct loans or bonds. By the end of the nineteenth century, their business was being backed by regional state banks (*landesbanken*), which widened their business scope. By 1908, cheque and bill transactions were allowed, which was an important premise for cashless salary and wage payments.

At that time, savings banks existed in almost every German town and district; in particular, the district savings banks (DSB) ran quite dense networks of branch offices, thus reaching the great majority of the people in Germany. These structures survived World War I and formed the basis for a successful development as non-profit universal banks, backed by the regional *Landesbanken*. Their business model differs significantly from the European pattern. In 1957, 871 West German savings banks were running 8,192 branches and balancing DM 18.7 billion of savings and a total turnover of DM 34 billion (Pohl, Schulz, and Rudolph 2005: 415ff.; for a European comparison, see Wissenschaftsförderung 1995a).

2. Co-operative banks emerged in the middle of the nineteenth century, driven by private interests, which had reservations against the public savings banks (see further Mooij in this volume). They were founded mostly by craftsmen, farmers, or retailers. In principle, they did the same business as the savings banks, also collecting small savings while their credit transactions focused on a local scale. In general, they did not run a branch network and they stayed quite small. They were backed by mutual regional

central banks, too, which gave them a broader activity range. The development was much more unstable than that of the savings banks. Anyway, they
became the sharpest competitors of the latter and were strong in personal
loans. In 1914, about 19,000 independent mutual banks existed. In the
mid-1950s there were still about 11,600 co-operative banks with around
2.4 million members.

3. Commercial private banks were organized on a national or a
regional level as joint stock or private companies. They started more or
less as investment or trade banks, but by the end of the nineteenth century
at least some of them had started private banking, including the savings business. Furthermore, the bigger players founded branch networks.
After World War II, the three largest private banks were each split into
several smaller companies under Allied occupation regulations, an act
that considerably hindered their development. They were only permitted to reunite in 1957. Additionally, in 1955, there were more than three
hundred locally or regionally rooted private banks. By 1960, the savings
bank sector held a market share of 36 per cent, the private credit banks
24 per cent, and the co-operative banks 8.6 per cent. All of them were
acting as universal banks, serving individuals, firms, and public institutions, and offering a broad service. With regard to all savings deposits,
the savings banks held DM 33.7 billion, the co-operative banks DM 7.5
billion, and the commercial banks DM 8.4 billion, the market shares adding up to 63, 14, and 16 per cent respectively. The 1960s and 1970s were
characterized by increased competition and a strong reduction of the
number of banks from 13,359 in 1957 to 4,940 in 1982, caused mainly
by mergers. On the other hand, the number of branches rose from 12,974
to 39,913; a result of the diffusion of bank services, which again boosted
technological requirements (Institut für bankhistorische Forschung 1984:
vol. 3, 231–73; Pohl, Schulz, and Rudolph 2005: 409–11; Ashauer 2005:
100–105).

IDENTIFICATION AND ANALYSIS OF THE IT PATH

Necessity to Act Rationally and the Impact of World War I

The mechanization of banking started at the very end of the nineteenth
century (Bonin and others in this volume) with mechanical calculating
machines to simplify addition, achieving a significant productivity gain of
up to 300 per cent, as historical estimations indicate (for details see the following). In 1898, a first Burroughs adding machine was documented at the
CSB in Kassel (Nehberg 1963: 22). Advertising for machines of this kind
first appeared in *Sparkasse*, a professional savings bank journal, in 1906.
From then on, book-keeping machines began to spread; they also printed
operations, including customers' savings books. Internally, printed ledgers

and reports began to replace manuscript entries. *Sparkasse* reported on their use in 1911 in the Berlin-Schöneberg savings bank as one of the German first-movers. The article describes the advantages as well: quicker customer service, fewer errors, better control, and reduced labour cost. Other institutions soon followed suit, especially because the number of savings accounts quite often topped twenty thousand (Mura 1995: 135–55; Wissenschaftsförderung 1995b: 19–32).[1]

During World War I, further reasons for machine application accrued:

1. There was an increasing scarcity of labour, especially because the great majority of banking staff were men.
2. New business fields, such as trading in (war) bonds, were opening up.
3. Consumption possibilities diminished and fostered savings.
4. Cashless payment was promoted because of the scarcity of cash.

As a result, savings and Giro accounts grew as well as the number of transactions. An important point in this context: Giro accounts at that time were no longer restricted to firms or wealthy individuals. The Prussian administration, for instance, had been transferring its employees' salaries—on demand—to bank Giro accounts since 1907. One year later, the savings banks were included in the cheque-transaction system by the *Reichsscheckgesetz* law. Many city and district governments immediately took up this service for their own officers and used it, of course, for their own transactions (Marx et al. 1961: 49; Mura 1995: 199). This must be seen as a further important milestone for the start of a typical German path (see in comparison Booth and Billings in this volume for Britain).

This means, then, that cost and mass incentives triggered the use of machines at that period to manage administration as well as costs, whereas the demand, in contrast, triggered the technological development. This hypothesis again fits in with the diffusion process, because savings banks, especially in bigger cities, such as Aachen, Bremen, Cologne, Hannover, Karlsruhe, and Munich, introduced machine book-keeping during World War I. Technological progress accelerated across many sectors and not only in financial institutions. In addition there was a growing general need for compatibility and unification (Mura 1995: 136ff., 204; Schulz 2001: 25). On the other hand, the number of Giro accounts was still relatively small compared with the savings accounts at that time. Meanwhile, the majority of banks and savings banks went on practicing their traditional "cameralistic" bookkeeping in combination with mental arithmetic or/and adding machines.

---

1. *Sparkasse* was the official journal of the German savings banks organization.

The "Race for Modernity" and the Rise of the Credit Industry in the "Roaring 20s"[2]

The end of World War I brought no fundamental changes with it. The savings banks defended their war-induced business fields against the commercial banks. A determining factor in the operational business was the "Great Inflation" that emerged after price restrictions ended with the war. Thus, "old" automation driving forces were supplemented by a new one that—as a side aspect—facilitated the financing of innovations, too. In general, we observe a veritable universal rationalization "hype" during the 1920s that literally overran not only the financial sector (see further Cortada 1996).

The common motto was: "machines at any price", and even in medium- and smaller-sized banks, cash register accounting machines spread widely. The umbrella organization of German savings banks, the DSGV, as well as the regional savings banks associations, campaigned intensively for an efficient and modern organization of the administrative processes in parallel to the automation of the business itself. We see here an attempt at coordinated systematic change management, backed by exhibitions and workshops. One central point of the campaigns was tabular bookkeeping, which facilitated the use of accounting machines and saved the need for a second bookkeeper, with the aforementioned results of easier control and better customer service. To give an example: a machine-booking clerk could manage 500 entries per day against 180 done by hand; an efficiency gain of nearly 300 per cent! Not surprisingly, the DSGV, for instance, had the big German engineering firm Krupp develop a machine as a reference model for all savings banks—with the intention of a nationwide strategy in mind. But a preliminary model was not ready until 1930. Meanwhile, a lot of institutions had bought machines without coordination (Höpker 1997: 180; Mura 1995: 137; Pohl, Schulz, and Rudolph 2005: 102ff.; Thomes 2008: 203; Schulz 2001: 26).

One interpretation says that the boards often succumbed to the machine sellers' wild promises. And indeed, a general "need" seems doubtful, especially as there was no scarcity of labor in the 1920s. Thus, the widely unquestioned "race for modernity" ended up in more than one so-called machine graveyard (*Maschinenfriedhof*).

On the other hand, an exemplary analysis clearly proves the need for technical equipment: the competing DSB Saarbrücken and CSB Saarbrücken savings banks[3] changed to tabular bookkeeping by means of Astra, Burroughs, and NCR machines almost simultaneously in 1927–1929, following the

---

2. In Germany the term *Goldene 20er Jahre* (Golden 20s) is used for the years between 1924 (currency reform, Dawes Plan) and 1929 (beginning of the world economic crisis) analog to the "Roaring 20s".

3. DSB (*Kreissparkasse* Saarbrücken), established in 1858; CSB (*Stadtsparkasse* Saarbrücken) established in 1909; for details see Thomes (2008).

suggestion by the regional savings banks organization. CSB modernized parallel to constructing a new building and invested around thirty-one thousand *Reichsmarks* in the equipment, which equalled 0.3 per cent of the liabilities. Soon, the whole booking system had been mechanized by hand-driven or electric-motor-driven machines. By 1933, the investment had been written off.[4]

The interesting point concerning the need—on which doubt was cast earlier—is that, in spite of rationalization, the number of employees grew significantly: between 1924 and 1930 the DSB Saarbrücken, for example, multiplied its staff from 23 to 145. Many of them were low-skilled "machine workers" without a banking education who worked in factory-like machine rooms. Many savings banks at that time employed their own mechanics, too (Thomes 2008: 207). The scale of fixed investment grew significantly. To sum up: this first automation wave deeply changed the composition of staff, the quality of work, and the capital intensity. In the 1920s, the banking business was turned into a banking industry, using complicated machinery, including first attempts to apply the Hollerith system, as is documented for banks in Hamburg and the region of Pomerania (Mura 1995: 143; Heide 2004). Concerning our general question, it is important to see that the path laid during World War I was consequently developed during the 1920s. The continued development of the savings banks towards universal banks with a large clientele and a great diversity of services made the use of machines indispensable, with reciprocal impacts on the producers of the machinery.

War-enforced Rationalization in World War II

The consequences of the world economic crisis, which began in 1929, were astonishingly slight in Germany with regard to automation aspects. The modernization process restarted in the mid-1930s, when the totalitarian Nazi regime was supporting saving as well as cashless payment in order to finance rearmament more easily. In addition, from 1936 onwards, due to the armament boom, mass unemployment was turned into full employment: a perfect situation, then, for pressing ahead with automation, as did many financial institutions, because this development coincided with the regime's needs, too (see further Thomes 1996).

Many studies in cost-accounting were launched. They covered the flow of work as well as aspects of general organization. As a result, both of our Saarsbrücken case study banks simplified current-account book-keeping and shifted the booking process from front to back office to minimize the term of employment. In 1940, CSB included its local branches in this system,

---

4. Records *Konferenzbezirk der Saarsparkassen* 1927, 106. AR CSB and DSB 1927/1933, passim; Mura (1995: 138ff.) gives an overview of the machines that were used.

whereas bookkeeping was centralized: an important prerequisite for data processing by punched cards or computers. Individual account files were also reorganized adequately. CSB's 1940 annual report says, for example, that reorganization compensated war shortages and that all transactions were still running smoothly. This positive experience was responsible for the continuation of the use of any opportunity to modernize.[5]

The development at DSB Saarbrücken was similar. They created their own department *Betriebsorganisation* (business organization), which would finally turn DSB into one of the foremost computing users in Germany. The measures immediately reduced manpower by about 15 per cent. Reputed costs of up to 100,000 *Reichsmarks* p.a.—as reports say—may be exaggerated. Anyway, both banks reveal a typical example of war-driven efficiency innovations.

Under general aspects, again the support from the national DSGV is worth mentioning, which was acting, of course, to conform to the Nazi regime's efficiency goals. The 1937 German savings banks convention, for instance, was accompanied by another office machine exhibition. And as the Saarbrücken example shows, the war did not stop but perpetuated the mechanization process. The result was quite impressive: by 1945, all intermediaries had implemented some kind of mechanization. Especially large banks were using advanced techniques, which mechanized the bookkeeping process completely, including balance sheets.

Another aspect of the war needs to be mentioned here. From 1943 on, the Allied Forces' air raids intensified and became increasingly well targeted, too. This means that a lot of the mechanical investments of the 1920s and 1930s had to pay their tribute to the war and were destroyed. This is an important fact because this destruction facilitated the transition to fully electronic computing during the post-war reconstruction period. To summarize: on the one hand, World War II generated the scope needed for further technological reforms and perhaps generated the basis for an international surge forward. On the other hand, the heavy destruction of equipment after 1943, in Germany especially compared to Britain, Spain, the Netherlands, or the Americas (see relevant chapters in this volume), created the conditions that made it easier to switch to data processing systems—at least, that is the theory.

The Data Processing Revolution of the 1950s

Post-war reality, however, was complicated. In fact, the results of World War II did not strengthen the modernization path thoroughly. The existing literature argues that after 1945 there was an intensified use of the

---

5. AR CSB (1937, 9); AR DSB (1937, 9, 18); Pohl (2001: 160ff., 181); Mura (1995: 139ff.); AR CSB (1940, 35).

techniques implemented during the Nazi period. It has been observed that there were strong innovative developments as well (Mura 1995: 140).

What we actually observe right after the war is that financial institutions had to use the equipment at hand. There was no choice because of the general situation, characterized by deprivation and disorder. Repairing was difficult because spare parts were rare, but procuring new machines was actually impossible. The reasons behind this are easily explained: most of the German machine manufacturers were situated in the Soviet occupation zone, which was out of reach. Foreign models at that time were too expensive; and even if they had not been, they would hardly have been available because of manifold occupation restrictions and a lack of foreign currency in Germany.

To cite our local example again: DSB Saarbrücken reported in 1945 that their machinery had survived to a large extent, but they deplored the loss of two expensive Continental 800 book-keeping machines. At the same time, 24 branches were still using calculating machines. The value of the bank's machinery was estimated at about 500,000 *Reichsmarks*. To bridge the gap between demand and supply, two local mechanics, who specialised in Astra booking machines, opened a repair service right in the DSB building in July 1946. At that time, the board was already considering a changeover to American machines (IBM, NCR) and shortly after, they did (Thomes 2008: 286–89, 308–13; MB DSB 1945, 1946; Kloevekorn 1958: 77ff.; Mura 1995: 141).

As early as 1947, the DSB board decided to switch to the Hollerith punch-card system and on 23 December 1947 a lease contract with *Deutsche Hollerith-Maschinen-Gesellschaft* (*DEHOMAG*) was signed (see Heide 2004; Ceruzzi 2003). As the minutes of the board prove, the board was quite assured about daring to take the step from mechanization to data processing as early as possible. When the system started work in 1948, it did so without substantial problems. By the end of the year, it was well established. Another aspect was new, too: leasing made the distribution of the innovation possible at a time when the savings bank would not have been in a position to pay for such a sophisticated system with its cash flow. Because the majority of institutions were (forced by the circumstances) still clinging to their traditional standards, this seems to have been an extraordinary decision. However, it was one with a path-setting referent power that coincided with the general positive innovation-friendly background mentioned earlier. In addition, there was a local factor for the decision making: personal know-how. Two highly interested and committed managers convinced the board of the economic potential of the data processing technology for mass business. (Thomes 2008: 263–75).

Promising results quickly justified the courageous decision: falling administration costs and a better customer service in terms of reliability and speed. We indeed see a real first-mover here. The local competitor, CSB, for instance, did not follow suit until 1955, whereas most of the institutions that opted for Hollerith did so much later, in the 1960s, when computing started a completely new automation era. Generally, the new technique was first applied in the work-intensive fields of general and current accounting as well as for the calculation of interest. As another automation consequence, machine receipts became valid with only one signature.

Meanwhile, the number of conventional non-Hollerith accounting machines was growing quickly, too. From 1953 to 1955, German savings banks bought 2,900 units. This seems on the one hand to have contributed to an over-mechanization of internal business procedures, similar to the situation during the 1920s. On the other hand, however, Deutsche Bank did not introduce the punched-card system until 1957 or 1958.[6]

As a result, we can identify two different modernization paths following World War II: a traditional, mechanical-based one and an innovative, punched-card-based, electromagnetic one. They finally became unified in electronic computing after the 1960s. Both paths had the same background. They resulted from fast-growing business and keen competition as well as from a tight labour market. The latter made it increasingly difficult and expensive to recruit employees. As the German economy grew quickly, real incomes and wages grew, too. Besides other aspects, both factors created positive effects for the financial industries (i.e. new customers) and these enabled corresponding automation investments.

On the other hand, we might raise the question of whether the switch-over to punched cards was necessary at all, or rather a costly change management detour on the way to digitalization. Our case study seems to prove the first hypothesis. It clearly shows that the use of punched cards made people aware of digital advantages. It was not by chance that Saarbrücken DSB and CSB were digital first-movers. The DSB was already combining punched-card machines and computers as an interim solution in 1957 and—after thirteen years of punched cards—was the first German credit institution to implement EDP with the same distributor—meanwhile trading in Germany as IBM—based on an IBM 1401 in 1961. In 1967 the CBS was one of the first financial intermediaries in Europe to successfully deploy real-time applications; but that is a different story which needs to be documented in detail in a separate chapter.[7]

Two further points have to be mentioned in this context: internal documentation and organization. Accounting had to become centralized—something that happened mostly in the 1950s—and there were some

---

6. See Mura (1995: 141, 143). Schulz (2001: 29–32), shows and describes different mechanical accounting machines; MB and AR, DSB and CSB 1957–1965, passim. For Deutsche Bank see Gall et al. (1995: 599). See also the general introduction in this chapter.

7. For the combination in general and the prospects, see *Der neue Teismann* (1960: 226). For online EDP statistics of the German savings banks, see Harmsen et al. (1991). For more details, see the following.

efforts to make data storage and handling more efficient. Thus, micro-filming of the slips was introduced, which allowed the documentation of 20,000 slips on a 30m film and reduced the required storage space to 1 per cent.[8]

Important in our respect is the fact that technical devices in the 1950s had been developed to such an extent that at least the bigger and some medium-sized savings banks were ready for a new dimension of mass business, which would change back office activities yet again. A German yearly merchants' guide prognosticated in 1960 quite far-sightedly, "Commercial administration will probably change profoundly in the near future" (*Der neue Teismann* 1960: 226). This indicates that computers were not only finding their way into the credit and insurance industries but, at the same time, into the manufacturing sector. This fact is important for our topic, because it changed administration and book-keeping structures in general, too; and as a result, it crucially affected the relationship between banking and commercial industry.

Another point to be made here to complete the arguments is that computerization was not without controversy; we can observe a broad discussion in all the relevant media since the late 1950s, which reveals quite a lot of diffuse reservations—none of which really slowed down the process or caused it to deviate from the described path, however.[9]

New Customer Services, the Rising Complexity of Tasks, and a Difficult Job Market as Catalysts of Computer Application in the 1960s

The savings banks, as the inventors of mass business in the German credit sector supplying the average person in the street with a bank account, headed the transformation process towards computers in this period, too. Commercial and co-operative banks innovated more slowly once more.[10] The latter still had a size problem (see Mooij in this volume), because the majority of co-operative banks were too small for individual computer use. The big commercial banks, however, were not really free to act until 1957, because only then were the occupation restrictions lifted. In addition, they started private banking and discovered the common private client and savings business. From then on, the big commercial banks grew fast and were

---

8. See Thomes (2008: 311) and Mura (1995: 224). For general commercial considerations, see Nehberg (1963: 130–49). He gives a very positive interpretation of the effects of the use of computers.

9. See, for instance, many relevant papers in *Zeitschrift für das gesamte Kreditwesen*; for Dresdner Bank, see Minske (1970).

10. In particular, the statements on co-operative banks for Germany are in a way provisional because their history has not been researched well enough yet. See Mooij in this volume for the Netherlands.

forced to close the modernization gap literally. To give an example: Jürgen Minske, manager of the Dresdner Bank, reports on the start of computer usage in the early 1960s—candidly, as he emphasizes: first, the salesman from the computer firm came, followed by the computer, followed by the conviction, and last but not least, there had to be plausible "excuses", such as the labour market and other circumstances not giving us any choice but to take the step into automation. In general, we see a mixture of external factors and personal convictions of locally acting people as the thriving forces behind computerization. And at least in the beginning, there definitely was no master plan, just uncoordinated automation efforts. The savings banks, however, by the end of the 1950s were ahead of the commercial banks for about one decade; many of them beyond the experimental phase and defining the general innovation path.[11]

Three developments at that time fostered the adoption and spread of computer technology in Germany: an empty labour market, government savings promotion programmes, and the broad introduction of cashless wage payment in industry.

In 1959, the German federal government launched a social programme to assist broad asset accumulation according to the concept of the German *Soziale Marktwirtschaft* (social market economy). Every taxpayer who saved a certain amount of money and invested it for five years got an extra pro rata bonus of 20 per cent from the State. This programme brought a lot of new clients into the banks. In the savings banks sector, the quantity of those special savings rose within ten years from DM 1 billion in 1959 to almost DM 12 billion in 1969. Of course, this development caused additional administration efforts and costs because the procedure was quite complicated. Even more relevant was the diffusion of Giro transfer, and with it an additional enormous rise in payment transactions. It started nearly at the same time as the social programme and was a broad dynamic movement, which seems to be unique in Europe (see related chapters in this volume). This combination is reckoned to have been the main motor behind digitalization in the financial services sector (Abelshauser 2004; Ellgering 2001: 95–99; Mura 1995: 37–44, 144–46; Pohl 2001: 244–46; Thomes 2008: 343).

The diffusion of EDP in industrial companies during the 1960s was one important precondition and had two main consequences: employees' salaries and workers' wages were transferred from traditional weekly payments into monthly payments. Parallel to this, there was the introduction of a non-cash payment mode. Both processes went hand in hand.[12]

---

11. Minske (1970); Marx et al. (1961: 34ff.). For the commercial banks, see *100 Jahre* (1970: 135–38), Gall et al. (1995: 597, 599) and Frost (2009: 18–76). For the development in general, see Cortada (1996: 129).

12. For a contemporary overview, see Kaiser (1960); Marx et al. (1961); Hohn (1964); for more analysis, see Wissenschaftsförderung (1995b: 51–64).

For employers, the new "modus operandi" brought about an essential organizational simplification and cost savings potential. For the credit industry, the system was attractive because of the opportunity to gain additional customers and additional "cheap" liquidity. In general, then, there should have been a strong impetus for both parties to implement clearing systems. However, there were reservations, especially in the commercial banking sector, which at that time was still suffering from a lack of automation, as explained earlier. The savings banks, however, saw a good opportunity to strengthen their position and took a chance on it (Gall et al. 1995: 595–98; Cortada 2006: 41).

Some facts will illustrate the momentum: in April 1960, all German savings banks were running 2.3 million Giro accounts; the other groups shared another 1.2 million. About half of them were wage or salary accounts. The majority of private clients belonged to the public service or were public firms, where cashless payments, as noted earlier, had started as early as 1908 and had, since the mid-1950s, been introduced systematically. Private firms, however, typically paid cash at that time. However, this ratio changed dramatically from then on. By the end of 1960, statistics show already six million savings banks Giro accounts. In 1965, the number was 9.9 million accounts, among them 6.5 million private accounts and 5.2 million bookings per day. In 1970, the result was 17 million accounts, among them 14.2 million private accounts and 9.7 million bookings per day. The latter were influenced by multiplied payment transactions, such as direct debits and standing orders, etc. The majority of employees—whether factory workers, clerks, or executive employees—had a bank Giro account by then, most of them with savings banks (Mura 1995: 231–36; Pohl, Schulz, and Rudolph 2005: 317–21; Marx et al. 1961: 65–71; AR GSBO 1961–1966).

To cite our local example again, cashless payments appeared on the DSD Saarbrücken board's agenda in 1957 for the first time. The final step was made in 1965, when the biggest regional employer, the government-run *Saarbergwerke* coal mining company, completely switched to cashless payments, and more or less parallel to that, several big steel companies. This wave generated several tens of thousands of Giro accounts simultaneously (MB DSB 1957; Thomes 2008: 359–62). For a comparative view, see Bonhage (2007: 97–99); Bonhage and Girschik (2005); and Zetti (2008).

These few figures give an impression of the huge need for investments in technology, standards, and staff, which were necessary to manage the fast and continually expanding transaction volume. Not surprisingly, there was a short but intense discussion between companies and banks as to whether customers should share in the costs. Employers especially argued strongly against fees, referring to expected significant monetary residuals in the clients' accounts, which would generate extra earnings for the banks and would pay for the cost of investment. In reality, interbank competition was so fierce that the savings banks would not charge their clients for the new services. Quite a few even paid moderate interest rates on Giro balances. And just as a side-note: in contrast to the U.S., for instance, there was no charging tradition in Germany. Within a relatively short period—accompanied by promotion campaigns—the new customers learned about the Giro advantages and the use of cheques, Giro transfers, or standing orders. Estimates prove the quick amortization of computer investments. Obviously, the cheap Giro balances as well as an intensified business activity with Giro clients compensated the high investment costs, whereas cost-benefit ratios developed positively. That applies especially to the savings banks, where the positive results created additional momentum to set the pace in the German financial services sector.[13]

Individual vs. Co-Operative Technical Innovation Solutions

The ways for optimizing IT efficiency, however, were heterogeneous. Again, the German savings banks umbrella association, DSGV, tried to coordinate actions by founding an *Institut für Automation* in 1965. It was successful but failed to achieve a state of nationwide unification. As one result we can identify two variations of the automation path since the 1960s:

1. intermediaries that went their own way by buying or leasing equipment
2. intermediaries that co-operated with partners in so-called book-keeping accounting processing centres (*Buchungsgemeinschaften*) to create economies of scale (Ellgering 2001: 99; Harmsen et al. 1991: 50; Mura 1995: 145–47; Pohl, Schulz, and Rudolph 2005: 319; for a comparative view, see Cortada 2006: 62)

The latter aimed at minimizing costs and risks in a fast-changing market. The first German booking centre not surprisingly was founded by co-operative banks in 1960 in Karlsruhe by FIDUCIA AG, a well-established securities custodian and bank accountancy firm. Others soon followed suit. In 1966, for instance, around 10 per cent of the German savings banks were affiliated with such centres. Two years later, in 1968, around two-thirds of the 857 savings banks were using computers, among them 200 as individual solutions and around 350 as members of 59 regional book-keeping centres. In 1976, only 111 out of 649 savings banks were running individual data processing devices. At that time, even remote data processing was part of the daily routine. This new dimension of regional

---

13. Marx et al. (1961: 18–20, 49–59). For a transatlantic comparative view, see Schmidt (1960). For an overview, see Mura (1995: 237–39), Gall et al. (1995: 597); and Thomes (2008: 359–62). For the general development, see Abelshauser (2004: 200–205, 288–94). For related aspects of a national case study, see Bonhage (2007, 2010) and Bonhage and Girschik (2005).

co-operation fostered co-operation in the credit sector in general, too, as well as unification efforts.[14]

The solutions chosen actually did not only depend on the size of the intermediaries, as is often argued (Cortada 1996: 163–65). Two examples of this thesis, which is supported by our Saarbrücken case study, may be given here: both medium-size institutions built up their own EDP capacities separately, although they were both using IBM equipment. They started with the transistorized IBM 1401 in 1961 (DSB) and 1963 (CSB). Incidentally, IBM was the German market leader with a share of about 60 per cent at that time. The DSB board must have been absolutely convinced by the possibilities of the new technology because they invested the remarkable sum of DM 230,000 in organizational and building facilities in addition to the leasing rates. Nevertheless, they expected monthly cost savings of around DM 5,000, mainly arising from the replacement of manual book-keeping, accounting, and balancing, whereas the "economized" employees got other tasks within the company. In this context, it should be mentioned that technological innovation at that time still did not reduce the number of employees.[15]

Actually the computer system did not operate at full capacity at first. As a reaction, in 1962 DSB started processing for two savings banks in the neighbourhood but not for the direct local competitor, CSB. In 1965, DSB took the next modernization step and ordered an IBM 360–30. The system's software had to be modified, but allowed broader and faster automation of routines and an intensified data processing for institutional clients like sport clubs or firms as an additional service. In June 1967, CSB counter-attacked in a spectacular way. It is reported that CSB was the first European credit institution to run a fully digital, real-time, in-house bookkeeping system.

Regarding that period, another observation can be made: it seems that rationality overran non-critical enthusiasm and started to play a major role in decision making about upgrading technical devices. At the same time, the German economy, after four decades of growth, plunged into its first post-war crisis, and the Saar district with it. In 1969, the savings banks of the Saar region formed an automation council, driven mainly by cost aspects, whereas shrinking margins favoured increasing standardization. The process ended in 1970 in a joint data processing centre for the regional

---

14. For concerns, widespread uncertainty, and the alluring perspectives of computer application, see *Bank-Automation* (1964). For an abstract concerning the role of payment transactions including book-keeping centres, see Harmsen et al. (1991: 45–57); Starke (1982); and Ashauer (2005: 120–22).

15. See *Bank-Automation* (1964). An IBM 1401 was sold in October 1959. The number of employees grew quite considerably until the beginning of the 1970s. For reciprocal effects between employees and automation concerning number, qualification, and tasks, see Thomes (2008: 367–72).

savings banks organization (MB 1961–1971; Mura 1995: 148; Thomes 2008: 325–31, 374–77). A comparable situation with a differing result is shown by the case of Aachen, a city comparable in size to Saarbrücken. The Aachen CSB outsourced its data processing at an early stage and switched to leased IBM machines in 1959. Similar to the Saarbrücken case, there was no contact with the local competitor, DSB Aachen. Both built up very individual and non-compatible EDP structures. This fact became somewhat painfully obvious when both savings banks merged in the beginning of 1993.[16]

To summarize: obviously, soft factors such as risk aversion, technical enthusiasm, prestige, and competitiveness of the locally acting people often played a determining role for the kind of digitalization. They generated individual variations of the path, which in some cases were followed for quite a long time until the end of the twentieth century. Size was not the only determining factor; the speed of technical development convinced even many successful and strong individual players to join processing centres in time (for a comparative view, see Cortada 2006: 62).

Meanwhile, co-operative and commercial banks caught up. As a result, in the 1970s the whole credit sector was acting on more or less the same IT level nationally and internationally as well (see also Bátiz-Lazo and Maixé-Altés, Mooij, and other chapters in this volume). To give some German examples: Deutsche Bank, for instance, started EDP in 1961 and ended the punched-card era in 1968. In 1967, Dresdner Bank established three long-distance data lines (200 km) by telephone. Online processing was introduced by Deutsche Bank in 1974 on an IBM 370 and a Siemens 4004. Finalizing changes at the bank counter started in 1983—but again later than in the savings banks sector (Gall et al. 1995: 599–604).

RESULTS AND CONCLUSIONS—DEFINING THE "GERMAN" IT PATH IN BANKING

The question of whether there is a specific German "computers-in-banking-path" in comparison to other countries has to be answered with a clear "yes".

Generally, the German development (like all other chapters of this volume) corresponds with Cortada's observations and conclusions. Concerning the outlines, he argues, "Nobody had a master plan, nobody had a clue" (Cortada 1996: 129). That is true, but who would have had a master plan for a new technology, including all its options and possibilities, which were unthinkable for most people even as recently as the late 1960s? In fact, learning by doing has been the name of this particular game, too, and

---

16. AR DSB Aachen 1992. A detailed study of this subject is in preparation.

locally acting people, who were strongly convinced of the new technology, pushed its application together with the suppliers of hardware and software, thus influencing the general development. As the main reasons for using computers in banking, Cortada identifies the following factors: "Labor [*sic*] efficiency, new customer services, complexity of tasks and prestige" (1996: 176). As shown earlier, these arguments played a role in the German development, too. However, this is not surprising because his arguments are virtually commonplace. His opinion that the main "barriers for entry for companies were insufficient capital . . ." has to be re-examined (Cortada 1996: 131). Suppliers seized upon the suggestions of their users and helped to spread their products, for instance, by attractive leasing offers, whereas the German example shows that users founded joint data processing centres at a very early stage.

The question to be answered is: why? One criterion in particular can be seen as shaping Germany's technical innovation path: the institutional structure of the financial services sector. It has been dominated by non-commercial savings banks (for a comparative view, see, for instance, Bátiz-Lazo and Maixé-Altés and Bonin in this volume). As the inventors of private banking they acted as universal banks. They integrated a great number of clients and created a mass business.

A second criterion is the long German tradition of private Giro banking starting early in the twentieth century. It was introduced broadly at the beginning of the 1960s. Its implementation would have been unthinkable without many years of experience with office machines. This had been fostered by both world wars. They forced especially German enterprises to adopt a strong sense of rationality and awareness of technical modernity because of an immense general lack of means. World War II additionally caused destruction of the existing equipment and triggered the introduction of new data processing technologies more effectively than in other states, as the case studies of this book demonstrate.

A third interacting path-forming criterion was the unique development of the German labour market in the 1950s and 1960s. As a result of the *Wirtschaftswunder* full employment generated an additional strong rationalization impetus because of high labour costs and a lack of able people.

This multidimensional interdependency explains the German path and the leading role of the savings banks in computerizing the banking business. They were unrivalled first-movers in the German banking sector. In none of the other European economies did such a development take place. Only in the late 1970s did the differences between the three German banking groups start to blur; there were also international discrepancies, because the process of diffusion was drawing to a close.

Knowing this background, Cortada's (1996, 2008) chronological computing scheme and the somewhat fuzzier scheme proposed by Bátiz-Lazo and Wood (2002) have to be scrutinized. These approaches help to create a broad impression of this process. In general, they reflect the

German development quite authentically, too. The reasons are obvious. U.S. and European trends are sketched quite closely to the IBM development scheme. As in the U.S. and other industrial countries, IBM was a market leader in West Germany, where it had been well established since the beginning of the twentieth century, and there was a strong U.S. influence on politics and business after World War II (Cortada 1996: 41, 161; 2006: 35, 38; Bátiz-Lazo and Wood 2002: 2; for Cortada's background, see Zetti 2007: 155–60).

However, this chapter shows that general analytic approaches have a limited reach in mapping reality. Innovation processes have been quite complex. Beyond technical innovations many other reasons—cultural, institutional, economic, and social ones—have played a role. The highly innovative German IT path in banking seems to prove this hypothesis. It was mainly dependent on an early integration of the common people into the banking system with the uniquely designed savings banks acting as the leading integration agents.

7 Organizational Change and the Computerization of British and Spanish Savings Banks, circa 1950–1985

Bernardo Bátiz-Lazo and
J. Carles Maixé-Altés

INTRODUCTION

This chapter reports on research into the role the mechanization and automation of practices within retail financial intermediaries aiming to contest bank markets. The financial service organizations, which are the topic of this chapter, were originally established as independent providers but all were guided by a common principle. This unifying concept dates to 1810 when the first "savings" bank was established in Ruthwell, Scotland (Horne 1947: 34). Savings banks grew throughout the United Kingdom and continental Europe. A change in government policy in the UK led to the amalgamation of independent savings banks into a single entity, which was floated in the Stock Exchange in 1986. It then merged with Lloyds Bank in 1995 to create the Lloyds TSB Group. Meanwhile in Spain, regulatory change during the 1980s positioned savings banks on the same footing as commercial banks while allowing individual savings banks to remain independent and maintain unique features of their corporate governance (including its philanthropic orientation). By the end of the twentieth century, Spanish savings banks had captured half the market for retail deposits and successfully contested many other markets that had been dominated by commercial banks.

British savings banks were late adopters of mechanical accounting when compared with clearing banks and building societies—the other main participants in British retail finance (see further Bátiz-Lazo and Wardley 2007). Technological evolution meant the use of mechanical and electromechanical devices was followed by automation in the form of mainframe computer technology. Initially, this evolution positioned savings banks in the UK as spearheading technological change when compared with Spanish savings banks. But later on, Spanish savings banks seemed to "close the gap".

Research in this chapter shows how increasing use of computer applications in Spain and the UK helped to develop data processing capabilities, which often were seen as a key element to resolving scale disadvantages.

However, Spanish savings banks adopted computer technology on the back of a diversified business portfolio. Early computerization in Britain primarily aimed to speed up transaction processing of low-value, high-volume deposits at retail branches. Spanish savings banks had developed organizational structures and created cradles of middle managers at head offices by promoting from within as early as the interwar period. At the same time, the ultimate step of career development in Britain meant becoming retail bank branch manager whereas staffing the head office in the 1970s and 1980s most often involved attracting talent from clearing banks and building societies. As a result, whereas Spanish savings banks went from strength to strength, "state of the art" computer systems were unable to make up for a lack of managerial capabilities when regulation allowed British savings banks to diversify across retail financial markets. This chapter thus shows how researching the uses and purposes of computer technology is every bit a business history (e.g. Haigh 2001; Cortada 2006; Yates 1999).

Before proceeding, five caveats must be considered. First, this chapter considers organizational forms with similar roots in their corporate governance to enable a degree of homogeneity in the analysis of technological change while articulating an international comparison (see also Booth and Billings, Thomes and Mooij in this volume). This premise enriches the understanding of financial organizations as users of technology while providing insights into the relative importance of aligning innovations of information and telecommunication technologies (ICT) with corporate strategy. However, in this chapter we focus on the evolution of mechanization and impact of computerization on the management of savings banks in Britain. But relevant aspects of mechanization and computerization in Spain are introduced to highlight the international dimension of technological change as well as enhance the understanding of the breath of opportunities technological innovation opened for "not-for-profit" financial organizations. As a result we are able to tell how the introduction of computers emerged from collaborative strategies by savings banks. The continuity of these strategies in Spain and their evolution to competitive collaboration help to highlight some of the idiosyncratic aspects of similar moves in Britain.

A second central tenet of our international comparison revolves around competitive dynamics associated with first-comer and late-comer advantage, which could be attributed respectively to Britain and Spain (see also Bonin and Thomes in this volume). The UK is characterised by a long industrial tradition and as a source of technological innovation whereas Spain industrialized well into the twentieth century and was typically a net importer of business applications of computer technology. When compared with other established providers of retail finance in their own milieu, neither British nor Spanish savings banks were early adopters of computers or applications of this technology. But whereas the adoption of computers and computer applications helped to address important management issues for British savings banks, on balance, Spanish savings banks benefited from a lack of legacy systems and the adoption of cheaper, thoroughly tested, and more powerful technology.

Third, without a doubt, the continuity in the evolution of ICT infrastructure noted by Chandler and Cortada (2000: 263) populates the competitive environments of North America and highly industrialized European nations like the UK. These and others aiming to support (or not) the Chandlerian view of the business organizations in Europe (e.g. Kay 2002; Whittington, Meyer, and Curto 1999; Whittington and Mayer 2002) move forward while focusing on large industrial organizations. This is also the case of those exploring the canons of the Chandlerian firm in financial intermediation (e.g. Channon 1977, 1978, 1988; Nightingale and Poll 2000). Research in this chapter contributes to this discussion by exploring similar ideas within non-bank intermediaries of "smaller" asset size with a clear retail focus and distinctive governance structure. British savings banks lived in a milieu where others were active contributors to the technological continuity; whereas Spanish savings banks were located outside of that continuity and were embedded in the "continental banking model", one that promoted loans rather than stock market finance as well as close links between manufacturing and financial intermediaries, to the extent that the Spanish savings banks even owned share capital of local firms (Maixé-Altés 2010). But in spite of that, Spanish savings banks seemed to have overcome the apparent disadvantage of being both late adopters as well as populating an environment outside of the technological continuity.

A fourth caveat has to do with the nature of mechanization and digitalization. The type of technology introduced to achieve "modernity" and competitive advantage is a significant part of this chapter (see also del Angel and Martin in this volume). Ours is not a tale of technological determinism. Rather we believe that savings banks in Spain and the UK attempted to assess the costs and benefits associated with the adoption of new technologies and act appropriately but, in so doing, were fully aware of the environment in which they undertook their business. Technology is seen as constructed primarily out of the interaction of policy decisions by senior bank staff and consumption decisions by banks' customers. Choice is therefore central to our tale of technological change (Malone, Yates, and Benjamin 1987; Yates 1999).

Fifth, during the twentieth century Britain and Spain changed in significant ways. Financial intermediaries played their part in fostering and responding to these changes, be they economic, legal, social, or political. Consequently, there are parts in this story for a number of factors in addition to the onward march of technological progress; among these are increased professionalism and the development of the managerial class; changing perceptions of gender; the impact of war; and the role of the State. Although new technology underpins these developments, these are the themes which also enlighten our story.

The narrative in this chapter builds upon news and trade publications from the period (e.g. *The Times, TSB Gazette, TSB Banknotes, Journal of the Savings Banks*), evidence to parliamentary committees, government papers and proceedings (e.g. TSB Inspection Committee, Anuario Estadístico de España), annual reports of the Confederation of Spanish Savings Banks (*Confederación Española de Cajas de Ahorro* or CECA), surviving business records, circulars, and other minutiae of both British and Spanish savings banks as well as interviews with those who designed the systems and who were their users in retail branches in Spain and the UK.

The remainder of this chapter proceeds as follows. The second section tells of the late adoption of mechanical accounting of British savings banks when compared with other participants in British retail financial markets. Section three considers the adoption of computer technology. Of particular importance is the creation of data processing capabilities. This is done by looking at how loose alliances of small and geographically dispersed intermediaries invest in computer technology and, in turn, achieve critical scale in retail bank markets. The fourth section analyses how Spanish savings banks and CECA embraced applications of computer technology (and specifically data processing infrastructure) to articulate viable solutions for cost reductions, offer alternative payment systems to cash, and facilitate greater diversification of their business portfolio within retail banking. The final section summarizes and forwards some conclusions.

MECHANIZATION OF THE TRUSTEE SAVINGS BANKS

For most of the first five decades of the twentieth century, savings banks in Britain and Spain relied on manual processes to conduct their business. Slowly but steadily, new devices were adopted to help transaction processing in the busiest retail branches. For instance, in 1948 a new system of mechanized accounting was announced in Belfast (see Figure 7.1). It wasn't until the 1950s that large and medium-sized Spanish banks (as measured in terms of assets) began to introduce mechanical accounting machines (Bátiz-Lazo and Maixé-Altés 2009).

Figure 7.1 shows how only a small portion of retail premises were dedicated to service customers (and this primarily through the mediation of human tellers or cashiers). A large space was used for performing a number of routine tasks which took place away from the counter (i.e. the "back office"). The image shows that the introduction of mechanical devices in trustee savings banks built on (cheap) female labour to perform repetitive tasks (Booth 2004, 2007; Wardley 2006). Figure 7.1 also suggests how savings banks' retail branches had adopted a number of labour-saving devices including typewriters, steel filling cabinets, mechanical adding machines, and as in the case of the Guernsey (not shown), electromechanical ledger posting machines.

Figure 7.1   The new system of machine posting at the Belfast Saving Bank, 1948.

Source: *TSB Gazette XVIII*, no. 4 (October 1948): 28. Courtesy of the Lloyds Banking Group Archives.

Other savings banks were to follow the example of Belfast. In some cases, the introduction of electromechanical devices mirrored an increased flow of deposits by customers at the teller. In other instances, the number of transactions had been reduced at the teller but not at the branch. This had been the case in Sheffield following the introduction of "direct transfer schemes" (that is, a fixed deduction from the payroll paid directly into the savings account).

In 1950, the Manchester and District Bank was the first to install accounting machines in all its branches. This took place while directors of other savings banks were quite happy to have escaped mechanization. They continued to rely on long-established processes and procedures as well as the manual and mental arithmetic skills of staff.[1]

---

1. Harry Read (director TSB Computer Services circa 1970–1988), interview with author, Milton Keynes, 17 July 2008; and Hayden Taylor (computer systems controller TSB circa 1970–1988), interview with author, Milton Keynes, 17 July 2008.

Mechanization, therefore, proceeded at the TSB in spite of currency controls, rationings, and other things that characterised the adverse economic climate in the British Isles during the years that followed the war in Europe. However, the rate of diffusion of mechanized accounting devices varied considerably from bank to bank and from region to region, as there was disagreement as to the advantages of such devices amongst the cadre of directors while, at the same time, each sought to reassert its independence. The National Debt Office (NDO) seemed to encourage the adoption of mechanical devices but some directors felt the gadgets were expensive as well as was not being "the way we do things here".[2]

Like in the UK, in Spain the processing information still relied on manual processes at most savings banks. It was not until the late 1950s when the Spanish savings banks started to consider the standardisation of accounting processes and the simplification of administrative routines (Maixé-Altés et al. 2003: 222–23). However, during the 1950s CECA introduced Swedish-made accounting machines to help with calculations, statistical estimates, and processing of ledgers. Changes in government policy had given CECA a mandate for individual banks to supply the necessary information for it to generate statistical reports and consolidated financial information for the whole sector. The reports were primarily used to inform managers at the banks, the central bank (*Banco de España*), and ministerial officers.[3]

Meanwhile, the response to increasing volumes of paper-based transactions in the UK was the creation of a "clearing house" for London-based savings banks in May 1953.[4] This was a simple system of settlement between a small group of banks, which kept customers' stationary unchanged and was built around the Surrey office.[5] The "clearing house" centralised settlement of travel credit payments, using a TSB Draft instead of cheque and (straightforward) transfers. The introduction of batching through summary ledgers helped increase efficiency by keeping labour costs under control. Specifically, the settlement of one week of transactions (i.e. some four thousand items) could be dealt with in one "man-hour". Reflecting on these results, participants speculated that new services (such as selling traveller

---

2. Read, interview with author, 17 July 2008; and Taylor, interview with author, 17 July 2008.

3. Namely, the Finance Ministry (*Ministerio de Economia y Hacienda*), National Statistics Institute (*Instituto Nacional de Estadística*), and National Economic Council (*Consejo de Economía Nacional*).

4. Unless otherwise stated this paragraph borrows freely from H.L.W. (1954).

5. Participating banks included Wessex, Oxford, Surrey, Thames Valley, Portsmouth, and South Eastern.

cheques)[6] could be easily introduced to the top of established administrative systems. Interestingly, the creation of a "clearing house" in the south-east mirrored better economic conditions in London and its immediate area. This was opposed to a declining industry base in the north-west of England where, at the time, Lancashire was the county with the greater number of savings bank offices.

Here it is interesting to note the "late" development of inter-savings-bank clearing in the UK when compared with other European countries. For instance, in Spain the Savings Banks Credit Institute (*Instituto de Crédito de las Cajas de Ahorro* or ICCA) was established in 1933 as a wholesaler of retail finance with clearing functions. A similar kind of institution had been developed in countries such as Finland (1908), Norway (1919), and Italy (1921) (Revell 1991). Then in 1971 inter-savings-bank clearing migrated from the ICCA and was centralised at CECA.

In 1959 some of the TSB head offices and one or two of the very big branches took further steps in the mechanization of accounting information by using Burroughs P600 equipment.[7] These were primarily adding machines to process the capital sums in the account and to solely process for accounts based in the branch in which they were housed. Interest had to be calculated through a manual process. In 1964 the Burroughs were replaced by NCR Class 31, as the latter could add the capital and calculate the accrued interest. But although it was the first machine that had been used by the TSB for multiplication, these operations were in fact additions, that is, the multiplication resulted from the operator providing an interest factor and then the machine adding a certain amount as many times as indicated by the factor.

By the mid-1960s transactions at retail counters were increasing around 5 per cent p.a. in the TSB whereas some savings banks and saving bank branches still worked with leather-bound ledgers. Hand-written record cards piled up in the thousands and even the most elemental source of managerial information (such as the annual balance sheet) was a huge task and in some banks it involved substantial amounts of overtime pay (Moss and Slaven 1992: 159). In summary, by the end of the 1960s organizational methods at most savings banks in both Britain and Spain remained not only antiquated but time-consuming. They were clearly badly in need

---

6. Offering traveller cheques and foreign currency for depositors was offered from 1965 onwards alongside other changes introduced by the Trustee Savings Bank Act 1964, namely, the payment of periodical charges, household bills, travel draft, current account, interbank and credit transfer schemes. See TSB Inspectors Committee No. 73 (1965), paragraph 30.

7. Unless otherwise stated this paragraph borrows freely from Ray Neal (director TSB Computer Services and TSB Trust 1959–1984), interview with author, Leicester, 16 March 2008.

of modernization and streamlining. Things were to change throughout the 1970s and these changes would create the ICT platform that enabled diversification in the 1980s.

EARLY COMPUTING IN BRITAIN

In the late 1950s savings banks became interested in the business applications of computer technology, among other things, thanks to the marketing efforts of Ferranti while trying to develop orders for its Pegasus (Stiles 1957). In 1960 representations were made for the mechanization of depositors' accounts at a central point but this proposal was turned down by the Inspectors Committee—whose mandate included overseeing capital expenditure at individual banks.[8] At the same time, inspectors were happy to allow for the mechanization of ledgers at the banks' head offices and the introduction of ledger posting machines in some branches.[9] For instance, a system of centralised posting in the London TSB started in February 1962 when the first punched card was prepared (Foster 1962). Information on the card included the account number of the depositor (made out of three digits for the branch, five for the account, and two for control), the value of the transaction, and type of transaction (credit transfer or standing order). A "Posting Unit" was created which centralised information from all branches and was responsible for a "master file" of customer data.

Increasing demands to replace manual systems for mechanized accounting of ledgers and to modernize obsolete accounting machines, combined with the impending decimalisation of sterling, the extension of administrative systems for the centralisation of customer information (at head offices of individual banks), and the increase in the numbers of transactions at the teller, resulted in the Trustee Savings Bank Act (1968) making provisions for financial assistance to be given to groups of savings banks for the acquisition of mechanical and electronic processing equipment.[10] The banks also noted the increase in salary costs, scarcity

---

8. TSB Inspectors Committee No. 69 (1962), paragraphs 4, 5, 11, and 26. At the time the members of the committee were A.R.B. Haldane (Trustee of the Edinburgh Savings Bank—Chairman), Anthony E. Barber (formerly Deputy Chief Accountant of the Bank of England—Vice-Chairman), John Fox (OBE, formerly Chief Registrar of Friendly Societies), Lt. Col. Oswald S. Francis (Deputy Chairman of Thames Valley TSB), W. Guy Densem (member of council and in representation of the Institute of Chartered Accountants of England and Wales), and Sir W. Bernard Blatch (MBE, member of council and in representation of the Law Society).

9. TSB Inspectors Committee No. 69 (1962), paragraph 26.

10. TSB Inspectors Committee No. 73 (1969), paragraph 20, and TSB Inspectors Committee No. 80 (1971), Premises and Computers, paragraph 30.

of staff, and the introduction of the Current Account Service as reasons for mechanization on an extended scale.[11] At the time, a London-based bank gained approval to explore the suitability of installing an IBM 1401 computer (which at the time was a ten-year-old technology and was soon to be superseded by IBM's System 360/370). The Inspectors Committee recognized its limitations in being able to provide adequate support for the purchase of capital equipment (in the form of computer technology) and thus called for the use of professional consultants to advise in the introduction of computers and mechanical accounting equipment in individual savings banks or groups of banks.[12]

The attitude of the Inspectors Committee was in sharp contrast with the practice in Spain, where in early 1960s the general manager of CECA, Luis Coronel de Palma, had taken the initiative to automate administrative and accounting processes inside of CECA. During the 1960s administrative processes changed to adopt batch-processing of information and these same processes were those meant to speed up when computers were adopted in the 1960s. The latter benefited from the availability of data transmission protocols over telephone lines developed elsewhere in Europe (primarily the Swedish savings banks), enabling Spanish savings banks interconnection and real-time, online processing before their European counterparts[13]—a claim to fame which the TSB also like to make.[14]

A group of computer experts were hired as full-time members of staff at CECA and this group would eventually grow to become the Computerization Department. On the one hand, this group helped create a shared technological platform that would speed up inter-savings bank clearing through the adoption of NCR 390 machines. On the other hand, this group interacted with developments at large savings banks and particularly the *Caja de Pensiones para la Vejez y de Ahorros de Cataluña y Baleares* (today "La Caixa"). It had taken steps to create the first online data interconnection network through telephone lines (while building on the telephone infrastructure provided by the national telephone company) with the aim of enabling the "hub and spoke" model, that is, speedy communication between main retail branch offices and their subsidiary sub-branches in urban areas.[15] For this purpose "La

---

11. TSB Inspectors Committee No. 74 (1970), paragraph 20.

12. TSB Inspectors Committee No. 73 (1969), paragraph 20.

13. José Esteve (director of CECA's Computer Department 1962–1995), interview with author, Madrid, 12 December 2007.

14. Neal, interview with author, 16 March 2008; Michael D. McQuade (branch manager and group manager TSB 1964–2000), interview with author, Leicester, 6 March 2008.

15. At the end of the 1960s, the cost of developing a data transmission network was out of reach for any one single private organization. However, interest in sharing such a network was made known to the national telephone company (Compañía

Caixa" adopted an IBM 360–40 mainframe, whereas other savings banks (such as the one in Granada) preferred NCR computers.[16]

The influence of "La Caixa" over CECA is key to understanding the structuring of automation at the Spanish savings banks. At the time Enrique Luño Peña was both the general manager of "La Caixa" and CECA's president. A second figure of interest was Jesús Ruiz Kaiser, one of the pioneers of electronic data interchange in Spain. He was also a full-time member of staff at "La Caixa" and often in secondment at CECA. In their dual roles these two persons influenced key decision at CECA (primarily aiming to ensure interbank compatibility in terms of technology already in place at "La Caixa"). This influence was articulated once a project for developing a common technological platform for all savings banks was launched in 1969 with the establishment of CECA's Organization, Automation, and Services Commission (*Comisión de Organización, Automatización y Servicios* or COAS). COAS provided the professional and organizational space for representatives of savings banks sharing and coordinating their activities for specific projects such as Interlex (April 1970); this continued in October 1971 through the Savings Banks Electronic Clearing System (*Sistema de interconexion de las cajas de ahorro* or SICA). Savings banks endeavoured to achieve interoperability in transactions and electronic clearing through a network of mainframe computers (hosted at individual banks, jointly owned and shared by groups of banks or computer bureau services supplied by CECA for the benefit of the smallest intermediaries) whereas CECA's central computer housed the main clearing function for all.[17]

Around this time the TSB also formally joined the computer age when a computer was used to produce a demographic analysis of customers taking up the TSB's first unit trust offer in 1968.[18] Shortly after, consent

---

Telefónica Nacional de España or CTNE). Commercial banks and most notably the Banco Español de Crédito (Banesto) actively encouraged the CNTE to develop a telephone-based data interchange network (*red telefónica conmutada* or RTC) while looking for a technological solution to reduce their growing exposure to cheque-based fraud and a lack of an appropriate regulation on the use of cheque-based payments (see further Ballarín 1985; Canals 1994; Channon 1988; Martín Tardío 2010).

16. In 1968, "La Caixa" had placed terminals linked to its mainframe in all of its 212 retail branch outlets, while servicing 1,658,051 customers and 5,267,425 transactions p.a. Some 44 per cent of retail branches were located within the city of Barcelona and its immediate province; the rest were distributed throughout Catalonia and the Balearic Islands. The electronic data interchange built upon an IBM 2970 terminal with a speed of 134.5 bytes per second (bps) and while running through nodes with the mainframe able to manage up to 1,200 bps.

17. CECA, COAS Secretaria Técnica: "Papers and Reports"; Esteve, interview with author, 12 December 2007.

18. *The Times*, 2 May 1968.

was given by the Inspectors Committee for the installation of a "Sensomatic computer" (i.e. electromechanical, programmable, ledger posting machine) in the south-east of England and for a group of Scottish banks to employ an independent consultant for a feasibility study leading to the introduction of a large computer.

The clearing centre near London considered the exchange of information (i.e. credit slips) with clearing banks.[19] This required the embossing of optical characters in magnetic ink at the bottom of credit transfer slips. The move was necessary as transaction volumes were growing so fast in London and elsewhere and there was no capacity at the branch level to cope with increased volume of paper-based transactions:

> [By 1968–1969] we simply could not manage the volume at the branch. To give you an indication, the branch in St. Martin's at Gray Friars [Leicester] had 250,000 accounts in the one branch and all of these were passbook accounts. On 20 November customers knew their annual interest was to be credited. But to copy over the interest to the accounts and rebalance the ledgers had to be done manually. It took us five days and five nights to do this manually. No transactions were posted to accounts during that week as the branch closed for the duration. We definitely needed computers to speed up processing.[20]

As was the case for some banks and many building societies, computer technology offered an attractive way to update individual accounts while sorting out the decimalisation of sterling. Decimalisation of sterling, therefore, was a second driver for computerization:

> The TSB had large numbers of accounts and transforming them by calculating the shillings and pence into decimal was seen as a formidable task. This was seen as the true spur to see if we could do it through computerized means. Initially, when computers were coming on the horizon, I was of the view that they were fine for complicated operations but not adequate for a series of small repetitive tasks. Memory was also very expensive. But cost came down while the possible use of computers also increased. So that made it for us worth exploring. We at the Nottingham Bank had done a bit on the computer of the Coal Board. But things got serious when we decided to take a huge load off the branches and get things ready by February 15, 1971, through computerization.[21]

---

19. Unless otherwise stated this paragraph borrows freely from McQuade, interview with author, 6 March 2008.
20. McQuade, interview with author, 6 March 2008.
21. Neal, interview with author, 16 March 2008.

But whereas clearing banks had already installed a number of computer installations by the mid-1960s, the mechanization of the British savings banks was largely incipient: most TSBs had just started to use mechanical and electromechanical equipment to speed up internal processes such as the accounting function.

The Savings Banks of Glasgow, Edinburgh, Aberdeen, Dundee, and Paisley jointly commissioned James Allen—a chartered accountant turned computer salesman—for a study of their accounting records to see what improvements could be achieved by automation (Moss and Slaven 1992: 159). The National Debt Commissioners granted permission for the research to be conducted, on the understanding that the findings of the report would be shared with all other savings banks. The resulting report recommended the purchase of Burroughs equipment. The savings banks then played a "Scottish card" (because Burroughs manufactured computers in Scotland) and overcame the Treasury's and the National Debt Office's reluctance to depart from the government's "Buy British" campaign.[22] Within two years four of the Scottish group jointly contracted to install a computer and create a computer centre in Anderston in Glasgow. The centre opened in 1969, and within two years it was servicing eight Scottish banks and processing 89 per cent of savings account transactions in Scotland (Moss and Slaven 1992: 160). By 1971, therefore, the main Scottish banks were brought into a regional computer network.[23]

Meanwhile, south of the border a speedy computerization using a bureau service was seen as a particularly attractive idea as it would help to deal with the cost of capital investment and the lack of technical skills. Most English and Welsh banks mapped to a bureau service supported by the National Data Processing Service (NDPS), a subsidiary of the post office (see further Billings and Booth in this volume). Rather than developing computer-related capabilities organically, the TSBs in the bureau service wanted to take advantage of the NDPS's twelve years of experience in computing and in servicing the National Savings Bank.[24] Press reports pointed to the NDPS using an ICL System 470 at the centre in Leeds.[25]

---

22. For details as to the British policy with regards to information technology, see Coopey (1999) and Ferry (2003). For a general discussion, international comparisons, and details of its impact on clearing banks, see Bátiz-Lazo and Boyns (2004); Booth (2007); and Coopey (2004).

23. The one exception was the Savings Bank of Aberdeen whose chairman, Richard Ellis, was resolute not "to keep up with the computer Jones" (Booth 2007: 83).

24. The post office got involved in computer technology as early as 1943 while designing and building ten high-speed, valve-based, single-purpose machines, individually called 'Colossus' (of which one of them was used at Bletchley Park to assist Alan Turing in his decoding work). See further Agar (2003).

25. *The Times*, 15 October 1970.

At retail branches, dedicated staff (called "processors" and usually females) were hired to digitalize standing order transactions.²⁶ This was done by transferring information onto punched tape. The tape was carried daily by dedicated courier to Leeds and processed overnight. The next morning large branches received a slip for each transaction (which would be sorted and filed manually by client to update passbooks) and a new tape. The processing of standing orders in smaller retail branches meant that on Monday each would receive a computer-generated printout with instructions. These would then have to be transferred manually to the branch ledger and updated in the customer's passbook. Whether the retail branch was large or small, the passbook would be updated until the customer next visited the branch.

Vendors of accounting equipment also took hold of the opportunity. NCR, for one, launched a dual currency model of the Class 31—one that could deal indistinctively with schillings and pence or decimal annotations. It also contracted the conversion of older machines to the new system as NCR accounting machines now populated all retail branches of the TSB (a process of conversion that took a good many years).²⁷

After decimalisation, operations were brought in-house and replaced by nine processing centres servicing forty-eight banks and some 1,550 retail bank branches: Manchester or MADCAP (six banks); West Midlands-Kidderminster (six banks); Bottle near Liverpool (eight banks); York (fourteen banks); Crawley in West Sussex (near Surrey, five banks); London (three banks); Glasgow (four banks); Belfast; and north of Edinburgh in Falkirk (Moss and Russell 1994: 266).

Lack of a coordinating centre meant that the loose association of TSB saw different solutions living together. For instance, the Manchester and the West Midlands-Kidderminster consortia committed to having their own computer centre running the same configuration system (built around an ICL System 4).²⁸ The system brought together the savings banks of Northern Ireland in September 1970, and was based on the combination of an undisclosed Burroughs mainframe and TC700 terminals.²⁹ Initially these were to service forty thousand of the Irish consortium's 560,000 deposit

---

26. The source also mentioned that in 1972 staff at large branches were fully trained in all back office procedures (i.e. 'the background of banking') before they were moved to face customers at the counter. Moreover, back office activities were seen as 'junior' whereas those at the counter as more 'senior'. Janet Shipley (retail branch staff TSB 1969–2008), interview with author, Leicester, 11 March 2008.

27. Ian Ormerod, e-mail to author, 16 March 2008.

28. Unless otherwise stated the reminder of this section borrows freely from Read, interview with author, 17 July 2008, and Taylor, interview with author, 17 July 2008.

29. Unless otherwise stated the reminder of this paragraph borrows freely from "New Computer System for Belfast Bank", *The Irish Times*, 9 September 1970, 15.

accounts and provide instantaneous communication to twenty-six of the forty-two retail branches.

Following developments around automation in both sides of the border, one observer then commented: "the savings banks are moving aggressively onwards to expand their clientele. Computerization is in progress throughout the [TSB] movement".[30] However, as had been the case for clearing banks a decade before and more recently for the building societies (see further Bátiz-Lazo and Boyns 2003, 2004; Bátiz-Lazo and Wardley 2007), the introduction of computers aimed to speed up established manual processes rather than redefine them for first principles. For many staff at branches the evidence as to the introduction and use of computer technology was limited to the weekly printout. A take-on team would then move branch by branch and decide, according to the volume of transactions, to convert the ledgers to online or off-line systems, that is, large branches would be fully automated (online, real time) and small branches in a mixed system of manual and automated (off-line).[31] But even when computer terminals made their appearance in the retail branch and position slips gave way to manual ledgers, for many a teller things changed little:

> It was all manual processing (including calculating the running credit and debit interest) and in a way it was good. We knew all of the processes so that when we were computerized we knew exactly what the computer was doing, because we could work it all out.[32]

DEVELOPING A COMMON INFRASTRUCTURE IN SPAIN

Both the TSB and the Spanish savings banks focused on servicing private individuals and had a dominant market position amongst lower-income customers. But in Spain, greater freedom to diversify their business portfolio resulted in the savings banks establishing themselves even more firmly in the retail credit market and attracting deposits from households. The economic crisis was followed by a large number of commercial bank failures, which together created an opportunity for saving banks to make inroads to service small and medium-sized firms as well as lending and

---

30. Lance English, "A Competitive Industry's Move to Expand Clientele", *The Times*, 25 April 1972.

31. McQuade, interview with author, 6 March 2008, and John Willars, e-mail to author, 7 March 2008.

32. Sarah Whitmore (retail branch staff TSB circa 1973–1980), interview with author, Leicester, 8 February 2008.

deposit-taking within the Spanish middle class.[33] The retail focus thus engendered a strong competitive base at the end of the 1970s when the savings banks gained even greater operative freedom.

Just as the TSB's adopted computer centres on a regional basis, through the COAS the Spanish savings banks set up bureau services in Torrente (Valencia) and Sabadell (Catalonia) in 1970. However, the rapid development of a new generation of computers, which were both cheaper and smaller, was to favour the computerization of individual savings banks and consequently there was an adjustment in COAS's information technology policy. The cost-sharing network of CECA worked well throughout the 1970s as it helped to achieve control at individual banks while providing a low cost-base that enabled them to deal with the long economic downturn associated with the international economic crisis of the late 1970s and the end of Franco's regime (Fanjul and Maravall 1985: 213; Caminal, Gual, and Vives 1990: 279).

A new phase began in 1979 when CECA and individual savings banks agreed on developing interconnectivity through SICA further. Specifically, they established a network directly linking mainframe and minicomputers (as appropriate) of different banks. This infrastructure enabled CECA and the savings banks to continue articulating a clearly defined policy with regards to shared systems for payment methods, cash machines, and point-of-sale terminals. But it was not until 1988 that all the saving banks were integrated into this online, real-time system.[34]

Between 1975 and 1985 the "big" savings banks actively engaged in CECA's activities as there were no major operational or strategy distinctions between them and the "small" savings banks. The association of "big" savings banks continued while all the savings banks could benefit from the troubles of the commercial bank sector, which resulted in the growth of advantages and profits for the savings banks (Ash 1987: 9). However, reduced rates of market penetration increasingly turned CECA into the defender of the smaller savings banks and this was accentuated when bigger savings banks pursued distinctive diversification moves such as their own international departments or the purchase of failed co-operative banks (c. 1987). The ominous trend for CECA changed in the mid-1990s and was associated with the savings banks having to update investments in information technology, a new general manager being named for CECA (Juan R. Quintás, a former management consultant), and renewed importance for CECA as the "central" Spanish savings bank.

---

33. Savings banks' share of total domestic loans grew from 21.2 per cent in 1980 to 34.3 per cent in 1990 (Boletín Estadístico del Banco España. Madrid: Banco de España, 1980, 1990).

34. CECA, COAS reports.

In sharp contrast to the development of CECA in Spain, throughout its history the Trustee Savings Banks Association failed to act as central provider of administrative functions to small independent savings banks (Bátiz-Lazo 2004; Bátiz-Lazo and Maixé-Altés 2009). Not surprisingly, a great number of the seventy-three banks in existence in 1975 did not have the critical scale to compete in British banking. The amalgamation of individual banks into purposely created regional banks and the establishment of a central board in 1975 brought about the use of resources to support the introduction of personal lending in 1977.[35] However, by 1979, the attempts to diversify across retail bank markets by the TSBs had failed. Together with the National Giro Bank and the Co-operative Bank the efforts of the TSBs to penetrate retail finance, from scratch in 1971, resulted in only £200 million in direct consumer loans in 1979 and this accounted for less than 3 per cent of total consumer lending that year.

In 1984 the government published a White Paper and a new TSB bill in which the quasi-federal decentralised structure was abandoned in favour of a central organization which was no longer legally unique but incorporated under the Companies Act. The aim was to give the then called TSB Group "a more effective operating structure and also establish clear guidelines for ownership and accountability, neither of which was clear under former legislation" (Marshall 1985: 41).

CONCLUSIONS

The research in this chapter was conducted through an historical evaluation of the role of computer technology within two loose confederations of non-bank participants in retail financial markets. On the one hand, computerization in Britain took place in tandem with the amalgamation into a single provider. Mechanization and automation were primarily adopted to achieve greater economies of scale. On the other hand, Spanish savings banks remained independent and came together to exploit opportunities offered by computer technology to achieve diversification in the product portfolio (i.e. economies of scope). On balance, the development of managerial and risk management capabilities, rather than the use of technology, seems to explain the relative success of Spanish savings banks in contesting bank markets. However, a large market share within lower-income individuals together with low transaction processing costs made the TSB an attractive target for amalgamation in the mid-1990s.

The evolution of British savings banks was quite different to that expected by the Chandlerian conception of the firm. Savings banks in

---

35. Committee of London Clearing Bankers or CLCB (1978: 230).

Britain remained a series of autonomous entities, many of them "unit banks" (where the whole organization was encapsulated within the premises of a single retail office) as late as 1970. Insipient collaboration accelerated to create a handful of small central service providers as larger banks wanted to take advantage of technological developments, but, ultimately, political rather than business agents led to the integration into a single large organization. Political considerations and regulatory change rather than effective implementation of corporate strategy also influenced the speed of diversification in the product/service portfolio (Maixé-Altés 2009). On balance, therefore, British savings banks used mechanical aids, computer, and other ICT applications to achieve economies of scale, that is, managing volume transactions with greater efficiency rather than redefining processes, procedures, transactions, and operations. There is little evidence that the initial use of computer applications aimed to redefine performance measures or supply directors with new and interesting forms of information.

Applications of ICT were critical in maintaining a long-term commitment to servicing Spanish retail financial markets while articulating diversification in the savings banks customer and business product portfolio, that is, in achieving economies of scope while many individual banks maintained a small scale of operation: active collaboration in technology-oriented projects under the aegis of a central service organization within their national trade association, namely, the CECA.

Yates (2005) makes a persuasive case for the need to consider entire industries, rather than isolated firms, as agents of computer adoptions and has documented the role of trade associations in creating a consensus on the nature and proper application of computers within an industry. The research this chapter briefly considers the behaviour of the Savings Banks Association in the UK is closer to the role attributed by Yates to the insurance industry in the U.S. Meanwhile in Spain, the CECA enabled individual and particularly small savings banks to assimilate ICT applications. The collaboration mediated through CECA offered a high degree of flexibility when confronted with alternative technological solutions as well as means to solve scale disadvantages.

Research results in this chapter support the idea that strategic alliances through trade associations and competitive collaboration (or the undertaking of joint projects by otherwise independent firms with the specific aim of challenging established providers) can enable the creation of interorganizational processes and procedures to distribute otherwise inaccessible information. The development and transformation of competitive capabilities of one or all of the partners, therefore, should be seen as the appropriate indicator for successful collaboration (Ross 2002). However, the intensity of competition could remain unchanged unless opportunities opened by collaboration are implemented successfully (Bátiz-Lazo 2004; Bátiz-Lazo and del Angel 2003).

Alongside the changing nature of competition and technological progress, philanthropy was another distinctive feature of savings banks in Britain and Spain when compared with other organizations populating retail financial markets in their host economies. In Spain, savings banks looked for ways to balance social, regional, and business dimensions. Although in Spain political considerations (and appointees) have played an important role in explaining the long-term survival of savings banks, their commitment to invest in the overall well-being of their host city or region is also undisputable.

Meanwhile, in Britain, savings banks remained dedicated to servicing the personal consumer while essentially being a vehicle for personal savings to finance government debt. From the 1960s onwards British savings banks began to change in response to a drop in market share as well as new trends in the behaviour of their customers (see further Marshall 1985). For the directors of British savings banks achieving the competitive advantage replaced educating the poorest of the poor in the habit of thrift as the main operating priority. As a result, British savings banks "forgot" their philanthropic principles to become ever-more commercial and business-like. By the time they were floated in the Stock Exchange in 1986, they resembled and had the same strategic aspirations as clearing banks.

In this chapter we have focused on the British savings banks while articulating a running comparison with developments of similar organizations in Spain. This meant we failed to address an important dimension of European savings banks: their active collaboration to present a common face to a number of issues. For instance, in 1984 CECA had became involved in an international project led by the *Instituto per L'Automatizacione delle Casse di Risparmio Italiane* (IPACRI) of Italy and the TSB (Maixé-Altés, forthcoming). Spanish, Italian, and British representatives presented a technical proposal to the European Savings Bank Group in 1985 that was developed in 1988. EUFISERV—an international partnership based in Belgium—was created in 1990 to start a pan-European project for the interoperability of cash-dispensing machines. A company called SEINCA (1988–1993) was created to articulate this collaboration by bringing together sixty-eight savings banks in Spain, CECA, IPARCRI, and two technology partners, namely, Ibermatica (a company financed by the Spanish savings banks) and ERITEL (a joint venture between Ibermatica and the Spanish telephone company).[36] It is a task of future research to document this collaboration at the pan-European level in greater detail.

---

36. CECA, Secretariat of COAS, papers and reports.

8 Techno-Nationalism, the Post Office, and the Creation of Britain's National Giro

Alan Booth and Mark Billings

INTRODUCTION

The focus of this chapter is the nexus of neo-mercantilist relationships between the British government, its most long-established trading agency, the General Post Office (GPO), and the British electronics industry to computerize some financial services and hasten domestic economic modernization. It is therefore a State-directed outlier in this volume, which is dominated by commercially driven examples of computerization, and indeed is one of the few examples in which IBM played only a cameo role. Elsewhere in this volume, however, Bonin has identified a neo-mercantilist preference among French financial services to support their domestic office machine suppliers in the 1930s and Thomes has noted the pressures from German financial services on Krupp to develop bookkeeping machines (see Bonin and Thomes in this volume).

The "national champion driven" pathway, one of the eight models of the twentieth-century diffusion of information technology identified by Cortada (2008: 6, 8–10), is distinguished by "the creation of a national (local) computer industry protected aggressively and preferred through government policy and action" (9). France pursued the strongest version of this strategy between the 1960s and 1980s, but Cortada notes that other European countries, including Britain, were also influenced by these ideas, which may have been reawakened by recession and financial crisis. Even in the U.S., federal government gave selected firms in defence-related industries generous financial and technical support. The idea of a national military-industrial-academic complex has been part of the social scientist's analytical armoury since the 1950s. Academic studies have tended to concentrate on the production side of State support for strategic industries, but governments also supported national champions through their purchasing power in procurement, and this chapter examines an intriguing British example.

The strategy of national champions is normally associated with the very large, strategically important industries like cars, electronics, and chemicals, but protection and support of British typewriters and other office machinery producers went back in some cases to the interwar years and was cranked up in the later 1940s.[1] There are obvious reasons why financial services should have been drawn into this supportive, neo-mercantilist web. As other chapters in this volume indicate, in the interwar years financial services were voracious users of office machinery, even to the extent of cross shareholdings and directorships in office machine-makers. During the first round of computerization of the British banks in the late 1950s and early 1960s, many elected to buy machines from companies that were also their own customers and key stages in the planning for computerization were delayed to allow British firms to develop hardware and software to the bankers' specifications (Booth 2007: 145–46). Thus, in the early 1960s both British government and some British banks favoured domestic producers of office machinery and computers.[2]

The high (or low) point of this neo-mercantilist, preferential moment in the computerization of Britain's financial services was the National Giro (Giro), which opened for business in 1968. Giro's role was to operate a national credit payments system, making use of the post office network, to provide an alternative to the traditional cheque-clearing system operated by the major commercial banks. As the chapters by Mooij, Thomes, and others in this volume make clear, many European countries developed such systems much earlier than Britain, where Giro's eventual creation owed more to political than commercial pressures. In the 1960s, British governments saw the large commercial banks as anti-competitive, inefficient hoarders of labour, with poor control over pay and a narrow middle-class customer base. After the Macmillan-Home Conservative government used the threat of a Giro to discipline the larger commercial banks, an exasperated Wilson Labour government went ahead. Giro's central office, the National Giro Centre, was established at Bootle, Merseyside, at the time an unemployment black spot and close to the prime minister's own parliamentary constituency.

Britain's Giro was thus very *political* with a wide range of goals, a full exploration of which is prevented by space constraints. In this chapter we focus on the role of Giro as a (relatively small) part of the efforts of Harold Wilson's governments' techno-nationalist efforts to use State spending to support Britain's computer industry. By the time Giro opened in 1968 the industry had effectively been reduced to one firm, International Computers Limited (ICL), the product of mergers encouraged by the Wilson governments (1964–1970) and a recipient of significant State development funding (Campbell-Kelly 1989: 335–42).

---

1. For the buy British policy on typewriters, see Prais (1981: 230–33). More generally, see Milward and Brennan (1996: 258–60).

2. During this first phase only Lloyds and the Westminster bought U.S. machines—both chose IBMs. See Booth (2007: 145).

We survey the historiography of the British State and high technology before looking at the efforts of the Wilson governments to assist the British computer industry and the part played by the GPO (the government department responsible for postal, telecommunications, and some savings and banking services) under its energetic and charismatic minister, Anthony Wedgwood Benn (now Tony Benn).[3] We then examine how Benn's proposals mapped onto the GPO's emerging understanding of computerization and automated data processing (ADP), especially in connection with its savings banking function and how this shaped Giro's technological strategy. Finally we draw conclusions.

TECHNOLOGY AND THE BRITISH STATE

Debates on the role of British governments in supporting high-technology industry have settled after much ferment. The traditional story has been of "two cultures", government and industry, which barely understood each other so that industrial policy at best neglected industry and at worst damaged its competitive performance (Allen 1976; Balogh 1959). The strongest version is Correlli Barnett's argument that twentieth-century British policymakers knew of, but failed to address, shortcomings in British manufacturing but instead pursued (at least until Thatcherism) welfare policies that ultimately crippled the productive economy (Barnett 1986). The "Barnett hypothesis" won immediate popular attention (as, indeed, had earlier versions of the argument that saw State expenditure as a huge millstone around the neck of private manufacturing) but has subsequently been undermined by professional historians (Edgerton 1991c; Harris 1990; Tomlinson 1997a).

The leading critic of the "two cultures" hypothesis has been David Edgerton, who has identified and underlined British governments' commitment to strategically important industries: naval shipbuilding, aircraft, electronics, and nuclear power (Edgerton 1991a, 1991b, 1991c, 1996a, 1996b, 2005, 2006). Edgerton has instead emphasized the creation of a "warfare state", assembled during and after the First World War, in which key government departments "sponsored" technologically advanced firms and industries. In Edgerton's eyes, State support of strategically important technologies—techno-nationalism—began with the creation of a military-industrial complex in the interwar years and lasted until the 1960s. The Wilson government slowly and painfully concluded that techno-nationalism had skewed the direction of research and development to the detriment of "civilian" industry and rapidly disassembled the support network.

---

3. Ian Martin's chapter in this volume highlights the importance of the GPO's telecommunications operations to computerization by Britain's clearing banks.

The tide of publications in the last decade has strongly favoured Edgerton over Barnett. Tomlinson (1994: 161–86, 263–74; 1997b: 68–93; 2004: 94–122) has explored attempts by the State to drive efficiency and technological dynamism in a range of British manufacturing industries that had no strategic importance other than in the trade balance. Milward and Brennan (1996) have explored the ways in which British governments of the 1940s and 1950s used import quotas to foster the development of key infant industries. Agar's (2003) provocative and still controversial study of the development of the computer has identified the Treasury, albeit its specialist management experts rather than the Oxbridge-educated high-policy generalists, as the main advocates of ADP in the UK, in the face of its information-handling problems.

There is, however, an issue concerning the dynamics and chronology of British techno-nationalism. Both Edgerton and Agar have concentrated on groups of technical experts in the British administrative system; Edgerton on the scientific officer class, particularly the "research corps" in the major military-scientific-industrial research establishments (Edgerton 2005: 108–190), and Agar (2003) on the Treasury's Organization and Methods (O&M) management specialists. Both identify the Wilson governments of 1964–1970, which promised to harness the "white heat" of the scientific-technological revolution to British industry, as the end of techno-nationalism. Edgerton notes the contraction of the research corps as Labour reduced "military" and encouraged the growth of "civilian science" (2005: 230–69). Agar (2003: 339) suggests that the creation of ICL in 1968 as a "national champion" allowed government to detach itself from the computer industry while changes in the machinery of government weakened the drive to computerize government administration.

But it is not difficult to identify the discourse of techno-nationalism after 1970 (as Cortada's analytical chronology would suggest). Pressure on British government to support high-technology sectors for their perceived military-strategic significance continued into the 1980s (Edgerton 1991b; Hartley 1996). Only after 1985, during the second Thatcher government, was the defence sector exposed to the combination of public expenditure cuts and much harder competitive forces especially from overseas (in effect, from the U.S.) that is commonly associated with the liberalizing strand in domestic economic policy (Dunne and Smith 1992: 92–98).

TECHNO-NATIONALISM, THE "WHITE HEAT", AND THE POST OFFICE

The techno-nationalist strand of British public policy is most strongly associated with Prime Minister Harold Wilson, who made technology policy the core of Labour's electoral strategy after becoming party leader in 1963. Wilson is often presented as the archetypal political opportunist, and his modernizing discourse as devoid of content (for the charge of opportunism, see Pimlott 1992: 254–55). However, Wilson prided himself on his role in the creation of the National Research and Development Corporation in 1948 to support technologically advanced private firms, especially its role in supporting the first-generation British computers (Wilson 1964: 46). On taking office in 1964 he initiated a review of support for manufacturing and created ministerial and official teams to review the technological state of key British industries.[4]

The computer industry was an important early interest of these groups. Although Wilson's political memoirs took an apocalyptic view of the condition of the industry, the ministerial group, including Frank Cousins, the Minister of Technology, was more sanguine. They noted that British computers were generally competitive but that U.S. producers had a definite edge in larger machines (those selling for around £500,000).[5] To support the industry, Cousins proposed in the short term a "buy British" policy in public sector procurement, even where the machines were more expensive, and, in the longer run, to explore the possibilities for Anglo-French collaboration to create an anti-American alliance in computers.[6] However, preferences were not unanimously welcomed at the ministerial table. Those, like the Minister for Pensions and National Insurance, who were anxious to press ahead with large-scale projects, feared delays and difficulty in realizing potential cost savings.[7] Other departmental agenda were threatened. The president of the Board of Trade, Douglas Jay, saw "buy British" as a threat to his efforts to encourage inward U.S. investment to the high-unemployment regions and, given the number of U.S. transplants operating in the UK, queried what "buy British" actually meant.[8]

From these debates, Cousins fashioned a workable policy. British government should "buy British" unless: "(a) no British machine can satisfy the requirement; or (b) the project for which the computer is required would thereby be delayed by [one year]; or (c) there is a disparity of 25 per cent or more between the tender prices of United Kingdom and foreign machines". A draft public statement on the proposed policy (never in fact published) did not set out the criteria in detail but referred to a "buy British" policy

---

4. National Archives, Public Records Office, Kew, London (henceforth NA, PRO). CAB 130/217. Prime minister's committee on technology, minutes, and memoranda.

5. Wilson (1971: 9) claimed that there was one month to save the British computer industry. The more sanguine conclusion is found in NA, PRO, CAB 129/121, C.(65)65, 27 April 1965. More generally, the early work of Cousins was laid out in NA, PRO, CAB 130/217, Cousins, "Tasks of the Ministry of Technology", 25 November 1964.

6. NA, PRO, CAB 129/121, C.(65)66, 29 April 1965.

7. NA, PRO, CAB 129/121, C.(65)67, 4 May 1965.

8. NA, PRO, CAB 129/121, C.(65)80, 1 June 1965.

in the absence of "unreasonable delay or excessive extra cost".[9] Cousins argued that the policy would create breathing space for the UK industry and that ". . . means of bringing together I.C.T. and English Electric [EE] computer interests should be considered further in the light of the outcome of the proposed Anglo-French project".[10]

After Wilson and Cousins, the third key figure in the formulation of Labour's techno-nationalism, and the minister most centrally involved in the Giro project, was Anthony Wedgwood Benn. In 1963–1964, Benn produced a series of articles for the *Guardian* surveying both broad political themes and more detailed, practical proposals for reform.[11] The best practical scheme concerned the GPO; it was stimulated by Wilson's own speeches on science policy and was sent to Wilson well before its final publication (Benn 1965: 72). The essence of the argument was the familiar techno-nationalist refrain that public enterprise should strengthen existing science-based industries and that the GPO, already a science-based enterprise, could make a major contribution. He identified the Post Office Savings Bank (POSB) as a "great area for development", not least because it could form the basis of a great working-class (Giro) bank into which welfare benefits could be paid and through which additional national savings could be mobilized.[12]

The article may have been enough to secure for Benn the role of Postmaster General (PMG) in a new Labour Government (Benn 1988: 67, 107, 130). It certainly identified Benn as a key member of the group formulating technology policy and he quickly learned the real technological potential of his new department. The telecommunications side offered huge opportunities to build a cluster of high-tech activities, from the enormously experimental (in satellite communications), to the enormously promising (the new generation of electronic telephone exchange equipment), to the more mundane (mass production by the state of telephone equipment). He had very ambitious ideas for a computer bureau service, based on the GPO's emerging business communications network, Datel, either to market spare capacity on other people's computers or in the longer run to acquire computers and run its own computer service.[13] More generally, the department had an extensive programme of computerization, with six or seven British computers to be operational

---

9. NA, PRO, CAB 129/121, C.(65)79, 31 May 1965.

10. NA, PRO, CAB 129/122, C.(65)115, 28 July 1965; Campbell-Kelly (1989: 248–49) discusses the Anglo-French Computer Project.

11. These articles were collected and republished as Benn (1965).

12. A.W. Benn, "The Future of the Post Office", *Guardian*, 19 June 1964, reprinted in Benn (1965: 137–40, quote from 137–38).

13. Royal Mail Archive, Mount Pleasant, London (henceforth RMA), Post 69/73. Post Office Board (henceforth POB) papers (64), third meeting, 25 November 1964.

by the end of 1965 and a further million pounds worth of computers under order each year from 1966–1967 onwards.[14]

Although some of this horrified Benn's civil servants, he quickly discovered that his department was more of a pioneer in computerization than the laggard he had portrayed to readers of the *Guardian*. The GPO's telecommunications side was at the cutting edge of scientific and technical development in many fields, notably at its Dollis Hill research laboratory, but even in the more mundane area of ADP the department was technologically progressive. The GPO was an early and substantial applier of computers to data processing operations (Agar 2003: 316, table 8.1). Two of the first eight government clerical computer projects were based in the GPO, and the second, the payroll operations of the London postal area, was regarded by the department's O&M experts as the biggest computer project in the UK.[15] Well before Benn's article, the GPO had considered computerizing key parts of the POSB's operations and had recognized both the great potential for transformation but also the enormity and interrelatedness of the task.[16] The GPO's planners estimated that a computerized POSB would require at least ten years to complete.[17] Equally interesting, given the parallel developments in the commercial banks, was an investigation of computerizing transactions at GPO counters.[18] The O&M planners also recommended the use of American-style credit cards to record POSB customer account details, and estimated very significant savings in labour, not least in balancing, reconciling, and checking figures, both at the counter and in the local accounts branches of each postal district. In this area, too, the GPO O&M specialists expected to spread the work over five to ten years.[19]

Thus, at roughly the same time as the British clearing banks were embarking on their first steps in computerization (that is, long before Benn's call for a computerized Giro), GPO planners suggested almost exactly parallel developments. The scale of the POSB exceeded that of any clearing bank, with very many more customers and a much, much bigger "branch" network, if the local post office can be seen as the equivalent of a bank branch. The timescales and basic procedures were very similar; the method of recording post office counter transactions was almost identical to the clearing banks in their first phase of computerization. As with the clearing

---

14. RMA, 1964, POB (64) fourth meeting, 9 December; NA, PRO, PREM 13/616, Benn to Cousins and Wilson, 13 January 1965.

15. RMA, Post 122/6480, "Training of Staff for Employment on the LEAPS Computer", "Appreciation Course for Directors", memorandum by A.H. Martin Smith, 5 September 1958.

16. RMA, Post 113/1, Report 156: "A General Description of Some Post Office ADP Projects", March 1961 (henceforth RMAR156), paras. 31–32.

17. RMAR156, para. 33.

18. RMAR156, para. 10.

19. For comparison with the clearing banks, see Booth (2008).

banks, the drivers were rising labour costs and staff retention problems, but GPO records offer no evidence of any sign of the clearing bankers' long-run drive to feminize routine clerical work.[20]

The most striking difference between the GPO and the clearing banks in their approaches to computerization in the early 1960s was the early appearance of doubts and scepticism in the public sector. The GPO's pioneering project in ADP, the computerization of its London payroll work, ran into the classic difficulties of late delivery with unreliable operation and the division of responsibility between the hardware manufacturer and in-house maintenance. This created problems that added to incompatibilities between the central processor and important peripherals, notably printers, supplied from a different manufacturer. The project lost more than half its core programming staff to better paid jobs in the private sector, all of which delayed programming, extended the time taken to load jobs onto the system (which was already delayed by equipment problems), and reduced potential financial benefits. From this catalogue of misfortunes, the GPO's central O&M staff concluded that the prime requirements of a successful computer project were that it had to be large scale, with a wide range of tasks that could be loaded simultaneously, or at least in a very short time, rather than sequentially.[21] These conclusions permeated all the (surviving) surveys of potential computer projects of the early 1960s.[22]

It is impossible to be precise about the full extent and impact of the disappointments with the payroll computerization because the survival of records from this period is somewhat haphazard, but the next phase of GPO O&M feasibility reports on the potential for computerized operations in its banking activities were much more cautious.[23] Planners recognized that much more advance work would be needed to prepare new systems and that parallel working of "established" and the "transition-to-computer" methods might not be feasible. Hence, the surviving records suggest (but can only suggest) that the evident enthusiasm for applying ADP to the POSB and related activities was dampened by the pessimistic lessons of

---

20. For a discussion on parallel developments in the clearing banks, see Booth (2004). These banks were computerizing rapidly to improve efficiency and cope with increasing business volumes, but also grappling with the problems this brought. See Bátiz-Lazo and Wardley (2007) for a comparison of developments in clearing banks and building societies.

21. RMA, Post 113/1, Report 157: "A Report on the Lessons to Be Drawn from Post Office Computing Experience", March 1961.

22. RMA, Post 113/1, Report 155: "A Report on the Future of ADP in the Post Office", March 1961.

23. During our research in the Royal Mail Archive an uncatalogued file of pieces on computerization was discovered (RMA, Post 119/1). It contains several O&M reports on ADP but the numbering and dating conventions indicate that many reports have not survived.

payroll computerization. Why, then, did the GPO agree to host the Giro, a bank that was computerized from the beginning?

STEPS TOWARDS THE GIRO

The most obvious stimulus to the introduction of the Giro was the report of the Radcliffe Committee on Britain's monetary system.[24] The Committee was established in 1957 in the aftermath of what appeared to be persistent failures of monetary policy to control inflation (Booth 2000; Cairncross 1987; Dow 1964, 90–103). Some members had already analysed the problem as "excess liquidity", where the public holds more liquid assets than it needs, and is induced to spend more at levels that initiate or sustain inflationary pressures.[25] A small, but significant, part in containing "excess liquidity" was the proposal to create a Giro system, on the continental European or Japanese model, as a means of settlement of accounts by the transfer of credits from payer to payee. Although very modest in conception, the Committee saw it as a potentially useful method of curbing the growth of the public's wish to hold bank-notes while simultaneously creating a flow of funds to the Treasury to ease its borrowing and debt management problems.[26] It recommended that: "... in the absence of an early move on the part of existing institutions to provide the services which will cater for the need we have in mind, there would be a case for investigating the possibility of instituting a 'giro' system to be operated by the Post Office".[27] There were two reasons for selecting the GPO: the Japanese and some European versions used their postal systems; and the GPO seemed the best-placed supplier of financial services to the working classes (the social stratum of most concern to the Committee) to take on the work. The Committee knew, however, that the GPO was extremely reluctant to take on the additional costs of processing frequent small transactions in accounts with low average balances.[28]

The GPO's response to the Committee's recommendation was a thirty-eight-page internal report in February 1960. This judged that a Giro would

---

24. UK Parliament, 1959. Report. Parliamentary Papers 1958–59, Vol. 17, Cmnd. 827. London: HMSO (Radcliffe Report).

25. Dow (1964: 308); Radcliffe Report, 15, 138–39, 170.

26. Radcliffe Report, 331.

27. Radcliffe Report, 332.

28. The Director of Savings of the POSB judged that his customers were using their accounts much more actively than pre-war, with many customers making close to one hundred transactions per year (UK Parliament, 1960. *Minutes of Evidence.* London: HMSO [Radcliffe Evidence], qq. 6854–63). As with the clearing banks, the growth of current account business had raised costs for the POSB (sixfold between 1946 and 1958 [Radcliffe Evidence, q. 6868]). The POSB, therefore, had limited the amount that could be deposited during the course of a calendar year to £500 (Radcliffe Evidence, q. 6880).

be attractive to organizations receiving large numbers of remittances (e.g. building societies, hire purchase companies, insurance companies, utilities, local authorities) but sounded a cautious note: "Before a decision was taken to inaugurate a giro system it would be desirable . . . to ascertain what actions the banks are planning to popularise banking". [29] The cost of processing small transactions in small accounts could, however, be overcome by computerization: " . . . it would not be feasible to handle on a manual system in one office the traffic level contemplated. A punched card system is out of the question for the same reason . . . Very substantial economies would be produced if this data conversion process [manual entry] could be avoided". [30]

Conservative governments tended to be wary of interfering in the internal management of the clearing banks, not least because some bank chairmen were very prominent in party circles. But Macmillan's government grew angry at the prominent role taken by bank staff pay settlements in breaking the "pay pause" introduced by Selwyn Lloyd in July 1961. [31] In effect, the government used the prospect of State-sponsored competition to discipline the clearing banks into more "responsible" pay policies. The message was understood: the threat of competition from the Giro featured regularly in the minutes of the clearing bankers' main policy-making committees. [32] The clearing bankers were most alarmed that the GPO document, to which they received privileged access, aimed for a monopoly in credit clearing. [33] Although the clearing banks were ambivalent about seeking new working-class customers, they were decidedly not prepared to surrender a new, potentially lucrative strand of business. [34] The banks were also "encouraged" to introduce a quasi-Giro system of credit clearing despite their reservations on its commercial viability. [35]

---

29. National Giro Archive, Alliance and Leicester plc Archive, Bootle, Merseyside (henceforth NGA) (1960, February). GIRO/R/P/1. "Report on the Practicability of Giro", paras. 23 and 40.

30. NGA, Report, 1960, paras. 50 and 53.

31. On the general position, see Blackaby (1978: 361–63).

32. Pre-publication rumours of Radcliffe's support for the Giro resulted in special meetings of bank chief executive officers (British Bankers' Association, Archive, Guildhall Library, London [henceforth BBA], M.32031, Vol. 11, 16 April 1959). In March 1962, the governor of the Bank of England had explicitly noted the possibility of the Giro when considering the banks' proposals to raise interest rates and reduce opening hours (BBA, M.32147, Vol. 1, 2 February 1962).

33. BBA, M.32031, Vol. 11, 15 October 1960.

34. See BBA, M.32147, Vol. 2a, "Banking Hours", 15 December 1963, for comments by the general manager of Barclays and the professional journal for a balanced review (*The Banker*, 113 [June 1963], 403–405, "How much do the banks want the 'little man'"?).

35. The clearing banks calculated in 1960 that they needed to charge 9d. (3.75 new pence) for each credit transfer (BBA, M.32031, Vol. 11, 3 November 1960). However, they became aware that the post office Giro proposed to charge 6d. (2.5 new pence) for such transactions and the banks reduced their charges accordingly

Simultaneously, they took government advice to reform their systems of pay bargaining to limit the possibility of further confrontation with government on wage and salary growth.[36]

The threat of the Giro had secured considerable gains and the actions of the clearing banks had clearly weakened the business case for the Giro. The Conservative government let the banks off the hook. Its Assistant PMG told the House of Commons on 4 March 1963:

> I think it is fair to say that two independent systems of transfer would probably prove less convenient than one and more expensive than one in the long run, and the present view of the Government is that the Post Office ought not launch into what may easily be a losing venture until it is clearer than it is now that the Clearing Bank system is incapable of developing so as to meet all the country's needs.[37]

This position could not withstand the energy of Labour's new PMG and the techno-nationalist sentiments of his ministerial colleagues after 1964. Benn quickly commissioned another GPO report. This concluded that a Giro, if it worked in collaboration with the clearing banks, could subsist alongside them, in part because it would initially take business away from existing GPO services.[38] The report reiterated the view that the steady expansion of instalment payments (hire-purchase, mail-order and credit shopping business, mortgages) offered significant growth potential. On ADP, the GPO now recognized that the complexity and range of its counter-operations precluded computerization at this stage, but the Giro would need centralized processing and a sophisticated mix of hardware and software to "read" the variety of paying-in and transfer forms that would be generated by the GPO and the many firms that might use its services. The Giro would therefore require more centralized computing power and less peripheral equipment than any clearing bank at the time, with an estimated

---

(BBA, M.32031, Vol. 11, 17 November 1960). In fact, the credit transfer system underperformed, and the banks had to promote it very heavily (BBA, M.32031, Vol. 18, 18 May 1967). Mooij's chapter in this volume notes that in the Netherlands the major commercial banks and two central farmers' credit banks established a separate Bankgirocentrale in 1967.

36. On pay reforms, see Cameron (1963). The Cameron Committee was established to help persuade the banks to grant independent union representation in pay bargaining. Simultaneously, the clearing banks were told that they would not be allowed to implement an increase in their charges to accommodate rising labour costs. BBA, M.32147, Vol. 2, contains the banks' proposal ("Strictly Confidential. Note for the Record. Interest Rating; Banking Hours", 11 December 1963) and the government's frosty response ("Strictly Confidential. Note for the Record. Interest Rating; Banking Hours", 16 December 1963).

37. Quoted in NGA, Report, 1965, para. 5.

38. NGA (1965, February), GIRO/PO/P/3, "Report".

demand for four large computers, forty punched-card machines, and one thousand new staff for the data processing tasks alone. There was sufficient encouragement in this report for the government to publish a White Paper, which concluded:

> . . . the case for establishing a Post Office giro is a strong one on economic and social grounds. It is likely to meet a real need cheaply and effectively and will not only modernise the existing remittance services of the Post Office, but also help to rationalise the nation's money transmission facilities generally using the most modern computer techniques. It thus demonstrates the way in which public enterprise can serve the more sophisticated needs of a modern society.[39]

The proposal had an easy, uncontentious passage through cabinet and parliament, apart from apparently minor controversies over whether to make welfare benefit payments through the Giro.[40] It would be helpful if we could analyse the decisions to purchase the Giro's main computers, but little documentary evidence about the ordering process survives at any of the archives holding Giro or computer-manufacturer material.[41] But the patchy survival of archival records offers much useful evidence as to the importance of techno-nationalist concerns among the many reasons for launching the Giro in the mid-1960s.

Before the Wilson government's new rules for ordering computer equipment in the public sector, the GPO, like many private sector computer users, had established "objective performance criteria" upon which to base its computer equipment purchases.[42] The computers selected by the GPO for the Giro, EE 4/70s, were exactly those large-scale machines that the government agreed to subsidize for British public sector purchasers. As far as peripheral equipment is concerned, the documentary sources demonstrate that Giro managers walked a tightrope between commercial and techno-nationalist needs. The case of optical character recognition (OCR) equipment

---

39. UK Parliament, 1965. *White Paper, A Post Office Giro*, Cmnd. 2751. London: HMSO, para. 21.

40. The failure to make such payments through the Giro undermined its commercial viability. The idea belonged to Peter Shore, whose contribution to techno-nationalism and the use of the State to drive the growth of science-based industries was substantial. The progress of the Giro through government and parliament is told in Benn (1988: 166, 173–74, 241–42, 294–95).

41. On the company consolidations leading to ICL, see Campbell-Kelly (1989: 244–74). The Giro material is concentrated at the Alliance and Leicester archive (as the Alliance and Leicester Building Society acquired Giro in 1990), but some material remains in the Royal Mail Archive. The ICL archive appears to have disappeared, apart from some technical material held at Imperial College London.

42. RMA, Post 113/5, Report 182: "Report on the Selection of Computers for Automatic Data Processing in the Post Office", August 1963.

provides a vivid illustration. As noted earlier, Giro depended upon forms (vouchers) that were generated at post office counters, received by post, or in the firms using Giro's services. Giro therefore needed OCR equipment that could "read" a wide variety of formats. Such equipment was made at the time only by a single (American) firm, Recognition Equipment Incorporated (REI), the recognized world leader, whose equipment was used by a number of financial service providers in the U.S. and Europe.[43] Commercial and efficiency considerations made REI equipment essential for Giro, but techno-nationalist considerations could not be forgotten entirely, and the GPO reached a messy compromise:

> To restrict expenditure in US dollars and to encourage British manufacturers to develop equipment conforming to our requirements, the initial order will be limited to the machines required to meet the level of traffic expected in the first few months of operation (with an option to purchase more if required). At the same time, an experimental order will be placed with the leading British contender.[44]

GPO tightrope walking was also evident in its response to the growing difficulties experienced by EE in developing the 4/70, derived from its long-standing and ruthlessly exploited technology-sharing agreement with the Radio Corporation of America (RCA; see Booth 2007: 33–34; Campbell-Kelly 1989: 240–41). In September 1967, EE indicated to the main customers for its top-of-the-range 4/70s that there would be delays in delivery and that reduced specifications might be necessary.[45] The Midland Bank, very concerned that these problems might frustrate its demands to introduce online branch banking by 1968, began exploring alternative sources of supply and within months switched to Burroughs (Booth 2004: 291–93). Giro, in contrast, stayed with EE (by now English Electric LEO Computers [EELC]) even though its own deadline was equally tight, and took EELC's temporary replacement machines (albeit from RCA), to limit the long-term damage to the British computer producer.[46] Giro had the advantage that it was a new organization, not bound by the conservatism and constraints of existing operations which inhibited the computerization of the clearing banks or of the Dutch Giro (Wit 1995).

More broadly, Benn's own account demonstrates how the Giro fitted in with the wider techno-nationalist themes. In July 1965, he recorded a

---

43. RMA, Post 122/10263, "Giro, Document Reading and Sorting", June 1967.

44. RMA, Post 69/80, POB (67)9, "Character Recognition and Document Sorting Equipment for the National Giro Centre", initialled A.W., 30 January 1967.

45. *Computer Weekly*, 21 September 1967.

46. RMA, Post 122/10263, "Operations Division: Progress Report GJCP 18/676", n.d. but November 1967.

conference organized by Labour's National Executive to discuss public enterprise and its role in the economy:

> Last night we had discussed financial targets and purchasing policy and this morning we considered the way in which public enterprise could be made to develop. We had a first rate discussion in which the most notable part was taken by Peter Shore, who also wound up the whole conference. It was Peter who really devised the entirely new approach by the Labour party to nationalisation. He was the man who thought of the idea of putting public money into the points of growth of the economy instead of just acting as a dustbin for private enterprise that had failed. Now at least we have a real chance to do this and of course that is the real significance of my Giro and the urgent necessity for the reorganisation of the Post Office as three nationalised industries. But few people understand this and it'll be a job to get the ideas carried through. (Benn 1988: 297)

The scale of computer purchases for this project was small in relation to total GPO spending on computers, much less for the public sector as a whole, but hardware expenditure told only part of the story. Programming the Giro computers was the largest single contract programming job that the British computer industry had seen.[47] Even so, the final piece of evidence for a techno-nationalist element in the Giro must rest on the wider pattern of GPO spending on new technology in the later 1960s, and we now turn to this theme.

BENN, THE POST OFFICE, AND EXPENDITURE ON COMPUTERS, 1960–1970

As suggested earlier, the GPO was among the first government departments to experiment with ADP projects. It is difficult to trace the long-term development of the GPO's spending on new technology due to minor changes in GPO finances arising from the 1961 Post Office Act, but in the early 1960s its technological priorities lay very squarely in telecommunications rather than posts.[48] Computer expenditure, however, was rising rapidly in the mid-1960s

---

47. NGA (15 August 1968). GIRO/T/F/ICL/1. ICL Press Release.

48. The public investment White Paper for 1961 listed the Post Office's priorities. Most were concerned with telecommunications but there was also a commitment to speeding up postal mechanization. Investment in plant and machinery amounted to £0.7 million in 1959–1960, rising to £1.7 million in 1962–1963 in the postal service, and £78.1 million in 1959–1960, rising to £94.8 million in telecommunications. In fact, this last figure represented more than 80 per cent of all projected investment by the GPO in 1962–1963 (Post Office, "Annual Report and Accounts", 1962, 19–20). The GPO spent just over £2 million on all furniture and office machines in 1960–1961 (Post Office, "Annual Report and Accounts," 1961, 51) but only a very small part of that sum was allocated to computers.

under the impetus of the applications prepared by the O&M branch. Benn's account of a lunch in December 1964 describes the O&M representatives as "a bright bunch", and refers to their computerization programme "which involves the purchase of two and a half million pounds worth of computers immediately and more computers at a rate of a million pounds a year" (Benn 1988: 196). Initially, Benn's main impact was on the tone of GPO public relations. Under the Conservatives, the GPO had presented itself as a technologically dynamic organization, often with photographs of the Goonhilly Downs satellite communications dish, the latest telephone equipment, and increasingly the plans for what was to become the GPO Tower.[49]

In its first annual report under Benn, the tone was now explicitly techno-nationalist, pointing out that the department should be seen as a science-based ministry of communications with demanding efficiency targets, and it was pursuing these twin tracks in large part through computerization.[50] It claimed that the order (placed under the Conservative government) for £2.5 million to purchase five new computers was the largest order placed in Europe for general purpose computers. This was more than simply mobilizing the lexicon of productivity growth, technological advance, and rates of return. In Benn's first months as PMG, GPO expenditure on British computers rose so rapidly that by the investment review of April 1965, the department was budgeting for £12.3 million to be spent on computers between 1964 and 1971, an increase in expenditure of roughly 50 per cent over inherited plans.[51]

Furthermore, Benn's idea of a GPO computer bureau drove expenditure on British computers still higher. The idea came originally from discussions at the Post Office Board (POB), and Benn received enthusiastic support from Wilson in the very early days of the new government (Benn 1988: 188). Ministerial responsibility for the service needed to be clarified because Cousins's plans for the Ministry of Technology included ambitious steps to accelerate the deployment of computers in British industry.[52] Only after these plans had been finalized, in the form of the National Computer Centre (NCC), could the relationship between the NCC and Benn's proposal for a National Data Processing Service (NDPS) be explored.[53]

Initially, Benn proposed to take the running of the NCC with the new NDPS into the GPO.[54] But his officials were concerned about the staffing and cost implications. The market for computer specialists was already

---

49. All these and more can be found in the report and accounts for the year ended 31 March 1962 (Post Office, "Annual Report and Accounts", 1962).

50. Post Office, "Annual Report and Accounts", 1965, 7–8.

51. RMA, Post 69/75, POB (65)35, "1965 Investment Review", Annex, April 1965.

52. NA, PRO, PREM 13/945, Cousins to Wilson, 15 December 1964.

53. The NDPS was used by some trustee savings banks, which competed to some extent with the POSB. See also Bátiz-Lazo and Maixé-Altés in this volume.

54. RMA, Post 69/79, POB (66) seventh meeting, 21 June 1966.

extremely tight and the ministerial members of the POB feared that they might lose GPO computer staff to both the NDPS and to the NCC. They were also worried that the capital cost of the NDPS would cut into the GPO's own computerization budget. But there were also changes that pressed the POB to welcome the proposal. The GPO was already establishing a regional computer network, and the suspicion is that these were large British computers whose capacity was determined as much by the techno-nationalist agenda as by the GPO's operational requirements. Again, documentary evidence is almost non-existent.

The other important factor was the imminent change of the GPO's status. Benn had decided early on that it was too big to be managed effectively as a single organization, especially given the projected demand growth of the telephone service. He proposed a three-way split into posts, telecommunications, and savings, with each part constituted as a separate nationalized industry subject to the same return on capital targets as other public corporations. This conclusion was endorsed by McKinsey, whom Benn had brought into the GPO at a very early stage. With these management reforms the department's culture had to undergo major changes and the GPO's senior officials may have chosen to pursue any revenue-raising opportunity in the new financial environment. The argument that had most leverage with GPO officials indicates a wholly new attitude within the department towards public expenditure and public investment:

> At an earlier stage it was in mind to carry out market research to determine the likely demand for the new facility. But this means carrying out a survey of potential customers who have no practical knowledge or experience of what a data processing service can do for them and who cannot really be given effective demonstrations: it would be rather like trying to sell a car on the basis of a specification to people who have not yet heard of a bicycle. An alternative approach would be to provide computer capacity in a selected area in excess of Post Office requirements, sell a data processing service as hard as it can be sold, and use the results to gauge the extent of the national market. This would be in line with the techniques already employed on the telephone side and approved by the Board, but it could not be started until the necessary legal powers had been obtained. It would not involve any risks, since the required computer capacity would be diverted to Post Office use as part of our developing computerisation programme if it were decided not to proceed with a NDPS.[55]

Thus, the reasons why the GPO became a major purchaser of British computers were not limited to the techno-nationalist drive from PMG Benn.

---

55. RMA, Post 69/79, POB (66)58. National Data Processing Service, Memorandum, June 1966.

However, we should not underestimate the strength of that drive nor Benn's conviction about the rightness of his strategy. As PMG he had transformed the receptiveness of senior GPO managers to new technology and had tied support for the British computer industry into the strategic technological decisions of the department. After becoming Minister of Technology in 1966, he became an even stronger advocate of British computer technology (and significantly of the EELC 4/70) and also played a very significant role in the final shape of ICL, the government-created "national champion" in British computer manufacturing.[56]

CONCLUSIONS

The Giro is a very curious beast indeed. It was always expected to have at best a modest commercial return, but its revenue-earning potential was an important argument for civil servants in the GPO who were becoming increasingly exposed to commercial pressures. Its role in disciplining the clearing banks was always marginal after the Conservative government of the early 1960s allowed the banks time to create a credit-clearing system that made it difficult for the Giro to build business quickly and effectively. Giro certainly fitted well with the Labour government's techno-nationalist agenda. In the House of Commons debate on Giro (21 July 1965) Benn argued that it ". . . will boost computer technology in this country, and will lead to a demand for more computers. It will meet the needs of a modern society".[57] Wilson argued that Giro:

> . . . included many new ideas and much new equipment which has been specially designed and produced by British industry . . . a striking example of the vitality of British technology and of what can be achieved from co-operation between those employed in the public sector . . . and those in private industry.[58]

Ministers, however, were aware that government computer procurement was a small proportion of total spending on computers, although for ICL "[b]etween 1968 and 1971 government purchasing . . . amounted to £36 million, 76 per cent of its total orders for computers; . . . some 10 per cent of turnover" (Mottershead 1978: 445–46). IBM, and American manu-

---

56. For Benn's role, see Benn (1988: 19–20). More generally, see Campbell-Kelly (1989: 12).

57. Hansard, Vol. 716, No. 158, cols. 1633–42, quoted in Thomson (1968: 196). Note that Thomson's book is modestly subtitled: "Whose First Book Helped to Persuade Parliament to Legislate for the National Giro".

58. NGA (18 October 1968). GIRO/OPEN/16. Prime Minister's speech at the National Giro Centre opening.

facturers overall, lost market share in Britain in 1968 and 1969 (Campbell-Kelly 1989: 250, table 12.1). But the percentage of computers of U.S. manufacture (including those made under licence) had risen from 20.5 per cent in 1962 to 55.4 per cent in 1967 among the UK computer population (Campbell-Kelly 1989: 254, table 12.2) and the UK's trade deficit on computers widened from £21 million in 1966 to £58 million in 1970 (Stoneman 1976: 187, table 8.15).

In this chapter, we have attempted to investigate the impact of techno-nationalist sentiment but recognize that mono-causal explanations are unsatisfactory. Cortada (2008: 9) has suggested, "The political policy factor must always be taken into account in describing any role of government in the deployment of IT". The case of the Giro is evidence of the importance of his argument, but also that "no nation adopted one diffusion model to the exclusion of all others" (Cortada 2008: 20). Indeed, if we are to find an answer to the question of why Britain had a Giro between 1968 and 1990, when it was sold to the Alliance and Leicester Building Society, we would have to locate its creation and weaknesses in the specific economic and political conditions of the late 1950s and early 1960s. These included concerns about the inflationary impact of working-class cash balances, government worries about the (in)efficiency with which clearing banks utilized clerical labour, the new financial rules imposed on the public sector, and the sector's potential to modernize British industry. A full investigation of why the Giro had such a short and unspectacular existence requires far more space than is available here.

9 Rabobank
An Innovative Dutch Bank, 1945–2000

Joke Mooij[1]

INTRODUCTION

Information processing plays a pivotal role in today's banking and finance. But the way financial information processing changed over the past decades is still hardly touched by banking historians. Dutch computer histories focus either on the technological development or on the interaction between technology and organizations. As far as banking is concerned most of these publications discuss the postal bank—as the Netherlands like Germany has a strong tradition of Giro payments—or the listed commercial banks. In 2004, De Boer and Frankhuizen published an inside history of forty years of automation at Rabobank, a co-operative bank. Still missing are comparative studies on mechanization and automation at Dutch commercial banks, savings banks, and co-operative banks. The same applies for the impact of automation on retail banking in the Netherlands.

This chapter presents an exploration of how mechanization and automation affected financial services of Rabobank, in the period from 1945 to 2000. In considering financial services, special attention is given to the Dutch payment system which—in an international context—has a number of unique characteristics. Moreover, in this period the Dutch payment system changed rapidly as new instruments were introduced for both face-to-face payments and remote payments.

Based on literature and archival research it will be shown here that from the start Rabobank's co-operative structure was of major influence on its information processing. In due course this enabled the bank to incorporate new technology to more easily offer state-of-the-art financial services.

Rabobank is a broad financial services provider based on co-operative principles. Its roots lie in the co-operative movement of the late nineteenth century. The co-operative organizational structure, whereby the

1. Views expressed are those of the author and do not necessarily reflect official positions of Rabobank Nederland. The author would like to thank colleagues and editors for their stimulating comments.

autonomous local banks are members of the central organization, gives Rabobank a unique vitality and has distinguished it from other banks from the very beginning.

Co-operative agricultural credit, modelled on Raiffeisen's principles, was highly successful during the first half of the twentieth century. Because of their limited size, the farmers' credit banks were relatively late adopters of mechanization for administration and accounting purposes. It was only in the third quarter of the twentieth century that the principal banking processes became automated, first centrally and later decentrally as well. The primary impetus can be attributed to the switch from cash to bank-to-bank payments by private households in the 1960s and 1970s.

Against the background of the fast-growing payment services market, what had once been small rural co-operative banks evolved to become modern co-operative financial services providers with automated payment processing systems. The technological possibilities of the day—combined with a desire to keep control of the costs of the payment system—led to a form of collaboration between all major Dutch banks. This collaboration also gave rise to new standardised payments products and instruments for the domestic market.

In 1972, expansion of services and increased competition in the banking sector led to a merger of the two central farmers' credit banks which resulted in Rabobank Nederland. In 1977 the bank chose to break new ground with a daring automation plan. Entirely in keeping with its co-operative structure, Rabobank—unlike most centrally managed banking organizations—opted for decentralised automation. This proved to be a fertile concept, and one that allowed Rabobank to incorporate new technologies into its own systems.

This chapter proceeds as follows. The following section provides a short history of Rabobank and some general background. In its third section, the chapter sets out how the mechanization of data processing progressed within the two banking organizations, both locally and centrally, in the period from 1900 to 1960. Alongside the many similarities, there were clear differences in both speed and methodology. The fourth section of the chapter deals with the period between 1960 and 1972, a time when banking activities were expanding and when the level of interbank transfers compelled the co-operative farmers' credit banks to seek further efficiency through automation. The chapter then covers the period 1972–2000 and brings together the aftermath of the merger, the explosive growth of Rabobank, the changing structure of domestic payment systems, and the rapid technological developments in both automation and communications which eventually led to new payment options. This chapter ends with some closing comments.

A SHORT HISTORY OF RABOBANK

In the Netherlands, *boerenleenbanken* (co-operative farmers' credit banks) were set up from the 1890s by rural folk who, with little access to the capital market, decided to help one another. These co-operative farmers' credit banks were modelled on the principles set out by the German mayor Friedrich Wilhelm Raiffeisen (1818–1888).[2] Just as was the case with the older German Raiffeisen movement, the co-operative agricultural credit movement in the Netherlands played an important role in the economic development of rural areas. The fledgling co-operative banks, with strong local roots, proved to be solid savings banks in which members of the farming community were happy to deposit their savings. The number of such banks rose quickly. In the first decade of the twentieth century the number of banks rose from sixty-seven in 1900 to 603 in 1910. From the 1920s onwards, 1,148 co-operative famers' credit banks could be found all over the Netherlands. At its peak there were over thirteen hundred banks. After the late 1960s the number of banks slowly decreased due to interbank mergers. In 2000 only 397 local banks were left. In a retrospect of the first hundred years, Sluyterman et al. (1998: 86–87) concluded that agricultural credit was responsible for significant innovation and renewal in both Dutch banking and Dutch agriculture.

Each farmers' credit bank was an autonomous co-operative with a geographically limited area of operation, its own board, its own responsibility for the balance sheet, and its own accounting records. The cashier who received and disbursed money was responsible for bookkeeping and correspondence, sometimes assisted by a member of the family. Being cashier was usually a part-time task, carried out in addition to a regular job. In the beginning, the cashier's house served as the bank's office. In this way overhead costs were very low. After the 1950s, the growth and expansion of services was accompanied by professionalization, and this led many banks to decide to move to proper banking premises. The cashier made way for staff who were trained in banking and administrative matters and were supervised by a general manager; but none of this affected the bank's involvement with the local economy and the community in any way (Schilte 2009).

The primary intention of the farmers' credit banks was to provide credit to local agricultural businesses at favourable rates. From the start, membership of the co-operative farmers' bank was a prerequisite for obtaining credit. At the annual general meeting, the members elected a board of directors and a supervisory board from their midst. Together they formed "the bank". The disadvantages of small-scale operations were alleviated by a central bank that acted as "banker's bank" for the local banks. Both central banks also supervised the affiliated banks and audited their books. They also advertised and promoted the co-operative banking sector.

---

2. Raiffeisen defined the five most important principles of co-operative banking as: (a) unlimited liability of the members; (b) unsalaried management; (c) reservation of profits; (d) a geographically limited working area; and (e) local autonomy, accompanied by affiliation to a central bank. These principles were defined in Raiffeisen (1888).

In 1898 two groups of farmers' credit banks had set up two separate central banks: the Coöperatieve Centrale Raiffeisen-Bank (CCRB) in Utrecht and the Coöperatieve Centrale Boerenleenbank (CCB) in Eindhoven. Both these central banks fitted in with the original Raiffeisen model, although they had slightly different backgrounds because of the socio-religious differences of the day (Lijphart 1968). The affiliated banks are not branch offices—although some of them do have branches—but they are legally autonomous entities working in a certain operating area. As members of the co-operative central bank they have a say in decisions that affect them all, such as investments and also automation. The members of the central banking organizations elected the board of directors and supervisory board in the same way as the local members did. Even though their structure and objective were almost identical, the two central banks differed in both organizational culture and methodology. From the beginning, CCB imposed a much stricter, more centralised form of management than CCRB. The latter was more inclined to emphasize the aspect of local autonomy. Both organizations flourished.

During what in Dutch historiography became known as the "second golden age"—the period between 1948 and 1973 the agricultural sector, the traditional domain of co-operative agricultural credit, became economically less important as a result of structural changes in the economy of the Netherlands. This period was characterised by scale expansion, mergers, and restructuring in industry, the financial sector, and the agricultural sector alike. Competition in the Dutch financial sector increased. Growth and expansion of their working areas, accompanied by the necessity to curb costs, compelled the farmers' credit banks in the direction of mechanization. But, at first, these banks were too small to make automation a real option. That would need to be a centralised service. In due course, both central banking organizations became major banks.

By 1962, with a balance sheet total of over one billion guilders (EUR 453.8 million), CCRB had become the largest bank in the Netherlands. According to the list of the five hundred largest banks in the world, published annually in the American magazine *American Banker*, it was ranked seventy-third worldwide. The smaller CCB was ranked 130th.[3] CCRB had outgrown many Dutch commercial banks. That situation changed completely because of the mergers of the four major commercial banks in 1964, giving rise to two new banks.[4] Subsequently, the merger of CCRB and CCB created the largest bank in the Netherlands, which then climbed to position forty-eight in *American Banker*'s worldwide listing.[5]

---

3. *De Boerenleenbank*, 1962, 1620–21.

4. In 1964 Nederlandsche Handel-Maatschappij and Twentsche Bank merged to become ABN and Amsterdam Bank and Rotterdam Bank merged into Amro Bank.

5. *De Raiffeisen-bode*, 1980, 8.

On 1 December 1972, the two central banks merged to form Coöperatieve Centrale Raiffeisen-Boerenleenbank. Since 1980 the new central co-operative bank, with head offices in Utrecht and Eindhoven, has been referred to as Rabobank Nederland. In subsequent years, many of the local Raiffeisen banks and farmers' credit banks also merged and took on the name Rabobank. That process resulted in a natural reduction in the number of member banks, and the inter-mergers of local banks as a result of upscaling prior to the 1972 merger merely added to the reduction.

The tasks of Rabobank Nederland were both advisory and supervisory, and the member banks had to seek permission for certain local decisions. Just as its predecessors had done, Rabobank Nederland monitored the liquidity and solvency of its member banks pursuant to the Act on the Supervision of the Credit System on behalf of De Nederlandsche Bank, the Dutch banking supervisor (Mooij and Prast 2003: 10–37). The original co-operative principles remained unaffected by the merger. In the course of time, however, it would prove necessary to modify the governance structures.[6] That applied equally to the member banks.

After the merger, Rabobank went through a period of strong growth and began to take on more and more characteristics of a "regular" commercial bank. At the same time it also gradually developed into an international player of some significance, but these international activities fall outside the scope of this chapter. The number of local member banks decreased rapidly during the 1990s. On the one hand, customers made fewer visits to the bank due to the evolution of cashless banking and automation but, on the other hand, the demand for advice and other banking services increased. It was decided that a further upscaling of the member banks was necessary to improve the quality of local services. This is a process which continues today: in November 2009 there were only 149 member banks, but each had a much larger operating area.

MECHANIZATION OF OFFICE TASKS

Up until the mid-1920s, the farmers' credit banks used hardly any form of office mechanization. The bank's cashier kept the books and conducted

---

6. In 1972 the new co-operative association consisted of five important bodies: (a) the annual general meeting of member banks; (b) the central delegates assembly, which had an important advisory role; (c) a board of directors; (d) an executive board, responsible for banking operations—although the executive board was and remains a management body, it has invariably carried out its tasks in close consultation with the board of directors although there is a clear delineation of tasks between the two; and (e) the supervisory board, charged with supervising the other executive bodies and with the appointment of the members of the executive board. This structure remained in place until it was changed in 2002.

the correspondence. Most of the farmers' credit banks had such a modest annual turnover (of loans and savings) that the purchase of a typewriter, adding machine, or calculator was not justified.

Except that they were much smaller, the work carried out at the two central co-operative banks was much the same as at any other bank (de Wit and van den Ende 2000: 87–118). Unlike the small local farmers' credit banks, however, they did have some manual typewriters, adding machines, and calculators. They also had a telephone, which was almost unheard of in the rural areas of the Netherlands before the Second World War because there were few places with the necessary infrastructure. As a result, contact between the central banks and their affiliated banks was generally carried out in writing. Compared to the urban-based commercial banks, this was all very modest. They had welcomed the first office machines (typewriters, adding machines, and calculators) around 1880. Nonetheless, despite their head start in office mechanization, even they remained primarily a manual bureaucracy until the 1920s (de Wit and van den Ende 2000: 88).

In the interwar years, larger farmers' credit banks implemented a degree of mechanization for bookkeeping and correspondence. In 1928 CCRB felt the need to warn its members against the "frivolous" purchase of expensive equipment. This would not, however, deter the larger banks from using machines for more complex calculations, and this saved their cashiers time. All this was still modest in comparison with the commercial banks, or even with the Dutch Postcheque- en Girodienst (PCGD; Post Office Giro Service), where modern American management techniques and punched-card technology were implemented during the 1920s. Attempts to combine centralisation and mechanization of processing at the rapidly growing PCGD in 1923 were, however, doomed to fail (de Wit 1994).

The mechanization of the administration and accounts at the farmers' credit banks was a gradual process, in which there was a degree of reciprocity between the administrative methods, the technical possibilities, and the volume of banking activities. The modest volume of banking activities was an especially crucial element in the decision process. For that reason, office mechanization in the co-operative credit sector progressed far more slowly than it did in the Dutch banking sector as a whole (van Oost et al. 1999).

MECHANIZATION OF DATA PROCESSING

During and after the Second World War, government interventions contributed to the expansion of interbank payments traffic. The currency reform of 1945 brought about an explosive rise in the number of bank and Giro accounts (Barendregt 1993; Sluyterman et al. 1998). Within the banking sector, the farmers' credit banks in particular benefited from a rush of new customers. Initially, the increase in banking activities gave these banks no reason to pursue further mechanization. In the early 1950s, less than 5 per cent of the farmers' credit banks, which then numbered over thirteen hundred, had even a calculator or bookkeeping machine. For most of the farmers' credit banks, the number of transactions to be recorded in 1961— savings, advances, and loans—was far below thirty thousand per year and therefore too low to justify the expense of a technically sophisticated bookkeeping machine (NLG 14,000 or EUR 6,000; see de Boer and Frankhuizen 2004: 17).

During the 1950s, the farmers' credit banks saw their cash flow gradually increase due to changes in the agricultural sector, the banks' main source of customers. In the areas with extensive market gardening, intensive use was made of interbank transfers. The rise of government subsidies to farmers, which were disbursed via the banks, also contributed to the growth on the current accounts (Zijlmans 1959: 123–42). When major customers such as the dairy co-operatives started to mechanize their milk registration systems as a way of reducing costs, a number of farmers' credit banks followed their lead and introduced punched-card technology into their back office processes. This in turn made it possible for the dairy co-operatives to deliver punched cards with the data for the settlement of milk deliveries directly to the bank; the banks could then process the data and distribute the dairy co-operatives' subsidies directly to the farmers. Manual work was thus reduced for both the dairy co-operatives and the banks, errors could be avoided and payments speeded up. On the other hand, the banks' operating costs rose. That particular factor was the cause of some local objections, but they were not strong enough to obstruct the process.[7]

The late 1940s saw the increase in interbank transactions and the growth of banking operations. The principal reason was the proliferation of stock-broking transactions. This compelled both of the central organizations to streamline their own administrative systems. They did so by installing the new punched-card machines which were designed to speed up processing. The two central organizations opted for different solutions. In the years between 1949 and 1951, CCB bought eight "modern" bookkeeping machines from the American manufacturer National Cash Register; in 1952 CCRB leased a number of Hollerith machines.[8]

Mechanical data processing called for new routines and different skills. Every bank, every customer, and every fund had to be given a code consisting of four digits between 0000 and 9999. Four separate sets of punched cards had to be maintained. This also marked the beginning of a new lexicon of technology-related jargon in the back offices.

---

7. Rabobank Nederland Archives (hereafter RNA), CCRB, Verslag van de Algemene Vergadering (Minutes of AGM), 25 May 1950.

8. RNA, CCB, Minutes of AGM, 8 May 1950; CCB, Notulen bestuursvergadering (Minutes of Board Meeting), 21 January 1960; CCRB, Minutes of Board Meeting, 13 June 1952.

At CCB, administrative streamlining was accompanied by a mechanization-tion programme, the design and implementation of which fell under the responsibility of the internal audit department. In 1959, five of the National machines were replaced by Exacta-Continental bookkeeping machines[9] with a punched tape attachment. This brought manual punch work to an end and also reduced the need for manual counting and checking.[10] Thanks to this new machinery, the processing of interbank transfers between the central organization and the member banks had been fully mechanized at both CCB and CCRB by 1962. The ongoing expansion of banking activities spurred both the central organizations to seek further efficiency improvements, and in 1962 CCB took the first steps towards automation.

THE FIRST COMPUTERS

In the early 1960s, there were less than two hundred computers in use in the Netherlands. The CCB's decision to take up automation was based on the expected growth of interbank funds transfers. In the 1950s, the number of bank accounts had almost tripled, but the turnover on current accounts had grown by a factor of five (Table 9.1). Both would grow even more rapidly in the years after 1960.

Another consideration was that, in the future, the computer could perhaps be used as a service for the affiliated banks. The local banks were

Table 9.1   Volume of Interbank Traffic via the Banks Affiliated to CCB, 1945–1970

Year	Number of accounts (* 1,000)	Turnover on current account (in millions of NLG)	Turnover on current account (in millions of EUR)
1945	15	298	135
1950	38	1,332	604
1955	63	3,064	1,390
1960	98	6,421	2,914
1965	147	14,570	6,612
1970	668	38,700	17,561

Note: No equivalent figures are available for Utrecht (CCRB).
Source: de Vries (1973: 167, table xxvii).

9. BOG Exacta Büromaschinen GmbH, later renamed Exacta-Continental GmbH, was established in Cologne in 1952.

10. RNA, CCB, Minutes of AGM, 13 May 1959; "Onder directeur Sonnenschein", *De Boerenleenbank*, 1964, 2150–51.

growing as well, and both central organizations looked for ways to improve efficiency at their affiliated banks. This led to recommendations for mechanization and automation. To reduce costs, certain routine administrative work could be carried out centrally.[11] So the first computers made an appearance before the mechanization process had been completed at the local banks. The hundreds of local farmers' credit banks were too small to take up automation independently.

With the approval of the supervisory board, the board of directors of CCB decided to lease an IBM 1440. In those days, IBM was market leader in the Netherlands (van Oost 1999: 138). Due to the great demand, there was an eighteen-month wait for delivery. In the meantime, a few employees were trained in the use of the equipment. The internal audit department made preparations for the transfer of the CCB's administrative records. The next step consisted of the automation of the savings records at the affiliated banks. Long discussions were held between the banks and CCB on this subject. In 1965, ten affiliated banks agreed to process their savings records on the CCB's IBM 360. The limited capacity of the mainframe delayed the transfer of other savings records. A new, more powerful mainframe arrived in 1966, and automation of the local banks' records could gradually be extended. At the end of that year, 635,000 savings accounts had been automated. The migration was completed in June 1967 and all the old mechanical equipment could be retired.[12] The next step would be the automation of the current accounts.

Use of computers at CCRB began in 1965 with the arrival of the latest IBM 1401. In that same year, the complete accounting records of twenty affiliated banks were being processed on this central computer. By 1968, more than forty banks had been converted. A number of local banks were reluctant to convert, but the rise of overhead costs and the substantial increase in work load compelled them to achieve greater efficiency. By 1969, the accounting records of no less than 104 affiliated banks were being processed on the CCRB's central computer.[13]

The switch from mechanization to automation progressed on much the same lines at both organizations, albeit at a different tempo and with a different organizational embedding. At CCRB, mechanization was initially the responsibility of the user, i.e. the Securities Department. In 1964 a separate Hollerith department was set up and a year later this was transformed into the Automation Department under the leadership of the former head of the Statistics Department. After the merger of the two organizations, automation became one of the directorates of Rabobank Nederland; this

---

11. RNA, CCB, Minutes of AGM, 16 May 1964; Ibid. Minutes of Board meeting, 14 December 1962; Ibid. Minutes of Supervisory Board, 21 December 1962.
12. CCB, "Annual Report", 1967, 27.
13. CCRB, "Annual Report", 1969, 33.

is a clear indication of the increased importance of automation. At CCB, mechanization was the responsibility of a special section, part of the internal audit department; this same department was initially responsible for automation but a dedicated automation section was set up in 1965.[14]

The mainframe computers ushered in a new era for agricultural credit. Automation meant more than simply the purchase of equipment; it had a profound effect on the administrative organization as well. Moreover, the first mainframe computers made specific demands on the environment in which they were used, including floor loads, cooling, and security. Special computer rooms had to be built on the bank's premises. As automation progressed, dedicated computer centres would be built.

WAGE PAYMENTS BY BANK TRANSFER

By the early 1960s, even the early forms of administrative automation were making it possible for employers to pay wages by bank transfer instead of in cash. Businesses and government alike saw opportunities to save costs on what had previously been a labour-intensive and therefore expensive weekly or monthly exercise. For the banks, automation offered an opportunity to manage the ever-growing stream of interbank transfers and administrative work. It was also known, from domestic and international surveys, that wage payments by bank had a positive effect on the average bank balances of account holders (Dankers, van der Linden, and Vos 2001; Lelieveldt 1989: 56). Through its own research, CCB knew that the West German Sparkassen had benefited from wage payments being made via the banks. According to Dankers, van der Linden, and Vos (2001), Dutch savings banks were keen to reap similar benefits. For more detailed information on the German savings banks, see the chapter by Thomes in this volume.

Dutch farmers' credit banks already had a solid savings base, but they could still make good use of the potential increase in the balances of private customers to respond to the increased demand for credit from business customers. That, of course, also applied to the savings banks and the commercial banks and it marked the beginning of the battle to attract and keep customers. In 1966, Dutch banks introduced current accounts as a way to tie customers to them.

At the end of the 1960s, banks in general became more visible when they expanded their office network. In 1968–1969, for example, the farmers' credit banks opened no less than 148 new branch offices, bringing the overall total to 2,779. That gave the farmers' credit banks the most banking offices in the Netherlands by far (see Table 9.2).

---

14. RNA, CCB, Minutes of Board Meeting, 29 September 1967.

Table 9.2   Increase in Number of Bank Offices, 1968–1969

Bank	1968	1969	Difference +/-
CCRB	1,601	1,679	+ 78
CCB	1,030	1,100	+ 70
ABN	433	474	+ 41
AMRO	571	613	+ 42
NMB	263	305	+ 42
Total	3,898	4,171	+ 273

Source: CCB, *Report of Annual General Meeting*, 28 May 1970.

Within a few years, the farmers' credit banks had captured approximately 25 per cent of the private payments market. This growth resulted in the need for new premises, and led to a general modernization of accounting records and an expansion of the workforce. Initially, these investments provided no tangible benefit to the farmers' credit banks because the simultaneous growth in the provision of services also came at a price; without automation, all this would probably never have been possible. The expansion of services did eventually lead to increased income from commission on securities transactions, insurance sales, and travel. The current account was, in fact, the main reason that potential customers went to the farmers' credit banks.[15] Initially, new account holders tended to withdraw—in full and in cash—any amount credited to their accounts. That was not due to lack of confidence, it was simply because most payments were still made in cash. This situation would change after 1967, as a result of joint action of the major Dutch banks (Peekel and Veluwenkamp 1984).

NEW PAYMENT METHODS AND INSTRUMENTS

Ever since the 1940s, the Nederlandse Bankiersvereniging (NBV), the most important interbank association, had been discussing the clearance of payments. In 1960, the major members of the NBV decided to put an actual clearing centre on the back burner for the time being, but to continue preparations and establish one as soon as technology allowed. They did, however, introduce standardised preprinted debit slips and each bank was allocated a unique code. In addition, a national account number system was introduced, one that could be used and processed by automated equipment; it also comprised built-in verification (Rudelsheim 1989: 134–50).

---

15. RNA, CCB, Minutes of Board of Directors, 26 November 1968.

Both CCB and CCBR were involved in these preparations, even though they were not yet members of the NBV (Wolf 1983: 27–32). After redesigning and modifying the banks' administrative systems, the farmers' credit banks were ready to link up to the national clearing centre by 1967.

The major commercial banks and the two central farmers' credit banks officially established the *Bankgirocentrale* (BGC) in 1967. BGC would facilitate the clearance of payments made by the customers of thirty-seven hundred banking offices across the Netherlands. Besides representing significant cost saving, the new central clearing institute for retail payments meant that the farmers' credit banks could more easily link up with the automation of banking data in the administrative systems of their business customers. The Dutch banking sector now had its own integrated and automated clearing system, alongside the one used by the PCGD. For a comparison with the situation in Britain, see the chapter by Booth and Billings in this volume. Integration of the two independent systems to form the National Payments Circuit was not actually effected until 1997 (Mooij and Dongelmans 2004: 71–73).

Efficiency drives and the new opportunities offered by automation and technology enabled Dutch banks to develop a completely new range of standardised credit transfers: standing orders with the bank, on fixed dates, for fixed amounts or for a named account, in-payment transfers (accept Giro), and automatic debits. All these originally paper-based payment instruments were suitable for mechanical processing, and the punched card as a data carrier played a crucial role in their successful introduction.

The intensive use of current accounts caused the costs of payments to rise. Dutch banks, particularly the commercial banks, looked for an alternative to curb these costs and to discourage the immediate withdrawal of all amounts credited to customers' current accounts; the solution needed to be acceptable to—and inexpensive for—both customers and businesses. It was decided that cheques and not credit cards would become the standard for domestic retail payments.[16] For this, the banks established a separate interbank firm which would introduce the new payment instrument as a national project in 1967. The new guaranteed cheque and the associated guarantee card had a uniform design, but allowed for the imprint of the name and logo of the issuing bank. CCB and CCRB were both closely involved in the preparations. Although the preparations of the new payment instrument by the farmers' credit banks took place centrally, its distribution was carried out locally.

Using the guaranteed cheques, account holders could make domestic non-cash over-the-counter payments and withdraw money from any bank.

---

16. RNA, CCB, Minutes of AGM, 6 May 1968, 6; "De ontwikkeling van het betaalchequeproject" ("Development of the Cheque Project"), *De Raiffeisen-bode*, December 1971, 12–15; Wolf (1983: 60).

Within a year the total number of cheques issued by the banks doubled: from nine million in 1968 to around eighteen million in 1969. The greatest increase was seen by the agricultural credit institutions.[17]

The increasing volume of cheques made further automation of the processing system essential. Although the amounts were usually small, the volume was enormous, and costs rose accordingly. The original cheques were not suitable for processing by means of optical character recognition (OCR). The new design, which could be used in combination with OCR equipment, was very similar to the original in terms of size and paper quality, and looked very much like the Eurocheque that would be introduced in 1974.[18] The Eurocheque would quickly replace the older domestic cheques. These cheques served as one of the main non-cash instruments in the 1970s and 1980s (Mooij and Dongelmans 2004: 77).[19] During the late 1980s, the use of cheques decreased as a result of the rise of Electronic Funds Transfer at Point of Sale (EFTPOS) payments. The rise of the cheaper EFTPOS payments combined with the high costs of processing cheque payments marked the end of the domestic cheques. Rabobank ceased issuing these cheques in 1990. The other banks followed, and by the end of 1994, these cheques had completely disappeared. The Eurocheque was phased out when the euro became legal tender in the Netherlands.

FARMERS' CREDIT BANKS AND EFFICIENCY

The surge of payment systems made further automation a serious consideration for both farmers' credit banks.[20] One innovation followed another in both organizations. In the 1960s they could hardly have been called trendsetters in the banking sector, but that would gradually change with the implementation of a major automation plan (de Boer and Frankhuizen 2004: 20).

After 1972 automation was set to take off, as reflected in the number of computers. In 1973 the Rabo organization had only six computers; five years later there were over sixty, spread around the country. By 1983 there were over six hundred. They processed not only fund transfers between the local banks and Rabobank and other Dutch banks, but they also processed various new forms of service such as home mortgages and insurance. The processing of administrative data became a 24/7 operation, in shifts, with many of the characteristics of an industry.

---

17. RNA, CCB, Report of AGM, 28 May 1970, 38.
18. *De Raiffeisen-bode*, April 1967, 19; "Het betaalchequeproject", *De Raiffeisen-bode*, November 1967, 14–15;"De ontwikkeling van het betaalchequeproject", *De Raiffeisen-bode*, December 1971, 570–75.
19. See also Bank for International Settlements (2003: 287–314).
20. RNA, CCB, Minutes of AGM, 6 May 1968.

Technical developments continually reduced the size and increased the capacity of computers. The aftermath of the merger, the explosive growth of Rabobank, the changing structure of domestic payment systems, and the rapid technological developments in both automation and communications, however, made Rabobank's automation process a very complex one (de Boer and Frankhuizen 2004: 39). Besides the automation of the large administrative systems, office automation also made an entrance and they would quickly replace the old mechanical office machines.

The downside of the increased dependence on computers was the concern about maintaining continuity of processing. Disruptions of any kind could have far-reaching consequences for services and for banking operations. A "backup centre" had to be arranged, a location where similar equipment was available so that the same processes could still be carried out.

THE MERGER AND THE MAJOR AUTOMATION PLAN, 1972–1985

After the merger, the executive board and the board of directors drew up a new automation policy. In the run-up to the merger, an Automation Working Party had been instituted. Its task was to investigate the opportunities for integration and harmonization of the automation of the two central organizations. The subsequent merger scenario included a plan for an integrated automated system, but in practice it did not prove quite as easy to integrate either the two fundamentally different systems or the ideas behind them (de Boer and Frankhuizen 2004: 27–39). Rabobank Nederland, the new central organization, kept the general managers of local banks apprised of the changes in the various administration systems in various ways. In the meantime, Rabobank Nederland was more or less being compelled—by the competition in the financial sector and by the complexity of the automation issue—to create a new automation plan.

In those days, the Rabobank organization had ten Technical Consultation Committees, made up of representatives of local banks and of Rabobank Nederland. Their aim was to deliberate on policy matters. It was a typical example of how the banks were involved in the overall policy-making. One such committee was for automation issues. In this way, the local banks were closely involved in the development of automated systems.[21]

In 1977, a daring information and automation plan was presented by the head of automation. Besides setting out technical aspects, the plan also

---

21. RNA, *Automatisering bij de Rabobank-organisatie*, 1985.

considered the possible social consequences of its implementation. The principle was that automation must not be allowed to impact on the overall number of jobs.[22] With time, of course, the nature of people's work would change, but that would be offset through retraining. It was a daring plan which made it abundantly clear that automation within the banking sector would have a significant impact on the growth of the sector in terms of job openings. The plan caused quite a stir, especially when its contents were made known prematurely on the TV news. The plan led to heated debates on automation and its social consequences; the trades unions were particularly concerned about the consequences that technological development would have on employment.

A UNIQUE AUTOMATION PHILOSOPHY

Unlike centrally managed banks, Rabobank opted for decentralised automation; this was entirely in keeping with its co-operative structure. In the Netherlands, that approach was new and unique. It meant that the systems to be developed had to be suitable for both small and larger local banks, and also for Rabobank Nederland. The designers of the plan took serious account of the ongoing developments in the domestic payments system, as agreed within the BGC.[23] Another thing that was special about Rabobank's automation philosophy was that back office processes (the administrative input processing) were included in the plan from the very beginning. It was well known that these often hindered automation. Other major Dutch banks had computers at a central location that were connected to terminals installed at the head offices by means of telephone lines. Input processing was therefore concentrated at one location. Rabobank, on the other hand, chose a decentralised approach: a network of locally installed computers to which dedicated terminals could be connected. In time, these local computers—every bank had at least one—were in turn linked to the computer centres in Zeist and Eindhoven (the latter was later moved to new premises a few miles away). Before that could all be realized, however, communication with the central computers was effected by means of a dedicated post delivery service. Every day after closing time, post vans collected diskettes with data from the local banks and delivered them to the computer centre in Zeist or in Eindhoven. There the data was transferred to magnetic tape for further processing. Data from the BGC also arrived every

22. *Rabobank*, 1984/2.
23. These innovations were aimed at reducing costs; they involved fewer loose sheets and thus less sorting. Customers would also no longer receive a statement after each transaction, but only after a certain number of transactions or a certain period of time. See further Sonnenschein (1974).

day. At night, the transactions for each bank were processed and the results transferred to diskettes again so that they could be delivered back to the local banks before opening time. The rise of telecommunications would eventually obviate the need for the special data deliveries, and they ended completely in the 1990s.

Before the automation plan was officially approved in 1978, it had been discussed at length throughout the organization. Those discussions took place at meetings of the central organization's boards, at works council meetings, and at meetings of general managers of the local banks.[24] The plan was implemented in phases between 1978 and 1985 (de Boer and Frankhuizen 2004: chap. 2). At first, implementation led to tensions within the bank organization, because the larger banks drew more benefit from the new developments than the smaller banks. The high costs made it uneconomical for smaller banks to take up the new developments.[25] Counter and cashier transactions were automated in the first and second phases. In the third phase, the computer systems of the local banks, Rabobank Nederland, and external parties were linked together. The fourth and final phase made real-time information possible.

In the 1970s, technical developments in telecommunications opened the way for the integration of computer and telephone (de Wit 2008). The result was information and telecommunication technology, or ICT. The telecom network in the Netherlands at the time, however, was not suitable for data communication between computers. That changed with Datanet-1 provided by the State-owned PTT for public use in 1982. The four largest financial service providers in the Netherlands, which included Rabobank, had been involved in the development of Datanet-1. Rabobank was also one of the first users of the network and for a long time it would be the only bank using Datanet-1.[26] In 1983, Rabobank managed one of the largest administrative systems in the world, with approximately fourteen million accounts, three million of which are private accounts. Every year, around six hundred million transactions were processed, an average of nearly 2.25 million each working day. In 1984 a trial was set up to connect three hundred banks to Datanet-1. It was an important step towards an information system through which Rabobank Nederland and the local banks were able to exchange information with each other. It marked the beginning of what became known as "customer-oriented banking". The systems that were being built not only processed data, but could also convert it into management and customer

---

24. RN Archives, Minutes of Central Delegates Assembly, 50/3–85.
25. *Rabobank*, 1984/2.
26. Ibid.

information.[27] During the 1980s, automation offered the opportunity to design new information products for business customers.[28] Information technology seemed to have less potential for private customers. Although the PTT did experiment with simple home terminals, called Videotext or Minitel, they were not a lasting success.

In June 1985 the last local Rabobank was connected to the computer network. At the end of the project, it was calculated that the automation plan had required an investment of NLG 90 million guilders (nearly EUR 41 million) for equipment and software. One door closes and another opens: Rabobank now faced new investment decisions in the domain of automation, including those for automated teller machines (ATMs).

THE ADVENT OF SELF-SERVICE BANKING

In 1982 Rabobank welcomed its first ATM. Fifteen years before, CCRB had investigated the possibilities offered by cash dispensers, as they were then called. Customers could themselves withdraw money from such machines without the aid of bank staff, using only a bank card and a secret identification number. Hardly any experience of such machines had been gained in the Netherlands, outside a few test set-ups.[29] Despite the alleged advantages—extra service for the customer, less waiting at the counter, and hopefully an increase of balances on accounts—the ATM was not really a commercially interesting proposition at the time. The limited size of the individual banks, and the correspondingly small number of account holders per local bank, would make this equipment relatively expensive and put substantial pressure on their operational costs.[30] CCB had also been interested in ATMs from the beginning. The main problem, however, was the perception that large-scale introduction of the ATM would negate the farmers' credit banks' advantage of a high-density office network.

The interbank fund transfer system worked very well, and this—in combination with guaranteed cheques and a high-density office network (one office per two thousand inhabitants in 1982)—was the main reason for the relatively late introduction of self-service banking in the

---

27. *Rabobank*, 1984/1.

28. This development is outside our scope here. In 1984, Rabobank offered businesses the opportunity to receive monthly statements. This would save them needing to keep a bankbook. Moreover, the bank could base its advice to the customer on the insights it gained from the customer's account movements (*Rabobank*, 1984/3).

29. Cf. Barclays Bank UK 1967; Philadelphia National Bank U.S. 1969; see also Bátiz-Lazo (2009).

30. RNA, CCRB, U03, Efficiency Dept., Report on Bank Note Machines (1968).

Netherlands. However, the rising costs of the retail payments systems would soon alter the situation. The plastic card which had initially been used for identification purposes would be equipped with a magnetic strip containing a personal identification number or PIN. Now, the cards could be used for two purposes: the cash dispenser (ATM) and the paying-in machine. Technically, much more was possible, but for the time being only these two applications were offered: withdrawing cash and making payments.

In April 1982, Rabobank Pey and Mariahoop in the south-eastern province of Limburg was the first to provide an ATM. Without really discussing the matter with Rabobank Nederland, the general manager of this local bank had ordered an ATM from the French firm Dassault. The reason was that the bank suffered from a severe shortage of space and customer service was not helped by the long queues. To start with, at least, it was only a trial. That same year, however, ATMs were installed at Rabobank Nederland. Despite positive reactions from customers, there were doubts at Rabobank Nederland about the impact of the machines on the relationship with the customer. That would become more anonymous, and the idea did not sit well with Rabobank's co-operative philosophy (de Boer and Frankhuizen 2004: 56–57). On the other hand, those same customers would no longer be constrained by the opening hours of banks, and service could be provided at any time and on any day. Two years later, a total of seventy ATMs were installed by Rabobank throughout the country. Via the data network at the local Rabobank, these ATMs were linked to the central computers. Rabobank was the first major retail bank in the Netherlands to draw up a long-term placement programme, and was the market leader of the day. This was only possible because of the network concept set out in the 1977 automation plan. At the end of 1985, thanks to agreements between the various retail banks, ATMs could be used by customers of other banks. Settlement was effected via BGC.

In 1987, Rabobank customers with a "euro bank card" could also withdraw money from ATMs in Spain, Portugal, and Denmark. Two years later, Rabobank was the first bank in the Netherlands to introduce the possibility of checking a current account balance via the ATM. Once again, an expansion of service was accompanied by a reduction of costs (due to fewer counter visits). In the years that followed, customer service would be one of the primary considerations when increasing the facilities available via ATMs.

In 1992 there were a total of thirty-three hundred ATMs in the Netherlands, nearly half of them operated by Rabobank (Hemelaar and Rudelsheim 1992: 122). Since then, the number has continued to increase steadily (Figure 9.1). As time went by, ATM facilities would continue to be adapted as new technology became available.

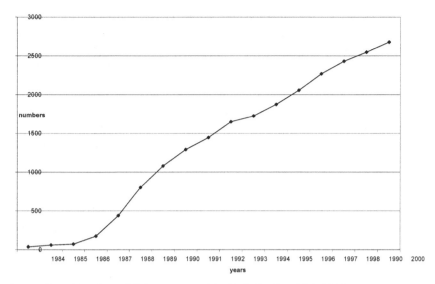

Figure 9.1   Number of ATMs operated by Rabobank, 1984–2000.

Source: Rabobank Nederland, "Annual Reports".

ELECTRONIC PAYMENTS

As in the case of the ATM, the Dutch banking sector was relatively slow in introducing electronic payments using a bank card fitted with a magnetic strip. Alongside the traditional cash register, shops and other places where payments needed to be made had to be equipped with a point-of-sale terminal (POS terminals) through which the PIN-protected bank card could be swiped. Electronic payment made it possible for banks to process large volumes of transactions very quickly. Plans had been discussed in the 1970s, but for various reasons it would be 1990 before electronic payments could be effected all over the country (Lelieveldt 1989: 34). To facilitate this new infrastructure, Dutch banks and Postbank (the former PCGD) set up a joint company, BeaNet. Its tasks would be to set the tariffs, decide on the specifications for POS terminals, and test equipment from various manufacturers. BeaNet was also an important link between the POS terminals and the computers of the participating banks (Hemelaar and Rudelsheim 1992: 142–43). In mid-1992 there were seventy-two hundred POS terminals in operation, and this number had increased to 165,000 by the end of 2001. Since the mid-1990s the use of debit cards for day-do-day retail payments has grown enormously. Most of these cards are equipped with a chip that can be used as an electronic purse.

During the years from 1989 to 1991, Rabobank was actively involved in the trial phase of the chip card. Unlike the PIN-protected card (a debit card), the chip card was a prepaid card. The chip card or electronic purse had to be "topped up" from the current account, and ATM facilities needed to be expanded once more. The same applied to POS terminals.

When it was introduced in 1991, Dutch banks had high hopes for the electronic purse. This was because the payment instrument—developed as a joint effort by the banks—was intended for small cash payments. The banks encouraged cashless forms of payment as these were cheaper, for the banks at least. A national promotional campaign was set up to encourage Dutch consumers to use the various payment methods more efficiently. It should be noted that in the Netherlands, the use of credit cards new became popular. One of the reasons may be that user costs are relatively high, especially for retailers (Bolt 2003). Despite all high hopes, and in contrast to the older debit card, the electronic purse would never become popular with consumers or with retailers.

CONCLUSION

Mechanization of administrative and bookkeeping systems was a gradual process for the agricultural credit banks. Between 1900 and 1960 there was a strong correlation between the nature and volume of banking activities, administrative methods, and technological possibilities. The first of these was of particular importance because the purchase of office equipment placed a heavy burden on the operating costs of the co-operative farmers' credit banks. As there are relatively few transactions involved in either loans or savings, the co-operative agricultural credit system was slow to implement office mechanization compared to the rest of the Dutch banking sector. From the 1950s to the mid-1970s, the increase in securities transactions and the increase of interbank transfers from businesses prompted far-reaching data automation, initially at a central level only. For a while mechanization and automation were two parallel processes because punched cards were also initially used as input for the computers. Apart from this, the capacity of the early mainframes was too small to accommodate the transfer of all the local accounting records to the centralised IBM equipment installed at CCB or CCRB. Although the end result was the same for both the central agricultural credit banks, their viewpoints and tempo were quite different in the decade before the merger in 1972.

The rise of interbank transfers by Dutch households in the 1960s and 1970s, and the accompanying growth of the volume of data to be processed, would eventually lead even the farmers' credit banks to streamline their administrative systems and turn to automation. Just like other Dutch banks, the farmers' credit banks tried to bind private customers and their balances to them by introducing a new product: the current account. The farmers' credit banks had the advantage of a large network of offices. Against the background of this growing public demand for payment services, what had once been small rural banks evolved to become modern co-operative financial services providers. The technological possibilities of the day—in combination with the need to control the costs of payment systems—led to a form of collaboration between major Dutch banks, including the two central farmers' credit banks. This collaboration also gave rise to new standardised non-cash payments products and instruments for the Dutch market. This was accompanied by a rise in the importance of banks in society: whereas people have little need for banks when payments are made in cash, they become an essential link in any cashless fund transfer system.

In 1972, expansion of services and increased competition in the banking sector led to a merger of the two central farmers' credit banks, which resulted in Rabobank Nederland. In 1977 Rabobank chose to break new ground with a daring automation plan. This put Rabobank in the spotlight in terms of automation. Entirely in keeping with its co-operative structure, Rabobank—unlike other major Dutch banks—opted for decentralised automation. This proved to have many advantages and allowed Rabobank to quickly incorporate new technologies into its own systems. As a result, Rabobank customers were able to make use of new electronic banking options sooner than customers of other banks were. This combined an expansion of service with a reduction of costs. Ever since the mid-1980s, Rabobank has been the frontrunner in the Dutch market in terms of offering new and innovative financial products and services (self-service banking), always against the background of its co-operative philosophy of serving customers in the best possible way.

Part IV

Socio-Historical Aspects of Digitalization

10 The Automated House
The Digitalization of the London Stock Exchange, 1955–1990

Juan Pablo Pardo-Guerra

INTRODUCTION

In 1971, Fischer Black, a key contributor to modern portfolio theory, published two articles that succinctly captured the imaginations of the future of corporate finance. In his assessment of the structure and operations of American financial intermediaries—from brokers and stock exchanges to over-the-counter trading services—Black concluded that, with a handful of changes, these could be:

> embodied in a network of computers, and the costs of trading can be sharply reduced, without introducing any additional instability in stock prices, and without being unfair either to small investors or to investors at large. (1971: 87)

Merely seven years after Black's articles on automation, Kenneth Garbade and William Silber provided empirical evidence connecting technology with improvements in the quality of market pricing. In their study of the telegraph and telephone in American and British stock markets, Garbade and Silber (1978) observed enhanced integration, reduced information delays, and a significant narrowing of inter-market price differentials after technological adoption. For Black and his contemporaries, technology was increasingly a handmaiden of the market, the visible skeleton of a global, invisible hand.

Illustrated by the preceding vignettes, the histories and imagined futures of finance—and particularly those of corporate finance—are written too often as triumphal sagas of efficiency, the collusion of tales of bold technological innovation and stories of decreasing trading costs, wider corporate ownership, and greater regulatory control. The subsection of this literature that deals with the digitalization of financial intermediaries and trading venues follows, indeed, the broad thrust of triumphalism. Systematic studies on the most recent wave of technological change within corporate finance approach the topic as a fundamental disruptive innovation, often leaving unexamined the nuances of technological development and its association with changing institutional arrangements. For instance, the relatively late adoption of computers and telecommunications in the securities industry is presented as the most important change in finance in the last century. Likewise, the structure of financial markets is deemed a consequence of the rise and consolidation of the (digital) information age and the technological networks upon which it is based (Cortada 2006; Castells 2000).

In presenting technology as a transformative force, however, authors have committed three omissions. First, following the basic metaphors of the neoclassical theory of production, they have presented information technologies as readymade inputs that emerge from the black box of the information age. Second, by rendering technologies as external inputs, they have tended to present financial organizations as adopters rather than developers, clients rather than designers. The financial services industry, it would seem, only embraced innovations "once it made economic sense to do so" (Cortada 2006: 187). Third, even in the rare instances when innovation is the explicit object of analysis, it has been portrayed as a linear process driven by the diverging telos of market demand or technological pull.

Examples of these omissions are numerous. Charles R. Geiss's history of Wall Street, for instance, conspicuously leaves technological change unattended (see Geiss 2004). Similarly, Ranald Michie's comprehensive history of the London Stock Exchange (LSE) mentions the proliferation of technological systems in the market almost in passing, without reference to the trials and tribulations of their development (see Michie 1999).

This chapter seeks to address these omissions by focusing on the history of the development of market information systems in the LSE between 1969 and 1992. These years bound an epoch of technological innovation within the City of London, inaugurated by the introduction of the first standardised market information dissemination system in Britain—the Market Price Display Service (MPDS)—and closed by the outsourcing of the Stock Exchange's technical services teams to Andersen Consulting.

In reconstructing the technological history of the LSE, this chapter contributes to a growing body of literature that engages with the minutiae of technological innovation in financial institutions, which is exemplified throughout this volume. Notably, it complements similar narratives that discuss in detail the development of the global communication networks that structure contemporary financial markets and serve as the material frames for economic calculation.[1] Inspired in the insights of science and technology studies,[2] this chapter stresses the co-evolution of markets, insti-

---

1. The former chief technology officer of the New York Stock Exchange provides a detailed account of the process of innovation within that organization. See Keith and Grody (1988). Similarly, Wells (2000) provides an interesting account of the adoption of computers in Wall Street.

2. Science and technology studies is a complex and illustrious tradition of intellectual engagement with the social world. An introduction to its approach in relation to the analysis of technology is given by MacKenzie and Wajcman (2003). Also see Williams and Edge (1996).

tutions, and technologies by presenting and contextualizing the often disguised innovation efforts of the technologists of the LSE.

The history presented in the following pages is the product of multiple sources. The *Stock Exchange Journal*, official publication of the Stock Exchange between 1955 and 1975, provided the narrative of early developments. Most of this chapter, however, is based on a series of interviews in the style of oral histories conducted by the author between 2006 and 2007 with former employees and members of the Stock Exchange. Internal Stock Exchange documents provided by the interviewees as well as articles from the *Stock Exchange Quarterly* were additional inputs.

The reminder of this chapter proceeds as follows: first there is a focus on the adoption of computer hardware. The second and third sections tell of the early mechanization of the LSE, the arrival of computer technology to the trading floor, and the creation of MPDS. The fourth section narrates the challenges for the expansion of MPDS. This section also helps to change the focus of the chapter from hardware to software. The fifth and sixth sections discuss the LSE fending off competition from a (failed) alternative system to MPDS, named Automated Real-Time Investments Exchange (ARIEL), and offer evidence of the role of the LSE's technical team in shaping the process of technological change as applications around MPDS evolve to create an electronic database of market prices (called Exchange Price Input Computer or EPIC). In the seventh section the LSE's technical team are given a mandate for the planning and development of new systems while being renamed the Special Systems Group (SSG). The eighth, ninth, and tenth sections tell of the travails of SSG to overcome the limitations of MPDS to respond to new requirements by users, the emergence of alternative providers of price information (such as Reuters and Datastream), and the loss of internal capabilities with the outsourcing of technological services to Arthur Andersen. The last section offers the conclusions to the chapter.

ANALOGUE DAYS ON THE FLOOR OF THE HOUSE

Throughout its history, the LSE has provided the largest and most important centre for dealing in British bonds and equities. Between its foundation in 1801 and "Big Bang" in 1986, the basic mechanism for making markets in the Stock Exchange changed little, providing a stable institutional reference for market practitioners and investors alike.

Although admittedly an idealization, the basic market mechanism of the Stock Exchange can be seen as constituted by three elements. The first was a division of labour known as single capacity. Formalized in 1909, single capacity separated the membership of the Stock Exchange into two groups. Stockbrokers provided advice to investors and took their orders to the market for execution. Conversely, jobbers acted as market-makers, buying and selling shares from brokers and profiting from the price differential between bids and asks. Under normal market conditions, brokers were prohibited from buying or selling shares on their account, whilst jobbers were not allowed to deal directly with investors.

The second element was thoroughly material. The business of creating a market occurred in a restricted space, the trading floor of the Stock Exchange. Located in a building that had undergone numerous alterations since its erection in the mid-nineteenth century (and known by the membership as "the House"), the trading floor was the physical centre of liquidity for the British securities market. On the periphery of the floor, brokers had "boxes" that served as a pied-à-terre, providing communication with their offices and the world at large. As orders arrived to the box, brokers or their authorized clerks took them to the trading floor. There, they would search for the best price available, walking from jobbing pitch to jobbing pitch. In effect, the process could be laborious: prices were seldom explicit, and brokers had to approach jobbers individually to obtain a quote. Only the most active shares were marked on whiteboards, and often the written prices differed from those ultimately provided by the jobbers.

The third element was intrinsically regulatory. The Stock Exchange not only defined the rules and regulations of its membership, it also acted as a trade association, a provider of settlement services, and a listing authority. The different roles occupied by the Stock Exchange transformed it into an undisputed point of passage for corporate information, having disclosure requirements that often exceeded those of the government.

With its large trading volumes, restricted admission, and privileged access to corporate information, the prices created on the floor of the Stock Exchange were valuable commodities in themselves. Indeed, for non-members such as merchant banks, access to Stock Exchange prices facilitated buying and selling shares without paying broking commissions or incurring in search costs.

COMPUTERS IN THE STOCK EXCHANGE

As such, the Council of the Stock Exchange—which since 1947 controlled the rules, regulations, and institutional policies of the organization—was not keen on mechanisms, technological or otherwise, that could reveal its prices to either domestic or overseas competitors. Such leaks could result in market fragmentation (namely, the emergence of alternative trading venues and the subsequent reduction in liquidity) and could potentially reduce the perceived quality of the prices of bonds and shares. Whereas the Exchange avoided the fragmentation of the market during the nineteenth century despite the introduction of the telegraph, telephone, and transatlantic cable in London, the digital technologies of the 1950s and 1960s presented a novel suite of challenges for the organization. Theoretically, they made practical the dissemination of prices off the trading floor of the Stock Exchange in real time, thus facilitating the consolidation of markets outside of its organizational and regulatory reach.

In the United Kingdom, the risk of fragmentation was enhanced by the fact that, by the 1940s, London and the provincial exchanges had established a stable division of labour within the market for bonds and shares.[3] Indeed, rather than seeking to expand its reach or compete with the provinces, the Stock Exchange's foray into computing responded to two broad incentives: first, the perceived economic benefits of rationalizing operations in the back office; second, as a mechanism to manage innovations within the marketplace in order to avoid the unregulated dissemination of information off the trading floor.

Computers thus entered the Stock Exchange through settlement, an area that was particularly amenable to technologies of record-keeping and arithmetic calculation. The adoption of computers in settlement followed trends initiated as early as 1949, when the Stock Exchange acquired Hollerith punched-card equipment to reduce the labour requirements of matching trades conducted on the floor. Effectively, settlement was a labour-intensive process that required considerable numbers of skilled personnel. It was, nevertheless, an activity that could be initially mechanized, subsequently computerized. Hence, the Stock Exchange purchased its first computer in 1966—an International Computer and Tabulators 1903—for use in the Settlement Department. This marked the beginning of an organizational trajectory that built in relation to the adoption of digital technologies for their use in and around the marketplace.[4]

Shortly after, the Council of the Stock Exchange introduced computing to other operational areas of the organization. For the Council, computers and modern telecommunications could be used to create—and, more importantly, control—a market-wide price and company news dissemination system. The proof of concept existed as early as 1956, when a handful of broking firms introduced a rudimentary service that recorded the prices on the trading floor with a conventional camera and transmitted the images to television screens in their offices. The system, however, depended on the state of the whiteboards on the floor, provided an unreliable service and, more importantly, was only accessible to a minority of

---

3. Although dominant, London was not the only financial centre in Britain. Since 1836, it had shared the market for British securities with exchanges in Birmingham, Manchester, Liverpool, Cardiff, Bristol, and Glasgow, among others. Provincial stock exchanges, however, tended to specialise in raising capital for, and trading shares in, regional companies. See further Thomas (1973).

4. A brief description of the Stock Exchange's early automation efforts in the Settlement Department is provided by Keen (1966).

firms. Whereas large firms were able to finance such systems, small firms could not afford the high costs related to installing and maintaining even the most rudimentary electronic price information systems. For the Council of the Stock Exchange, such imbalance was dangerous, as it could lead to an erosion of confidence within the organization and, in an extreme case, to a fracturing of the membership. A system sponsored by the Stock Exchange would provide not only higher levels of technical reliability and uniformity in the visualization of market prices; such a system would also guarantee both institutional control and the equality of access to all member firms—or at the very least, to those willing to pay for a subscription.

In 1969, the Council of the Stock Exchange announced the introduction of a new price and company news dissemination service based on state-of-the-art British computing. Developed jointly by Ferranti, the computer manufacturer, and the Stock Exchange's Computer Services Group (*Stock Exchange Journal*, 1970a), MPDS was designed to broadcast the middle prices of approximately 650 stocks (out of approximately two thousand traded shares) on sixteen black-and-white channels through closed circuit television within the City of London. Subsequently, the design was expanded by adding four channels, two featuring the prices of new issues, special stocks, currencies, and commodities, and two dedicated to company announcements and other relevant pieces of information.[5]

MPDS consisted of two broad elements: first, the visualization system that took the shape of a coaxial network that transmitted images to a number of black-and-white television screens; second, an information capturing and processing system composed of input terminals located on the trading floor of the Stock Exchange that were linked to a central computer. Data from the floor would be processed by the computer only then to be distributed to the screens in the network.

The development of MPDS ensued in a planned and careful fashion. The service initially operated on a restricted number of channels (sixteen, solely for prices) and during a limited period in the day (from 9:30 to 15:30). As testing and debugging continued, and as the suggestions from the users were compiled and analyzed, both the number of channels and the time of operation expanded. By the time it was formally introduced in early 1970, nearly one thousand MPDS television receivers were operating in 220 offices of member firms, the result of seventy thousand hours of work by 250 engineers. In October of the same

---

5. The development and operative scope of MPDS was a matter of several articles in the *Stock Exchange Journal*, including "House Notes", *Stock Exchange Journal* 14, no. 1 (1969), and "House Notes", *Stock Exchange Journal* 15, no. 1 (1970).

year, the service reached 145 member firms and twenty-two institutions, including press agencies, insurance companies, an arbitrage house, and merchant banks, who were reportedly very satisfied with the operation of the price and news announcement channels of MPDS.[6]

MPDS was an immediate success. As Margaret Hughes reported in the *Stock Exchange Journal* in 1971, in little over a year, the city's brokers became a group of "push button devotees" (Hughes 1971). Success came despite the odd fact that the service was more an instrument of convenience than a tool for trading: as the former broker Scott Dobbie recalled, the service was "extremely crude"[7]; the mid-prices displayed on the television screens of MPDS were useless for dealing and the floor remained the undisputed source of market prices. MPDS was neither the result of technological push nor the product of a pre-existing market demand. Technological change derived, rather, from an organizational imperative to provide equality of access to market services to all member firms.

MPDS GOES TO THE COUNTRY

The development of MPDS had two consequences. First, it demonstrated that investments in sophisticated technological services were profitable: soon after its introduction, MPDS became the source of a secure income stream for the Stock Exchange. In 1970, the annual subscription to the service was £500 for members and £1,000 for non-members (members were the predominant users of the system, although some merchant banks and institutional investors were early subscribers). Additional television receivers were charged at £50 each, per annum, and subscribers covered both the equipment and the installation costs. The costs of developing and maintaining the system were recovered in little time.

Second, MPDS introduced a standardised mechanism for collecting and processing quotes from the jobbers on the floor. To keep the prices on MPDS "as fresh as possible", the Stock Exchange devised a system whereby price collectors would update the computer of MPDS throughout the trading day according to a preset routine.[8] The standardization of price collection made MPDS a source of reliable information.

The system was limited, nonetheless, and in 1973, its technical specifications were tested by a reorganization of the British securities industry. In particular, the amalgamation of the LSE with provincial exchanges

---

6. See "Stock Exchange Information Computerised", *Accountancy* 81, no. 924 (1970); also "House Notes", *Stock Exchange Journal* 20, no. 4 (1970).

7. Scott Dobbie, interview with author, London, February 2008.

8. Ian McLelland, interview with author, York, October 2007.

(which created the Stock Exchange of Great Britain and Ireland) entailed guaranteeing access to the services offered in London across the regional financial centres of the United Kingdom. MPDS was no exception. Nevertheless, based on a coaxial distribution network that was limited to the City of London, the expansion of the service in its existing design was prohibitive.

The eventual solution to MPDS's expansion came from the development of remote data entry terminals for settlement. Although the introduction of computers in the 1960s reduced the labour requirements of the Settlement Room, checking remained physically centralised. Before feeding data into the 1903 (replaced in 1973 by an IBM 158) for batch-processing daily and fortnightly accounts, the details of the deals struck on the floor had to be checked and ordered by specialized clerks (Grimm 1977).

In order to decentralize the scrutiny of individual tickets (whereby the trades conducted on the floor were matched in order to settle the accounts between buyers and sellers) and to reduce the number of clerks working in settlement, the Stock Exchange designed an electronic system that allowed each firm to report bargain details (that is, the details of trades) from their offices. Larger firms possessing computerized management systems of their own could enter the information of the bargains by sending their magnetic tapes and punched cards directly to the Stock Exchange Computer Centre on Wilson Street. For firms that could not afford investments in computing, the Stock Exchange developed the equivalent of a banking terminal that connected their offices to the Stock Exchange's dedicated settlement computer.

With checking and reporting decentralized, the Stock Exchange reduced the costs of settlement services. However, the new system required examining and processing inputs before submitting them to the central computer. This intermediate step involved validating data so as to maximize the use of the dedicated computer. A Digital Equipment Corporation (DEC) PDP-11/40 minicomputer hosted the validation processes by providing a flexible architecture to the remote data entry system.

Designed by the Stock Exchange in co-operation with Logica, a firm of computer consultants, the expansion of MPDS—known as Country MPDS (cMPDS)—used the remote data entry architecture of settlement to overcome the obstacles of space. Whereas the original design of MPDS relied on a distribution network of coaxial cables, the verification system used in settlement that used PDP-11s could transmit signals through conventional telephone networks. By installing a PDP-11/40 in each of the regional centres, the Stock Exchange could distribute digital feeds from its Argus 400 (the computational core of MPDS) across the country via dedicated telephone lines. In each regional centre, the PDP-11/40s would transform the digital feed of the Argus 400 into an analogue signal that could be distributed to the local users, "creating the so-called fairness with everybody seeing the same thing".[9]

ARIEL

A critical event overshadowed the introduction of cMPDS in 1974. In the early 1970s, the growing body of British institutional investors showed clear signs of discontent with the restrictive practices of the LSE. Their inability to access the market other than through a stockbroker together with the fixed commission structure established by the Council of the Stock Exchange were increasingly objects of resentment.

Challenging the centrality of the Stock Exchange, a select group of merchant banks known as the Accepting Houses Committee proposed in 1971 creating an alternative electronic trading platform based on the architecture of Instinet's bloc-trading system. The threat was real and imminent. In May of 1972, the Issuing Houses Association (formed by members of the Accepting Houses) announced the introduction of the computerized dealing system ARIEL, providing "an inexpensive efficient trading market which will transcend National boundaries". The seventeen merchant banks that initially subscribed to ARIEL found inspiration in the fragmented markets of the United States. If Americans had managed to compete with technology, so could British firms. The system, set for introduction in 1974, was envisioned to capture 10 per cent of the institutional business, equivalent to 4 per cent of the total equity market (Littlewood 1998; Kynaston 2002).

Opposition to ARIEL did not take long to emerge and consolidate around a common discourse. For the Stock Exchange, ARIEL was simply "incompatible with the established methods of dealing in securities in this country". By ignoring the separation of functions that defined securities dealings in London, they argued, ARIEL jeopardized the fairness of the market, reducing "the effective establishment of fair prices", and avoiding the regulatory disciplines "which are imposed on the members of the Stock Exchange in the interests of the whole securities industry".[10]

Although ARIEL subsequently failed to command much influence on the market, it catalysed the consolidation of the Stock Exchange's information services. In effect, as Dundas Hamilton, former deputy chairman of the Stock Exchange, wrote, ARIEL led the Council to press for the development of instruments that would obtain "the maximum advantage in the distribution of dealing information to institutions [by creating] a system which instantly recorded prices at which deals

---

9. Michael Newman, interview with author, London, November 2007.
10. Council of the Stock Exchange (1973).

took place and a further communication system through which brokers could inform institutions of their interest in lines of stock" (Hamilton 1986: 5).

THE EPIC MARKETPLACE

The computer that fed the screens of MPDS, however, was not an adequate platform upon which to erect new, sophisticated services. Whereas the Argus 400 could handle the mid-prices on a limited number of shares, its architecture made further expansions technically undesirable. Critical, however, was the fact that the analogue signals sent to the MPDS television receivers across the country could not be processed by in-house computer systems. In a sense, they "were only used on that system. They could not be put to any other use".[11] With views to expand the repertoire of services offered by the Stock Exchange, both the Council and the technologists deemed that time had come to upgrade the system.

The upgrade of MPDS became an independent project involving the replacement of the Argus 400 with a PDP-11/70 from DEC.[12] The new computer allowed for a critical innovation, namely, the construction of an electronic database of market prices. The project, initially labelled EPIC, was a joint financial venture between the Stock Exchange and Exchange Telegraph, a long-standing provider of information services of the City of London.

Although Extel & Co. participated in name (the "E" in EPIC referred indistinctly to Extel & Co. or the Stock Exchange), the ultimate design of the system was in the hands of the Stock Exchange's technical team. Given their experience in managing and maintaining MPDS, the organizational template for EPIC came from the known and tested collection protocol of MPDS, where current prices were entered from the market via price input terminals on the edge of the trading floor. The system, however, went further than MPDS. As the project evolved, other types of information (including company announcements and, later on, regulatory news) were added to the service, leading to is renaming as EPIC. EPIC incorporated such elements as market-related news items and headlines, and specialised programmes that managed official publications requiring accurate and up-to-date data.

---

11. McLelland interview.

12. By the mid-1970s, the engineers and technologists of the Stock Exchange had developed a strong commercial relationship with DEC. The previous mash-up of IBM, International Computers and Tabulators, Olivetti, and Ferranti systems took a new shape: whereas IBMs were used primarily in settlement, DECs were used mostly in real-time market applications (Newman interview; Peter Buck, interview with author, Dartford, September 2007).

Particularly important to EPIC's design was the ability to create malleable data feeds for the press, a task that had been impossible under the architecture of the Argos 400. EPIC, for instance, facilitated the production of the *Stock Exchange Daily Official List* (SEDOL)—containing the official prices of all the securities in the market. In effect, guaranteeing the smooth production of SEDOL was not merely an issue of internal bureaucracy. All tax, probate, and portfolio valuations carried out in the United Kingdom referred to the prices in the *Official List*. Before EPIC, maintaining the list was a laborious task, involving record-keeping of thousands of shares. EPIC, however, automated the production of SEDOL and facilitated other editorial tasks, such as the creation of the *Weekly Official Intelligence* (WOI), a collection of company announcements and news deemed relevant for the market (Buck 2008).

EPIC went online in 1977 amid little pomp. For the users of the Stock Exchange, the introduction of the system was surreptitious: EPIC did not transform the screens of MPDS nor the quality of the documents published on a daily and weekly basis by the Stock Exchange. Everything seemed to be the same.

At the level of infrastructure, however, EPIC embodied a change in the role of information technologies within the Stock Exchange. In particular, EPIC demonstrated that digital data feeds could become the core of the financial marketplace. EPIC was able to gather within a single computational unit the different inputs from the floor—from prices to company announcements—moulding them into data feeds that reached distant corners of the British Isles through cMPDS and overseas countries through the distribution networks of Extel. Centralisation of services and information, it seemed, could be achieved through the computer.

SPECIAL SYSTEMS GROUP (SSG) AND BEYOND

The development of EPIC was correlated to a significant organizational innovation within the Stock Exchange, that is, the creation of a specialized group charged with the planning and development of new systems. Established circa 1977, the SSG was constituted by a few dozen technologists that, for all intents and purposes, defined the Stock Exchange's technological policy for the next fifteen years. The creation of SSG responded to an internalization of the technological efforts at the Stock Exchange: whereas MPDS and cMPDS were built in co-operation with external service providers (Ferranti and Logica, respectively), the development of EPIC—the cornerstone of the new suite of services offered by the Stock Exchange—was driven almost in its entirety by internal staff.

The SSG was not the first division of the Stock Exchange to deal with market technologies, though. The acquisition of punched-card equipment and computers for settlement in the 1960s, for instance, had led to the creation of the Computer Services Group (CSG), which took part of the development of MPDS and survived until roughly 1971.

The expansion of settlement and market information services in the early 1970s encouraged the establishment of the Directorate of Information Systems and Settlement (DISS), headed initially by Michael Jenkins and subsequently by George Hayter. As a directorate, DISS had more freedom and resources than its predecessor, the CSG, and enjoyed a dedicated channel of communication with the Council of the Stock Exchange in Patrick Mitford-Slade, the chairman of the Information and Communications Committee.

In 1979, and only two years after the establishment of the SSG, DISS was rebranded as Technical Services (similarly, the Information and Communications Committee became the Technical Services Committee). Finally, in 1984, a splinter of the SSG headed by Peter Bennett established a small, blue-skies research team, the Advanced Systems Group (ASG).

Whereas the organizational diagram of the Stock Exchange changed considerably from 1970 to 1992, the core group of technologists and engineers behind the development of the Stock Exchange's systems remained relatively stable. At its apex, technology in the Stock Exchange was commanded by two individuals: Peter Bennett, who joined in 1971, and George Hayter, hired in 1976 from the British Overseas Airways Corporation to lead DISS. In addition to Hayter and Bennett, innovations were driven by John Scannell, in charge of systems operations (engineering) and who joined from Olivetti circa 1972; Michael Newman, hired in 1975; Ian McLelland, seconded from Logica in 1975; Peter Cox, hired from IBM in 1979; and Peter Buck, trained at Imperial College London, and who joined in 1979.

The success of the innovations of the early and mid 1970s provided the SSG and DISS the undivided trust of the Council of the Stock Exchange. The technologists "could do no wrong. I mean, they gave me more or less a carte blanche to automate everything inside", recalled Bennett. Indeed, for Patrick Mitford-Slade, the process was "definitely bottom up", with ideas coming from people who "knew what technology was available", particularly, the Peter Bennetts and George Hayters of the world. Built upon trust, the systems of the Stock Exchange thus continued to expand.[13]

---

13. Patrick Mitford-Slade, interview with author, Hampshire, November 2007.

Table 10.1 History of Market Information Systems at the London Stock Exchange, 1968–1992

	1969–1970	1974–1975	1979–1980	1985/6–1992
Systems	Market Price Display Service (MPDS), 1969–c. 1980			
		Country MPDS (cMPDS), 1974–c. 1980		
			Exchange Price Information Computer, 1977–c. 1992	
			Teletext Output by Price Information Computer (TOPIC), 1980–c. 1992	
				Stock Exchange Automated Quotations (SEAQ), 1986–1990s
Technologies	Ferranti/Olivetti/DEC		DEC	
Departments	Computer Services Group, c. 1966–1971			
	Directorate of Information Services and Settlement (DISS), 1971–c. 1979			
			Special Systems Group (SSG), c. 1977–c. 1984	
			Technical Services Department, 1979–c. 1990	
People	Peter Bennett			
	John Scannell			
	Michael Newman			
	Ian McLelland			
	George Hayter			
	Peter Cox			
			Peter Buck	

A TOPIC OF CONVERSATION

The expansion of finance in 1970s Britain provided the Stock Exchange with an incentive to replace MPDS.[14] The old system was marvellous "as far as it went", recalled Mitford-Slade. "It only had twenty-two pages of information, and it was really just listing the shares on those twenty-two pages with an up-to-date market price on it". The growth of data services—from Reuters to Hoare and Govett's Datastream—provided strong incentives for the modernization of MPDS. Effectively, what the Stock Exchange needed was a system capable of dealing with "an unlimited amount of information".[15]

The SSG was particularly aware of the technical limitations of MPDS and had considered as early as 1975 "moving the system forward".[16] There were, nevertheless, important technical roadblocks to overcome. Increasing the number of channels was prohibitive due to the architecture of the system. The twenty-two channels already "squeezed every available bandwidth [...] so much so that the gap between [them] started to get almost blurred." MPDS was "absolutely at its limits".[17]

Pressure to expand the system only increased with time. As new instruments entered the market, users of MPDS demanded more from the service. For instance, when the Stock Exchange introduced traded options into the floor, SSG had to implement a time-sharing system on the channels in MPDS. The data displayed on the screens would switch every ten seconds between market sectors, allowing for the visualization of the prices of traded options while keeping the system at twenty-two channels. However, "people really didn't like it, because if you were trading you didn't want the bloody thing to switch on to the other page when you were looking at the stock prices".[18]

The replacement of the visualization systems of MPDS came as a serendipitous confluence between real-time computing and Prestel, the data-dissemination standard developed by the British Post Office. Prestel was a "marriage of industries, technologies, processes and skills" in "telecommunications, the telephone, the computer, and publishing".[19] A service that integrated colour television, conventional telephone lines, dial-up modems,

---

14. From the mid-1960s onwards, the financial services sector in the City of London grew both in volume of trading and in the complexity of operations. The consolidation of Eurobonds, for instance, represented the emergence of a new market and new financial actors that required ever-expanding information services. See Michie (1999) and Kynaston (2002).

15. Mitford-Slade interview.

16. John Scannell, interview with author, London, November 2007.

17. Newman interview.

18. Ibid.

19. For an example of the promissory language surrounding Prestel, see Fedida and Malik (1979).

and digital computing, Prestel provided a bidirectional interactive video-text system for the delivery of information.

Prestel, however, did not meet the technical requirements of the Stock Exchange. The architecture of the service made updating pages both slow and expensive. To meet user specifications, Bennett and the SSG adapted Prestel's design, making it "formal and reliable".[20] The system developed, and known as Teletext Output of Price Information by Computer (TOPIC), utilised EPIC as the source of market data. Whereas EPIC was the source of information—from prices to company regulatory announcements—terminals built by the Belgium electronics manufacturer BARCO served to navigate, access, and visualize the digital repository of the central computer. Connected to colour television screens, the terminals allowed users to update the information on their screens at will.

For the Council, TOPIC "was quite an investment to launch into [requiring] quite a lot of persuasion", recalled Mitford-Slade. To convince the Council of the need of the investment, Mitford-Slade found inspiration in a well-known slogan for Heineken. "TOPIC", he assured, "reaches parts MPDS cannot reach". Trust in the SSG and the DISS, however, was strong, leading to the ultimate approval of the project. "In fairness to them", mentioned John Scannell about the Council, "we'd got the proper documentation. They were quite confident we knew what we were doing. Their own firms were suffering because they'd really needed this equipment for their business, so it was very interesting times".[21]

Introduced in 1979, the only restriction to the number of pages available in TOPIC was the storage capacity of EPIC. Soon, the twenty-two channels on MPDS became several hundred pages on TOPIC. The sixteen channels of prices moved to a "magazine" of one hundred pages; the four channels for company news and announcements became more than one hundred pages; and pages for indices, currencies, and traded options proliferated throughout the new system.[22] TOPIC was "ahead of anything that Reuters was running at the time",[23] providing a completely novel service for the market. Introduced in 1980, TOPIC was an immediate success. Within two years, the four hundred terminals initially authorized by the Council grew to more than five thousand.

CHANGE AT THE EXCHANGE

The digital ambitions of the technologists did not stop with TOPIC. In 1979, what initiated as a relatively innocuous review of the settlement

---

20. Peter Bennett, interview with author, London, July 2007.
21. Scannell interview.
22. McLelland interview.
23. Bennett interview.

mechanisms for government-issued debt transmuted into a unique opportunity to standardize and integrate the mash-up of systems run by the Stock Exchange. Conceived by George Hayter and Peter Bennett, the plan envisioned reassembling the heterogeneous networks of market information and settlement systems under a single technological umbrella, creating a general purpose network to replace those in place.

In May 1982, the Council of the Stock Exchange embraced the strategy of an integrated data system for the British securities industry. A year later, in 1983, the upgrade in settlement effectively became the first step in the ambitious development of an Integrated Data Network (IDN). As George Hayter announced, the IDN was set to have "a widespread impact on the working of the Securities Industry over many years" (Hayter 1983). Based on the growing communications method of packet switching, IDN responded to the "proliferation of networks" within the Stock Exchange which, in the views of the Technical Services department, resulted in "high cost, inflexibility and inconvenience to service users". Offering a unique communication platform, IDN would permit the interoperability of the existing systems at the Stock Exchange, providing "faster, easier and cheaper communications" for the UK securities industry through the use of "a common data network operating to a set of recognized international standards" (Hayter 1983).

With its forward-looking design and its overtly strategic intent, IDN became the flagship project of the Stock Exchange, acknowledging the importance of owning and controlling the principal communications facilities used for business in order to facilitate the Stock Exchange's regulatory control over the market and its member firms. Standardization meant not only a more fluid, efficient, and reliable operation of the marketplace; it symbolized too the centralisation of services and the possibility of real-time surveillance.

IDN would have been a tremendous technological feat had it come to fruition. On paper, the system made a cost-effective use of the most sophisticated systems available at the time. The plans integrated the "IBM personal computer, or one of its look-alikes [as] the basis for [a new] terminal system". Brokers, jobbers, and clients of all types should have been able to use a single terminal, or a limited range of terminals, for a multiplicity of functions. Finally, IDN would have freed users from the costs and time involved in building and maintaining their own communications networks by providing a common dealing, settlement, and market information platform (Hayter 1983).

Times were difficult, nevertheless. Since the challenge of ARIEL in the early 1970s, the Stock Exchange had been under great political pressure to open its markets, reform its membership, and alter fundamentally its organizational structure. In effect, in 1974 the *Rules and Regulations* of the Stock Exchange became an object of governmental evaluation, following complaints from users in the City of London that considered fixed commissions, closed membership, and other practices uncompetitive. In 1978, the organ in charge of the review—the Office of Fair Trading—identified seventeen restrictions to competition and referred the Stock Exchange to the Restrictive Practices Court. Several years of negotiation eventually led to an agreement between the chairman of the Stock Exchange, Sir Nicholas Goodison, and the secretary of state for Trade and Industry, Cecil Parkinson, to bring the court case to a halt. Reached in 1983, the agreement created a nonnegotiable deadline: the court case would be dismissed if and only if the Stock Exchange "[dismantled], by stages and with no unreasonable delay, all the rules which at present prescribe minimum scales of Commissions, and to complete this dismantling by 31 December 1986" (Michie 1999).

The political realities of the 1980s cooled the technological ambitions of IDN. The network in its complete incarnation would have to wait, if not be completely forgotten. On account of time, the efforts of the Stock Exchange shifted to pragmatics. The deadline on 27 October 1986, known as Big Bang, was less than two years away, and implementing an integrated data network was too risky a route to follow. Indeed, the market of the future was terra incognita for the Stock Exchange. Big Bang implied more than the removal of fixed broking commissions. It encompassed abandoning single capacity, allowing firms to act as brokers and market-makers, and opening the membership to foreigners and banks. For Hayter, there was "a wide river to be crossed and time only to build a Bailey bridge initially". Time was scarce for blue-sky innovation. The Stock Exchange needed a system delivered in time for Big Bang. However elegant and ambitious, IDN was not the Bailey bridge to cross the turbulent waters of a market in constant reform.

With hindsight, the technological trajectory of the Stock Exchange was fixed years before Big Bang with the selection and design of TOPIC and EPIC. In late 1984, Hayter presented London's newest bridge. Initially code-named SEMANTIC (for Stock Exchange Market and Trade Information Computer) and later known as SEAQ (for Stock Exchange Automated Quotations), the system implied a modification of TOPIC and EPIC that allowed the bidirectional distribution of bid/ask prices (quotations) from either the trading floor or the offices of member firms. Whereas SEAQ served as a mechanism for capturing quotations and reporting deals, a modified version of TOPIC enabled the visualization of market prices. Under the version of SEAQ introduced ultimately for Big Bang, competing market-makers (formerly known as jobbers) were required to keep continuous quotes for the securities in which they traded. Rather than being uttered on the floor, these quotes were entered into SEAQ terminals. Upon seeing a satisfactory quote on the screen, a broker would phone a jobber to close the deal.

Such radical transformation of the market's structure entailed some modifications to the systems of the Stock Exchange, however. The PDP-11/70s that served as computational core of EPIC, for instance, were replaced by VAXes, also from DEC. EPIC was also transformed: in the new arrangement, the database would be subjected to a constant influx of quotations and trades, putting great strain on the system. Existing technologies—such as relational databases, which are at the core of well-known programmes such as Microsoft Access—were simply too slow. As Peter Buck, development manager for SEAQ, recalled:

> We talked to [to several vendors], and the new version of Oracle [was] coming out [soon] and they could guarantee on a VAX 80–600 [. . .] an average of a transaction a second, on a good day, with a trailing wind. [. . .] One transaction a second was where it was at.

Experience in developing systems, however, provided the technologists of the Stock Exchange with the instruments necessary for finding a solution. In particular, by transforming EPIC into a memory-resident database, the system introduced by the Stock Exchange could handle more than one thousand transactions per second, "a little bit more than Oracle".[24]

Yet from an engineering perspective, SEAQ was "not exactly rocket science", recalled Peter Buck. "It was it was just TOPIC and EPIC brought together. [The system was] two legacy systems [put] together essentially, which was actually quite a safe route".[25] As Hayter explained in December 1984, in arriving at this design, the Technical Services department:

> had to face up to a number of practical problems. Firstly, we have a short time scale in computer developments [which] will not allow us to build radically new services from scratch with any degree of confidence that they will work effectively and reliably under high volumes of loading from the first day of the new market. Secondly we have a fundamental uncertainty about the real requirements of the system. [. . .] Finally we have little idea about the absolute level of trading which is likely to take place and the consequent level of system activity. (Hayter 1984: 23)

SEAQ responded to the constraints faced by the Stock Exchange, basing the platform of the future market on "solid and reliable systems", and adopting a "low-risk implementation plan". For technologists like Hayter, Big Bang had become a series of "scarcely discernible pops".[26]

BEYOND REVOLUTION

On 27 October 1986, the harmony of planning gave way to the cacophony of reality. Thirty minutes into Big Bang, TOPIC was overloaded with a

---

24. Buck interview.
25. Bennett interview.
26. *Guardian*, 3 April 1985.

"tidal wave" from users. Then standing in one of the operations rooms, the chief of engineers, John Scannell, recalled the scene:

> Eight o'clock comes and the systems all come up. And we're look-ing at the page response request and it goes up to 1.7 million almost immediately, which is a little bit bloody worrying. Then it crept up to sort of two million, three million, and four million. What's go-ing on? This is quarter past eight. Then it got to five million, then everything is going berserk. Bells, and whistling, and ringing, and popping and banging.

It took some clever on-site programming, a restart of the system, and bring-ing the government-debt market off-line to establish order. Dealers in the government securities were not amused. "'It's the government's market, you can't take it off the system', they said. But we said 'You've been dealing perfectly satisfactorily without the system for god knows how many years, you can continue without it for a little bit longer' and of course they did, to satisfaction".[27]

As the trading day came to a close, the chairman of the Stock Exchange reflected on Big Bang. "The fact that the system worked at all this morn-ing was a triumph", said Sir Nicholas Goodison.[28] As the days followed, normality kicked in. Glitches continued to surface from time to time, but SEAQ remained the core of the market. "So much for being a Bailey bridge. It was still there some years later".[29]

With Big Bang behind them, the technologists of the Stock Exchange continued their relentless expansion into the market. Indeed, investments in computing and telecommunications were essential: catalyzed by the introduction of SEAQ, dealings in bonds and equities went off the floor in March 1987, transferred to the dealing rooms of member firms and their rows of telephones and screens. As Ian McLelland remarked:

> It was literally while one release were being developed, we got the programmers working on that as soon as we could, the designers would be looking at what are the next stages, and you either had like a major requirement coming or we had what we called change requests which would drive us. Then we said, "okay, what's the next release going to look like" and start designing that. And we could even have three releases on the go. You know, once we'd got a release into testing whereby we were supporting any fixes that had to be done, we'd probably have a team working on the next release and the designers working on the release after that, so it was kind of like a

---

27. Mitford-Slade interview.
28. *The Times*, 21 October 1986.
29. Buck interview.

continuous cycle because this is what the Exchange and its membership demanded.[30]

The Stock Exchange was more than ever before a technological marketplace. While Hayter and his team concentrated on expanding the
repertoire of services offered to the membership (which including the
development of a small order automated execution system, SAEF, in
1989[31]), Bennett's team—the Advanced Systems Group—sought to
enlarge the technical horizons of the organization, experimenting with
artificial intelligence, satellite communications, and the possibilities
offered by the personal computer.

Expansion, however, came at a price. The initially compact group
of technologists had grown into a veritable army. George Hayter alone
commanded over two thousand people (out of three thousand Stock
Exchange employees) responsible for specifying, designing, developing,
implementing, managing, and selling systems to the membership of the
Stock Exchange. Organizationally, the Technical Services department
was experiencing the problems of scale: whilst the technological services provided by the Stock Exchange continued to generate revenues,
margins decreased by the year and were pushed to the limits in times
of crisis.

The technological culture of the Stock Exchange was likewise com-
promised. The interim Bailey bridge, recalled Ian McLelland, became the
cornerstone of future systems. Services that departed too much from the template of SEAQ "would not be developed; we would build on the existing limited capability due to time pressure". The growth of the technical staff also
presented problems. Developers spent much more time in meetings, updating designs, reporting developments, and involved in "all the bureaucracy of
big organizations". Critically, the "rapid development culture" of the Stock
Exchange was "lost". "Developers were no longer allowed to develop without a long process of approval. For many [. . .] it was time to move on".[32]

The crash of October 1987 and the ensuing reorganization of the
securities industry marked the beginning of the decline of the Stock

---

30. McLelland interview.

31. The development of SAEF was a symptomatic of problems faced by the technologists of the Stock Exchange. Inspired by IDN, SAEF was built as a compromise
with SEAQ. Given their investments in the lead up to Bog Bang, member firms were
unwilling to install systems that deviated from SEAQ. The design of SAEF was thus
subordinated ultimately to SEAQ. This, however, presented technical problems that
translated into a long development cycle. Programmed to go live in 1987, SAEF was
only introduced in 1989, despite similar products developed by member firms in a
matter of weeks—notably, BZW's small order automated execution system, TRADE
(Nic Stuchfield, interview with author, London, November 2007).

32. McLelland, personal communication.

Exchange's Technical Services department. Expenditure continued to increase while income fell from 1987 onwards (see Figure 10.1). In late 1989, the Stock Exchange incurred its first loss.[33] Tensions mounted, and the autonomy of the technologists became a liability. For the new Stock Exchange, development was not a priority. For them, Bennett recalled, large investments in innovation were "not the way to run an exchange".

The *coup de grâce*, however, came in 1990. With mounting pressure from member firms to reduce expenditure, the spiralling cost of technological development, and the continuing influence of the technologists on the Stock Exchange's policies, Peter Rawlings, the chief executive, commenced a two-year process of outsourcing. "In a funny way", reminisced Hayter in 2007:

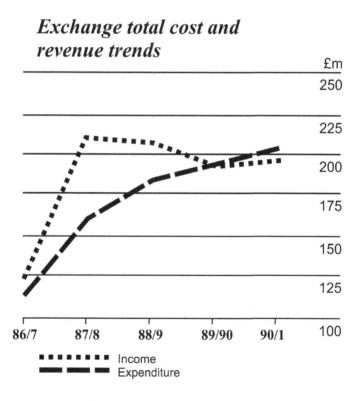

Figure 10.1   Stock Exchange expenditure vs. revenue, 1986–1991.

---

33. Scannell interview.

the Big Bang which everybody said was going to rid us of the club mentality and make the whole thing more commercial ended up coming full circle to the point where the members were saying "We don't want the Stock Exchange to do commercial things. We want it to just be the place that coordinates the regulation of the market, and not very much else".[34]

The ranks of the Technical Services department were slowly depleted. In April 1992, *The Times* reported that an agreement was reached between the Stock Exchange and Arthur Andersen whereby latter would "run the exchange's market support systems" and take on the "312 exchange staff".[35] The exodus began, and soon enough the original members of the SSG had left.

CONCLUSIONS

With hindsight, the images heralded by Fischer Black and his peers in the 1970s seem prophetic. More than two decades after Big Bang, the LSE is one among many competing electronic marketplaces, providing execution facilities to investors located in every corner of the world. Indeed, a cursory glance at the Stock Exchange might seem to confirm "traditional" views on technological change in finance, presenting innovation as a process driven by the market and fuelled by the pervasive yet ultimately alien emergence of modern information and telecommunication technologies.

Upon closer examination, however, the smooth road that created the digital present reveals many pebbles and particles from the past. Above all, the history of the Stock Exchange demonstrates that technological change in finance involved armies of individuals, batteries of things, and centuries of work-hours, shaping the marketplace through the everyday politics of the trading floor, the Council chambers, and Britain at large.

The history presented in this chapter provides three specific lessons on technological change in modern finance that highlight some omissions encountered in accounts of the digitalization of financial institutions.

The first is relatively straightforward: to be effective in day-to-day operations, technologies (particularly large-scale, sector-wide systems) require implementation (Fleck 2003: 244–57). Although based on components that were commercially available at the time, the market information services introduced by the Stock Exchange were implemented to meet the specifications of the Council. In the Stock Exchange's technological history, there were no such things as off-the-shelf solutions. MPDS involved adapting the

---

34. Hayter interview. Gloucester, November 2007.
35. *The Times*, 12 April 1992.

Ferranti Argus 400—initially designed for use in missile control—to process and transmit data from the market floor. To make the Argus 400 an operational piece of financial technology, however, the Stock Exchange had to transform the computer, design new organizational routines, and adopt additional systems including coaxial cables and television receivers.

Importantly, the fact that technological systems require some degree of implementation makes their origin relevant. Because it involves working with external providers to reconfigure devices for specific uses, implementation entails forging commercial relations that can affect future decisions within the firm. For instance, whereas the first information services introduced by the Stock Exchange involved different providers—including International Computers and Tabulators, IBM, Olivetti, Ferranti, and DEC—the market information systems launched after 1977 relied primarily on DEC minicomputers. As Ian McLelland recalled, the Stock Exchange's technical teams "worked very closely [with DEC] particularly on the technology changes". On the contrary, IBM systems, widely used in Wall Street, were deemed too "rigid" and "hierarchical",[36] explaining their ultimate confinement to settlement where batch-processing was seen as the technical norm. These path dependencies in the technological trajectory of the Stock Exchange were not the product of some inherent technical quality of the system; rather, they originated from the networks of relations formed between the Stock Exchange's engineering teams and particular technology suppliers.[37]

The second lesson is equally simple: technological adoption creates new types of work—for instance, routine maintenance. In providing market information services, the Stock Exchange hired computer and telecommunication engineers that guaranteed the reliable operation of its systems (perhaps recognizing that the implementation and use of technologies requires local, tacit forms of knowledge). Yet as demand for the systems grew, and with it the pressure for increased reliability, the number of technologists climbed. Decisions to update systems only accelerated the process, leading the Stock Exchange to increase the size of the Technical Services department and expand the expertise of the organization, hiring analysts, programmers, managers, developers, and support staff. The work associated with the market information services transformed the Stock Exchange into a centre of technological innovation. Growth was not inconsequential, though, as Figure 10.1 demonstrates. By the early 1980s, recalled Bennett, technologists "were effectively setting policy".[38] In a very tangible way, the sheer size of the Technical Services department implied a deep modification the organizational politics of the Stock Exchange facilitated, in part, by the income streams generated from the provision of market information services.

---

36. Newman interview.
37. A sociological analysis is provided by White (2002).
38. Bennett interview.

Innovation was nevertheless a rocky enterprise. Despite the armies of technologists, updates to the Stock Exchange systems often departed from plans. That technological change is not a smooth linear process is the third and final lesson. The technological trajectories of the Stock Exchange were as much products of organizational imperatives, economic justifications, and technological design as they were reactions to external political pressures and the fixed investments of users. Notably, the deadline set by Big Bang altered the plans for the Stock Exchange's IDN, transforming EPIC and TOPIC into the unexpected core of the new market. A regulatory decision "locked in"[39] the systems at the Stock Exchange, making SEAQ the obligatory—and in some people's opinion, suboptimal—referent for market participants. The road from floor to screen, from the analogue stock exchange to its modern digital incarnation, was indeed technological. Yet, as other technological histories, the digitalization of the LSE was a product of sweat, blood, electrons, and artifice.

---

39. Processes of lock-in can be conceptualized in line with David (1985).

11 Historicizing Consumer Credit Risk Calculation

The Fair Isaac Process of Commercial Scorecard Manufacture, 1957–circa 1980

Martha Poon

> The invention of a new financial tool and its introduction into the commercial world may sound boring, but it is hardly that to those who are trying to do it. (Lewis 1992: xi)

INTRODUCTION—INSTRUMENTS AS THE CARRIERS OF RISK INTO MANAGEMENT

Financial institutions are highly specialised in risk management. This observation has become so taken for granted that the origins of the tools, models, and expertise being used to do the managing have largely been obscured. This chapter seeks to demonstrate that the rise of calculated risk information in consumer finance—as in other financial sectors—is not the result of any spontaneous or necessary shift brought on, for example, by the advent of digital infrastructures. As computing historian, James Cortada, has emphatically pointed out that "the most important story about computing is its applications, not its technological evolution" (2006: xi). Following this assertion, this research examines the earliest application of computing to the problem of calculating consumer credit risk. It begins from the observation that financial managers cannot do their work without being equipped with specialised risk management tools. The argument is that credit managers have the ability to conceptualize and act upon particular kinds of risks because of specific and often commercially developed instruments whose material histories can be traced and told.

Treating risk computation, a derivative of computers, in historical perspective is an extension of a research objective laid out by business historian, JoAnne Yates. Her research on the insurance industry has amply demonstrated that in order to understand "how today's businesses adopt and use computers requires us first to understand how these businesses used yesterday's information technologies" (2005: 1). Similarly, in this chapter I will suggest that to understand how the finance industry adopts and uses risk calculation requires us first to understand how financial institutions have used yesterday's risk management devices. The sheer physical space that early machines occupied—discussed by both Ian Martin and Hubert Bonin in this volume—has given historians a striking entry point for narrating the important organizational work that has supported the introduction of computers into banking. The effort involved in raising calculation, generally thought of as a theoretical function black-boxed inside of machines, proves to be somewhat more opaque. Respecting that financial risk assessment has been developed as a distinct application of computing requires that we disentangle calculation, and give it a separate but analogous history to the history of business computing.

Just as the history of computing cannot be separated from the description of machines, the history of financial risk calculation cannot be separated from the design and implementation of particular risk management devices. To demonstrate that risk calculation practices have situated histories, this chapter considers the early development of a device called a "scorecard", a centrepiece of risk assessment in consumer finance.[1] In its most generic description the scorecard is an algorithm that allows managers to associate the likelihood of a defined event, such as default, with the profile of a consumer. Scorecards work by placing input in relationship to a record of proven outcomes. The device compares information on an individual case to empirical patterns found at the level of a population, captured from an accumulated archival source.[2] By standardising information requirements (set questions with a defined selection of answers), passing these data through a problem-specific algorithm, and expressing an output on a numerical scale, this technology provides managers with probabilistic information upon which to make operating decisions. Funnelled through scorecards, credit accounts are treated as units of a greater population which allow managerial intervention to occur at the level of the aggregate portfolio. When fully digitized, the use of scoring in account management gives rise to a form of batch-processing that facilitates economies of scale by mechanizing the execution of executive policies for credit control.

---

1. This contribution is an adaptation of the first chapter of the author's dissertation on the history of commercial credit scoring. The research traces the transformation of credit quality into a piece of information expressed through numeric scores by a company called Fair Isaac. This project differs from previous studies of credit scoring in that it gives consumer default risk calculation a specific history, rather than treating it as a terrain on which to explore broader themes such as rationalisation (Guseva and Rona-Tas 2001), digitalization (Leyshon and Thrift 1999), or governmentality (Marron 2007). For a general summary of the technology's evolution, see Poon (2007).

2. These kinds of techniques fall into a category of tools that Stephen Collier has named 'statistical-archival'. Collier (2008) demonstrates that this is only one among a number of categories of calculative rationality for treating risk.

Scorecards were first introduced into consumer finance in the late 1950s through the commercial initiatives of the firm Fair, Isaac and Company Incorporated (Fair Isaac).[3] Given their ubiquitous and proliferating application within today's sophisticated electronic environments, it may sound implausible to trace the origins of this device to a single firm. Yet, the scorecard could not have, and indeed did not spout up spontaneously from within the credit industry. This is because the problem-framing and problem-solving approaches at the heart of risk assessment were completely unfamiliar to consumer financiers of the post-war period. To build the original scorecards—a relatively simple technology, initially designed to capture the risk of consumer default when screening credit applications—Fair Isaac acted as a second-party technology provider, adapting techniques from the field of operations research.[4] Traditional credit managers would collaborate in the process of scorecard development, but they did so from their position as technology customers.[5] So although finance companies had to provide the technical team with access to the field, and their staff would contribute domain expertise about the intricacies of lending, the tool was essentially conceived of, executed, and delivered by Fair Isaac.

What is remarkable is that the scorecard was innovated prior to the widespread use of computers and digital infrastructures in business. The metaphorical term "data mining" is increasingly being used to refer to an infinite number of creative searches taking place in air-conditioned cubicles that seek to harness the information content of vast electronic repositories of electronic information. As the chapter will describe, however, to carry out a statistical analysis of a consumer finance operation the Fair Isaac team's first objective was to compose the very pools of data that the proliferation of data mining

---

3. The company changed its name to the Fair Isaac Corporation in 2003. In March 2009, it publicly rebranded to the simple acronym FICO. I conserve the original (and legal) company name, Fair Isaac, to emphasize the historical nature of this research. Whereas other methods and firms can provide credit analytic solutions, Fair Isaac has dominated the U.S. marketplace for quantified consumer-level credit information since 1957, a position that went unchallenged until at least the early 2000s. In 2004, Fair Isaac had made the *Forbes* list of Top 200 U.S. Small Companies ten times in the previous eleven years. It placed nineteenth on the Business 2.0 ranking of the one hundred fastest growing technology companies in 2003; it was named one of the top two hundred IT companies globally for 2002 by *BusinessWeek*; and until recently all of the top ten *Fortune 500* companies are reported to have relied on some kind of Fair Isaac technology.

4. Operations research was introduced to business enterprise as a science for executive decision making in the 1940s (see Herrmann and Magee 1953; Horvath 1948). In science and technology studies, the history of the field has been discussed by Fortune and Scheweber (1993) as well as by Mirowski (1999).

5. Early Fair Isaac preferred the term 'customer' over 'client' when referring to the purchasers of scorecards. The company felt that 'customers' involve a simple one-time transaction whereas 'clients' imply a repeated, long-term, and open-ended engagement. I have conserved this convention in this text.

presupposes. In the late 1950s, data, a prerequisite for getting an empirical hold on what had transpired in the past, had to be extracted out of a morass of idiosyncratically kept administrative records that were not predestined to support statistical analysis. The image of Fair Isaac personnel digging through paper records does resemble the act of panning for gold in quite a literal way. But to describe credit scoring as a simple case of "data mining" is to beg the historical question because the very conditions of unlimited consumer data that are often presumed to be driving practices of quantified managerial techniques were not yet in existence.

Drawing on oral histories and company memoirs, this chapter will record the unique arrangement of technology manufacture which was required to make early credit scoring technology possible. I use the word "manufacture" not only to underline that scorecards are part of a commercial enterprise,[6] but also to emphasize that the rise of consumer risk calculation has involved a genuine process of product innovation and commercial technology production.[7] Focusing on the manufacture and delivery of instruments is a useful empirical method for narrating the situated labour behind the rise of risk management and new information technologies in the financial industry. As the chapter shows, quantitative consumer credit risk assessment was not spearheaded by either an abrupt or a spontaneous shift towards calculative control. Although statistical credit scoring would dramatically transform what was happening in manual underwriting, the existence of statistical scoring was never completely alien from a manual setting.[8] It was a physically demanding manual environment, not a fluid

---

6. Whereas numerous historians have studied the histories of corporate research laboratories within firms (for an excellent review see, Dennis 1987), very few have discussed how specialised firms provide scientific and technological products to client industries. One notable exception is Geoffrey Bowker's (1994) study of how Schlumberger had established a form of information infrastructure among oil companies through the production of its geophysical information. Another is JoAnne Yates's (2005) study of how tabulation technology was adapted to the insurance industry.

7. This is the meaning of manufacture as it is used in Knorr-Cetina (1981), a foundational work in the sociology of science. Based on a year-long study of a government-funded (and not industrial) biochemical research centre Knorr-Cetina sought to show that "what happens in the process of [scientific] construction is *not* irrelevant to the products we obtain" (5). Beyond the title, however, the term *manufacturing* is invoked metaphorically in this work to refer to science as a generative act.

8. Mary Poovey has written extensively about the historical processes that led to the separation of narrative forms of knowledge from more privileged numerical representations of facts. The description in this chapter of the transition from written records, capable of capturing more complex narratives, to quantitative information, can be read as an ethnographic response (that is, an account of how an equivalent separation has occurred in financial practice) to what Poovey has observed by examining literary genres (see further Poovey 1998).

digital environment that furnished the raw materials for the first score-cards, a past that marks their design and construction to this day.

INVENTING A DEVICE FOR ASSIGNING
AN ODDS OF DEFAULT

Credit scoring technology was developed at Fair Isaac, which began as a two-person firm founded by William R. Fair and Earl J. Isaac in 1956. The business plan the partners devised upon leaving the employment of the Stanford Research Institute (SRI) was to set up shop as independent computer consultants who would apply operations research techniques to civilian problems. Some projects would involve assisting firms to install and utilise computers, but others, like credit scoring, would involve executing computation on behalf of firms who did not have access to a computer of their own. In 1957, Fair Isaac began to do concerted work on what it called "the credit granting problem", the specific problem of "account origina-tion" or "client selection" in consumer finance. Bill Fair unhesitatingly gives credit to the company's first scientific employee who was also from the SRI, "a gentleman by the name of Earl Follett" (Fair 1991) for having introduced the idea. When Follett joined Fair and Isaac he had already done work on the potential usefulness of multivariate statistics in consumer credit screening. Eventually, the more general goals of computer consulting would give way to a tight specialisation in credit scoring tools, which were only one among many of the company's first projects.

In a memoir written in 1977, Fair recorded how he and his partners had originally formulated the credit granting problem. The trio's initial instinct was that "a competent analysis of the large number of factors appear-ing on a credit application would permit the construction of an accurate odds quoter of the applicant's future payment behavior [*sic*]" (Fair Isaac & Company Incorporated 1977). The general premise was that with access to a rich source of data, it would be possible to statistically summarize the known behaviour of previous borrowers in support of forward-looking decision making. Insofar as an imprint of the past was captured by the kinds of information that were being conserved within a lender's adminis-trative records, the assumption was that a pattern of performance could be mapped, and then used as a guide to future credit granting action. In keep-ing with the principles of operations research, scorecards were presented as a means of using quantitative analysis of performance data to quickly and mechanically replicate the choices that had previously been made by a lending operation.

In its original conception the tool would be a simple aid "used by a credit grantor in deciding which risks he would be willing to accept and which he would prefer to reject" (Sawyer c. 1992). Assisted by way of statistics, the Fair Isaac team suggested that a credit organization might not only replicate its previous set of choices, but might further control and reduce the rate of loan defaults. Armed with a summary of their own past experience represented through integers printed on a card, credit managers would be able to use this information to avoid originating the kinds of accounts that had already led them to a negative experience, while pursuing more of the ones that resembled those known to have resulted in acceptable repayment outcomes.[9] In comparison to the sophistication of today's quantitative risk management practices the purpose of the original scorecards was modest in the extreme. With increasingly mechanized data capture, credit scoring tools have been adapted to assist in a number of complex credit management tasks.[10] Through to the mid-1970s, however, the utility of cardboard scorecards was limited solely to the problem of account origination, that is, to assisting in a decision framed as a binary question of whether to originate a loan or not.

To launch its initiative, Fair Isaac sent letters to fifty of the nation's top consumer credit lenders, a range of both banks and finance companies. The communication not only explained the concept of quoting odds, but it also solicited "[the lender's] views as to how it would operate in practice" (Sawyer c. 1992). In an oft-repeated story, only one firm, the local subsidiary of the fourth largest finance company in the nation, bothered to respond. For its first scoring job, Fair Isaac was received by the Public Finance Company of Missouri which operated under its parent company, American Investment.[11] The team arrived on location not as product vendors—because no product had yet been developed—but as "specialists in mathematics and in the use of electronic computers".[12] By 1958, the world's first commercially produced "odds quoters" for the prediction of consumer default had been developed and installed. One odds quoter was put in place for screening clients in Public Finance Company's home base of St. Louis and its sur-

---

9. To emphasize the modesty of the original scorecard, it is worth mentioning that decreasing default is a distinct goal from increasing returns or widening profit margins, even though the latter are a heavily implied result of the former. This is to say, it is one thing to show that the tool decreases default, as Fair Isaac strived to do from the outset; it is a separate proof to show that (and how) the tool serves to increase revenue which may or may not, depending on the operating costs consumed by managing the increase in revenue, result in greater profits.

10. These tasks include, among others, account management, line limit changes, revenue projections, marketing response assessments, and segmented pricing strategies.

11. Several reports published at that time named American Investment Company as the fourth largest operation in the nation. See Cottle and Mickelwait (1959) as well as A.L. Kraus, "Scoring System Begun on Credit", *New York Times* (9 July 1961), F1.

12. See Zaegel (1962). The author of this trade journal paper was listed as the director of research at the Public Finance Company of St. Louis, Missouri, which was presumably a regional arm of the American Investment Company.

rounding areas. Another was developed for use in the neighbouring state of Louisiana, which was deemed to be a distinct population of borrowers and therefore merited a separate statistical analysis.[13]

By 1969, Fair Isaac had engineered seven geographically distinct odds quoters covering the American Investment Company's eight hundred operations nationwide. Buoyed by this initial success, Fair Isaac formed a subdivision called The Risk Evaluation Corporation (TRECORP) which focused exclusively on promoting the sale and production of these credit granting devices. TRECORP was eventually reabsorbed back into the parent company. So although they continued to dabble in a number of other types of consultancy projects throughout the 1960s, gradually, the major offering of Fair Isaac was a specific product solution, a table of statistically derived points embedded in a stiff sheet of cardboard that served as an on-site calculating tool for probabilistically sorting applicants for consumer credit. The complete product, which "included the credit scoring table and the voluminous statistical information necessary for its effective use" (Lewis 1992: 8), was subsequently renamed a "scorecard". If the odds quoter was the bold initial "idea" for the technology, the scorecard could be considered the pragmatic outcome of its progressive material realization.

Making the first scorecards would prove to be a tedious and physically laborious proposition. It is important to recognize that, unlike consultants, early Fair Isaac was not in the business of selling disembodied intellectual analysis or theory-based scientific expertise. Instead, their value proposition was deeply anchored in their mastery of the material world. In the Fair Isaac method, analysts culled credit data from paper files at finance field offices; transported the contents of these documents to Fair Isaac's specially equipped central office; processed the raw materials into digital data through multiple sequential stages; and then deployed expensive computational machines adapted to credit scoring which the customer had neither the means nor the skill to own. As Bonin points out, mechanization cannot work if it is not accompanied and supported by the very functions that Fair Isaac performed on behalf of their customer: data processing, streamlining, and standardisation (see Bonin in this volume). Finally, Fair Isaac delivered a refined analytic product back to the scorecard customer in a tangible, practical, and useful form. As with all technical projects, scientific efforts would have been useless unless the findings could actually be taken up by consumer financiers and put to use (Oudshoorn and Pinch 2005; Yates 2005).

---

13. In a previous publication, I misreported that the city of St. Louis in question was located in Louisiana. What should have been reported has been restated here. It was also misreported in that piece that the nationwide system was a single comprehensive scorecard when in fact it involved geographical segmentation (see further Poon 2007).

THE SCORECARD DESIGN FOR DELIVERY
AND IMPLEMENTATION

The first credit scoring devices were to be deployed in small towns and in rural America, often at the point of sale. This meant that clerks positioned at the retail level would be required to calculate credit scores by hand. For this reason, the tool's final presentation had to be simple enough to be adopted by people with no knowledge of statistics and no access to calculating machines. In addition to performing statistical analysis, then, Fair Isaac had to engineer a stand-alone tool to make results relevant to the everyday practices of lending operations. The choice of an appropriate statistical method as well as the table format for delivering the outcomes were both worked out "in the field" through an experimental process of trial and error. Fair Isaac would, moreover, change the name of the tool such that it pointed to the two most obvious features of the technology's manual design: the numerical *score* output and the physical *card*. Instead of providing an intimidating description of what the device was doing—that is, calculating an empirical likelihood of default for a prospective credit client—calling the tool a scorecard presumably helped to render it familiar by associating it with the point systems in various sports.

The original credit scoring systems were carefully constructed so that responses provided by a credit applicant to a series of questions could be quickly situated according to the differentiating categories embedded on the printed card (Table 11.1). Applicants' answers, assessed either face-to-face or from a written form, were classified on a table of point distributions representing the statistical assessment of the algorithm. For each of the possible answers to the questions, the algorithm assigned a numerical figure that contributed towards the calculation of a likelihood of defaulting. In simple terms, the scorecard worked as a kind of mathematical analogy. The statistical formula determined which people an applicant most closely resembled from among the base of clients with whom the lender had already completed dealings in the past. The algorithm or model then calculated a probability of default—a numerically expressed estimate of the odds that a person of these qualities would repay a loan—according to how the groups represented in the algorithm were already known to have behaved. This is how past experience drawn from archival data was communicated forward as an aid in ongoing decision making through the final score.

The statistical content of the scoring apparatus was strongly shaped by practical considerations and was intimately linked to the easy-to-use form of the tool's final presentation. Trying "to minimize the error of the people doing the scoring" turned into "a big consideration when we developed a scorecard",[14]

---

14. Interview A by author with retired Fair Isaac employee, a first-generation analyst and senior executive, 22 June 2004.

Table 11.1 "The Example Bank—Scorecard", 1977

CHARACTERISTICS	ATTRIBUTES				
Years on Job	1 yr to 4.5 yrs 30	Less than 1 yr 35	4.5 to 12.4 38	12.5 or more Retired 52	
Finance Company	Any 0	None Listed 22			
Department Store	None listed 10	One 15	Two 23	Two or more 26	
Years at Address	Less than 3.5 Not Ans. 30	3.5 to 7.49 38	7.5 or more 42		
Bank Account	No Bank 10	Savings Only 20	Check Only 28	Check and Save 34	
Total Income	Less than $600 30	$600–699 42	$700– 1,199 47	$1,200 or more Not Ans. 59	
Worst Bureau Rating	None 16	No Rating 5	One derog -13	Two or more -40	
No. Inquiries (6 mo.)	None or One 10	No Record 7	Two -2	Three -4	Four or more -10

Notes: This example scorecard has been reproduced from a newsletter called *Viewpoints*, distributed by Fair Isaac from 1977 onwards. The purpose of the newsletter was to communicate information on best practices to scorecard customers in lay terms. The point values are representative of actual results, although the table is probably a composite rather than a faithful presentation of a single empirical case. Sample scorecards were frequently used as teaching tools in the newsletter, but it is unclear whether the visual presentation of these tables is similar to the scorecards that were being employed by clerks in day-to-day retail transactions.

Source: *Viewpoints* I, no. 2 (Winter 1977): 3.

recalled one senior executive. Doing addition *in situ* was possible, but spur-of-the-moment multiplication proved to be somewhat problematic. What is more, the team soon also discovered that in a manual environment, "the fewer attributes you had [in the model] the easier to score".[15] It was only when the number of questions remained manageable—ten to twelve was found to be ideal—that the points associated with each response could be reliably summated by hand. The key consideration in design, therefore, was neither statistical

---

15. Ibid.

nor technical sophistication. It was that "the form of the model had to be simple enough that somebody could just ask a question look up something write down a single number write down the question look up something write down another number at the end of which, draw a line and add it up".[16] For the tool to work in the manual setting, statistical complexity had to yield to the demands of the existing business environment.

Although credit scoring changed the working routine for the clerk, the final system did not look or feel substantially different from what the consumer was used to experiencing. As the *New York Times* explained when reporting on the novel use of scorecards at American Investment Company, "A prospective borrower is asked the familiar questions about his age, marital status, whether he owns or rents a home, how long he has been on the present job, whether he has a telephone, and the like".[17] In one basic version of the tool the user made reference to a permanent laminated copy of the table. They recopied the appropriate point values and performed the addition on a separate sheet of paper. In another, stacks of disposable tables were printed up and the calculations were done directly on a fresh page for each applicant. The kinds of things that counted in a scorecard were transparent because the applicant clearly knew what questions they were being asked, although to preserve the efficacy of the system users were advised not to advertise the exact point values associated with each of the possible answers.

If the table has been the main calculative aid for some forty-five hundred years of human history (Campbell-Kelly et al. 2003: 1), then it should come as no surprise that the original Fair Isaac scorecard is also an enduring technical form. When pressed as to whether rudimentary manual scoring systems continued to be relevant today, a senior credit scoring analyst enthusiastically responded, "Absolutely. They were scoring by hand in '85. They were scoring by hand in 1990! And I bet there are some still scoring by hand in some other countries".[18] From humble beginnings, the scorecard has been passed down and globally diffused through generations of specialised credit scoring practitioners that have been trained at Fair Isaac. What is more, despite the loss of one of its two key features through digitalization[19]—the physical card— numerous internal and taken-for-granted features of scorecard algorithms

---

16. Interview B by author with former Fair Isaac employee, a career analyst and current industry entrepreneur, 9 September 2005.

17. A.L. Kraus, "Scoring System Begun on Credit", *New York Times*, 9 July 1961, F1.

18. Interview C by author with former Fair Isaac employee, a career analyst and product innovator, 31 January 2007.

19. There are moments in digital scoring where the scores have also disappeared. For example, software can be hardwired to carry out score-based policies such that the only output a retail agent using computer relationship management (CRM) software might see is a final decision to offer a product, accept or reject an application, or seek additional information with regard to a client. For an ethnographic study of the use of CRM in Hungarian retail banks, see Vargha (2009).

continue to be inherited from the original Fair Isaac methods of design and production. "[I]t is kind of ironic isn't it", marvelled a current credit scoring innovator and intellectual legatee of the company, "that the most sophisticated credit decisions these days are easily made based on a model form that started from a small finance company in the South".[20]

THE PROCESS OF SCORECARD MANUFACTURE (c. 1960–1980)

At the core of this chapter is the claim that it is meaningless to treat the rise of consumer risk management as a spontaneous event or an intellectual discovery. Some readers may be puzzled by the emphasis on acts of physical labour at the expense of statistical formulas in this account. Indeed, formulas, rules, and theorems are obvious ways of capturing what it means to do risk calculation. But these are not the only languages through which to communicate how statistics have been put to use in the evaluation of consumer credit risk. To think about score calculation in terms of commercial manufacture is to focus on the daily activities that were carried out at the company which brought the first credit scoring tools into being, and to render these movements palpable and visible. Captured here are the deliberate but ephemeral gestures and the organizational routines behind innovation that are distilled out of esoteric formulas, and are seldom if ever admitted into the records of scientific and technological achievement.[21]

COLLECTING SAMPLES FROM CREDIT OFFICES

As late as the mid-1970s digital information infrastructures did not routinely exist in financial institutions. In technical terms, the "performance [of a loan] was on ledger cards as opposed to on an automated accounts receivable".[22] What this means in practice is that Fair Isaac worked with paper records. "A big part of projects was actually getting the data into the model. You know, 80 per cent of the task was that a lot of what was coming [was] on paper and had to go through data processing and so on".[23] When a scorecard contract was signed, a team would be sent out to collect the data for statistical analysis.

---

20. Interview B by author with former Fair Isaac employee, a career analyst and current industry entrepreneur, 9 September 2005.

21. For an account of how science is turned into written text through the selection of modalities see Latour and Woolgar (1979). See also Knorr-Cetina (1981).

22. Interview D by author with a career Fair Isaac employee, a first-generation analyst and senior executive, 9 September 2006.

23. Interview E by author with a retired Fair Isaac employee, a first-generation analyst and senior executive, 5 September 2004.

Their job was to bring it back and concentrate it in a single location, the centre of calculation (Latour 1987), the place where analytic activity was concentrated—just north of the San Francisco Bay, in the city of San Rafael (Marin County). Just as grain, livestock, and timber once poured into Chicago from rural areas through waterways and railroads, to be processed and shipped back out again, boxes full of raw credit data poured into San Rafael by parcel post from remote parts of the country to be analysed, mulched, and returned to customers as finished scorecards.[24]

The key scientific and organizational figures in the process of producing a Fair Isaac scorecard were called "analysts". Once a contract was made with a finance company (the main type of scorecard customer along with mail-order outfits and some retail firms), the primary task of the analyst was to figure out how best to constitute a sample of cases on the ground which could be used to build a predictive statistical model. Scientists and project managers all in one, analysts were accorded by far the most prestige in the hierarchy of production. This was not only because of esoteric textbook knowledge achieved through higher education—early analysts were required to have or nearly have attained a PhD in either engineering or operations research—but also because they were responsible for numerous strategic decisions that would affect how sampling was to be done.[25] A practical and cost-effective means of case selection was achieved by an imperfect method of cluster sampling, usually by selecting a few offices deemed representative of the overall operations of the finance firm through close consultation with management.

Because the goal was to statistically differentiate the past performance of both "good" (consumers that had repaid more or less consistently and in full) and "bad" borrowers (consumers that had a record of disrupted repayments or of failing to repay in full), analysts selected consumer files which had a lengthy enough history from which to extract two "snapshots" of data. These snapshots were used to establish a statistical relationship between characteristics assessed at the moment of application (first snapshot) and an outcome of default or repayment some time later (second snapshot). The data had to come from closed (and not current) credit accounts, so drawing a statistically adequate sample required digging deep into storage spaces to assemble defunct files from lists generated in co-operation with the scorecard customer. One of the old guard described it this way: "[I]n those days, every shopping centre [*sic*] had a loan office, and you'd go in and get an instalment loan [. . .]. They kept everything on little cards, all

---

24. As Cronon (1992) has shown, the city and the rural have been inextricably connected through industrialization by the continuous traffic of raw materials and produced goods passing back and forth between them.

25. There are several prominent female analysts and executives in Fair Isaac history but they do not appear until the 1980s.

handwritten".[26] To access these files, analysts visited suburban strip malls to locate and copy ledger cards as well as application forms that had (hopefully) been conserved. Where there was no archival record, there could be no scorecard.

In July 1974, Larry Rosenberger made his very first such sampling trip as a "kid out of school" to fulfil a contract with Spiegel's, the Chicago-based mail-order firm. He packed his bags and followed fellow analyst John Woldrich, so that he could be taught everything he needed to know. The road trip "lasted a total of 10 days and covered Swissvale, PA, a suburb of Pittsburgh, Ironton, KY, Anderson, IN, Maumee, OH, Willowick OH", and, as an internal Fair Isaac history records with what could be read as a hint of Californian snobbery, "several other bright spots in the heartland." Somewhere along the way, one of the microfiche cameras broke down. Woldrich, the senior member of the team set out in the rental car to find a repair shop some fifty miles away, leaving a baffled Rosenberger behind with barely any experience working the machine. Before he left, Woldrich reminded his pupil "that all he had to do was to be sure to adjust the exposure for the different colors [*sic*] of the ledger cards and everything would be OK." His words were hardly reassuring. "I went to school 19 years", Rosenberger thought ruefully to himself when left alone to contemplate his future in credit scoring, "to be able to take pictures of ledger cards" (Sawyer c. 1992).

This particular story was often repeated at Fair Isaac not only because it was somewhat typical, but because Rosenberger would go on to succeed Bill Fair as chief executive officer, whereas Woldrich would eventually become chief operating officer. What was striking in conversations with this first generation of analysts, who eventually became the Fair Isaac executives in the 1990s, is that the most vivid part of early scorecard projects was sample collection, with little or no mention of the sanitized intellectual work usually associated with statistical analysis. Far from the idealized image of the ivory tower, doing scientific work at Fair Isaac involved manual participation. No one, not even a freshly graduated star PhD student of Robert Oliver coming out of Berkeley's IEOR (Industrial Engineering and Operations Research) program, could escape the mundane task of hauling boxes of data out of dusty storage rooms, some of which were being sequestered in some "pretty unsavory [*sic*] places". Recalling his trips to finance offices, another retired senior vice president noted that "At that time some of them were located in the worst parts of cities. [. . .] It could be, not intimidating, but certainly not the most pleasant thing, it's not the most glamorous thing to do, [. . .] driving around to these strip malls and storefronts".[27]

---

26. Interview E by author with a retired Fair Isaac employee, a career analyst and senior executive, 5 September 2004.

27. Interview F by author with a retired Fair Isaac employee, a first-generation analyst and senior executive, 8 August 2006.

To strain matters more in the field, the aid offered by the finance company's local staff was often less than forthcoming. Clerks and office workers often had little regard for the disruptive intrusion of an alien scientific activity. "Some of the people who worked there might have a high school education. [. . .] These people don't particularly want to help you, right? They have their other jobs to do there and things like that" (Sawyer c. 1992). In a small technology firm with a handful of employees, run with the intimacy of a family business, when something had to get done everyone was expected to do their part. It the early years it was not uncommon for spouses to travel with Fair Isaac analysts (and in at least one case a teenaged son), to provide companionship through long, hot, and dusty days on the road. Unsalaried, spouses assisted in the grunt work that kept the company going. Incidents of accidentally destroyed records, waterlogged files, inaccessible or misplaced archives, and boxes shelved just out of reach, not to mention the occasional necktie caught in rolling microfiche feeders, all added to the challenge of assembling a workable sample.

The scorecard business grew slowly, but contract by contract, firm by firm, it did grow. Eventually, when the process was ironed out into a semi-skilled task, the sample collection trips would also be carried out by non-scientific Fair Isaac personnel. "So, can you imagine", explained one former female employee, "going around to all these locations and shoving paper [a machine] bigger than a printer".[28] "It was hard work", contributed another. "Once we hit the ground there was no joy. You would go in and you would go into the customer's files and in many cases, you would have to sometimes pull 'em out of there if they didn't already have them arranged for you". Then "you would just keep passing the document through. Booorrring. Unstaple, then restaple. Then, bloody hands."[29] Once located, selected files continued to be photographed page by page, and by hand in the field. Thick undeveloped rolls of film were then sent back to California in metal canisters by post. "That was a real scary thing" about sampling, recalled a senior executive with a mischievous grin, "because you didn't really know whether you had a good sample until you got it back." [30]

HIRING HOUSEWIVES TO PROCESS THE DATA

Manual activity and moment-to-moment problem solving continued in scorecard manufacture well after the fieldwork had been completed. When

---

28. Group interview G by author with former Fair Isaac homecoders who became career employees, 24 August 2006.

29. 29 Ibid.

30. Interview F by author with a retired Fair Isaac employee, a first-generation analyst and senior executive, 8 August 2006.

the film collected over a week finally arrived at the head office in San Rafael it was developed and printed on long rolls of paper that had to be torn by hand and restapled to resemble the original credit files. The samples were precious and potentially information-rich materials, but in their raw state they were not as yet useful for statistical analysis. To make them into useable data the documents underwent a multistage process through which they were gradually converted into a crisp, clean, and uniform database. Once reassembled, the culled credit documents had to be coded into a mechanically readable form. At first, Fair Isaac's six full-time office staff were asked to do the initial stages of this work, which they managed to squeeze in between their regular administrative duties. By the late-1960s, however, after a large contract was signed with the Chicago retailer Montgomery Ward, a full-time arrangement for coding was clearly needed.

Fair Isaac hired a young woman named Carol Veris to manage the situation because there was, as yet, "neither the space, budget, nor consistency of workload to make hiring permanent coders possible" (Fair Isaac & Company Incorporated 1977: 6). To solve the problem in a way that would control costs Veris resorted to an age-old solution in tradition manufacture called domestic production or "putting-out".[31] That is, she placed an ad in the newspaper and contracted the work out on a piece-rate basis to local Marin County housewives willing to work on a flexible schedule, many of whom had husbands employed at the Hamilton Field Air Force Base in Novato. Under the homecoding arrangement, when a scorecard contract was signed by Fair Isaac, any number of women from a roster of about two hundred might be offered work preparing the data. The women would come into the office and pick up a batch of applications along with special preprinted data sheets designed by the project analyst in co-operation with the head of coding.

In combination with the sampling strategy performed by analysts, the meticulous work of the homecoders was the backbone of the scorecard because it was their job to interpret the writing on the ledger cards and convert it into the standardised numerical codes demanded by the analytic process. The quality of the final product depended in large part on the ability of the coders to perform this task reliably, which would require a form of distributed collective action. Veris developed the basic theory and rules for coding. Those who succeeded her in the position of head of coding were mandated to instruct the coders on what they were doing. One woman

---

31. Chandler (1977) has described how before the 1840s, "Entrepreneurs distributed work for processing in the homes or neighboring families" (51). Along with hiring specialised apprentices and journeymen, and acquiring simple machinery, the domestic production system was one of the three ways early manufacture could be expanded. Although it never reached the level of development that it did in England, Chandler notes that in the U.S. domestic production was frequently used for producing shoes and boots.

remembered that "[w]e went to these classes and they gave us these print-outs. There was lots that we had to look at." The head of coding was also responsible for preparing extensive reference books. "Oh yes", confirmed one woman when asked whether they received any ongoing guidance. "We had big binders. We went page by page. So we had to read and code for each project".[32] Candidates were subject to serious training to absorb a consider-able range and content of codes. "There were occupation codes. Housewife was HH. Fireman, Policeman", rattled off one coder. "Then there would be groups. For how many years did they live [at an address] you would just put the year".[33]

The purpose of this first stage of data processing was to pull, reduce, and standardise information from the mass of paper that had been sampled. After the initial training, a common data sheet distributed to the women indicating which pieces of information were deemed relevant to the project at hand was the basic material aid in coordinating action. Equipped with a pen and stack of forms, each woman would do this transfer work independently, filling the nooks and crannies of her personal schedule at home. "You know", explained one woman, "we'd just sit there and do it on these sheets of paper. They all had the heading of what you were supposed to put, where."[34] Another level of coordination involved organizing the women into working groups of five. Four unit members did the initial coding while one was assigned as a "checker" to review for accuracy behind the others. From kitchen tables and parked cars, between loads of laundry and shuttling children to school, this diligent labour force scoured personal finance files one after the next. This is how coding work became a visible part of the Marin County community. One woman amusedly recalled that "you'd go certain places . . . I was by the campfire and could see somebody doing this and I walked over and I said, well you have got to be working for Fair Isaac!"[35]

If analysts were quick to point to the unexpectedly manual aspect of their jobs, for their part, coders soon revealed the intellect and judgment required of their labour. Former coders drew attention to conditions that were equally true for both parties: "It was a lot of work. We had to make a lot of decisions because of the different rules." Looking back on the process what these women emphasize is that in practice, selecting codes that corresponded with raw credit files involved its own form of tacit decision making that was far from obvious. Former coders make it clear that "[t]here was some interpretation on all of this.

---

32. Group interview H by author with former Fair Isaac homecoders and other female employees, 21 August 2006.

33. Group interview G by author with former Fair Isaac homecoders who became career employees, 24 August 2006.

34. Group interview H by author with former Fair Isaac homecoders and other female employees, 21 August 2006.

35. Informal conversation recorded over dinner with a group of retired female Fair Isaac employees that meets periodically in Marin County (21 September 2006).

You couldn't just copy it. That was the hard part, coding it. [. . .] They didn't just say he's been three times thirty days late in nice English".[36] Because there was no standard format for record-keeping in the credit industry, different customers and offices (or even credit officers) could keep their files in idiosyncratic ways. For example, "[w]e had to read these logs of payments and every company didn't do the same thing, and we'd get so confused".[37] Not everyone could function under these demanding and constantly shifting conditions. A person who "just couldn't get it" was not kept on for very long.

Coding was beset by its own set of seemingly trivial but enormously hampering problems which not only slowed data processing but also threatened scorecard quality. A coder explained, "The [customer] wouldn't let go of the originals. They were afraid that if something happened they would be liable". So in addition to illegible writing and unusual responses, homecoders often did battle with substandard copies. Mining copies, the primary material for the production of light and mobile credit data, was a burden that was borne heavily by the coders. Even the slightest inconsistencies were not tolerated. As Bill Fair noted, "We knew we had to be attentive to correctness but we had very little idea of the sensitivity of the results to error" (Fair 1991: 489). To overcome routine challenges, Fair Isaac coders developed their own organizational hierarchy, subroutines, forms of problem-solving expertise, policies, and rules of thumb. So although coding might be considered a mundane task because of its overtly repetitive appearance, upon closer inspection it is clear that the work demanded constant learning and could not simply be offloaded onto the unskilled.

Although coding required skills it could not be contracted to an occupational group considered to be skilled. This is because, in addition to technical coordination, there is another component of coding that is equally as important—the economic element. Coding depended on the willingness of all of these women to do the work of data capture at a cost that was not prohibitive to the overall endeavour. At a piece-rate of seven cents per credit file, ranging up to twenty depending on the amount of data to be gleaned (checkers only made two cents per application), the goal was to complete at least ten applications an hour. A first paycheck of $17.50 was certainly something to be proud of. "The only way you'd earn money [was] to be very fast. Otherwise you didn't get very much".[38] Even though they were not officially required to memorize the codes, in fact, "you did sort of have to memorize it if you were going to make any time at all, if you were going to get through one of

36. Group interview G by author with former Fair Isaac homecoders who became career employees, 24 August 2006.

37. Ibid.

38. Group interview G by author with former Fair Isaac homecoders who became career employees, 24 August 2006.

these applications".[39] The use of home labour to reduce salaries and human memory to informally maximize production, as well as the presumption that coding remained unskilled labour even as women workers became highly experienced workers are only two example of the situated ways in which the production cost of scorecards was absorbed by Fair Isaac and controlled.

The second stage of data production was key punching in which the assigned codes were transferred from paper forms onto eighty-column, machine readable punched cards. The key punching machine was "like a typewriter, you put your IBM cards in—they're about five by seven—and you have to sort them. If we punched a certain digit that would mean [occupation]: housewife."[40] Once again, some women keyed while others checked behind for errors. Getting to and through these application files was a time-consuming process that absorbed the bulk of the production period. Bill Fair himself would find fit to record years later, "Data entry was demanding and tedious in the extreme. [...] Getting a deck of cards ready for a run was a matter of weeks of work counting the time it took to encode it before keypunching could begin" (1991: 489).[41] This two-step process continued until April 1975, by which time Fair Isaac acquired the technology which permitted codes to be directly entered into computer terminals and saved in an electronic format. It was at this moment that data entry became an internal unit of the company. The homecoding function was replaced by a permanently staffed, and with few exceptions all female, Cathode Ray Tube (CRT) Department.[42]

The women for the CRT Department were handpicked according to new and stringent performance requirements, and only those with the skills to work the machines could "make it" in the transition from home to office. By machine "[y]ou had to deal with the same type of information but at a certain degree of speeds. Any type of typing information certainly helped you. Because otherwise the keyboard was like Greek, I would think." To increase the pace of processing the organizational structure of the coders was reworked. A new department called "sample control" was established "that would go through all the documents and try to find the ones that were readable and those that were not, and then bundle them into groups of fifty".[43] And because "[y]ou

---

39. Group interview H by author with former Fair Isaac homecoders and other female employees, 21 August 2006.

40. Group interview G by author with former Fair Isaac homecoders who became career employees, 24 August 2006.

41. In addition to the cards containing the sample data, programming cards which held the programme the analyst designed also had to be punched and fed into the computer.

42. Women employees played a central role in preparing the programming cards, and as time went on a woman took charge of managing the iterative data analysis runs. Later, when transfer technology changed and cards of data became magnetic tapes, the position of tape librarian was filled by a woman as well.

43. Group interview G by author with former Fair Isaac homecoders who became career employees, 24 August 2006.

couldn't be on the machines and try to interpret information all day", three shifts of four hour duration were created: 7 to 11 a.m., 1 to 5 p.m., and the self-styled "ladies of the night" who worked from 5 p.m. to 10 p.m.[44] Remuneration was made hourly rather than per piece. No one can remember precisely what the rate was, but it was somewhere in the ball park of $2.50 to $3.50 per hour. Raises came in increments of five cents, and eventually a health care package was provided for anyone working at least part-time.

Women's labour has only recently been included into accounts of science and technology.[45] As the turn towards the study of scientific practice has made clear, if the extension of science and technology into the everyday is to be explained, something more has supported it than the cognitive genius emanating from a few great men. In the rise of distributed systems, practical considerations of execution matter. This has proved particularly true for the routine operation of data-driven systems and calculative infrastructures where scores of working women—the first "calculators"—have consistently played an important role.[46] The production of scorecard technology and its spread into consumer finance is no exception. Fair Isaac records report that on 23 December 1977 at precisely 10:47 a.m. Fair Isaac's spirited data entry unit officially celebrated the processing of their millionth credit application to the sound of a ringing bell.[47] The event was carefully staged by upper management, who, in recognition of this milestone, pro-

---

44. Ibid.

45. As an historian of science, Shapin (1989) has remarked, because histories of science have tended to focus on its marvellous effects rather than on the details of scientific production, the role of technicians as scientific actors has generally been neglected. Following on this insight, several case studies have sought to restore the vital role of women, who are often not considered scientists, to accounts of scientific and technological change. See, for example, Casper and Clarke (1998) and Oreskes (1996). The female clerk has long been associated with office work (see Strom 1992). So, just as they have in science, women have also played an important historical role in the rise of information management. There are telling photographs that capture the prominence of women in raising early information infrastructures (Yates 2005: 24). This is confirmed in the banking sector where the role of women in the adoption of new information technologies has frequently been noted. See Bonin and Pardo-Guerra in this volume as well as Bátiz-Lazo and Wardley (2007). That the importance of women's labour might easily be overlooked in the history of computing, as it was in the history of science, may not be entirely surprising given the very tendency of information infrastructures to become mundane and to sink into the background (see Star 1999).

46. For a historical reference to how women were organized in a factory-like arrangement, serving as human calculators in the manufacture of logarithmic tables, see Daston (1994).

47. *Viewpoints* II, no. 1 (Fall/Winter 1977). *Viewpoints*, the major historical reference for tracing Fair Isaac's activities, was a quarterly newsletter initiated by yet another prominent woman at Fair Isaac, Mary Pellegrino, who ran the series for twenty years. This unpretentious publication written in accessible, non-technical language diffused best practices to customers covering a range of topics from

vided commemorative paperweights and cake for all. Until well into the 1990s this is how the information infrastructures for credit scoring systems were built up—upon the movement of pencils over paper, and millions of tiny decisions, revisions, and keystrokes.

FAIR ISAAC'S CORNER ON COMPUTING AND ANALYSIS

After sampling and data processing the next stage in the production process was analysis, the set of activities that is most readily associated with statistical expertise and computing. When Fair and Isaac set up shop as operations research consultants a computer was still a relatively inaccessible thing. In order to offer computing assistance they rented time on machines available around San Francisco (their initial work was tailored for the IBM-650), for example, at Standard Oil of California, during off-peak hours. It was the late 1960s by the time Fair Isaac was able to lease a machine for itself. The model, an IBM-1130, was a low-budget desk-sized system with direct access programme storage expressly "designed for on-the-job problem solving by engineers, scientists and business people".[48] When the stack of punch codes prepared by the coders was complete, it was carried to the computer room where it met a second deck of programming cards that held the instructions written by the analyst for the parameters that were to be extracted from the data set. But with one machine for everyone, computing time continued to be a limited resource. While one card run was proceeding the other analysts had to wait, working on weekends and overnight in order to gain access to the machine.

When the two carefully prepared decks of cards were finally joined the process of producing statistics would begin. The first set of information the analyst sought to extract from the data was a basic set of tabulations which it spit out on long rolls of paper. Based on this initial breakdown the analyst would engage in a task Fair Isaac called "classing" in which they would impose some modest groupings to simplify the distinctions in the data. The act of classing was not analytically neutral. It reduced the information content of the data because it decreased the granularity at which the description of an individual could be made. Classing was, therefore, as one senior analyst

management strategies to regulation. The series continues to be published today but has been converted into a vehicle for marketing and brand promotion.

48. See http://www-03.ibm.com/ibm/history/exhibits/1130/1130_4513PH03. html. Information on the IBM-1130 is available at this online IBM archive. Although I have only mentioned one transition here, Fair Isaac would bear the cost of adopting new computing systems numerous times (including one transition to a UNIVAC 1108). Instead of consulting externally on computer usage, the business model of scoring had them exercising sophisticated computing expertise internally, to port, update, and maintain their proprietary programme called INFORM.

put it, "Very, very important. It's crucial to the outcome because from that point on, everything depended on that".[49] Knowing when it was appropriate to sacrifice information and when it was not, respecting empirically detected patterns in the data, being able to read for significant shifts in performance and retain them, demanded seasoned judgment. The work was so critical that inexperienced analysts were advised that they should "have the next guy down the hall look at the way you're classing that data for a while until you're really good at it".[50] Finely classed data was then tested through Fair Isaac's proprietary scoring software, called INFORM, to select factors and build the statistical model that would become the scorecard.[51]

Over the years, the process of scorecard manufacture would change as the consumer finance industry's command of information technology evolved. For example, the Fair Isaac coders were eventually replaced by reels of magnetic tapes loaded with data coded elsewhere. Many of these tapes were sent from the second-party information processors charged with handling the wealth of data that would be produced by the flow of credit card transactions whizzing through Visa's electronic payment system, whose function is described by David Stearns in this volume. Data would also be transferred to Fair Isaac on reels of tape from the newly digitized credit bureaus which aggregated credit data on consumers from multiple lenders and public sources. (It is this arrangement—a marriage of bureau data with Fair Isaac analysis—that produces the analytic product called a FICO score, the gold standard of consumer credit risk assessment in today's U.S. credit markets.) What is noteworthy, however, is that even as the transition towards routine electronic data capture obviated the need to manually access paper records, and the rise of information infrastructure the need to physically transport it at all, the separation of risk calculating capacity (at Fair Isaac) from data management (at the firm or processor) is a structural feature that was largely conserved.

The original Fair Isaac's business model was fundamentally dependent upon the company's ability to sequester default risk calculation and statistical analysis away from data producers, an arrangement that was

---

49. Interview 1 by author with former Fair Isaac employee, a career analyst and product innovator, 28 September 2006.

50. Ibid.

51. The statistical function of INFORM was based on logistic regression, but what made the software proprietary was that it permitted numerous functions that were specific to treating and interpreting credit data. For example, one of the functions would allow the analyst to force the points associated with a factor to increase or decrease monotonically even if the data did not produce this result. This is useful for ensuring that if age is a factor that appears in a scorecard, applicants over the age of sixty-two receive the greatest number of points regardless of empirical outcomes, as per the Equal Credit Opportunity laws passed in the 1970's. A repertoire of such functions accumulated within INFORM as Fair Isaac gained progressive experience in the field over the years.

permitted by the initial scarcity of computers. It was only in the late 1970s that Fair Isaac would face its first true competitor, a free-standing analytics company called Management Decision Systems (MDS). The stakes of the credit scoring business would heighten over the next decade as the major banks rushed to raise the kind of score-supported, mass-market credit card operations that had overtaken instalment retail and small personal loans. Whereas banks had traditionally been hesitant to provide direct consumer credit because of the managerial costs of managing small accounts by hand, at the end of the twentieth century they would seize upon the power of statistical credit control managed through electronic systems. Banks would push forward this high-volume form of production alongside a new species of monolines that used the new statistics to start credit operations from the ground up.[52] Both banks and monolines would thrive by setting up home teams of statisticians to exploit the masses of data at their command. The credit bureaus would do the same, with Experian, most notably buying out MDS. This move among the institutions that generated and owned credit data, to internalize not only computers but also statistical competence, signalled the beginning of a profound erosion of Fair Isaac's corner on the production of basic credit scoring algorithms.

As the company lost its material hold, first, over data processing, and later, with the emergence of specialised statistical software, statistical calculation, it would have to redefine its value proposition in order to maintain a competitive edge. It began to foster brand loyalty and to market its products based on the exclusivity of an intangible proprietary value: the distinctive nuance that decades of accumulated experience lent to its credit data analysis. To access this specific expertise banks and bureaus could continue to purchase and install Fair Isaac products; but they could also hire personnel who had received analytic trained at the company. So although Fair Isaac continued to be a major fount of innovation in the domain of consumer finance data analysis, its influence now circulated in many ways— through the sale of a number of well-delimited products, but also through an informal social web of circulating expertise in which former employees carried embodied forms of know-how with them out into the burgeoning world of scoring. Thus unfolded a process of dematerialization in the business of credit risk analysis, pushing it away from the manufacture of a tangible, proprietary, and monetized technological products, and towards

---

52. Information-based lending strategies supported, for example, by Fair Isaac's credit bureaus scores opened the market to monoline credit card issuers. The case of Capital One's 'information based strategy' (IBS) to direct market credit cards has been enthusiastically discussed in business school case studies, although they fail to mention the role of Fair Isaac in providing the basic information infrastructure that permit this type of lending to emerge (see Chang 2005; Anand, Rukstad, and Paige 2000).

a struggle to command an increasingly non-appropriable, non-rival, and universally acknowledged scientific good.[53]

CONCLUSION—CALCULATING CONSUMER DEFAULT RISK IN THE ABSENCE OF DIGITAL INFRASTRUCTURE

In a world flattened by digital infrastructures it can seem as though information is travelling at light speeds and that risk calculations can be performed at no significant organizational cost. Although the efforts involved in raising calculative systems are more difficult to discern within sophisticated electronic environments, examining the way consumer credit scoring was carried out in the past is a cogent reminder that the costs of calculation cannot have disappeared. It is noteworthy that credit scoring techniques were put into practice prior to and not as a result of mass computerization, which makes this case a particularly informative one for observing and exploring the kinds of rich organizational (re)arrangements that risk assessment demands. As the chapter shows, if consumer credit risk has come to exist in the practical managerial encounter, it is because of Fair Isaac's firm-by-firm initiatives to identify and assemble data, to work out methods for analysing these, and to implement computer-enabled calculation to the industry in a stable and useable form. The design of the tools that have and are still being used for consumer credit risk assessment are the fruit of these forgotten commercial efforts.

A history of instruments as a means of tracing the rise of risk management practices finds its strength in the close coupling between tools and action, between risk calculation and managerial intervention. Once introduced, the scorecard's presentations of default risk reconfigured the industry around the key decision-making moment that it, itself, mediated. With a metric of default risk in hand it became possible not only to assess default risk; by using the tool to mechanize screening decisions it was further possible to make changes to reduce that risk at the aggregate level. The study of early scorecard manufacture contributes to an understanding of how consumer finance made its first step towards quantitative forms of operational control. What is remarkable is that the original Fair Isaac scorecards were not extraneous to the existing methods of credit underwriting. Rather, through an intricate organizational arrangement crisscrossing the boundary between lending firms and an independent technology provider, an empirical definition of consumer default was extracted out of the available paper records, translated into a statistical expression through electronic computers, and presented back to credit managers embedded in a simple cardboard device.

---

53. For an incisive discussion of how the non-appropriable, non-rival, and universal qualities of scientific information, defined by the new economics of science by Arrow and Nelson, are achieved only at the price of costly investments, see Callon (2002).

To assume that risk calculation is a spontaneous response to digitalization is to take the nature of calculation for granted and to isolate it from history.[54] In contrast, treating calculation as a specific material arrangement implies that there are multiple ways of calculating and constituting risk. This is not to say that a method for assessing default risk could not have been innovated at a later period from within an electronic environment, but it is to suggest that under different conditions its statistical structure, pattern of circulation, and information content would certainly have worked out differently. As this chapter traces, having to build default risk calculation out of the manual records and the practices of mid-century consumer finance has mattered with continuing effects on their contemporary form. In this view, mechanization is not just the one-to-one replacement of an existing function that substitutes machines for human beings. Through technical innovation, processes of mechanization generate historically situated possibilities of novel financial action that actors may exploit and develop. (This position is shared in this volume by Juan Pablo Pardo-Guerra and David Stearns.)

If calculation is historically situated, then the historian's purpose is to trace the points of connection where organizational contexts get translated and woven into technical content in the adaptation of innovations into practice (Callon and Law 1989). In this regard the story of credit scoring resembles JoAnne Yates's account of how insurance companies adopted pre-computerized information-processing technology at the turn of the century. To understand the move towards digitalization in the insurance industry, Yates (2005) has methodically traced several instantiations of information management systems beginning with mechanical tabulating equipment. What her study shows is that specific organizational arrangements influence the design of technologies every bit as much as technologies influence organizations. Similarly, my research seeks to show that risk calculation has had a distinctive trajectory within the consumer credit industry. Demonstrating that the move towards statistically assisted account selection was a gradual rather than abrupt shift, profoundly shaped by the mid-century operational environment of consumer finance, confirms and reinforces Yates's general findings.

Because credit scoring is a perpetually evolving technology, this chapter does not seek to capture a single definitive description of what the technology is, nor does it propose a fixed definition of what it should be (Poon 2007). Instead, for the sake of producing a technically attentive historical

---

54. The material nature of calculation in practice has been a topic of extensive study in science and technology studies. For an early discussion, see Latour (1987); for two case studies see Lave (1988) and Verran (2001); for a more recent treatment with regards to the relationship between markets and calculation see Callon and Muniesa (2002); and for a brief and more philosophical introduction to the topic see Latour (2008).

memory which might inform as to the study of contemporary digital information systems in finance, it has merely sought to recreate a detailed and momentary snapshot of this calculative science as it once was. The scorecard took form through a "distributed organizational arrangement" (Hutchins 1995) that responded to a particular economy of computerization in which computing capacity was as yet a scarce resource in financial firms. The emergence of early default risk calculation was predicated upon the commercial encounter between data-generating credit institutions and a specialised engineering firm with knowledge of statistics and access to computers. It was by looping a manual environment back onto itself and passing through Fair Isaac computers—and not by transitioning financial institutions to a digital environment—that consumer credit origination was first reconfigured, mechanized, and refined by consumer credit risk assessment. Thus, the Fair Isaac scorecard was a substantive product of its era and cannot be said to have arrived before its time.

12 Automating Payments
Origins of the Visa Electronic Payment System

David Stearns

INTRODUCTION

Most anywhere in the developed world, I can walk into a shop and use a small plastic card to pay for goods and services. The merchant and I may speak different languages, and the face of my card may look quite different from those issued locally, but the merchant will still accept it, partly because we both recognize and trust the small logo in the lower-right corner of the card. The merchant's account and mine might be measured in different currencies, but from our perspectives the transaction is no different than one conducted between locals. Although my bank might be on the opposite side of the world, the merchant can insert my card into a small, relatively inexpensive terminal and in a few seconds receive a confirmation code that is literally a guarantee of payment.

It is perhaps a sign of the increasing rate of technological change that we, after such a short time, have ceased to be surprised by this. Sixty years ago, paying for consumer goods and services outside your local area typically required the use of local currency in the form of cash, and once you ran out, your options for obtaining more were costly and limited. Using a small plastic card to transfer funds directly between accounts during the course of a consumer transaction has quickly become something we do without reflection, much like flipping on an electric light-switch, or turning on a water faucet. It has become such an unreflective part of our everyday lives that we now view it as "common", "normal", or even "natural".

However, this was not always the case. To borrow a metaphor from Harry Collins, we tend to think of these systems like ships in bottles, complete, frozen in time (Collins 1975). We rarely consider that they were at one point simply a pile of sticks, and often fail to see how those finished "ships" were significantly shaped by the process of putting them together. How do new payment systems arise? How do they become widely adopted, and how are they shaped and altered by that process of adoption? How do they reshape our social relations once they are widely adopted? How does the application of new technologies, such as computers and telecommunications, then alter the dynamics of the system?

This chapter begins to answer these questions by examining in detail the origins of one system in particular: the electronic payment network known today as VISA.[1] Specifically, I will describe how the system initially formed, how it became widely adopted, and how it transitioned from mostly paper-based to fully electronic processing. Along the way, I will point out ways in which the technologies that make the system function were shaped by the surrounding social dynamics, and the ways in which those technologies then began to reshape those social relations in return.

The narrative in this chapter is built upon original primary research conducted for my PhD dissertation (Stearns 2007). Primary sources include news and trade publications from the period; interviews with those who designed, built, and participated in the Visa payment system; and a selection of primary documents that I was able to obtain.[2] By combining these three types of sources, I was able to triangulate a highly accurate account of the period while also infusing events with the meanings ascribed to them by the actors involved. The period covered by this narrative was the most significant and prolific period of Visa's development, and is the most useful for demonstrating the social-shaping of this technological system.

My analytical lens when commenting on the narrative is borrowed from the Social-Shaping of Technology (SST) and Actor-Network Theory (ANT) perspectives.[3] These approaches emphasize the ways in which artefacts and technological systems are significantly influenced by the social dynamics surrounding their design, implementation, and adoption. Instead of treating the current form of the system as given, natural, or inevitable, scholars in these traditions show how contingent these systems are on their historical context. From our vantage point, we often assume that a system's current forms were obvious or "the best" solutions to well-understood problems, but actors at the time often construct the problems they think need solving and choose amongst multiple possible solutions. Actors also commonly disagree about what the best solution is, as they value different things and bring different interests and goals to the situation.

I should also point out that my focus on payment systems is not unique. Evans and Schmalensee's (1999) book on the multisided economics of payment card systems is perhaps the most well known. Historians of money, such as Davies (1994), Chown (1994), Einzig (1966), Eagelton and Williams (2007), Robertson (2005), and Weatherford (1997), have traced the

---

1. VISA is technically a recursive acronym for "Visa International Services Association". In this chapter, I will follow the tradition of other authors by simply referring to it as "Visa" in all subsequent uses of the name.

2. All interview sources had already retired from Visa before the interview, and were reminded to honour any non-disclosure agreements they may have signed with the organization.

3. For SST, see MacKenzie and Wajcman (2003). For ANT, see Latour (1987).

origins of earlier monetary artefacts such as coins, paper money, and written transfer orders (e.g. bills of exchange and modern cheques, see Maixé-Altés and Iglesias 2009), often discussing how the designs of these physical artefacts were shaped by the social forces surrounding them and how their introduction altered those social relations in return. Historians of business and finance, such as Mandell (1990), Howels and Hine (1993), Kirkman (1987), Frazer (1985), Wonglimpiyarat (2004), Booth and Billings (in this volume), Mooij (in this volume), and Bátiz-Lazo and Maixé-Altés (in this volume) have recounted histories of early credit cards, ATMs, Giro payments, and other Electronic Funds Transfer (EFT) systems. Sociologists such as Guseva (2008) have demonstrated how social networks involving both individuals and institutions are key to understanding the development and adoption of new payment systems, especially in post-communist states. Legal scholars such as Mann (2006) have begun to investigate how laws and court decisions influence the spread and adoption of new payment systems. My hope is that this chapter contributes a rich and detailed empirical case of a ubiquitous electronic payment system to this growing body of literature.

WHAT IS VISA?

Before I discuss Visa's origins, it might be helpful to briefly explain what Visa currently is. Many readers may be surprised to learn that Visa itself does not actually issue cards. Visa itself is not a bank, nor is it a governmental institution. It does not extend credit to cardholders nor maintain cardholder accounts. It does not recruit merchants to accept those cards, nor does it maintain accounts for the merchants that do. It does not even develop those small point-of-sale terminals that read the magnetic stripe or the chip embedded in those cards that it does not issue. So what *is* Visa exactly, and what does it *do*? Visa's 2008 initial public offering was the largest in U.S. history (their market capitalization reached U.S.$45 billion by the end of the first day), so it clearly must do *something* to justify all that attention.[4]

Essentially, Visa is an enabling organization; it developed and continues to operate the legal, financial, and technological infrastructure necessary to facilitate the processing of payments involving multiple financial institutions, which, in some cases, may be located in different countries and subject to different banking regulations. The core Visa organization is the central hub of a vast network of participating financial institutions, each of which has agreed to play by the same set of jointly maintained rules. Visa

---

4. "Visa Has a $45 Billion Debut on Wall St.", *New York Times*, 20 March 2008, http://www.nytimes.com/2008/03/20/business/20visa.html (accessed 15 July 2010).

makes money *move*, and for its trouble, takes a small percentage of that money in fees. The percentage may be small, but a small amount of four trillion dollars annually (an amount that continues to grow each year) is enough to get the attention of many investors.

Interestingly, the Visa system makes no assumption about how a given transaction is funded. Although its history is rooted in the bank-issued credit cards of the 1960s, the founder of Visa intended to build an electronic system for the exchange of any kind of value a cardholder might posses: deposits, investments, a line of credit, etc. Visa's founder began speaking publicly about this "asset card" only three years after the organization formed, and their first debit card product (the Entrée card) was first put into production in 1975. Contrary to popular assumption, the Visa system has been processing more debit transaction than credit since 2003, and the ratio has continued to rise.

Although Visa recently restructured into a publicly held stock corporation, for most of its history it operated as a non-profit membership association, owned and governed by the same financial institutions that it served.[5] Visa's primary function was, and still is, to establish and adjudicate the rules by which transactions are processed, and to provide the technological infrastructure necessary to process those transactions entirely in electronic form. Visa's highly reliable computer systems enable cardholders to make guaranteed purchases at anytime and from "everywhere you want to be".[6]

ORIGINS OF THE VISA ORGANIZATION

The organization known as Visa today traces its roots back to the BankAmericard programme started by Bank of America (BofA) in 1958. Despite its rocky beginnings, the BankAmericard was the first truly successful bank-issued credit card, becoming a profitable business by the early 1960s. BofA was able to succeed where other banks had failed, primarily because California banking regulations allowed it to operate branches across the state, and by 1958 it had some kind of banking relationship with

---

5. Visa was legally organized as a for-profit, non-stock membership association. However, because it did not issue stock and was solely owned by the same institutions that provided its operational funding, it effectively operated as a non-profit. Any accumulated net revenue amassed by the organization was either put back into operations or was used as a settlement reserve in compliance with the Basel accords.

6. Visa's "Everywhere You Want to Be" ad campaign, which was one of their most successful attacks against American Express, also nicely illustrates Visa's third responsibility: promotion of the Visa brand through worldwide advertising. See Visa's corporate biography in Chutkow (2001). For a discussion of Visa's dependability, see Stearns (2006).

an estimated 60 per cent of the state's population (Nocera 1994: 18–20). This enabled BofA to quickly build the cardholder and merchant acceptance base that is necessary to kick-start any new payment system.

However, the federal banking regulations of that time prohibited BofA from operating across state lines, and thus it lacked the relationships necessary to expand the system beyond California. In 1966, BofA began to license the card programme to banks in other states, hoping to create a nationwide credit card system that would eclipse Diners Club and American Express, both of which threatened the banking industry's domination of the nation's payments mechanisms. After only two years, the licensing programme appeared to be a resounding success: the number of licensee banks had grown from the initial eight to 254; cardholders had increased threefold, from two to six million; and merchant acceptance had expanded nearly eight times, from twenty thousand to 155,000 locations.[7] However, this impressive growth masked several fundamental flaws in the system that led to a near collapse in October of 1968.

Operational Problems

There were two critical operational flaws in the BankAmericard licensing system that were quickly exposed by the increasing sales volume. First, the authorization process established by BofA could not adequately protect against the rising amount of fraudulent transactions. One of the salient differences between bank-issued credit cards and cheques is that the former are *guaranteed* from the merchant's perspective. This introduces a certain amount of risk to the issuing bank, and in an ideal world, it would want to authorize every transaction. However, this was not a realistic option in 1968, as the labour and telecommunication costs would easily outweigh the revenue gained from the commonly low-value transactions. It was also technically infeasible—at this time, merchants telephoned human authorizers who manually looked up account numbers in large printed reports and made written annotations as transactions were authorized. Cardholders were willing to endure this delay occasionally for high-value transactions, but requiring it for every transaction would no doubt have encouraged cardholders to use a different form of payment.

Instead of authorizing every transaction, the BankAmericard system borrowed the concept of a "floor limit" from the merchant-specific credit card systems of the 1920s.[8] The floor limit was the amount under which the merchant could accept a transaction without calling for authorization

---

7. "Card Plans Show Big Gains", *Burroughs Clearing House* 52, no. 5 (February 1968).

8. Bill Powar, former Visa employee, interview with author, November 2005. See also Mandell (1990).

(literally, the amount the shop "floor" could accept on its own). The specific amount varied depending on the merchant's business and the type of card (wealthy and important customers were given cards with a gold star on the front, signifying a higher floor limit). The floor limit technique is essentially a cost/risk trade-off, but criminals quickly learned that they could continue to use a stolen or counterfeit card for several months simply by keeping purchases under the merchant's floor limit.

The second critical operational flaw involved how transactions were cleared and settled between the licensee banks. As in the case of checks, the bank representing the merchant (the "acquirer") may be different than the bank that issued the card, so the system must define a mechanism by which transactions can be interchanged. In the checking system, the Federal Reserve acted as a centralised clearing house for most banks, but it refused to handle BankAmericard transactions.[9] Technically, it would have required some modifications to their mechanical sorters and tabulators: the BankAmericard sales drafts were eighty-column IBM punched cards, larger in size than most cheques of the day; and information was encoded on them using punched holes rather than magnetic ink. However, the technical reasons were secondary to a more strategic reason: BankAmericard transactions were cleared at a discount, a practice the Fed had been trying to eliminate from the checking system for several decades.[10]

With the Fed's refusal to handle BankAmericard transactions, one might have expected BofA to create their own centralised clearing house. Unfortunately for BofA, it chose instead to let banks perform peer-to-peer clearing, sending the sales drafts directly to each other via the post. However, to actually settle the transactions (i.e. transfer "good and final" funds from the issuer to the acquirer), acquiring banks submitted what amounted to a cheque for the total amount, drawn on the issuer's account, to the Fed's clearing house. Although this allowed the licensee banks to leverage their existing funds-transfer mechanisms, it created a timing problem that jeopardized the issuing bank's ability to reconcile. When the issuing bank received payment notice from the Fed, it would enter that amount into a suspense ledger and wait for the individual sales drafts to arrive in order to reconcile and bill the cardholder. Unfortunately, this often took quite a long time. This is how Dee Hock, Visa's founder described it:

---

9. Chuck Russell, former CEO of Visa, interview with author (14 October 2005). Dee Hock, "Electronic Funds Transfer or Electronic Value Exchange?" Speech given at the Federal Reserve Bank of Boston Conference, Melvin Village, New Hampshire, October 1974.

10. Clearing "at a discount" refers to the practice of paying less than the face value for a payment instrument such as a cheque or credit card sales draft. In the BankAmericard system, the acquirer would receive approximately 98 per cent of the draft amount from the issuer, and would credit the merchant somewhere between 93 per cent and 94 per cent.

> Meanwhile, the merchant bank, having already been paid and under immense pressure to handle its own cardholder transactions, had no incentive to process foreign [i.e. interchange] transactions and get them to the issuing bank for billing to the cardholder. Since each bank was both a merchant-signing bank and a card-issuing bank, they began to play tit-for-tat, while back rooms filled with unprocessed transactions, customers went unbilled, and suspense ledgers swelled like a hammered thumb. It became an accounting nightmare. (Hock 2005: 77)

This immense backlog in the system also compounded the fraud problems discussed earlier. Issuing banks would have no way of knowing if sub-floor-limit fraud was occurring on a card until the actual sales drafts arrived and were processed. By the time they arrived, thousands of dollars worth of fraud could have taken place.

Organizational Problems

Although these operational problems may have had potential solutions within the existing BankAmericard licensing framework, the organization had problems of its own that further compounded the operational difficulties. When BofA created the licensing structure, it retained not only ownership of the BankAmericard name and marks, but also all the organizational power. The licensees had little to no say in the governance of the system, and they fundamentally distrusted BofA—it was the nation's largest bank at the time, and would likely move into the licensees' territories if the banking regulations ever allowed it.[11]

Although BofA retained the power to set the operational rules for the system, their power to enforce and modify those rules was neutered by two critical flaws in the license contracts. First, the contracts lacked mechanisms for financially punishing banks that skirted or bent the operating regulations, nor did they contain a method for resolving grievances between the licensee banks. The only recourse BofA had was to revoke a bank's license, but because most of these banks held large correspondent deposits with BofA, and were dominant in their geographic area, this was not likely to happen. Second, the contracts also lacked a clause allowing BofA to change the operating regulations in response to new developments. If BofA needed to modify or add a rule, they had to renegotiate a new contract. Again, BofA had no recourse if banks simply refused to sign the new license, which they often did if the rules were not in their best interests.[12]

---

11. Several interviewees commented on the nature of this relationship. See also Hock (2005).

12. Bennett Katz, former general counsel of Visa, interview with author (26 October 2005).

The fundamental distrust and the flaws in the contracts created a number of organizational instabilities. The most significant and pernicious was the tension over the interchange reimbursement fee, which was paid by the acquirer to the issuer during the settlement of an interchange transaction. At this time, the intent of the fee was to compensate the issuer for the cost and risk of extending the cardholder credit for the transaction. The rule established under the licensing system for interchange fees was essentially unenforceable. This is how Bennett Katz, Visa's long-time general counsel described it:

> When I came on board, the rule was . . . if a customer of your bank goes into a merchant belonging to another bank, outside of that territory, then the bank that signed the merchant has a choice as to what it sends to the issuer. It could send the amount of the discount that it received from the merchant less a processing fee (for processing the transaction), or if it didn't want to calculate each and every one . . . it could send the average discount it was getting from all of its merchants less a processing fee. Well they would say "my average is two per cent." How are you going to audit that? And if the merchant put up a big deposit, their merchant discount might be close to zero, and the issuer would get almost nothing!
>
> So the issuer has all the costs because he's extending the credit and eating defaults, but he was getting almost nothing when the customer travelled. The losses were horrendous. It was literally chaos in the BankAmericard system.[13]

Tensions Come to a Head

In October of 1968, BofA called a special meeting of the licensees to discuss the operational problems facing the BankAmericard system. The meeting did not go well, and by the second day, it had devolved into an "acrimonious argument", with licensees threatening to leave the system or form a new one without BofA. In a last-ditch attempt to save the system, BofA allowed the licensees to form a committee of their own to investigate the problems. However, the member selected to lead that committee, Dee Ward Hock of Seattle's National Bank of Commerce, already had a sense that a more radical restructuring would eventually become necessary (Hock 2005: 84).[14]

---

13. Katz interview.

14. Although Hock's autobiography is written in retrospect, his motivations and ideas expressed in it were confirmed by transcripts of speeches he gave at the time, as well as those interviewed who worked with him in the early 1970s.

DEE HOCK, ORGANIZATIONS, AND MONEY

To Hock, the BofA licensing arrangement was a classic example of what he called "mechanistic, command-and-control organizations". These types of organizations are typified by the centralisation of power, the creation of bureaucratic hierarchies, and the use of technology and highly rationalised rules to control an increasingly specialised and deskilled set of workers. For Hock, this concept of organizational design was bred from "industrial age thinking", where an organization is viewed as a sort of machine with humans as the cogs and wheels. In these kinds of organizations, "purpose slowly erodes into process", "procedure takes precedence over product", and "the doing of the doing" causes nothing of substance to get done. Furthermore, Hock argues that command-and-control organizations are actually incapable of dealing with their increasingly complex and dynamic challenges, and because this is still the dominant organizational form, we are in "the midst of a global epidemic of institutional failure" (Hock 2005: 36–38; see also Appelquist in this volume).

Hock eventually developed a different model for organizations based on his observations of natural systems. He refers to these new kinds of organizations as "chaordic", a neologism he defines as: "The behavior of any self-organizing and self-governing organism, organization, or system that harmoniously blends characteristics of chaos and order" (2005: 13). In contrast to the command and control organizations, chaordic organizations are decentralised, self-organizing, self-governing, exhibiting emergent properties. The obvious implication is that they are also more flexible and adaptive. Although, this concept was still rather nascent in Hock's mind at this time, his design for Visa was his first, albeit still flawed, attempt at working out these ideas in practice.

In addition to his desire for a new kind of organization, Hock had also been slowly coming to the realization, as had many others, that "money" had become nothing more than "socially guaranteed alphanumeric data" and that a bank is nothing more than an "institution for the custody, loan, and exchange" of this data. Furthermore, that data was increasingly being stored and manipulated by computers, and would eventually "move around the world at the speed of light at miniscule cost by infinitely diverse paths". This, for Hock, represented an amazing opportunity:

> Any organization that could guarantee, transport, and settle transactions in the form of arranged electronic particles twenty-four hours a day, seven days a week, around the globe, would have a market—every exchange of value in the world—that beggared the imagination. The necessary technology had been discovered and would be available in geometrically increasing abundance at geometrically diminishing cost. But there was a problem. No bank could do it. No hierarchical, stock corporation could do it. No nation-state could do it. In fact, no existing form of organization we could think of could do it. On a hunch I made an estimate of the financial resources of all the banks in the world. It dwarfed the resources

of most nations. Jointly they could do it, but how? It would require a transcendental organization linking together in wholly new ways an unimaginable complex of diverse institutions and individuals. (2005: 98–99)

NATIONAL BANKAMERICARD, INC.

In Hock's mind, the fundamental problem with the BankAmericard licensing system was not a lack of applied technology or formal procedures: it was the organizational design itself. Computer and telecommunication technologies would certainly be needed to solve the operational problems, but if the organizational problems were not addressed, the system would still collapse. The operational and the organizational were all part of the same system, and both needed to be redesigned and implemented as a cohesive whole. Hock turned his attention first to the organizational design.

Over the next year, Hock formulated the structure for a new co-operative organization that he felt could build and operate a worldwide electronic system for the exchange of value. It would be a membership co-operative where the members would also be the joint owners. In essence, the customers and owners would be the same, so there would be no divided loyalty. It would be non-stock, and membership would be non-transferrable, so that ownership and participation would forever be linked. Membership qualifications would be set by the board, but then any organization meeting those criteria must be allowed membership. Both membership fees and voting rights were determined by the amount of volume a member generated, linking taxation and representation. Operating regulations dictated not only how inter-member work was to be accomplished, but also how members would be penalized when they violated them. But most importantly, members would agree to abide by a common set of bylaws and operating regulations "as they now exist or are hereafter modified" (Hock 2005: 124). Thus Hock ensured not only that the new organization could enforce the rules, but also that they could modify and extend them as needed without renegotiating contracts.

The exact legal description of the new organization was a "for-profit, non-stock membership corporation". This rather unusual classification is actually quite important. Banks at this time were not allowed to own stock in anything but a Bank Service Corporation (BSC), but BSCs were also subject to stringent regulation. By creating NBI as a non-stock membership corporation, Hock enabled the banks to "own" it through membership, but completely avoided government regulation of the core National BankAmericard Incorporated (NBI) organization.[15]

---

15. Katz interview. Issuing banks were, of course, still subject to government regulation, and several laws passed in the U.S. during the early 1970s sought to regulate the practices of their credit card programmes. See Mann (2006).

Convincing the BofA to relinquish control of the system was difficult to say the least, but they actually had little choice. The system was clearly falling apart, and there was a very real danger that the licensees could organize a new competing system on their own and exclude the BofA, or simply join the rival Interbank network.[16] In 1970 the new organization was legally formed as a Delaware membership corporation named NBI. The BofA became just another member, although they retained five special seats on the board for the first few years to recognize their unique contribution in forming the original system.

The NBI organization was a watershed event in the history of Visa. It created the structure in which multiple, competing financial institutions could co-operate, just enough, to provide a payment service that none could have realistically provided alone, even with the best technology available in the late 1960s. Although Hock claims it was a radically new kind of organization, it was not an entirely novel form. Its structure was similar to the existing Interbank network, and somewhat akin to the Federal Reserve System.[17] However it did solve the aforementioned organizational problems in the BankAmericard system, enabling it to address the operational problems in a coordinated manner.

However, NBI did not include any of the international licensee banks. By 1972, banks in fifteen countries had licensed the BankAmericard programme, and after witnessing the creation of NBI, asked Hock to help form an international version of the organization. Hock eagerly complied, and the resulting organization, known as IBANCO, was incorporated in 1974 (Brooke 1974b). The entire NBI system joined the international licensees as members of IBANCO, whose operating regulations stipulated the rules for international settlement. To better reflect their international status, IBANCO was renamed Visa International Services Association (forming the recursive acronym VISA) in 1976, and NBI became Visa USA, Inc.[18]

ELECTRONIC AUTHORIZATION

Although NBI alleviated the organizational issues mentioned earlier, the operational issues were still waiting to be solved. The most critical of these, according to the actors involved at the time, was authorization. This was for two reasons: first, the delay and hassle involved in obtaining an

---

16. Interbank was a competing association of bank credit card programmes, which eventually renamed itself to Master Charge, and then again to MasterCard.

17. This kind of organizational structure appears in other industries as well. For example, Multiple Listing Services in the U.S. are often organized in a similar manner.

18. "'Visa' Will Replace 'BankAmericard' Worldwide", *The Nilson Report* 147:2.

authorization was beginning to affect consumers' desires to use the card, and merchants' willingness to accept it; second, the floor limits, which were intended to ease the former concerns, were simultaneously making it difficult to control the increasing levels of fraud, which was in turn further eroding consumer confidence. Without the continued participation of both cardholders and merchants, the system would quickly collapse.

In Hughes's terms, the authorization process had become a "reverse salient", that is, an element holding back, or even thwarting, the development and growth of the overall system (Hughes 1983: 79). Hughes argued that when confronted with a reverse salient, actors seek to correct it by constructing one or more "critical problems", the articulation of which often guides them towards, or even directly implies, certain solutions. In the case of bank card authorization, the industry leaders constructed two critical problems. First, the local *authorization decision* was too slow, and often not available, because it required *human intervention*. Second, *interchange authorizations* were too slow because they required manual "two-legged" calls or telexes between the acquiring and issuing centres. The solution implied by the first problem was replacing the human authorizers with automated, computerized logic. The solution implied by the second problem was enabling electronic communication between the centres, eventually linking their host computers directly together. Building an effective nationwide payment card system ultimately required solving both problems, but the specifics of the solutions were not immediately obvious or given.

Automating the Authorization Decision

National Data Corporation (NDC) of Atlanta seems to be the first processor to offer some sort of computerized authorization to its subscribers. NDC began operations in 1968 as the primary processor for the Chicago-area Interbank members, but eventually expanded to handle processing for a number of merchant-specific card systems, oil industry cards, and two NBI member banks. NDC also provided "after-hours" authorization services for banks that wanted to operate their own centre during the normal working hours. Because NDC was a processor for many issuers and acquirers, they took the approach of centralising all cardholder data onto one computer system from which they could make automated authorization decisions. Merchants called one of NDC's four regional authorization centres, where less-skilled, clerical operators keyed the transaction information into terminals, which in turn communicated over twenty-four hundred baud modems with NDC's central computer (a UNIVAC 494) in Atlanta.[19]

---

19. "National Authorization Joint Feasibility Study Final Report" (29 January 1971), provided by a member of the committee.

The key aspect of this system was that *the authorization decision was entirely automated*; subscribers could define the rules used to make the decision, but the rules were then executed without human intervention. Most subscribers opted for "negative authorization", meaning that card numbers were simply checked against a "derog" file, which contained accounts on which purchases should not be authorized. However, some took advantage of NDC's scheme for "positive authorization", which maintained an "open to buy" amount for the particular account, as well as a history of transactions over the previous seven days. Automated decisions significantly sped up the authorization process, resulting in an average local authorization time of just twenty-two seconds. However, NDC's system could authorize transactions only for cards issued by one of their subscribers—interchange authorizations required an additional, "two-legged" call to the issuer's centre.

Several other banks began experimenting with computerized authorization in the early 1970s. Credit Systems Incorporated (CSI, which later developed Interbank's authorization system) offered a service similar to that of NDC, but merchants could use a Touch-Tone telephone to enter transaction details, guided by voice prompts, and receive a pre-recorded response message.[20] Omniswitch, the centralised authorization service for New York Merchants, took this one step further by deploying point-of-sale (POS) authorization terminals, which could read the card details from a magnetic stripe and send the information over telephone lines to the authorization computer.[21] NDC also began supporting POS terminals in 1971, although theirs optically read the embossed account number and expiration date printed on the front of the card.[22]

City National Bank and Trust of Columbus Ohio also ran a well-publicized test in October of 1971 that was designed to ascertain the feasibility of not only computerized authorization, but also consumer acceptance of the very idea of electronic payments. This test was similar to other "cashless society" experiments, where residents of a small suburb were asked to use cards for all their payments at participating merchants. On the whole, the technologies performed well, but the consumer acceptance was lukewarm at best. Only twenty thousand transactions were completed in the first one hundred days, only one per card issued. The bank's spokesperson declared that "the public will adapt to change": not eagerly accept it (Brooke 1971a: 1).

However, these early tests did convince issuers of the feasibility and benefits of replacing human authorizers with computerized logic. Many organizations

---

20. "Fast Credit Card Authorization is Offered to Banks and Merchants by CSI", *American Banker*, 6 January 1971, 8.

21. C. Frederic Wiegold, "Omniswitch Tests System of Merchant-to-Bank Authorization to Aid Card Use, Reduce Fraud", *American Banker*, 18 June 1971, 1.

22. "NDC Credit Authorization Pilot Underway", *Payment Systems Newsletter*, July 1971, 7.

continued the trend by computerizing their local transactions in a similar manner throughout the rest of the 1970s. Interchange authorizations still required a manual, two-legged call or telex, resulting in multiple-minute authorization times for those travelling outside of their area. One system that promised an innovative solution to this problem was Omniswitch.

Automating Interchange Authorizations

The Omniswitch organization was originally formed in 1969 to provide New York merchants a single, centralised authorization service for all Master Charge cards. The New York metropolitan area was one of those where banking regulations and competition made it relatively common for the merchant and cardholder to be represented by different banks. Most of the Interbank members in that region belonged to the Eastern States Bankcard Association (ESBA), who also performed their processing, but the First National City Bank (FNCB, later Citibank) did not, as they already had their own processing centre. Omniswitch eliminated the need for merchants to determine which centre to call, providing them with one point of contact for all Master Charge authorizations, regardless of issuer. Omniswitch began offering this service in June 1970.[23]

Because FNCB was uninterested in transferring their cardholder data to ESBA's computer, Omniswitch developed the innovative approach of "switching" the authorization request messages to the appropriate computer system, similar to how a networking switch routes packets to the appropriate node on a computer network. Merchants called Omniswitch's data centre in Lake Success, New York, where operators keyed the requests into an interactive computer terminal. The Omniswitch computer (an IBM 360/40) then used the first few digits of the card number to determine the appropriate destination: the ESBA computer, which was literally across the room; or the FNCB authorization computer, which was about nine miles away. The Omniswitch computer transmitted the messages to the issuer's computer system, where they were processed without human intervention.

This switching technique had two important advantages over the consolidation approach taken by organizations such as NDC. First, it made it *politically* easier to expand the geographic reach of the system, as banks and processors could maintain control over their cardholder data and local authorization decisions, but utilise Omniswitch to process interchange authorizations at nearly the same speed. Second, it also made it *technically* easier to expand the system, as supporting a new processor required only the development of a relatively simple bridging program, what we would today call a "driver". Processors could and did use a wide variety of

---

23. Information on Omniswitch comes from interviews with Tom Schramm, former VP of Operations, and Brooke (1971c).

computer hardware and software for their local processing, but they could still communicate through Omniswitch to other issuers, as Omniswitch provided all the necessary protocol conversions.

The Attempt at a Joint National Authorization System

Omniswitch established a model for how to build a decentralised national authorization system by networking together the existing local centres and switching authorization requests between them. This was something NBI, Interbank, and American Express all wanted to provide, and during Omniswitch's first year of operation, representatives from each of the payment card networks met to discuss the possibility of developing one joint computerized system that could provide authorizations anywhere, at any time, for any card programme. From a systems engineering perspective, it seemed wasteful to develop separate authorization systems for each card network, as they would all need to do essentially the same task. It seemed far more "logical" to combine efforts and build one shared system.

The participants formed an advisory team, which investigated the technical feasibility of such a system and compiled their final report in January 1971.[24] In it they concluded that such a system was indeed feasible, and recommended using the message-switching technique developed by Omniswitch. They estimated that a single switching centre could be operational in eighteen to twenty-four months, and two more could be added by 1976 to handle the expected increase in volume.

A shared system may have been technical feasible, but was it politically so? Hock was vehemently opposed to it because he thought that a single, shared system was antithetical to his vision. However, it is equally possible that Hock was simply opposed to any such system that he did not completely control. Hock's more ambitious goals required a large-scale computer network similar to what the joint feasibility study was proposing. If he did not control it, he would lack the ability to dictate the development of the system to ensure that his goals could be achieved. Once a shared system was in place, it would also become difficult to convince banks to fund a second, private network to deliver the services Hock ultimately wanted to provide. It would also make it difficult for his new, smaller organization to compete against Interbank.

At the June 1971 Charge Account Bankers Association conference in the Bahamas, Hock announced that NBI would abandon the joint effort, take a "unilateral approach" to national authorization, and develop its own private system.[25] Interbank followed suit, and the joint effort effectively dissolved.

---

24. "National Authorization Joint Feasibility Study Final Report".

25. "Card Groups Take Own Authorization Paths", *American Banker*, 29 June 1971, 1.

NBI's BASE

Having decided to develop their own system, NBI did what most firms at that time did: hire a consultant and put out a Request for Proposals (RFP). Of the sixty vendors interested, NBI invited twenty-one to attend a meeting on 8 October 1971, where NBI presented their needs. At this time, NBI was primarily interested in buying an existing system in order to offer a national authorization service in the shortest amount of time possible. In fact, the RFP required that any proposed system must be operational within twelve months (Brooke 1971b).

Although the requested system, which was given the tentative name of "BankAmericard Authorization System Experimental" (BASE), was primarily intended to provide authorization services, the RFP revealed that Hock already had much larger plans. National authorization was merely "the first phase of a more comprehensive nationwide bank information processing system". Building BASE would create a computer network connecting the seventy-six existing BankAmericard centres and processors spread across the nation, and once that network existed, authorization was only one of the many possible services NBI could offer. From the beginning, Hock was intending NBI to be the electronic hub through which all electronic value exchange transactions flowed.

Thirteen vendors submitted proposals in November 1971, and at the time NBI was confident it could offer a nationwide authorization service by the second quarter of 1972. However, in late February 1972, NBI announced that it had rejected all thirteen proposals as none "satisfied enough of [their] functional needs" (Brooke 1972: 1). This very careful statement attempted to gloss over a much worse reality that Hock later admitted: even the best bid was several times more than their allocated budget, twice as long as their desired schedule, and "no vendor was willing to warrant the performance of the system". Hock was told that this was customary in the computer industry and that he should just go back to the NBI board and ask for more money and time. But that would have been antithetical to Hock's personality, not to mention damaging to his reputation, and quoting Emerson's "Trust thyself", he declared that NBI would design and build their own system within the budget and timeframe already approved by the board (Hock 2005: 171).

However, NBI needed help, as they did not have the necessary staff in 1972 to design and build a large-scale computer system. In fact, NBI's complete staff totalled less than twenty employees. They contracted with TRW, one of the thirteen vendors who had submitted a proposal, to design and coordinate development of the system, and hired a few of their employees to manage the effort.[26]

---

26. Aram Tootelian, project manager of BASE, interview with author (6 March 2006), and Win Derman, former Visa technologist, interview with author (28 September 2005). See also Brooke (1972).

Hock assigned them a formidable task: establish a nationwide computer telecommunications network; install terminals in each of the BankAmericard centres around the country and train each centre's staff on how to use them; obtain all the necessary computer and networking hardware; build a data centre to house that hardware; install four regional concentrator minicomputers; write, test, and debug software that could provide online switching of authorization messages twenty-four hours a day, seven days a week; and staff a call centre that could take merchant calls after the local card centres closed for the night. And all of this had to be done by 1 April 1973, just nine months away. Despite the usual association with that day of the year, Hock was not joking.

NBI and TRW busily began development. At the heart of BASE was a redundant pair of Digital Equipment Corporation (DEC) PDP-11/45 minicomputers, housed in NBI's newly constructed data centre in San Mateo, California, just down the peninsula from their San Francisco headquarters. This central computer acted as a real-time switch for authorization requests, which could either come from acquiring authorization centres or directly from the electronic cash register systems of large national merchants. Acquiring centres entered their request into a Harris-Sanders model 804 terminal (often shortened to "Sanders terminal"), which could queue up to ten messages in its internal memory. Periodically a regional concentrator (a DEC PDP-11/20) polled the terminals in its area, collected all pending requests and sent them on to the central switching computer. The switch would determine the issuer from the first few digits of the card number, and forward the request to the appropriate destination.

NBI's choice of DEC PDP minicomputers was atypical for the banking industry, which had standardised on IBM mainframes. Although the DEC machines were perhaps better suited for real-time processing, the primary reason for this choice was Hock's personal feud with "Big Blue" at the time. Sources differ as the exact cause, but all agree IBM had promised support to the fledgling NBI but later reneged. This infuriated Hock, who considered NBI to be the future of computerized banking, and he swore never to do business with IBM again. He later softened when the PDP's could no longer keep up with the transaction volume, and they were forced to port the system to an IBM mainframe.

The issuers also had a Sanders terminal in their authorization centre, on which new requests would appear. However, because many issuers experienced such low interchange volumes at this time, it was common that nobody would be sitting in front of the Sanders terminal to see the incoming authorization request. To remedy this situation, NBI asked Sanders to add a small bell to the terminal, the clapper of which could be triggered electronically when a new request arrived. Convincing Sanders to add the bell proved to be surprisingly difficult task, but Sanders eventually relented, and issuing authorizers learned to jump to their terminals when they heard the bell ring.

After making the authorization decision (either by using their own computer system or printed reports), the issuing authorizer typed the response into the terminal, which was then routed back to the acquirer's terminal through NBI's central switch. A few of the more technically advanced issuers established direct computer-to-computer interfaces with BASE, which as one might expect, greatly improved the speed of authorization. However, this was rather difficult to achieve, as most of these banks ran IBM mainframes, and thus had to translate the DEC communication protocol, as well as the authorizations messages, into their own systems' native formats.

Despite a few minor mishaps (such as the terminal key caps having square pegs whereas the Sanders keyboards had round holes), the system was completed within the original three million dollar budget and on time. On 4 April 1973, the system was put into limited production, and by 1 May it was used twenty-four hours a day, seven days a week. After it ran successfully for a few months, NBI held a formal press conference to announce the system, which was then renamed to the more assured "BankAmericard Service Exchange". However, NBI employees and member bankers would continue to refer to it by its acronym: BASE (Brooke 1973a; O'Neil 1973).[27]

Once BASE began operation, it generated some immediate, noticeable effects. Because NBI could "stand in" and approve authorizations when the issuing bank's centre was closed, merchants could now authorize transactions twenty-four hours a day, seven days a week, regardless of the issuing bank's time zone. Furthermore, an interchange authorization that previously took four to five minutes could now be obtained in just fifty-six seconds. Although fifty-six seconds seems like an eternity from our current perspective, in 1973 this made the system *fast enough* to be a viable competitor to cash and cheques, removing one of the critical barriers to adoption. Lastly, BASE provided a platform upon which the system could expand and improve. In the case of a multisided platform like payment cards, an inability to grow and adapt could actually cause a system to collapse (Evans and Schmalensee 1999: 131–58).

In the 1980s, NBI also played an active role in stimulating the development of electronic authorization terminals that could use standard dial-up telephone lines, and encouraging their adoption by merchants. These terminals allowed merchants to quickly authorize every transaction, greatly increasing the speed of authorization while also reducing the amount of fraud. These terminals were soon enhanced with storage and printing capabilities, allowing merchants to submit transactions electronically to their acquiring bank for clearing and settlement.[28]

---

27. Key caps story from "BASE Is a System of People", *BankAmericard World*, June 1973, 2.

28. Interviews with Bill Powar, Frank Fojtik, Win Derman, and Roger Pierce (all former Visa employees); see also Visa USA, "Visa Dial Terminal Project Final Report" (April 1982).

ELECTRONIC CLEARING AND SETTLEMENT

As noted earlier, the other major operational problem facing the BankAmeri-card system was the lack of a centralised clearing house. Although BASE had computerized interchange authorizations, the members were still required to sort and mail the physical sales drafts to the appropriate issuing bank each day. The member banks were able to cope with this process while the volumes remained low, but as more banks joined NBI, and the sales volume increased by 30 to 40 per cent each year, so did the number of interchange transactions. During 1972, the NBI member banks exchanged ninety-five million drafts, and they projected that this would rise to 225 million by the end of 1975.[29] It was clear that without an automated, centralised clearing house, the BankAmericard system would grind to a halt.

As noted in the previous section, computerizing interchange authoriza-tions was just the first phase of Hock's overall plan to build an electronic value exchange system. Once BASE was put into operation in 1973, Hock quickly began the second phase, which was aptly named BASE II. In this phase, he intended to automate the clearing and settlement of interchange transactions, but instead of using high-speed Magnetic Ink Character Rec-ognition (MICR) readers and sorters as the Fed had done with cheques, he wanted to "truncate" the paper, transforming the sales drafts into elec-tronic records and clearing them through a centralised computer system. Using this approach, interchange transactions could be cleared and settled as early as the night after they were deposited.

Descriptive Billing

However, building an electronic clearing system would require engineer-ing not only the computer and telecommunication systems, but also con-sumer acceptance of a process known as "descriptive billing".[30] In the early 1970s, most banks were still performing "country-club billing", which is the practice of returning the actual punched-card layer of each sales draft to the cardholder, much like banks had always done with cheques. These cancelled drafts were not only a visual memory of the transaction, but also a legal proof of payment.

Country-club billing was actually advantageous for smaller issuers. Because the drafts were punched cards, they could be sorted, tabulated, and collated by rather simple mechanical devices, instead of expensive mainframe computers. Summary bills could be generated using rudimen-tary software developed by BofA, which was still given to new members

---

29. "NBI Planning Paperless Card Drafts", *American Banker*, 18 December 1973, 1.
30. My language here draws upon Law (1987).

when they joined NBI. Additionally, because the drafts were returned to the cardholder, the issuer did not need to capture the merchant names and locations in electronic form, as they were printed directly onto the drafts.

Descriptive billing differed from country-club billing in that the customer received only a description of the transaction. This billing method was preferred by issuers with larger volumes because it required handling the paper only once, which greatly reduced their labour and postage costs. It was also preferred by NBI because it did not require the movement of paper from acquirers to issuers. Ultimately, NBI wanted to truncate the paper at the acquirer and clear the transactions in electronic form, but this would be impossible if cardholders continued to demand the original drafts.

However, neither Hock nor his staff at NBI believed that all cardholders were actually *demanding* the original drafts; they were, instead, merely *accustomed* to receiving them. Although some cardholders were no doubt reassured by the original, most would probably not notice if they received something that merely *looked like* the original, as long as it contained the most important information: the merchant name and location, the date of the transaction, and the amount. In fact, cardholders already received on occasion a clone of the original draft if it was badly mangled by the merchant or the punched-card readers.[31] If the issuer could print what NBI called a *facsimile draft*, based upon transaction information electronically transmitted from the acquirer, most customers might not even notice the difference; and even if they did, the facsimile would still be an adequate evidence of payment. If the cardholders accepted the facsimile drafts without serious complaint, the bank was then one step closer to implementing descriptive billing.

To test this hypothesis, NBI conducted an experiment with six of its more technically advanced banks starting in early 1973.[32] Acquirers of interchange drafts captured the descriptive billing information in electronic form and transmitted it to the issuer. The issuer then computer-printed the transaction information onto the punched-card layer of a new, blank sales draft and sent that to the cardholder with their summarized bill. The facsimile looked nearly the same as the original, but did not contain any details of the purchased merchandise or the cardholder's signature. If a customer could not recognize the charge, or needed the original for some other purpose, the customer could still request it from their issuer. The issuer would then request it from the acquirer, who would send it through the mail. Effectively, the movement and return of physical sales drafts became the exception instead of the rule.

---

31. Denny Dumler, former card manager at a member bank, Visa employee, and VP of the Plus ATM network, interview with author (9 December 2005).

32. "NBI Finds No Major Problems with Facsimile Drafts", *American Banker*, 10 October 1973, 81.

In October 1973, NBI announced that "neither its member banks nor cardholders have related any major problems or objections to the facsimile drafts".[33] Again, it was not that cardholders were *delighted by* the facsimile drafts; they simply did not care enough to complain about them to any significant extent. After a few months, they also became accustomed to them, and requests for originals were infrequent. During the test, cardholders requested only one original for every five hundred facsimiles. Forty-five per cent of those were due to the cardholder not recognizing the acquirer's processing name for the merchant, which often differed from the merchant's trade name, but this could easily be adjusted. Nineteen per cent were requested for business purposes, typically for employers who were wary of the facsimiles, and those cardholders quickly learned to keep the customer receipt layer of the original draft. The remaining 17 per cent were requested by the issuer for fraud analysis and prosecution.[34]

In essence, this test was the key to determining if BASE II was *culturally* possible. NBI could engineer the computer systems and telecommunication networks, but if they could not also "engineer" the cardholder acceptance of facsimile drafts (which were just descriptive billing in a more recognizable form), cardholders would have demanded so many of their originals as to negate the benefits of an electronic clearing and settlement system. The 1973 test showed that facsimile drafts would be acceptable to the current cardholder base, allowing NBI to continue with the design and implementation of BASE II.

Design of BASE II

In essence, the BASE II design was a computerized version of the clearing house concept developed by the London clearing banks in the 1770s (Campbell-Kelly and Aspray 1996: 15–18). Although BASE II was not the first implementation of this idea, commonly called an "automated clearing house" (ACH), it was by far the largest and most ambitious, the first with a national scope, and the first in the domain of bank cards.[35] Members

---

33. "NBI Finds".

34. A later story from December quotes Hock as saying that one in three hundred were requested, so either the ratio increased somewhat over the two-month period, or it was reported incorrectly. See "NBI Planning Paperless Card Drafts", *American Banker*, 18 December 1973, 1. Either way, the ratio was still small enough to justify building BASE II.

35. In the late 1960s, the California commercial banks organized the Special Committee on Paperless Entries (SCOPE), which resulted in the creation of the California Automated Clearinghouse Association (CACHA; Pete Yeatrakas, President of WesPay, formerly CACHA, interview with author [9 December 2006]). This organization, with the help of the Federal Reserve Bank of San Francisco, began operating what seems to be the first ACH in the U.S. on 13 October 1972. See Brooke (1973b).

would now settle *with the clearing house* instead of each other as they had done under the BankAmericard licensing system. Furthermore, BASE II would perform "net settlement", meaning that the amount each member owed the clearing house would be subtracted from the amount the clearing house owed the member, and the member would pay or receive only the difference, greatly reducing the amount of money transferred each day.[36]

Data Capture

However, in order for all of this to work, the acquirers needed to encode the paper sales drafts into an electronic form that could be transmitted to NBI's data centre. This process, known as "data capture", could be accomplished either by manual entry or by scanning the drafts using an Optical Character Recognition (OCR) device. The latter promised to be faster and more accurate than the former, but even in the ideal case, the OCR scanners of the early 1970s could capture only half of the information. The card and merchant numbers were printed in a standard OCR font, but the transaction date and amount were typically hand-written on the draft by the merchant.[37]

Eventually imprinters with adjustable embossed wheels for the date and amount became available, allowing the OCR scanners to read the entire draft automatically. However, these imprinters were not widely adopted, as they were more expensive and consumed more counter space. In fact, many of the largest acquirers continued to use manual data capture until the widespread adoption of electronic merchant POS terminals in the mid-1980s.

Edit Package and TTUs

After acquirers captured the draft information in electronic form, they could then easily separate interchange transactions from local ones and submit the former to the BASE II central computer for clearing. After validating the transaction records using an NBI programme called "the edit package", acquirers copied them onto a magnetic tape, which was then mounted onto their "tape transmission unit" (TTU). The TTUs were custom-engineered DEC PDP-11/10 minicomputers equipped with a tape drive, modem, and a bell (explained later). NBI contracted with DEC to install and maintain one of these devices in each of the eighty-eight BankAmericard processing centres in the U.S.

---

36. Although this was new for the BankAmericard system, it was by no means the first occurrence of the idea. Most other clearing houses already used the net settlement technique to reduce the amount of funds transferred. See Campbell-Kelly and Aspray (1996).

37. "What Credit Card Executives Should Know about OCR Readers", *The Nilson Report* 174:1.

The Central Clearing Computer

At the core of the BASE II system was a redundant pair of large mainframe computers (IBM System/370 model 145s). Each night, starting at 5 p.m. Pacific Time, the central computer would begin calling each of the TTUs according to a schedule established with the processing centres. For five hours the central computer initiated connections to each TTU and read all the transactions contained on each tape. During the validation process, the edit package inserted verification amounts onto the tape so that the mainframe programme could ensure that the information was transmitted accurately; if it had not, the TTU could automatically back up to the last checkpoint and resume transmission. At the end of a successful transmission, the central mainframe then sent an instruction to the TTU that triggered it to ring the aforementioned bell. This bell told the operator in the processing centre to unmount the tape containing the outgoing transactions, and mount a new blank tape for the incoming transactions and summary reports.[38]

The central computer then moved into a two-hour sort and calculation phase. It first calculated the amount owed to each acquirer, which was the total of their submitted transactions minus the interchange reimbursement and NBI's processing fees (1.95 per cent and 2.5 cents per item, respectively). Next, it sorted the transactions by issuer and calculated how much each issuer owed. Finally, it computed the net amount each member owed or was due from the clearing house. This information was then printed by NBI for use in the actual settlement, as well as auditing and accounting.

For five more hours, the mainframe again established connections with each of the TTUs and streamed back all the interchange transactions for which that bank was the issuer. The member banks could then extract these transactions using the edit package and incorporate them into their own billing systems. In addition to the incoming transactions, the central system also transmitted a full clearing report (which the member could use for bookkeeping and reconciliation), as well as the net settlement amount for that bank. By 5 a.m. Pacific Time the next morning, each bank had all the information they needed to bill their cardholders and settle with the clearing house.

The actual movement of "good and final funds" was still accomplished with clearing drafts, but now NBI completed these drafts on behalf of the members. After the clearing drafts were prepared, an NBI employee literally got in her car and drove them to a BofA branch located just down the hill from NBI's data centre. By 1980, the settlement process was also

---

38. Derman interview; Brooke (1974a). The tapes at this time did not have enough room to store both the outgoing and incoming transactions.

computerized by transmitting the net settlement amounts electronically to a clearing bank.

Truncating the Paper

With the help of IBM, NBI completed BASE II by 1 November 1974, within its allocated budget of seven million dollars.[39] On that day, every NBI issuer began receiving electronic interchange transactions via BASE II, but some slow-to-automate acquirers were allowed to continue mailing paper drafts through the Christmas season. By 1 March 1975, all interchange transactions in the NBI system began to be cleared electronically, and overnight the movement of paper sales drafts became the exception instead of the rule (Brooke 1974a).

BASE II altered the BankAmericard system in five important ways. First, BASE II dramatically reduced the time it took to clear and settle interchange transactions. Under the manual system, it took an average of six to eight days for sales drafts to reach the issuer, where they often failed to reconcile with the already paid clearing draft; with BASE II, all sales drafts were now cleared and settled, in batch, overnight.

Second, the reduction in clearing time resulted in a corresponding reduction in float, mostly for the acquirers, but also for the issuers. BASE II essentially forced the acquirers to implement an automated data capture system, enabling them to submit transactions to interchange much more quickly, and thus recover the funds they had already credited to their merchants. Issuers received the transaction details electronically at the same time they paid the acquirers, which not only eliminated the painful reconciliation process, but also provided an easy way to import the transactions into their billing systems in order to recover funds from the cardholder.

Third, automating the interchange process dramatically reduced the labour and postage costs associated with the clearing and settlement of interchange transactions. NBI estimated at the time that BASE II saved the members between fourteen and seventeen million dollars in gross clearing costs during its first year of operation alone (Brooke 1974a). Although the exact amount would have been difficult to substantiate, as so many aspects of the business were in constant flux, there is no question that the labour costs alone would have made the existing manual process uneconomical as the number of interchange transactions increased.

Fourth, faster clearing also meant that issuers now received fraudulent interchange transactions in a more timely manner. Although BASE I stopped many fraudulent transactions, until the mass adoption of POS terminals in the 1980s, it only saw those that were over the merchant's floor limit. The issuer would have no way of knowing that fraud was occurring

---

39. Hock (2005).

until those transactions were cleared through interchange. The faster transactions were cleared, the faster the issuer could detect fraud and take steps
to cancel and recover the card.

Lastly, BASE II established a platform upon which NBI could offer other
batch-oriented data transfer services between the members, just as BASE
I provided a platform for *on-line* message exchange. From its inception,
BASE II allowed members to transmit other administrative transactions
such as charge backs, reversals, and requests for originals, in addition to
interchange drafts. BASE II was later extended to include other kinds of
clearing messages as well, such as rewards for recovering stolen cards or
reimbursements for telex costs incurred by foreign acquirers.[40] With the
combination of BASE I and II, NBI could now facilitate any type of data
exchange between its members. These two systems became the information-processing backbone upon which Hock could eventually provide his
"premier system for the exchange of value".

Although BASE II virtually eliminated the movement of paper between
acquirers and issuers, merchants in the 1970s still filled out paper sales
drafts and physically deposited them at their bank. As those merchants
began to adopt POS terminals that could electronically store and submit
transactions, the paper largely disappeared from that leg of the transaction
as well. Merchants are still required to keep the signed receipts printed by
those terminals and produce them during a dispute, but the original transactions are authorized, captured, submitted, cleared, and settled entirely in
electronic form.

CONCLUSIONS

In the introduction, I posed a series of general questions concerning payment
systems, and this chapter has offered some specific answers by recounting
Visa's origins and its transition from paper-based to fully electronic processing. I described how the Visa membership association structure arose out
of the BankAmericard licensing programme and was designed to address
specific organizational problems identified by the principal actors involved.
I explained how various actors sought to solve what they thought to be the
most pressing operational issue (authorization) in a variety of ways, and
how Visa's BASE was shaped by the earlier efforts of Omniswitch and the
National Joint Authorization System discussion. I showed how Visa needed
to "engineer" consumer acceptance of descriptive billing in order to solve
the issues with clearing and settlement, and how that solution was shaped
by the pre-electronic practice of country-club billing. Finally, I argued that

---

40. Ingrid Kollmann, former Visa employee, interview with author (18 May
2006).

the computerization of these two functions not only solved some of the operational problems plaguing the system at the time, but also created a platform upon which the system could grow and expand.

This chapter is the beginning of an effort to construct a more general socio-technical theory of payment systems. Although consumer payment card systems like Visa and MasterCard are widely adopted and used today, we have already seen in the last decade the introduction of several new consumer-oriented payment systems (e.g. PayPal, mobile payments) that pundits think will pose a significant challenge to these two payments giants. Whether these new systems become widely adopted, or whether they go the way of countless other failed payment systems that we no longer remember, is impossible to predict, but a deep understanding of the social and technical dynamics behind all payment systems will help us identify factors that commonly make the difference between those that become widely adopted and those that do not.

Part V

Wrapping Up and Grand Conclusion

13 Retail Banking and the Dynamics of Information Technology in Business Organizations

Lars Heide

INTRODUCTION

The contributions to this book document the breathtaking change in the scale and scope of bank services across Western Europe and North America throughout the twentieth century. In different ways and in various places, applications of information technology made essential contributions to this change by facilitating the transformation of the organization of work in financial institutions. It has, of course, made the work more efficient, but it has also occasioned a reshaping of jobs of employees and a redesign of the layout of retail bank branches. Gone are the bars that separated customers from cashiers. Many cashiers have been replaced by automated teller machines (ATM) and Internet transactions, and an unobtrusive, open layout has become a familiar sight: fewer cashiers, less tellers, and a greater number of customer service people working at separate desks, each with a personal computer and several chairs for customers. The chapters of this volume chart this transformation of banks and other financial intermediaries throughout the twentieth century, change that has adopted greater intensity since the end of the Second World War.

These chapters document three general characteristics of the dynamics of information technology in this industry:

1. Financial institutions applied three types of information technology: key-set office machines (since the early twentieth century), batch processing technologies (since the 1920s), and computers beyond batch-processing (since the 1970s). Financial institutions acquired established technology, but they also contributed to the development of technological innovation.
2. New technology provided new organizational and strategic opportunities that were seized in similar ways across countries. Each technology was used to support several opportunities that could be conflicting.
3. Key-set office machines and batch-processing technology facilitated Taylor-style rationalization of work, and post-batch-processing computer technology facilitated a broader scope of jobs for the individual. However, they were also used for different modes of work.

The histories of the development of information technology in banks and other financial intermediaries in Western Europe and North America illustrate several general features of the wider role of this technology in business. Typewriters, adding machines, and other stand-alone office machines diffused in businesses in the industrialized world beginning in the early twentieth century. They allowed new and less-trained people to perform various tasks, contributing to the routinization of jobs and the building of taller hierarchies. The batch-processing technologies—punched-card machines and early computers—accelerated this process. Since the 1960s, computers have been contributing significantly in shaping theories of the firm and actual products, production processes, organizations, and work (Aylen 2009; Boyns 2008). This volume is the first attempt to outline this development of a single industry across the Western World.

This is a rich and promising research area for business and government, and a few examples will suffice to indicate the work that has paved the way for this volume: James W. Cortada (2004, 2006, 2008) has written an overview of the computerization in business and private organizations in the United States since 1950. JoAnne Yates (2005) studied information technology in the shaping of the U.S. life insurance industry. Daniel M.G. Raff (2000) analysed the role of information technology in the transformation of book retailing in America in the last quarter of the twentieth century. Jon Agar (2003) has studied the discourse about the mechanization of government work in the United Kingdom from the nineteenth to the twentieth century. He focused on the rise of "expert" movements, groups whose authority has rested on their expertise, which they linked to the adoption of new information technology.

The chapters of this volume raise a number of issues that continue this conversation. In this afterword, I begin by surveying the three phases of mechanization and then discuss the dynamics of mechanization strategies in banks and their impact on banks and other financial intermediaries. I then address the impact on the work of bank clerks.

BANK MECHANIZATION TECHNOLOGIES

The use of information technology by banks in the twentieth century was driven largely by innovation in office machines. First, adding machines and other key-set office machines were introduced, followed by punched-card machines and, since the 1960s, computers in various forms. Joanne Yates (2005) has shown how the U.S. life insurance companies not only adopted but contributed to the shaping of punched-card and mainframe computer technology. Her analysis illustrates the important role of the user in shaping technology and business (Pinch 2001). The history of the LEO computer, built by Britain's J. Lyons Company in the 1950s, was a user-driven innovation where the company designed and implemented systems and technology to serve its specific business needs for organizing and managing complex inventories and operations (Caminer et al. 1996).

Generally speaking, banks preferred to adopt established technology. However, they constituted an important office machine market, which influenced the producers' design and production, and banks were instrumental in developing information technology in several instances. In the years around 1930, the Bank of Alsace and Lorraine was a key actor in a failed project to establish a production of punched-card machines in France based upon designs from Remington Rand in the United States (Heide 2009: 192–94). Cheque clearing was a major task in banks across Western Europe and North America in the 1950s. In California, Bank of America collaborated intensely with a research institution to design a machine for handling cheques, which General Electric came to produce (McKenney, Copeland, and Mason 1995; Fisher and McKenney 1993; McKenney and Fisher 1993). In England, the Powers-Samas Company developed a cheque reader in order to establish a competitive advantage for its equipment (Campbell-Kelly 1989: 178). In the late 1960s, the project of establishing a British National Giro bank was a key element in Minister Tony Benn's project of establishing a British national computer producer champion, which produced International Computers Limited (ICL) in 1968 (Booth and Billings in this volume). Further, banks were major agents in the emergence of ATM technology in several countries from the 1960s to the 1970s (Bátiz-Lazo and Reid 2010). These examples illustrate the importance of approaching information technology as a factor in shaping business, which users and customers at the same time contributed to the shaping of. It was not just a given, external factor.

This observation suggests structuring analysis of information technology according to type of use, both for analyses of information technology in organizations and of the development of information technology and industry. This volume on retail banks and other financial intermediaries suggests three types of information technology: key-set office machines, batch-processing technologies, and computers beyond batch-processing.

Key-set Office Machines

Already before the First World War, banks in several countries adapted key-set office machines, early adding machines, multiplication machines, and typewriters. In the 1930s accounting machines followed, which facilitated distributing transactions between several accounts (Bonin and Thomes in this volume). The key-set office machines were stand-alone machines with few organizational requirements beyond the training of operators (e.g. Seward 1904). They were simple to use, easy to introduce, and produced higher-quality computations and prints.

Batch-Processing Technologies

Punched-card systems contrasted to key-set machines by requiring much wider organizational changes (e.g. Bátiz-Lazo and Wardley 2007; Heide 2009). They were based upon several machines and required strict standardization of information to be processed. Batch-processing was based on handling sets of many standardized little jobs, which resembled conveyor-based industrial production. For example, the calculation of individual interest accrued for a large set of a bank's accounts. Batch-processing facilitated faster execution of manual jobs, but required all tasks to be standardized. Updating the interest on a particular account, for example, had to wait until the next batch job rather than at the customer's request.

Punched-card machines were available since the 1880s, but the early machines only displayed the results of calculations. These had then to be copied manually. Banks only started using punched cards in the early 1920s, when manufacturers added facilities to print lists of selected information, from punched cards and outcome of calculations. During the 1920s, punched-card machines got improved calculation capability and gained the possibility of printing alphabetical characters. These facilities opened for access the extensive use of punched cards in banks in Germany and France in the 1920s and 1930s, which further grew in the 1950s (Bonin and Thomes in this volume). In the 1950s, financial retail intermediaries in other countries also adopted punched-card processing. A downside was that it required several machines and therefore a great deal of space; they were also noisy, which forced them to be located in back offices or at wholly separate locations. Banks used punched-card processing to handle deposit administration, credit administration, monitoring holdings, and frequently producing account statements for current account holders (Heide 1996: 110–12; 2009: 192–93).

The first commercial mainframe computers were produced in the early 1950s. A decade later, computers had attained reliability and a somewhat lower price enabled several banks to start acquiring them. However, they still had restricted calculating capacity because of limited storage. Punched cards, punch tape, and magnetic tape were the only large-scale memory and data entry media. Therefore, inputting data required punching or keying it unto magnetic tape and banks had to operate through batch-processing, which to a large extent made computers just advanced punched-card machines. Large banks and associations of smaller banks established computer centres away from their main customer offices (Appelquist and Bátiz-Lazo and Maixé-Altés in this volume). Initially data were exchanged between banks and computer centres through shipment of vouchers, punched cards, magnetic tapes, and printouts. Subsequently, various kinds of hierarchical data links were established between banks and their computer centres (Martin, Thomes, del Angel, and Mooij in this volume). Banks focused on jobs suited for batch-processing, like calculation on interest of accounts with many transactions and handling the fast-growing number of cheques which customers issued between the 1950s and the 1980s.

In the 1950s, cheques became a general alternative means of payment in the industrialized parts of North America and Western Europe. This made mechanization of cheque clearing urgent in banks as volumes increased. Banks in North America and Western Europe standardized cheque designs with magnetic ink character cheque numbers to ease manual handling and facilitate machine reading (one design for continental Western Europe and a different design for Great Britain and North America; see Heide 1996: 268). In California, Bank of America found cheque handling onerous and costly and, in 1952, they engaged in developing a mechanical cheque-handling machine. It became operational in 1961, linked to an IBM computer (McKenney, Copeland and Mason 1995: 41–75). At the same time, IBM developed its own cheque reader and cheque sorter, which became a major sales argument in the 1960s (Bashe et al. 1986: 498–500; Nerheim and Nordvik 1986: 127).

Credit cards emerged in the 1950s and became widespread in the 1960s and 1970s. They were based upon paper processing, which implied the information was keyed in or read by an optical reader for the clearing operation. Visa and MasterCard originated as means to get around regulations in the United States that a bank could operate in only one state. This regulation was abolished in the 1980s, and simultaneously magnetic strips in credit cards were introduced and facilitated machine processing without manually assisted data entry. Banks and credit card organizations established complex batch-processing-based clearing of credit card receipts and cheque transactions between banks in the United States and beyond (del Angel and Stearns in this volume).

Computers Beyond Batch-Processing

Online processing by cashiers and other bank employees opened for real-time processing, which advanced banks data processing beyond batch-processing. Since the early 1970s, banks have introduced three phases of online processing, which has had a large impact on customer services and employee tasks.

The first phase of online processing was the introduction of online terminals for mainframe computers, which appeared in the late 1960s and became common in the 1970s. They gave the cashier access to the customer's actual credit balance, which simplified the operations of endorsing and registering transactions. First, the banks used cash register terminals with small one- or two-line displays. Later, video terminals diffused in banks. They had a virtual dialogue, resembling a personal computer today, and were subsequently used for other purposes than recording transactions. Banks applied central and decentralized computer configurations. In a central computer configuration, all terminals in the bank were permanently linked to the bank's main computer, which gave real online information about the actual credit balance on all accounts, but the bank's operations depended on the reliability of the net connections and permanent net connections across a country were costly. The alternative was a decentralized configuration with the terminals in each branch office linked to the branch's own computer. Once every twenty-four hours the branch office computers exchanged data with the bank's main computer. The outcome was information from the day before on customers' credit balance. This configuration reduced the bank's dependency on the national data net and its transmission costs (Mooij, Thomes, and Bátiz-Lazo and Maixé-Altés in this volume).

In addition to internal mechanization of bank jobs, they worked to simplify transactions between separate banks both within a country and internationally. The Eurocheque was introduced in 1968 and was planned by the German banks to facilitate customer payments across national borders (Bonhage 2010). In 1973, the Society for Worldwide Interbank Financial Telecommunication (SWIFT) was established in Brussels, Belgium, with the mission of creating a shared worldwide data processing and communications link and a common language for international financial transactions. It started transferring money in 1977, when 518 banks in fifteen countries were SWIFT members and made 3.5 million interbank transactions.

Also, the London Stock Exchange used information technology to mechanize production of settlement accounts for its members. In the 1970s, the Exchange developed software to circulate its market information in real time beyond the Stock Exchange building, which subsequently facilitated broadening the number of organizations trading at the exchange, both geographically and in number (Pardo-Guerra in this volume).

The second phase of online processing was based on the computer industry's introduction of personal computers and microprocessors in the early 1980s. They supported more powerful mainframe computers and decentralized networks, which contrasted with the older networks, where all the bank's terminals linked to its main computer. Local Area Networks (LAN) of personal computers linked to a server in each branch office improved speed and reliability because the computer system ceased to rely on one single computer. In addition, the information industry introduced relational databases, which facilitated improved interactive computer operations for employees in banks (Bergin and Haigh 2009: 38–39). This increased the possibility that a bank employee could access selected information on a customer and general information on the bank's products (Mooij, Appelquist, and Bátiz-Lazo and Maixé-Altés in this volume).

The other major technical investment at that time was an extensive expansion of ATMs, which were developed largely independently in several countries. The first were installed in the late 1960s, and ATMs became common across Europe and North America in the late 1980s (Bátiz-Lazo and Reid 2010). The ATM was the first device to shift routine bank jobs from the teller to the consumer.

The third phase of online processing was the introduction of telephone and Internet banking. This has grown steadily since the mid-1990s, closely linked to an increased focus on self-service. Simultaneously, personal computers replaced the 'dumb' terminals and became standard work stations for bank employees, which increased the employee's access to structured information (foreign exchange rates, available mortgage arrangements, Stock Exchange quotations, etc.) and sophisticated information process tools. This changed the employees' jobs and the layout of many retail banks (Appelquist in this volume).

DYNAMICS IN BANK MECHANIZATION

The mechanization of retail financial intermediaries rested both within the intermediaries themselves and among vendors and competitors. Gunnar Nerheim and Helge W. Nordvik documented IBM's endeavours in Norway, which included the selling of punched-card and computer equipment to banks (Nerheim and Nordvik 1986: 123–26). The quick early diffusion of computers among British banks indicates a dynamic factor outside each of the banks, like vendors or networks of banks (Martin in this volume). In France, the introduction of office machines in the interwar years was based upon information about mechanization in banks in Germany, Belgium, the Netherlands, and England (Bonin in this volume). This volume focuses on the internal development in financial institutions and several chapters document the dynamics of mechanization through growing demand from customers for specific services which caused rising costs (Mooij, Bonin, and del Angel in this volume).

For establishing and operating punched-card and computer applications, the cases emphasize the role of the financial institutions' own employees, which seem to coincide with the "Organization and Method" (O&M) discipline promoted in Britain and the Netherlands in the first half of the twentieth century as a way of improving administrative efficiency by people within the organizations working to improve office work (Guerreiro-Wilson 2008: 321–23). In Britain, when computers came on the scene, the O&M experts claimed to have the ideal expertise to introduce the computer into the offices. However, they lost their position to purely technical experts who came mostly from outside their organization and who would come to control the introduction and use of computers. In contrast, in the Netherlands similar experts found a new field of application in the diffusion of electronic computers (Guerreiro-Wilson et al. 2004).

In addition, changes in bank mechanization were centred around vendors and external experts. Scholars describe IBM as an efficient sales organization, and the history of IBM Norway is based upon vendor material and emphasizes the vendor's role in establishing punched-card and computer applications (Engelbourg 1976; Nerheim and Nordvik 1986). The stories of several banks in Britain, Spain, Mexico, and the Netherlands focus on the role of bank employees and bank officers in establishing computer applications (Martin, del Angel, and Bátiz-Lazo and Maixé-Altés in this volume). The history of the British savings banks included acquisition of external expertise (Bátiz-Lazo and Maixé-Altés in this volume). This illustrates the role of consultants, who took advantage of the growing complexity of information systems and machines. Matthias Kipping (2002) has shown how information technology—and its adaptation to client organizations— became an increasingly important part of consulting services.

The various office machine technologies played varying dynamic roles in the development of bank organizations. This raises the important issue of what happened when a job or task was transferred from one setting to another? Nicholas Rowland and Tom Gieryn's (2008) analysis on a different field shows that the organizational process that accompanied the transfer of some technology from one organizational setting to another reshaped the technology. This volume illustrates the location and character of these transformations. Key-set office machines seem to have had little impact on the structure of the main office and branches of banks. In contrast, the batch-processing technologies—punched-card systems and the early mainframe computers—tended to relocate operations to back offices and separate locations. Punched-card machines were noisy and mainframe computers were bulky and produced much heat and their locations required extensive air conditioning (Bonin and Martin in this volume).

Some banks used the batch-processing technologies to enhance central control, whereas others used the same technology to establish several regional computing centres or emphasized the role of local offices. Bancomer and Banamex in Mexico established regional computer centres because the country's telecommunications infrastructure did not yet facilitate reliable national online networks (del Angel in this volume). Savings banks in Britain, Germany, and Spain originated as small, local savings banks. These banks and many small rural banks in the Netherlands introduced punched cards and computers by establishing new shared computer centres as separate organizations because they found a need for batch-processing mechanization and each was too small to be able to afford their own installation (Mooij, Thomes, and Bátiz-Lazo and Maixé-Altés in this volume). A less costly alternative was to acquire punched-card and computer service from the service bureaus operated by non-banking organizations. This alternative was used by savings banks in England and Wales (Bátiz-Lazo and Maixé-Altés in this volume). After the many small rural banks in the Netherlands had established a shared computer centre that standardized data processing between its members, the computer centre became an important element in bank mergers in the 1980s (Mooij in this volume).

The introduction of post-batch-processing computer systems in the 1980s facilitated both centralizing and decentralizing strategies among banks, which provides possibility for future research. The introduction of ATMs, telephone, and Internet banking reduced customers' visits to their retail branch and the less frequent visits were used to justify a diminishing number of retail branches. Simultaneously, the increasing use of applications of information technology in selling retail services facilitated the marketing of a larger range of products and services, including mortgage and insurance. Once bank regulation allowed this growing scope, banks established financial supermarkets through mergers with insurance companies and mortgage institutions. Computer-based tools enabled employees to manage a broad range of issues and the banks to delegate decisions committing the bank, like granting of loans. Donald McKenzie (2006) studied the impact of the emergence of computerized mathematical models on financial intermediaries and their customers. He showed how financial models influenced and shaped the world they tried to understand. But these models did not only influence the way bank people appreciated the business environment, they were the basis for the computerized tool that bank employees applied in dealing with customers.

Martha Poon (in this volume) tells how the operations research firm Fair, Isaac & Company developed consumer credit risk calculation. The original technology was a relatively simple algorithm embedded in a cardboard table that allowed credit managers to associate an empirically assessed risk of defaulting with a consumer. Poon describes how the cardboard scorecard was shaped. Subsequently, tools like consumer credit risk calculation became the basis for computer-mediated risk management. Her chapter illustrates the role of commercial scientific actors in the process. Similar tools were the basis for establishing risky subprime lending that became a central element in the U.S. credit crisis in 2007.

This volume demonstrates that retail banks and other financial intermediaries seized the organizational and strategic opportunities of new information technology in similar ways across countries. Each technology was used to support several opportunities that could be conflicting. This is a central observation for further studies into the role of information technology in the shaping of business and government.

MECHANIZATION AND WORK

Likewise, this volume demonstrates that the introduction of information technology by retail banks and other financial intermediaries had a similar impact on the individual's work across countries. Key-set office machines and batch-processing technology facilitated Taylor-style rationalization of work, and post-batch-processing computer technology facilitated a broader scope of jobs for the individual. However, the impact of new technology went beyond victimization. It provided opportunities for individuals which some were able and ready to utilize. This observation should also apply for studies of other businesses and government.

The key-set office machines were simple to introduce and produced higher-quality computations and print. They allowed banks to use less-skilled clerks, notably in German banks during the two world wars (Thomes in this volume). In this perspective, individual labour can be seen as passive recipients of the changes wrought by new systems and technology. In the most notable cases, this passivity equated to victimization. Harry Braverman's (1974) thesis on the "deskilling" of labour by technology was an important exponent of the idea that technology users were being exploited. However, literature on the development of office work and the changing role of women in offices in the late nineteenth century see women users of the new technology of the typewriter as having a certain agency in the use of that technology. Early female users of typewriters were not passive and not victims; they were women who were seeking to carve out an occupational niche for themselves that they deemed to be superior to shop-work or factory work (Guerreiro-Wilson 1998: 238, 279–80).

The office machine producers developed punched-card machines and early mainframe computers to be used to attain economic scale efficiency along the lines suggested by Taylorism in the production industries. The implementation of the Tayloristic mode of organization in industrial production made it possible to use less-skilled workers and still achieve sharp rises in productivity. However, the downside was more routine-based production (Appelquist in this volume). The introduction of online cashier terminals in the 1970s—they eventually became the first post-batch-processing computer technology—was probably exclusively reasoned as yet another improvement to attain additional scale efficiency. And it could readily be applied in this way. Online terminals facilitated simple ways to control the cashier's efficiency.

The facilities to look up information about the bank's accounts and other information only came gradually into general use. The introduction of relational databases, personal computer work stations, and LAN increased the ability of bank employees to access selected information on the current customer and general information on bank products, rates of interest in other banks, current rates of exchange, possible mortgage arrangements, Stock Exchange quotations, etc. This increased the scope of clerks' jobs and provided additional freedom in their work, which reduced simple managerial control. Therefore, banks could apply the new technology to attain improved economic efficiency or they could focus on development of capabilities, applying a longer-term perspective.

In Sweden in the period from 1975 to 1985, several banks decided simultaneously to change work processes in a way that led to the creation of new, more qualified positions in which a greater number of tasks were performed by each employee and deskilling was avoided. This was the outcome even though an increased number of routine-based tasks were being introduced (Appelquist in this volume).

The information and computer technology investments since 1985 supported the strategic change in the Swedish banks, which focused on self-services in order to reduce the need for routine transactions. Moreover, these investments enabled an increase in the number of personal bankers selling more complex financial services, which generated greater revenues. This turned the focus to the personnel's understanding of the products they were marketing. First, they had a broad, but shallow, understanding of new products and services. A move towards specialization then took place among employees. Banks started demanding expert knowledge in more narrowly defined areas. The reasons were the increased use of Internet banking and the rise in the number of services offered through them, as well as the increased demand for more qualified financial services. Indicators of a development towards increased specialization included the increase in the share of employees in positions requiring higher–level skills, and the fast-growing numbers of employees with a university education.

The history of technological change in banks and other financial intermediaries, then, illustrates several key features in the operation of our computerized society and how it has developed since the end of the Second World War. Information technology provides an entry into understanding work in business organizations and how organizations operate and develop across countries. This complements management and labour perspectives on these developments.

References

100 Jahre Commerzbank 1870–1970. 1970. Frankfurt am Main: F. Knapp.

Abelshauser, W. 2004. *Deutsche Wirtschaftsgeschichte seit 1945*. Munich: Beck.

Abrahamsson, M., and L.O. Grönstedt. 1985. *A New Terminal System—A Case Study in Decision Making*. Handelsbankens Småskriftserie 24 (Intra–bank Work Series). Stockholm: Svenska Handelsbanken.

Ackrill, M., and L. Hannah. 2001. *Barclays: The Business of Banking, 1690–1996*. Cambridge: Cambridge University Press.

ADB för Bankmän. 1970. Malmö: Banco Information AB and Hermods.

Agar, J. 2003. *The Government Machine: A Revolutionary History of the Computer*. Cambridge, MA: MIT Press.

Allen, G.C. 1976. *The British Disease: A Short Essay on the Nature and Causes of the Nation's Lagging Wealth*. London: Institute of Economic Affairs.

Anand, B.N., M.G. Rukstad, and C.H. Paige. 2000. "Capital One Financial Corp.". *Harvard Business School Cases* (April): 1–28.

Anaya, L. 2002. *Colapso y reforma. La integración del sistema bancario en el México revolucionario 1913–1932*. Mexico City: Universidad de Zacatecas-Miguel Ángel Porrúa.

Angel, G. del. 2002. "Paradoxes of Financial Development. The Construction of the Mexican Banking System". PhD dissertation, Department of History, Stanford University, CA.

———. 2006. *The Corporate Governance of the Mexican Banking System. A Historical Perspective: 1940–2000*. Mexico City: CIDE, Documento de Trabajo DE 373.

———. 2007. *BBVA-Bancomer. 75 años*. Mexico City: El Equilibrista.

Appelquist, J. 2005. *Informationsteknik och Organisatorisk Förändring -Teknik, Organisation och Produktivitet i Svensk Banksektor 1975–2003*. Stockholm: Almqvist and Wiksell International.

Ash, N. 1987. "Cajas Cash in by Concentration". *Euromoney (Supplement)* 1 (September): 8–9.

Ashauer, G. 2005. *Sparkassen und Banken im Wettbewerb. Strukturwandel im deutschen Kreditgewerbe*. Stuttgart: Deutscher Sparkassenverlag.

Austrian, G. 1982. *Herman Hollerith. Forgotten Giant of Information Processing*. New York: Columbia University Press.

Autor, D.H., F. Levy, and R.J. Murnane. 2002. "Upstairs, Downstairs: Computers and Skills on Two Floors of a Large Bank". *Industrial and Labor Relations Review 55*, no. 3: 432–47.

Aylen, J. 2009. "'You've Got to Roll with It': Radical Adoption of Computers and Changes to Managerial Routines at Llanwern Steelworks, South Wales". Presented at IT in Shaping Work Processes and Organizations, SHOT SIGCIS

Conference in honor of Michael Mahoney, The Pittsburgh Meeting, 15–18 October.

Ballarín, E. 1985. *Estrategias competitivas para la banca*. Barcelona: Ariel.

Balogh, T. 1959. "The Apotheosis of the Dilettante". In *The Establishment*, edited by H. Thomas. London: Anthony Blond: 83–126.

Banamex. 2004. *Banco Nacional de México. Su historia (1884–2004)*. Mexico City: Banamex.

Bank-Automation in Vormarsch. 1964. *Zeitschrift für das gesamte Kreditwesen* 19: 905–907.

Bank for International Settlements. 2003. "Payments Systems in the Netherlands". *Red Book*, 287–314.

Barendregt, J. 1993. *The Dutch Money Purge. The Monetary Consequences of German Occupation and Their Redress after Liberation, 1940–1952*. PhD dissertation, Vrije Universiteit, Amsterdam.

Barnett, C. 1986. *The Audit of War: The Illusion and Reality of Britain as a Great Nation*. London: Macmillan.

Bashe, C.J., L.R. Johnson, J.H. Palmer, and E.W. Pugh. 1986. *IBM's Early Computers*. Cambridge, MA: MIT Press.

Bátiz-Lazo, B. 1998. "Internal and External Influences on Innovations in Commercial Banking, PhD dissertation, University of Manchester, Manchester.

———. 2004. "Strategic Alliances and Competitive Edge: Insights from Spanish and UK Banking Histories". *Business History* 46, no. 1: 23–56.

———. 2009. "Emergence and Evolution of Proprietary ATM Networks in the UK". *Business History* 51, no. 1: 1–27.

Bátiz-Lazo, B., and T. Boyns. 2003. "Automation and Management Accounting in British Manufacturing and Retail Financial Services, 1945–68". Paper presented at the workshop on The Information Systems and Technology in Organisations and Society, Barcelona, Universitat Pompeu Fabra.

———. 2004. "The Business and Financial History of Automation and Technological Change in 20ᵗʰ Century Banking". *Accounting, Business and Financial History Journal* 14, no. 3: 225–32.

Bátiz-Lazo, B., and G. del Angel. 2003. "Competitive Collaboration and Market Contestability: Cases in Mexican and UK Banking (1945–75)". *Accounting, Business and Financial History* 13, no. 3: 1–30.

Bátiz-Lazo, B., and J.C. Maixé-Altés. 2009. "Managing Technological Change by Committee: The Origins of Data Processing Networks in Spanish and British Savings Banks (c. 1960–1988)". Presented at the European Business History Association-Business History Conference Joint Meeting, Fashions: Business Practices in Historical Perspective, Milan, 11–13 June.

Bátiz-Lazo, B., and R. Reid. 2010. "The Development of Cash Dispensing Technology in the UK". *IEEE Annals in the History of Computing* 32: no. 2. Available at http://www.ieeexplore.ieee.org/stamp/stamp.jsp?tp=&arnumber=5396280 (accessed 10 August 2010).

Bátiz-Lazo, B., and P. Wardley. 2007. "Banking on Change: Information Systems and Technologies in UK High Street Banking 1919–69". *Financial History Review* 14, no. 2: 177–205.

Bátiz-Lazo, B., and D. Wood. 1999. "Management of Core Capabilities in Mexican and European Banks". *International Journal of Service Industry Management (Special Issue on Service Management in Latin America)* 10, no. 5: 430–48.

———. 2002. "An Historical Appraisal of Information Technology in Commercial Banking". *Electronic Markets* 12, no. 3: 1–12.

———. 2003. "Strategy, Competition and Diversification in European and Mexican Banking". *International Journal of Bank Marketing* 21, no. 4–5: 2002–16.

Belden, T.G., and M.R. Beldena. 1962. *The Lengthening Shadow: The Life of Thomas J. Watson*. Boston: Brown and Company.

Benn, A.W. 1965. *The Regeneration of Britain*. London: Victor Gollancz.

Benn, T. 1988. *Out of the Wilderness: Diaries, 1963–67*. London: Arrow Books.

Bergin, T.J., and T. Haigh. 2009. "The Commercialization of Database Management Systems, 1969–1983". *IEEE Annals of the History of Computing* 31, no. 4: 26–41.

Bergström, R. 1996. "Nordiska Terminalprojektet—Datasaabs Perspektiv". In *Tema Bank—Datasaab och Bankerna*, edited by H. Tord-Jöran. Linköping: Datasaabs vänner: 20–34.

Berthau C. 1928. "Étude sur l'organisation mécanographique des services 'position' et 'comptes courants' du Crédit Nantais". *Banque*, 326–27.

Black, F. 1971. "Toward a Fully Automated Stock Exchange". *Financial Analysts Journal* 27, no. 6: 23–87.

Blackaby, F.T. 1978. "Incomes Policy". In *British Economic Policy 1960–74*, edited by F.T. Blackaby. Cambridge: Cambridge University Press: 360–401.

Boer, S. de. 2003. "Rabobank's Domestic and International Strategies, 1972–2002". *Popular Banking and the Financial System*. EABH Proceedings from the Conference Hosted by National Bank of Slovakia, Bratislava (May).

Boer, S. de, and J. Frankhuizen. 2004. *Een eigenzinnige reus; Veertig jaar automatisering bij de Rabobank*. Utrecht: Rabobank.

Böhle, K., and A. Arbussà. 1999. *Electronic Payment Systems in European Countries. Country Synthesis Report*. Karlsruhe: Forschungszentrum Karlsruhe GmbH.

Bolt, W. 2003. "Retail Payments in the Netherlands: Some Facts and some Theory, De Nederlandsche Bank". *Research Memorandum WO 722* (January): 1–40.

Bonhage, B. 2007. "Befreit im Netz. Bankdienstleistungen im Spannungsfeld zwischen Kunden und Computern". In *Vernetzte Steuerung. Soziale Prozesse im Zeitalter technischer Netzwerke*, edited by S. Kaufmann. Zürich: Chronos: 95–108.

———. 2010. "Eurocheque: Creating a 'Common Currency'. European Infrastructure for the Cashless Mass Payments". In *Materializing Europe. Technologies of Transnationalism*, edited by A.W. Badenoch and A. Fickers. London: Palgrave Macmillan: 182–97.

Bonhage, B., and K. Girschik. 2005. "Die Selbstbedienungsgesellschaft". *Akkumulation* 21:1–11.

Bonin, H. 1988. "L'informatique française en quête d'entrepreneurs et de marchés (1963–1983)". *Revue Historique* 567:53–89.

———. 1997. "Les banques & la ive République". *Historiens-Géographes* 357–358:291–305.

———. 2000. *Les banques françaises de l'entre-deux-guerres*. Paris: Plage.

———. 2002. *La Banque nationale de crédit. Histoire de la quatrième banque de dépôts française en 1913–1932*. Paris: Plage.

———. 2004. "The Development of Accounting Machines in French Banks from the 1920s to the 1960s". *Accounting, Business and Financial History* 14, no. 3: 257–76.

Booth, A.E. 2000. "Inflation, Expectations and the Political Economy of Conservative Britain, 1951–64". *Historical Journal* 43:827–47.

———. 2004. "Technical Change in Branch Banking at the Midland Bank, 1945–75". *Accounting, Business and Financial History* 14, no. 3: 277–300.

———. 2007. *The Management of Technical Change: Automation in the UK and USA since 1950*. Basingstoke: Palgrave Macmillan.

———. 2008. "Technological Change and Gender in the Labour Policies of British Retail Banks, 1945–70". In *Managing the Modern Workplace: Productivity,*

Politics and Workplace Culture in Post-War Britain, edited by J. Melling and A.E. Booth. Aldershot: Ashgate: 101–24.

Börnfors, L. 1996. *Bankmannen*. Lund: Historiska Media.

Bowker, G.C. 1994. *Science on the Run: Information Management and Industrial Geophysics at Schlumberger, 1920–1940*. Cambridge, MA: MIT Press.

Boyer, R., and M. Freyssenet. 2002. *The Productive Systems. The Conditions of Profitability*. London and New York: Palgrave-MacMillan.

Boyns, T. 2008. "Accounting, Information, and Communication Systems". In *The Oxford Handbook of Business History*, edited by G. Jones and J. Zeitlin. Oxford: Oxford University Press: 447–69.

Boynton, A., and T.G. Milazzo. 1996. "Post-Fordist Debate: A Theoretical Perspective to Information Technology and the Firm". *Accounting, Management and Information Technologies* 6, no. 3: 157–73.

Brand, S. 1995. *How Buildings Learn: What Happens after They Are Built*. New York and London: Penguin Group.

Braverman, H. 1974. *Labour and Monopoly Capitalism: The Degradation of Work in the Twentieth Century*. London: Monthly Review Press.

Brooke, P. 1971a. "City NB&T, Columbus, to Test Point-of-Sale Card Authorization, Data Capture in Suburbs". *American Banker*, 14 July, 1.

———. 1971b. "NBI Plans to Sign Pact for Nationwide Authorization System by Year's End". *American Banker*, 4 November, 1.

———. 1971c. "Quigley Describes Operation of Omniswitch; Urges Cooperation in National Development". *American Banker*, 11 August, 6–7.

———. 1972. "BankAmericard Schedules April Start for 24-Hour National Card Authorization". *American Banker*, 21 August, 1.

———. 1973a. "Electronic Data Transmission Net Linking All US BankAmericard Centers is Operative". *American Banker*, 11 May, 1.

———. 1973b. "In Past Year, EFTS Concepts Shift from Theory to Action". *American Banker*, 4 June, 13.

———. 1974a. "BankAmericard Begins Electronic Interchange of Drafts". *American Banker*, 6 November, 1.

———. 1974b. "IBANCO, Ltd., Organized to Manage Worldwide BankAmericard Program". *American Banker*, 20 September, 1.

Brooks, A.W. 1965. "The People Concerned in Automation". In *Automation in Banking*. London: The Institute of Bankers: 19–36.

Buck, S.P. 2008. *EPIC and the Use of State Tables: Recollections 30 Years on*. Unpublished manuscript.

Bullock, N. 2002. *Building the Post-War World*. London: Routledge.

Cairncross, A.K. 1987. "Prelude to Radcliffe". *Revista di Storia Economica (Second Series)* 4:1–20.

Callon, M. 2002. "From Science as an Economic Activity to the Socioeconomics of Scientific Research". In *Science Bought and Sold: Essays on the Economics of Science*, edited by P. Mirowski and E.M. Sent. Chicago: University of Chicago Press: 277–317.

Callon, M., and J. Law. 1989. "On the Construction of Sociotechnical Networks: Content and Context Revisited". In *Knowledge and Society: Studies in the Sociology of Science Past and Present*, edited by L. Hargens, R. Alun Jones, and A. Pickering. Greenwich, CT: JAI Press: 57–83.

Callon, M., and F. Muniesa. 2002. "Economic Markets as Calculative and Calculated Collective Devices". *Organization Studies* 26, no. 8: 1229–50.

Cameron, Lord. 1963. *Report of the Inquiry into the Complaint Made by the National Union of Bank Employees (Cmnd. 2202)*. London: HMSO.

Caminal, R., J. Gual, and X. Vives. 1990. "Competition in Spanish Banking". In *European Banking in the 1990s*, edited by J. Dermine. Oxford: Blackwell: 271–324.

Caminer, D., J. Aris, P. Hermon, and F. Land. 1996. *User-Driven Innovation: The World's First Business Computer.* London: McGraw-Hill.

Campbell-Kelly, M. 1989. *ICL. A Business and Technical History.* Oxford: Oxford University Press.

———. 1992. "Large-Scale Data Processing in the Prudential, 1850–1950". *Accounting, Business and Financial History* 2:117–39.

———. 1998. "Data Processing and Technological Change: The Post Office Savings Bank, 1861–1930". *Technology and Culture* 39, no. 1: 1–32.

———. 2003. *From Airline Reservation to Sonic the Hedgehog.* Cambridge, MA: MIT Press.

Campbell-Kelly, M., and W. Aspray. 1996. *Computer: A History of the Information Machine.* New York: Basic Books.

Campbell-Kelly, M., M. Croarken, R. Flood, and E. Robson, eds. 2003. *The History of Mathematical Tables.* Oxford: Oxford University Press.

Canals, J. 1994. *Competitive Strategies in European Banking.* Oxford: Clarendon Press.

———. 1997. *Universal Banking.* Oxford: Oxford University Press.

Cantarell, A., and M. González. 2002. *Historia de la computación en México.* 3 vols. Mexico City: Hobbiton Ediciones.

Capelins, P., and N. Rogovsky. 1994. "New Work Systems and Skill Requirements". *International Labour Review* 133, no. 2: 203–20.

Carmille, R. 1938. "La mécanographie au service de l'évolution économique". *Revue d'Économie Politique* 52, no. 4: 1121–39.

Casper, M.J., and A.E. Clarke. 1998. "Making the Pap Smear into the 'Right Tool' for the Job: Cervical Cancer Screening in the USA, Circa 1940–95". *Social Studies of Science* 28, no. 2: 255–90.

Castells, M. 1996. *The Information Age: Economy, Society and Culture. The Rise of the Network Society.* Vol. 1. Malden, MA: Blackwell.

———. 2000. "Information Technology and Global Capitalism". In *On the Edge,* edited by A. Giddens and W. Hutton. London: Jonathan Cape: 52–75.

Ceruzzi, P.E. 2003. *A History of Modern Computing.* Cambridge, MA: MIT Press.

Chandler, A.D. 1977. *The Visible Hand: The Managerial Revolution in American Business.* Cambridge, MA: Belknap Press.

———. 2001. *Inventing the Electronic Century.* Cambridge, MA: Harvard University Press.

Chandler, A.D., and J.W. Cortada. 2000. *A Nation Transformed by Information.* Oxford: Oxford University Press.

Chang, V. 2005. "Capital One Financial Corporation: Setting and Shaping Strategy". *Stanford Graduate School of Business* Case SM-135: 31.

Channon, D.F. 1977. *British Banking Strategy and the International Challenge.* London: Macmillan.

———. 1978. *The Service Industries: Strategy, Structure and Financial Performance.* London: Macmillan.

———. 1988. *Global Banking Strategy.* New York: John Wiley and Sons.

Chown, J.A. 1994. *History of Money: From AD 800.* London: Routledge.

Chutkow, P. 2001. *VISA: The Power of an Idea.* Chicago: Harcourt.

Collier, S. 2008. "Enacting Catastrophe: Preparedness, Insurance, Budgetary Rationalization". *Economy and Society* 37, no. 2: 224–50.

Collins, H. 1975. "The Seven Sexes: A Study in the Sociology of a Phenomenon, or the Replication of Experiments in Physics". *Sociology* 9:205–24.

Committee of London Clearing Bankers. 1978. *Evidence of the London Clearing Bankers to the Committee to Review the Functioning of Financial Institutions (General Memorandum of Evidence to the Wilson Committee).* London: HMSO.

Coopey R. 1999. "Management and the Introduction of Computing in British Industry, 1945–70". *Contemporary British History* 13, no. 3: 59–71.
———. 2004. *Information and Technology Policy: An International History.* New York and Oxford: Oxford University Press.
Cortada, J.W. 1993. *Before the Computer: IBM, NCR, Burroughs and Remington-Rand, and the Industry They Created, 1865–1956.* Princeton, NJ: Princeton University Press.
———. 1996. *Information Technology as Business History.* Westport, CT: Greenwood.
———. 2004. *The Digital Hand, Volume 1: How Computers Changed the Work of American Manufacturing, Transportation, and Retail Industries.* Oxford and New York: Oxford University Press.
———. 2006. *The Digital Hand, Volume 2: How Computers Changed the Work of American Financial, Telecommunications, Media and Entertainment Industries.* Oxford and New York: Oxford University Press.
———. 2008. "Patterns and Practices in How Information Technology Spread around the World". *IEEE Annals of the History of Computing* 30, no. 4: 4–25.
Cottle, S., and K. Mickelwait. 1959. "Composite Earnings Performance of the Major Consumer Finance Companies". In *SRI Project, no. I-2737.* Menlo Park: Stanford Research Institute: 6.
Council of the Stock Exchange. 1973. "ARIEL—the Council's View". *Stock Exchange Journal* 23, no. 2: 6.
Cronon, W. 1992. *Nature's Metropolis: Chicago and the Great West.* New York: W.W. Norton and Company.
Dankers, J.J., J. van der Linden, and J. Vos. 2001. *Spaarbanken in Nederland; Ideeën en Organisatie, 1817–1990.* Amsterdam: Boom.
Darrieulat, O. 1992. "Histoire de la Compagnie des machines Bull (1931–1945)". PhD dissertation, University of Paris 10-Nanterre, Paris.
Daston, L. 1994. "Enlightenment Calculations". *Critical Inquiry* 21:182–202.
Daumas, M. 1996. "La filiation des machines à calculer contemporaines". In *Histoire générale des techniques, tome 5: Les Techniques de la civilisation industrielle—Transformation, communication, facteurs humains,* edited by M. Daumas. Paris: Presses Universitaires de France: 434–72.
Davenport, T.H., and J.E. Short. 1990. "The New Industrial Engineering: Information Technology and Business Process Redesign". *Sloan Management Review* 11 (Summer): 11–23.
David, P. 1985. "Clio and the Economics of QWERTY". *American Economic Review* 75:332–37.
Davies, A.E. 1953. "Banking by Electronics". In *The Institute of Bankers in Scotland Lectures, 1953–1954.* Edinburgh: The Institute of Bankers in Scotland: 5–21.
Davies, G. 1994. *A History of Money: From Ancient Times to the Present Day.* Cardiff: University of Wales Press.
Degos, J.G. 1998. *Histoire de la comptabilité.* Paris: Presses universitaires de France.
Dennis, M.A. 1987. "Accounting for Research: New Histories of Corporate Laboratories and the Social History of American Science". *Social Studies of Science* 17:479–518.
Der neue Teismann. Der rechte Hand des Kaufmanns. 1960. 32 ed. Essen: W. Girardet-Verlag.
Dewett, T., and G.R. Jones. 2001. "The Role of Information Technology in the Organization: A Review, Model, and Assessment". *Journal of Management* 27:313–46.

Dottelongue, P., and C. Malaval. 1996. *Caisse centrale des Banques populaires, 1921–1996. 75 ans d'histoire*. Paris: ClioMedia.

Dow, J.C.R. 1964. *The Management of the British Economy, 1945–60*. Cambridge: Cambridge University Press.

Dunne, P., and R. Smith. 1992. "Thatcherism and the UK Defence Industry". In *The Economic Legacy, 1979–1992*, edited by J. Michie. London: Academic Press: 91–112.

Eagleton, C., and J. Williams. 2007. *Money: A History*. Buffalo, NY: Firefly Books.

Edgerton, D. 1991a. *England and the Aeroplane: An Essay on a Militant and Technological Nation*. London: Macmillan.

———. 1991b. "Liberal Militarism and the British State". *New Left Review* 185:138–69.

———. 1991c. "The Prophet Militant and Industrial: The Peculiarities of Correlli Barnett". *Twentieth Century British History* 2:359–79.

———. 1996a. *Science, Technology and the British Industrial 'Decline', 1870–1970*. Cambridge: Cambridge University Press.

———. 1996b. "The 'White Heat' Revisited: The British Government and Technology in the 1960s". *Twentieth Century British History* 7:53–82.

———. 2005. *Warfare State: Britain, 1920–1970*. Cambridge: Cambridge University Press.

———. 2006. *The Shock of the Old: Technology and Global History since 1900*. London: Profile Books.

Einzig, P. 1966. *Primitive Money in its Ethnological, Historical and Economic Aspects*. Oxford: Pergamon.

Ellgering, I. 2001. "Von der Buchungsmaschine zur virtuellen Bank". In *Technik und Management in der Sparkassen-Finanzgruppe, Sparkassenhistorisches Symposium 2000*, edited by Wissenschaftsförderung der Sparkassenorganisation. Stuttgart: Deutscher Sparkassenverlag: 95–111.

Ellis, H.F. 1962. "Give Me Back My Ledger". *Punch*, 14 March, 430–32.

Engelbourg, S. 1976. *International Business Machines. A Business History*. New York: Arno Press.

Espinosa Yglesias, M. 2000. *Bancomer. Logro y destrucción de un ideal*. Mexico City: Editorial Planeta.

Evans, D., and R. Schmalensee. 1999. *Paying with Plastic: The Digital Revolution in Buying and Borrowing*. Cambridge, MA: MIT Press.

Fair, W.R. 1991. "Inform History". Unfinished memo, Saturday, 27 April (collection of the author: M. Poon).

Fair Isaac & Company Incorporated. 1977. "History of Fair Isaac and Co.". (Collection of the author: M. Poon.)

Fanjul, O., and F. Maravall. 1985. *La eficiencia del sistema bancario español*. Madrid: Alianza Universidad.

Fedida, S., and R. Malik. 1979. *The Viewdata Revolution*. New York: Halsted Press.

Ferry, G. 2003. *A Computer Called LEO: Lyons Tea Shops and the World's First Office Computer*. London: Harper Perennial.

Fincham, R., J. Fleck, R. Procter, H. Scarbrough, M. Tierney, and R. Williams. 1994. *Expertise and Innovation: Information Technology Strategies in the Financial Services Sector*. Oxford: Oxford University Press.

Fisher, A.W., and J.L. McKenney. 1993. "The Development of the ERMA Banking System: Lessons from History". *IEEE Annals of the History of Computing* 5, no. 1: 44–57.

Fleck, J. 2003. "Learning by Trying: The Implementation of Configurational Technology". In *The Social Shaping of Technology*, edited by D. MacKenzie and J. Wajcman. Maidenhead: Open University Press: 244–57.

Fortune, M., and S.S. Scheweber. 1993. "Scientists and the Legacy of World War II: The Case of Operations Research (OR)". *Social Studies of Science* 23:595–642.

Foster, R. 1962. "Electronic Data Processing". *TSB Gazette* XXX, no. 3 (June): 151–52.

Frazer, P. 1985. *Plastic and Electronic Money: New Payment Systems and Their Implications.* Cambridge: Woodhead-Faulkner.

Freyssenet, M. 2000. *Les systèmes productifs.* Paris: La Découverte.

Frost, R. 2009. *Wünsche warden Wirklichkeit. Die Deutsche Bank und ihr Privatkundengeschäft.* München: Piper Verlag.

Galison, P., and E. Thompson, eds. 1999. *The Architecture of Science.* Cambridge, MA: MIT Press.

Gall, L., G.D. Feldman, H. James, C.L. Holtfrerich, and H.E. Bushes. 1995. *Die Deutsche Bank 1870–1995.* Munich: Beck.

Garbade, K., and W. Silber. 1978. "Technology, Communication and the Performance of Financial Markets: 1840–1970". *Journal of Finance* 33, no. 3: 819–32.

Gardener, E.P.M., and P. Molyneux. 1990. *Changes in Western European Banking.* London: Unwin and Hyman.

Geisst, C. 2004. *Wall Street: A History, from Its Beginnings to the Fall of Enron.* Oxford: Oxford University Press.

Géry H. 1932. "Étude des machines et du matériel nécessaires à une organisation rationnelle des services de banques". *Banque* (March): 197–201.

Gieryn, T. 2002. "What Buildings Do". *Theory and Society* 31, no. 1: 35–74.

Goldring, M.S. 1953a. "Electronics and the Banks I—Could Computers Help". *The Banker* (January–December): 140–44.

———. 1953b. "Electronics and the Banks II—Costs of Electronic Accounting". *The Banker* (January–December): 205–8.

———. 1953c. "Electronics and the Banks III—Cheque-Sorting for Clearing". *The Banker* (January–December): 285–90.

Grimm, E. 1977. "London Town". *IBM THINK Magazine* (September–October): 40–45.

Guerriero-Wilson, R. 1998. *Disillusionment or New Opportunities? The Changing Nature of Work in Offices, Glasgow 1880–1914.* Aldershot: Ashgate.

———. 2008. "'The Machine Should Fit the Work': Organisation and Method and British Approaches to New Technology in Business". *History and Technology* 24:321–33.

Guerriero-Wilson, R., L. Heide, M. Kipping, C. Pahlberg, A. Tympas, and A. van den Bogaard. 2004. *Information System and Technology in Organisations and Society (ISTOS), Review Essay.* Unpublished manuscript.

Guseva, A. 2008. *Into the Red: The Birth of the Credit Card Market in Postcommunist Russia.* Stanford, CA: Stanford University Press.

Guseva, A., and A. Rona-Tas. 2001. "Uncertainty, Risk and Trust: Russian and American Credit Card Markets Compared". *American Sociological Review* 66, no. 5: 623–46.

H.L.W. 1954. "A Clearing House for Trustee Savings Banks". *TSB Gazette* XXIV, no. 1 (January): 6–9.

Haigh, T. 2001. "The Chromium-Plated Tabulator: Institutionalizing an Electronic Revolution, 1954–1958". *IEEE Annals of the History of Computing,* 23, no. 4: 75–104.

Hally, M. 2005. *Electronic Brains: Stories from the Dawn of the Computer Age.* London: Granta Books.

Hamilton, J.D. 1986. *Stockbroking Tomorrow.* London: MacMillan.

Hammer, J. 1958. *Problèmes d'organisation administrative dans la banque.* Paris: Les Cours de droit.

Harianto, F., and J.M. Pennings. 1988. *Technological Innovation through Inter-firm Linkages*. Working Paper of the Reginald H. Jones Center, WP 88-24, Philadelphia, PA, Reginald H. Jones Center, Wharton School, University of Pennsylvania.

Harmsen, D. M., G. Weib, and P. Georgieff. 1991. *Automation im Geldverkehr. Wirtschaftliche und soziale Auswirkungen*. Opladen: Westdeutscher Verlag.

Harris, J. 1990. "Enterprise and Welfare States: A Comparative Perspective". *Transactions of the Royal Historical Society (Fifth Series)* 40:175–95.

Hartley, K. 1996. "The Defence Economy". In *Britain in the 1970s: The Troubled Economy*, edited by R. Coopey and N. Woodward. London: UCL Press: 212–35.

Hayter, G.A. 1983. *The Stock Exchanges Integrated Data Network—A Service for the Securities Industry*. London: Online Publications.

———. 1984. "The New Market Machinery: System Strategies for a Changing Market Place". *Stock Exchange Quarterly* (December): 20–25.

Hedberg, B. 1976. *The Design and Impact of a Real-Time Computer System—A Case Study from a Swedish Commercial Bank*. Företagsekonomiska Institutionens Rapportserie 70 (Working paper series).

Heide, L. 1994. "Punched-Cards and Computer Applications in Denmark, 1911–1970", *History and Technology* 11:77–99.

———. 1996. *Hulkort- og edb i Danmark, 1911–1970*. Århus: Systime.

———. 2004. "Between Parent and 'Child': IBM and its German Subsidiary, 1910–1945". In *Multinationals in Dictatorships*, edited by P. Hansen and C. Kobrak. New York: Berghahn Books: 149–73.

———. 2009. *Punched Card Systems and the Early Information Explosion 1880–1945*. Baltimore, MD: The Johns Hopkins University Press.

Hemelaar, A., and H. Rudelsheim, eds. 1992. *Betalingsverkeer in Nederland; stand van zaken en perspectief*. Amsterdam: Het Financieele Dagblad.

Herrmann, C.C., and J.F. Magee. 1953. "'Operations Research' for Management". *Harvard Business Review* (July–August): 100–112.

Hock, D. 2005. *One from Many: VISA and the Rise of Chaordic Organization*. San Francisco: Berrett-Koehler.

Hodder, H.G. 1934. *Principles of Bank Book-Keeping*. London: Isaac Pitman and Sons.

Hohn, H. 1964. *Die bargeldlose Lohnzahlung*. Düsseldorf: Verlag Handelsblatt.

Höpker, H., ed. 1997. *Die deutschen Sparkassen, ihre Entwicklung und Bedeutung*. Stuttgart: Deutscher Sparkassenverlag.

Horne, H.O. 1947. *A History of Savings Banks*. London: Oxford University Press.

Horvath, W.J. 1948. "Operations Research—A Scientific Basis for Executive Decisions". *American Statistician* 2, no. 5: 6–8, 18–19.

Hoschka, T.C. 1993. *Cross-Border Entry in European Financial Services: Determinants, Regulation and the Impact of Competition*. Oxford: St. Martin's Press.

Howells, J., and J. Hine, eds. 1993. *Innovative Banking: Competition and the Management of a New Networks Technology*. London: Routledge.

Hughes, M. 1971. "Shares Prices by Push Button Catch On". *Stock Exchange Journal*, 24–25.

Hughes, T. 1983. *Networks of Power: Electrification in Western Society, 1880–1930*. Baltimore, MD: The Johns Hopkins University Press.

Hunter, L.W., A. Bernhardt, K.L. Hughes, and E. Skuratowicz. 2001. "It's Not Just the ATMs: Technology, Firm Strategies, Jobs, and Earnings in Retail Banking". *Industrial and Labor Relations Review* 54, no. 2A: 402–24.

Hutchins, E. 1995. *Cognition in the Wild*. Cambridge, MA: MIT Press.

Institut für bankhistorische Forschung. 1984. *Deutsche Bankengeschichte*. Vols. 2 and 3. Frankfurt am Main: Knapp.

Joerges, B. 1999. "Do Politics Have Artifacts?" *Social Studies of Science* 29:411–31.

Jungerhem, S. 2000. *"Arbetskraft och konkurrenskraft i den svenska finansiella sektorn"*. *Bilaga 21, till Finansmarknadsutredningen*. Stockholm: Fritzes Förlag.

Kaiser, F. 1960. *Bargeldlose Lohnzahlung. Probleme, Erfahrungen, Möglichkeiten*. Neuwied: Verlag der Raiffeisendruckerei.

Kay, N.M. 2002. "Chandlerism in Post-War Europe: Strategy and Structural Change in France, Germany and the UK, 1950–1993: A Comment". *Industrial and Corporate Change* 11, no. 1: 189–97.

Keen, G. 1966. "Stock Exchange Computer One". *Stock Exchange Journal*, 12–13.

Keith, C., and A. Grody. 1988. "Electronic Automation at the New York Stock Exchange". In *Managing Innovation: Cases from the Services Industries*, edited by B. Guile and J.B. Quinn. Washington, DC: National Academy Press: 82–107.

Kipping, M. 2002. "Trapped in their Wave: the Evolution of Management Consultancies". In *Critical Consulting: New Perspectives on the Management Advice Industry*, edited by T. Clark and R. Fincham. Oxford: Blackwell: 28–49.

Kirkman, P. 1987. *Electronic Funds Transfer Systems: The Revolution in Cashless Banking and Payment Methods*. Oxford: Blackwell.

Kloevekorn, F. 1958. *100 Jahre Kreissparkasse Saarbrücken 1858 bis 1958*. Saarbrücken: Kreissparkasse.

Knorr-Cetina, K. 1981. *The Manufacture of Knowledge*. Oxford: Pergamon Press.

Körberg, I. 1987. "Bakgrunden till Spadabs bildande". In *Från fjäderpenna till microchip—den tekniska utvecklingen i sparbankerna*, edited by I. Körberg. Stockholm: Spadab: 69–78.

Kynaston, D. 2002. *The City of London: A Club No More 1945–2000*. London: Pimlico.

Larsson, M., and H. Sjögren. 1995. *Vägen till och från bankkrisen*. Stockholm: Carlssons.

Latour, B. 1987. *Science in Action: How to Follow Scientists and Engineers through Society*. Cambridge, MA: Harvard University Press.

———. 2008. "The Netz-Works of Greek Deductions". *Social Studies of Science* 38, no. 3: 441–59.

Latour, B., and S. Woolgar. 1979. *Laboratory Life: The Construction of Scientific Facts*. Princeton, NJ: Princeton University Press.

Lave, J. 1988. *Cognition in Practice: Mind, Mathematics and Culture in Everyday Life*: Cambridge: Cambridge University Press.

Law, J. 1987. "Technology and Heterogeneous Engineering: The Case of Portuguese Expansion". In *The Social Construction of Technological Systems: New Directions in the Sociology and History of Technology*, edited by W. Bijker, T. Hughes, and T. Pinch. Cambridge, MA: MIT Press: 111–134.

Law, J., and M. Callon. 1988. "Engineering and Sociology in a Military Aircraft Project: A Network Analysis of Technological Change". *Social Problems* 35, no. 3: 284–97.

Lean, T. 2008. "From Mechanical Brains to Microcomputers: Representations of the Computer in Britain 1948–1984". In *Science and Its Publics*, edited by A. Bell, S. Davies, and F. Mellor. Newcastle: Cambridge Scholars: 181–202.

Lelieveldt, S. 1989. "Elektronisch betalen goed geregeld? Een multidisciplinaire studie naar de inrichting van elektronisch betalen in Nederland". Afstudeer scriptie, University of Twente, Twente.

Levy, S. 2001. *Hackers: Heroes of the Computer Revolution*. London: Penguin.

Lewis, E. 1992. *An Introduction to Credit Scoring*. San Rafael, CA: Fair, Isaac and Co.

Leyshon, A., and N. Thrift. 1999. "Lists Come Alive: Electronic Systems of Knowledge and the Rise of Credit-Scoring in Retail Banking". *Economy and Society* 28, no. 3: 434–66.

Lijphart, A. 1968. *The Politics of Accommodation. Pluralism and Democracy in the Netherlands*. Berkeley: University of California Press.

Littler, C.R. 1978. "Understanding Taylorism". *British Journal of Sociology* 29, no. 2: 185–202.

Littlewood, J. 1998. *The Stock Market: 50 Years of Capitalism at Work*. London: Pitman Publishing.

Lowe, G. 1987. *Women in the Administrative Revolution. The Feminisation of Clerical Work*. Toronto: Toronto University Press.

Löwstedt, J. 1989. "Projektets bakgrund, syften och fallstudier". In *Organisation och teknikförändring*, edited by J. Löwstedt. Lund: Studentlitteratur: 59–85.

Lybeck, J.A. 1994. *Facit av finanskrisen*. Stockholm: SNS Förlag.

MacKenzie, D., and J. Wajcman, eds. 2003. *The Social Shaping of Technology*. Maidenhead: Open University Press.

Maixé-Altés, J.C. 2009. "Enterprise and Philanthropy: The Dilemma of Scottish Savings Banks in the Late Nineteenth Century". *Accounting, Business and Financial History* 19, no. 1: 39–59.

———. 2010. "Competition and Choice: Banks and Savings Banks in Spain". *Journal of Management History* 16, no. 1: 29–43.

———. Forthcoming. "Diversity in Banking Systems: France, Italy and Spain (19th and 20th Centuries)". In *Banking and Finance in the Mediterranean: A Historical Perspective*, edited by J. Consiglio, J.C. Martínez Oliva, and G. Tortella. Aldershot: Ashgate.

Maixé-Altés, J.C., and E. Iglesias. 2009. "Domestic Monetary Transfers and the Inland Bill of Exchange Markets in Spain, 1775–1885". *Journal of International Money and Finance* 28, no. 3: 496–521.

Maixé-Altés, J.C., M. Vilar, and E. Lindoso. 2003. *El Ahorro de los Gallegos. Orígenes e historia de Caixa Galicia (1876–2002)*. A Coruña: Fundación Caixa Galicia.

Malone, T.W., and J.F. Rockart. 1992. "Information Technology and the New Organization". Proceedings of the Twenty-Fifth Hawaii International Conference on System Sciences (HICSS '92), Koloa, HI, 9 January.

Malone, T.W., J. Yates, and R.I. Benjamin. 1987. "Electronic Markets and Electronic Hierarchies". *Communications of the ACM* 30, no. 6: 484–97.

Mandell, L. 1990. *The Credit Card Industry: A History*. Boston: Twayne.

Mann, R.J. 2006. *Charging Ahead: The Growth and Regulation of Payment Card Markets*. Cambridge: Cambridge University Press.

Marichal, C. 1997. "Obstacles to the Development of Financial Markets in Mexico". In *How Latin America Fell Behind?* edited by S. Haber. Stanford, CA: Stanford University Press: 118–45.

Marquardt, R. 2000. *Finansmarknad i förändring*. Stockholm: Svenska Bankföreningen.

Marron, D. 2007. "'Lending by Numbers': Credit Scoring and the Constitution of Risk within American Consumer Credit". *Economy and Society* 36, no. 1: 103–33.

Marshall, I. 1985. "Strategic Issues for the Trustees Savings Banks". *Long Range Planning* 18, no. 4: 39–43.

Martin, C.D. 1993. "The Myth of the Awesome Thinking Machine". *Communications of the ACM* 36, no. 4: 120–33.

Martín Tardío, J. 2010. *Albores y primeros pasos de la transmisión de datos en España, 1965–1974*. Available at http://www.telefonica.net/web2/jesustardio/Zips/Td.pdf (accessed 15 April 2010).

Marx, A., et al. 1961. *Monatliche bargeldlose Lohnzahlung—ein Vorteil für alle.* Frankfurt am Main: Verlag für Bürotechnik.

Mayer, M. 1997. *The Bankers—The Next Generation.* New York: Truman Talley Books/Plume.

McGoun, E. 2004. "Form, Function, and Finance: Architecture and Finance Theory". *Critical Perspectives on Accounting* 15, no. 8: 1085–1107.

McKenney, J,L. 1995. "Developing a Common Machine Language for Banking: The ABA Technical Subcommittee Story". *IEEE Annals of the History of Computing* 17, no. 4: 61–75.

McKenney, J.L., D.C. Copeland, and R.O. Mason. 1995. *Waves of Change: Business Evolution through Information Technology.* Boston: Harvard Business School Press.

McKenney, J.L., and A.W. Fisher. 1993. "Manufacturing the ERMA Banking System: Lessons from History". *IEEE Annals of the History of Computing* 15, no. 4: 7–26.

McKenney, J,L., R.O. Mason, and D.G. Copeland. 1997. "Bank of America: The Crest and Trough of Technological Leadership". *MIS Quarterly* 21 (September): 321–54.

McKenzie, D. 2006. *An Engine, Not a Camera. How Financial Models Shape Markets.* Cambridge, MA: MIT Press.

McRae, H., and F. Cairncross. 1973. *Capital City: London as a Financial Centre.* London: Eyre Methuen.

Medwick, P.A., and M.S. Mahoney. 1988. *Douglas Hartree and Early Computations in Quantum Mechanics. The History of Computing in the History of Technology*, Secaucus, NJ: Springer.

Meuleau, M. 1992. "Les HEC et l'évolution du management en France, 1881-années 1970". PhD dissertation, University Paris 10-Nanterre, Paris.

Meyer, D.R. 2006. *Network Machinist.* Baltimore, MD: The Johns Hopkins University Press.

Michie, R. 1999. *The London Stock Exchange: A History.* Oxford: Oxford University Press.

Milward, A.S., and G. Brennan. 1996. *Britain's Place in the World: A Historical Enquiry into Import Controls, 1945–60.* London: Routledge.

Minske, J. 1970. "Eine gute Verbindung. Automatisierte Datenverarbeitung bei der Dresdner Bank AG". *Data Report* 5:14ff.

Mirowski, P. 1999. "Cyborg Agonistes: Economics Meets Operations Research in Mid-Century". *Social Studies of Science* 29, no. 5: 685–718.

Misa, T.J. 1994. "Retrieving Sociotechnical Change". In *Does Technology Drive History?: The Dilemma of Technological Determinism*, edited by M.R. Smith and L. Marx. Cambridge, MA: MIT Press: 114–41.

Montréer, G. Le. 1928. *La "rationalisation" des banques en Allemagne.* Paris: Dalloz.

Mooij, J., and T. Dongelmans. 2004. *Mogen wij even afrekenen? Twee eeuwen betalen in Nederland.* Amsterdam: Boom.

Mooij, J., and H. Prast. 2003. "A Brief History of the Institutional Design of Banking Supervision in the Netherlands". In *Banking Supervision and the Crossroads*, edited by T. Kuppens, H. Prast, and S. Wesseling. Cheltenham: Edward Elgar: 10–37.

Moss, M., and I. Russell. 1994. *An Invaluable Treasure: A History of the TSB.* London: Weidenfeld and Nicolson.

Moss, M., and A. Slaven. 1992. *From Ledger Book to Laser Beam: A History of the TSB in Scotland from 1810 to 1990.* Edinburgh: TSB Bank Scotland.

Mottershead, P. 1978. "Industrial Policy". In *British Economic Policy 1960–74*, edited by F.T. Blackaby. Cambridge: Cambridge University Press: 418–83.

Mounier-Kühn P. 1989. "Bull, a Worldwide Company Born in Europe". *IEEE Annals of the History of Computing* 41:279–98.

Mura, J. 1995. *Entwicklungslinien der deutschen Sparkassengeschichte*. Stuttgart: Deutscher Sparkassenverlag.

Murillo, J.A. 2005. "La banca después de la privatización. Auge, crisis y reordenamiento". In *Cuando el Estado se hizo banquero. Consecuencias de la nacionalización bancaria*, edited by G. del Angel, C. Bazdresch, and F. Suarez. Mexico City: Fondo de Cultura Económica: 247–90.

Murphy, M. 2002. *Organisational Change and Firm Performance*. STI Working Paper 2002/14, OECD.

Nehberg, K. 1963. *Der Sparverkehr der Sparkassen*. Stuttgart: Deutscher Sparkassenverlag.

Nerheim, G., and H.W. Nordvik. 1986. *'Ikke bare maskiner'. Historien om IBM i Norge 1935–1985*. Oslo: Universitetsforlaget.

Nightingale, P., and R. Poll. 2000. "Innovation in Investment Banking: The Dynamics of Control Systems within the Chandlerian Firm". *Industrial and Corporate Change* 9, no. 1: 113–41.

Nisbet, R., A. Tucker, and S. Wagg. 1990. *Money Matters: A Critical Look at Bank Architecture*. New York: McGraw-Hill.

Nocera, J. 1994. *A Piece of the Action: How the Middle Class Joined the Money Class*. New York: Simon and Schuster.

Omnès, C. 2003. "La mise en oeuvre de la rationalisation au Crédit lyonnais dans l'entre-deux-guerres". In *Le Crédit lyonnais, 1863–1996*, edited by B. Desjardins, M. Lescure, R. Nougaret, A. Plessis, and A. Straus. Geneva: Droz: 211–44.

O'Neil, M. 1973. "Charge-Card Networks Are Working". *ABA Banking Journal* 66, no. 3: 116ff.

Oost, E. van. 1999. "Toepassingen van computers: een nieuw avontuur". In *De opkomst van informatietechnologie in Nederland*, edited by E. van Oost, G. Aalberts, J. van den Ende, and H.W. Lintsen. The Hague: Ten Hagen en Stam: 136–59.

Oost, E. van, G. Aalberts, J. van den Ende, and H.W. Lintsen, eds. 1999. *De opkomst van de informatietechnologie in Nederland*. The Hague: Ten Hagen en Stam.

Oreskes, N. 1996. "Objectivity or Heroism? On the Invisibility of Women in Science". *Osiris* 11:87–113.

Oudshoorn, N., and T. Pinch, eds. 2005. *How Users Matter, the Co-Construction of Users and Technology*. Cambridge, MA: MIT Press.

Peekel, M., and J.W. Veluwenkamp. 1984. *Het girale betalingsverkeer in Nederland*. Amsterdam and Deventer: Postgiro-Rijkspostspaarbank.

Pennings, J.M. 1992. *Technological Innovation and Organisational Performance*. Working paper of the Reginald H. Jones Center, WP 92–06. Reginald H. Jones Center, Wharton School, University of Pennsylvania, Philadelphia.

Pennings, J.M., and F. Harianto. 1992. "The Diffusion of Technological Innovation in the Commercial Banking Industry". *Strategic Management Journal* 13, no. 29: 29–46.

Pimlott, B. 1992. *Harold Wilson*. London: HarperCollins.

Pinch, T. 2001. "Why You Go to a Piano Store to Buy a Synthesizer: Path Dependence and the Social Construction of Technology". In *Path Dependence and Creation*, edited by R. Garud and P. Karnoe. Mahwah, NJ: Lawrence Erlbaum Associates: 381–400.

Pineau R. 1928. "Application de la mécanographie dans la conservation des titres". *Banque*, 265–73.

Pohl, H. 2001. *Die rheinischen Sparkassen*. Stuttgart: Steiner.

Pohl, H., G. Schulz, and B. Rudolph. 2005. *Wirtschafts- und Sozialgeschichte der deutschen Sparkassen im 20. Jahrhundert*. Stuttgart: Deutscher Sparkassenverlag.

Poon, M. 2007. "Scorecards as Devices for Consumer Credit: The Case of Fair, Isaac & Company Incorporated". *Sociological Review* 55, no. 2: 284–306.

Poovey, M. 1998. *A History of the Modern Fact, Problems of Knowledge in the Sciences of Wealth and Society*. Chicago: University of Chicago Press.

Powell, W.W. 2001. "The Capitalist Firm in the Twenty-First Century: Emerging Patterns in Western Enterprise". In *The Twenty-First-Century Firm*, edited by P. DiMaggio. Princeton, NJ: Princeton University Press: 33–68.

Prais, S.J. 1981. *Productivity and Industrial Structure: A Statistical Study of Manufacturing Industry in Britain, Germany and the United States*. Cambridge: Cambridge University Press.

Raff, D.M.G. 2000. "Superstores and the Evolution of Firm Capabilities in American Bookselling". *Strategic Management Journal* 21:1043–59.

Raiffeisen, F.W. 1888. *Die Darlehnskassen-Vereine*. Düsseldorf: Neuwied (Druck und Verlag von Raiffeisen u. Cons.).

Rambow E. 1930. "Pourquoi et comment la Dresdner Bank a rationalisé ses services". *Banque* (November): 810–13.

Rannemo, A. 1987. "Spadab—25 år i sparbankernas tjänst". In *Från fjäderpenna till microchip—den tekniska utvecklingen i sparbankerna*, edited by I. Körberg. Stockholm: Spadab: 79–167.

Regini, M., J. Kitay, and M. Baethge, eds. 1999. *From Tellers to Sellers: Changing Employment Relations in Banks*. Cambridge, MA: MIT Press.

Revell, J. 1991. "Consecuencias de los cambios recientes en las cajas de ahorro de Europa occidental". *Papeles de Economía Española* 46:173–202.

Rietz, A.L. du. 2003. *Dynamics of the Internet—A Transformation Analysis of Banking and Finance*. Eskilstuna: Mälardalens högskola.

Robertson, F. 2005. "The Aesthetics of Authenticity: Printed Banknotes as Industrial Currency". *Technology and Culture* 46:31–50.

Rodgers, W. 1971. *L'empire IBM*. Paris: Robert-Laffont.

Ross, D.M. 2002. "Penny Banks in Glasgow, 1850–1914". *Financial History Review* 9:21–39.

Rowland, N.J., and T.F. Gieryn. 2008. "Transfer Troubles: Outsourcing Information Technology in Higher Education". In *Living in a Material World. Economic Sociology Meets Science and Technology Studies*, edited by T. Pinch and R. Swedberg. Cambridge, MA: MIT Press: 375–91.

Rudelsheim, H. 1989. "Banken met elkaar aan de slag voor ontwikkeling van het binnenlandse betalingsverkeer: dertig jaar overleg". In *Veertig jaar Nederlandse Bankiersvereniging 1949–1989*, edited by J.J.M. Schipper, R.J. Schotsman, and C.A.M. Wijtvliet. Amsterdam: NIBE: 134–50.

Sandal, K. 2004. "The Nordic Banking Crises in the Early 1990s—Resolution Methods and Fiscal Costs". In *The Norwegian Banking Crisis*, edited by T.G. Moe, J.A. Solheim, and B. Vale. Oslo: Norges bank: 77–115.

Saville, R. 1996. *Bank of Scotland: A History, 1695–1995*. Edinburgh: Edinburgh University Press.

Sawyer, B. c. 1992. *A Brief History of Fair Isaac*. Unpublished manuscript (collection of the author: M. Poon).

Schilte, E. 2009. *Menselijk kapitaal. Honderdtien jaar personeelsbeleid bij de Rabobank*. Utrecht: Rabobank.

Schmidt, H. 1960. *Die bargeldlose Lohn- und Gehaltszahlung*. Stuttgart: Deutscher Sparkassenverlag.

Schulz, G. 2001. "Der Sparkassenbetrieb bis in die fünfziger Jahre des 20. Jahrhunderts". In *Technik und Management in der Sparkassen-Finanzgruppe, Sparkassenhistorisches Symposium 2000*, edited by Wissenschaftsförderung der Sparkassenorganisation. Stuttgart: Deutscher Sparkassenverlag: 21–55.

Scranton, P. 1996. "The Significance of Spatial Theory for Business Historians". *Business and Economic History* 25, no. 1: 65–71.

Seward, G.H. 1904. "Mechanical Aids in Factory-Office Economy". *Engineering Magazine* 27 (July): 605–625.

Shapin, S. 1989. "The Invisible Technician". *American Scientist* LXXVII:554–63.

Sluyterman, K.E., J.J. Dankers, A.A.M. van der Linden, and Zanden, J.L. van. 1998. *Het coöperatieve alternatief. Honderd jaar Rabobank 1898–1998.* The Hague: Sdu Uitgevers.

Smith, C., J. Agar, and G. Schmidt, eds. 1998. *Making Space for Science: Territorial Themes in the Shaping of Knowledge.* New York: St. Martin's Press.

Smith, V. 1997. "New Forms of Work Organization". *Annual Review of Sociology* 23:315–39.

Sonnenschein, L.J.H.M. 1974. "De nieuw geautomatiseerde administratieve systemen voor de aangesloten banken". *Rabobant* 8:11–13.

Star, S.L. 1999. "The Ethnography of Infrastructure". *American Behavioral Scientist* 43:377–91.

Starke, W. 1982. "Sparkassenautomation". In: *Handwörterbuch der Sparkassen,* vol. 4, edited by Günther Flemming. Stuttgart: Deutscher Sparkassenverlag: 57–65.

Stearns, D. 2006. *In Plastic We Trust: Dependability and the Visa Payment System. Social Studies of Finance Working Paper, School of Social and Political Studies,* Edinburgh. Available at http://www.sociology.ed.ac.uk/finance/Papers/StearnsDIRC06.pdf (accessed 13 August 2010).

———. 2007. "'Think of it as Money': A History of the VISA Payment System, 1970–1984". PhD dissertation, University of Edinburgh.

Stiles, C.R. 1957. "Mechanisation". *TSB Gazette* XXVII, no. 3 (June): 99–105.

Stoneman, P. 1976. *Technological Diffusion and the Computer Revolution: The UK Experience.* Cambridge: Cambridge University Press.

Strom, S.H. 1992. *Beyond the Typewriter: Gender, Class, and the Origins of Modern American Office Work, 1900–1930.* Urbana: University of Illinois Press.

Stymne, B. 1989. *Information Technology and Competence Formation in the Swedish Service Sector.* Stockholm: Stockholm School of Economics.

Taylor, F.W.W. 1911. *Scientific Management.* New York: Harper and Brothers.

Thomas, W.A. 1973. *The Provincial Stock Exchanges.* Oxford: Frank Cass.

Thomes, P. 1996. "Sparen und Sparsamkeit im Nationalsozialismus—Gedanken zur Pervertierung einer Institution". *Zeitschrift für bayerische Sparkassengeschichte* 10:63–81.

———. 2008. *Da, wo Sie zu Hause sind. 150 Jahre Sparkasse Saarbrücken.* Saarbrücken: Sparkasse Saarbrücken.

Thomson, F.P. 1968. *Money in the Computer Age.* Oxford: Pergamon Press.

Tilly, C. 1991. "Reasons for the Continuing Growth of Part-Time Employment". *Monthly Labour Review* 114, no. 3: 10–18.

Tomlinson, J. 1994. *Government and the Enterprise since 1900.* Oxford: Oxford University Press.

———. 1997a. "Correlli Barnett's History: The Case of Marshall Aid". *Twentieth-Century British History* 8:228–38.

———. 1997b. *Democratic Socialism and Economic Policy: The Attlee Years, 1945–51.* Cambridge: Cambridge University Press.

———. 2004. *The Labour Governments, 1964–70. Volume 3: Economic Policy.* Manchester: Manchester University Press.

Torres, F. 2000. *Banquiers d'avenirs. Des Comptoirs d'escompte à la naissance de BNP Paribas.* Paris: Albin Michel.

Touchelay, B. 2005. "A l'origine du Plan comptable français des années 1930 aux années 1960, la volonté de contrôle d'un État dirigiste?" *Comptabilité, Contrôle, Audit* (July): 61–88.

———. 2008a. "De la mécanographie à l'informatique en France (années 1890-années 1960): la formation d'une nébuleuse propice aux transformations technologiques en marge de l'État". *Économie et Sociétés, Série Histoire Économique Quantitative*, AF 38, no. 3: 647–76.

———. 2008b. "La normalisation comptable en France. Un mariage de raison pendant l'Occupation". *Revue Française de Gestion* 188:383–401.

Touchelay, B., and P. Verheyde. 2009. *La genèse de la décision. Chiffres publics, chiffres privés dans la France du XXe siècle*. Pompignac-près-Bordeaux: Bière.

Travers, D.S. 1965. "The Actualities of Bank Automation". In *Automation in Banking*. London: The Institute of Bankers: 1–18.

Trueblood, B. 1990. *125 años de Banco Serfin*. Mexico City: Banca Serfin.

Turrent, E. 2000. *Historia del Banco de México. 1940–1946*. Mexico City: Banco de México.

Vargha, Z. 2009. "Technologies of Persuasion: Personal Selling and the Production of Markets in Consumer Finance". PhD dissertation, New York, Columbia University.

Vernay, J. 1989. "IBM France", IEEE *Annals of the History of Computing* 11, no. 4: 299–311.

Verran, H. 2001. *Science and an African Logic*. Chicago: University of Chicago Press.

Vries, Joh de. 1973. *De Coöperatieve Raiffeisen- en Boerenleenbanken in Nederland 1948–1973: van exponent tot component*. Utrecht: Rabobank.

Wallander, J. 1994. "Bankkrisen". In *Bankkrisen—Rapporter av Håkan Lindgren, Jan Wallander, Gustaf Sjöberg*, edited by J. Wallander. Stockholm: Bankkriskommittén: 67–180.

Walter, I. 1997. "Universal Banking: A Shareholder Value Perspective". *European Management Journal* 5, no. 4: 344–60.

Wardley, P. 2006. "Women, Mechanization and Cost-Savings in Twentieth Century British Banks and other Financial Institutions". Presented at the XIV International Economic History Conference, Helsinki, 21–25 August.

Warf, B., and S. Arias, eds. 2008. *The Spatial Turn: Interdisciplinary Perspectives*. London: Routledge.

Watkins, J. 1998. *Information Technology, Organisation and People—Transformation in the UK Retail Financial Services Sector*. London: Routledge.

Weatherford, J. 1997. *The History of Money*. New York: Three Rivers.

Wells, W. 2000. "Certificates and Computers: The Remaking of Wall Street, 1967 to 1971". *Business History Review* 74 (Summer): 193–235.

White, H. 2002. *Markets from Networks: Socioeconomic Models of Production*. Princeton, NJ: Princeton University Press.

Whittington, R., and M. Mayer. 2002. *European Corporation Strategy, Structure and Social Science*. Oxford: Oxford University Press.

Whittington, R., M. Meyer, and F. Curto. 1999. "Chandlerism in Post-War Europe: Strategy and Structural Change in France, Germany and the UK, 1950–1993". *Industrial and Corporate Change* 8, no. 3: 519–51.

Williams, R., and D. Edge. 1996. "The Social Shaping of Technology". *Research Policy* 25:856–99.

Wilson, H. 1964. *The New Britain: Labour's Plans Outlined by Harold Wilson*. Harmondsworth: Penguin.

———. 1971. *The Labour Government, 1964–70: A Personal Record*. London: Weidenfeld and Nicolson.

Winner, L. 1988. *The Whale and the Reactor*. Chicago: University of Chicago Press.

Winter, S.J., and S.L. Taylor. 2001. "The Role of Information Technology in the Transformation of Work". In *Information Technology and Organizational Transformation—History, Rhetoric and Practice*, edited by J. Yates and J. van Maanen. Thousand Oaks, CA: Sage Publications: 7–34.

Wissenschaftsförderung der Sparkassen organisation, ed. 1995a. *Europäische Sparkassengeschichte*. Stuttgart: Deutscher Sparkassenverlag.

Wissenschaftsförderung der Sparkassenorganisation, ed. 1995b. *Der Zahlungsverkehr der Sparkassenorganisation*. Stuttgart: Deutscher Sparkassenverlag.

Wit, D. de. 1994. *The Shaping of Automation. A Historical Analysis of the Interaction between Technology and Organization 1950–1985*. Hilversum: Verloren.

Wit, O. de. 1995. "Caught between Historical Experience and High Hopes: Automation at the Dutch Postal Cheque and Clearing Service, 1950–1965". *IEEE Annals of the History of Computing* 17, no. 2: 9–21.

———. 2008. "De convergentie van computertechnologie en telecommunicatie 1980–2000". In *De eeuw van de computer: de geschiedenis van de informatietechnologie in Nederland*, edited by A. van den Bogaard, H. Linster, F. Veraart, and O. de Wit. Deventer: Kluver bv: 214–36.

Wit, O. de, and J. van den Ende. 2000. "The Emergence of a New Regime: Business Management and Office Mechanisation in the Dutch Financial Sector in the 1920s", *Business History* 42, no. 2: 87–118.

Wit, W. de. 1991. "Review [Untitled]". *Journal of the Society of Architectural Historians* 50, no. 4: 450–52.

Wolf, H. 1983. *Betalen via de bank—van verleden tot heden. Serie Bank- en Effectenbedrijf* 18. Amsterdam and Deventer: Kluwer.

Womack, J.P., T. Daniel, and D. Roos. 1990. *The Machine that Changed the World*. New York: Rawson Associates.

Wonglimpiyarat, J. 2004. *Strategies of Competition in the Bank Card Business: Innovation Management in a Complex Economic Environment*. Brighton: Sussex Academic Press.

Woolgar, S., and G. Cooper. 1999. "Do Artefacts Have Ambivalence? Moses' Bridges, Winner's Bridges and Other Urban Legends in S&TS". *Social Studies of Science* 29, no. 3: 433–49.

Wootton, C., and B. Kemmerer. 2007. "The Emergence of Mechanical Accounting in the US, 1880–1930". *Accounting Historians Journal* 37:91–124.

Yates J. 1989. *Control through Communication: The Rise of System in American Management*. Baltimore, MD: The Johns Hopkins University Press.

———. 1993. "Co-Evolution of Information-Processing Technology and Use: Interaction between the Life Insurance and Tabulating Industries". *Business History Review* 67, no. 1: 1–51.

———. 1999. "The Structuring of Early Computer Use in Life Insurance". *Journal of Design History* 12, no. 1: 5–24.

———. 2005. *Structuring the Information Age: Life Insurance and Technology in the Twentieth Century*. Baltimore, MD: The Johns Hopkins University Press.

Zaegel, R.J. 1962. "Credit Scoring System". Paper presented at the Consumer Credit Symposium, The Consolidated Reporting Company, New York.

Zetti, D. 2007. "Handlungsreisen. James W. Cortadas The Digital Hand". *Nach Feierabend. Züricher Jahrbuch für Wissensgeschichte*, 155–60.

———. 2008. "Personal und Computer. Die Automation des Postscheckdienstes mit Computern, ein Projekt der Schweizer PTT". *Preprints zur Kulturgeschichte der Technik* 22, ETH Zürich. Available at: www.tg.ethz.ch/forschung/produkte/preprints.htm (accessed 26 July 2010).

Zijlmans, H.H.A. 1959. "Het boerenleenbankwezen in het betalingsverkeer". In *Landbouw en bankwezen: Opstellen uitgegeven ter gelegenheid van het zestig-jarig bestaan van de Coöperatieve Centrale Boerenleenbank te Eindhoven*, edited by H.W.J. Bosman. Eindhoven: s.n.: 123–42.

Zuboff, S. 1988. *In the Age of the Smart Machine—The Future of Work and Power*. New York: Basic Books.

Contributors

Joakim Appelquist holds a doctorate in ECONOMIC history from Lund University. His research focuses on the interaction between innovation, organizational change, and productivity. He has also worked for International Organization for Knowledge Economy and Enterprise Development (IKED), guiding national agencies on issues regarding monitoring and evaluation of research funding. Appelquist is currently working for the Swedish Governmental Agency for Innovation Systems (VINNOVA) as a programme manager in charge of the "Innovation System Research on R&D and Growth" research programme.

Bernardo Bátiz-Lazo read economics (at ITAM, Mexico, and Autónoma de Barcelona, Spain), history (Oxford), and received a doctorate in business administration (Manchester Business School). He has been studying financial markets and institutions since 1988.He joined Bangor University as Professor of Business History and Bank Management after appointments at Leicester, London South Bank, Open University, and Queen's University of Belfast. He combined full-time appointments with consulting and executive training in Europe, Asia, and Latin America.

Bernardo was elected to the council of the Association of Business Historians in 2008 and fellow of the Royal Historical Society in 2010. He is a member of the editorial board of traditional outlets of international stature in history (i.e. *Business History, Journal of Management History, Economic History of Developing Regions*), business and management (*International Journal of Bank Marketing, Quest—Indian Journal of Management and Research, Cuadernos de Gestión*), and edits a weekly report on new working papers in business, economic, and financial history (see http://lists.repec.org/mailman/listinfo/nep-his).

Mark Billings read economics (at Sheffield) and financial management (London). He was then admitted to the Institute of Chartered Accountants in England and Wales (ICAEW) in 1985. After several years in industry (which included posts at Peat, Marwick, Mitchell & Co., now KPMG, and financial controller of a Japanese investment bank) he joined academia at the School of Financial Studies and Law, Sheffield Hallam University in 1995. He was also a research assistant at City University Business (today Cass Business School) and after returning for some time to Sheffield Hallam he joined Nottingham University Business School in 2005.

He has published in a number of outlets of international standing and this includes noteworthy contributions and co-authored work with Forrest Capie (in *Business History*, *Financial History Review*, *Accounting, Business and Financial History*, and *European Review of Economic History*).

Hubert Bonin is professor in modern economic history at Sciences Po Bordeaux and a member of the GRETHA research centre at Bordeaux 4-Montesquieu University. He is a specialist of the history of services companies (Suez Canal company, colonial and overseas trading houses and their maritime affiliates) and moreover of French banking history (regional banks or Paris deposit and investment banks, with several monographs and a few handbooks). He is completing a large history of *Société générale* (from 1864 to the 1940s) in a few volumes (the first published in 2006). He has been responsible for the research programme *Ford in Europe* (1903–2003) and the programme *American Firms in Europe* and is taking part in several research projects in banking and business history along French, European, and Asian perspectives. He supervises about a dozen doctoral research students.

He is a member and treasurer of the Association francaise des Historiens Économistes and of the Société Francaise d'Histoire d'Outremer. He is also a member of the academic advisory council of the European Association for Banking and Financial History, and of the scientific committee of *Enterprise and Society*; and he has also been a member of the Council of the European Business History Association (2000–2007).

Alan Booth received a first-class degree in economic and social history from the University of Kent, where he later pursued a doctorate in the same area with a thesis entitled "The Timing and Content of Government Policies to Assist the Depressed Areas, 1920–1939". Since 2006 he has been Professor of History and Lead Academic at the School of Humanities and Social Sciences, University of Exeter, Cornwall Campus.

His major research interest is in twentieth-century British economic history, in both national and comparative frameworks, with particular emphasis on systems of production and work in the manufacturing and service sectors. He also has a strong teaching interest in patterns of economic, social, and political development since the 1800s, especially in the Far East.

Major recent publications since 2000 include *The British Economy in the Twentieth Century* (Basingstoke: Palgrave, 2001), *The Management of Technical Change: Automation in the UK and USA since 1950* (Basingstoke: Palgrave, 2007), and, with Joseph Melling, *Managing the Modern Workplace: Productivity, Politics and Workplace Culture in Post-War Britain* (Ashgate: Aldershot, 2008).

Gustavo A. del Angel Mobarak read economics (at ITAM, Mexico, and Pompeu Fabra, Spain), and received a doctorate in history (Stanford University). He is currently a professor of the Department of Economics at the Centro de Investigación y Docencia Económicas (CIDE). He has been Professeur Invité *Alfonso Reyes* at Universite de Paris III- Sorbonne Nouvelle (2006) and researcher at the Center for U.S.–Mexican Studies, University of California-San Diego (2000–2001), as well as consultant on rural financial services and director in Mexico for the CIDE–Ohio State University programme on rural finance. He is a member of the Mexican Academy of Sciences (since 2007) and non-executive director at Prodesarrollo Financiera del Sector Social and Development Alternatives Mexico.

His publications include *La experiencia Mexicana del seguro agropecuario* (Mexico City: CIDE: 2008); *BBVA-Bancomer. 75 Años* (Mexico City: Editorial El Equilibrista, 2007); *Cosechando progreso. 50 Años de FIRA* (Mexico City: Pinacoteca 2000; FIRA, 2004); with Carlos Bazdresch and Francisco Suárez Dávila, *Cuando el Estado se hizo banquero. Consecuencias de la nacionalización bancaria en México* (Mexico City: Fondo de Cultura Económica. Colección Lecturas del Trimestre, 2004); *La Banca en América Latina. Lecciones del pasado, retos al futuro* (Mexico City: CIDE, 2003).

Lars Heide is associate professor at the Centre for Business History at the Copenhagen Business School (CBS). Before joining CBS in 2000, he held managerial positions and fellowships at various universities and a museum. He has written and published extensively on development and application of information technology in various countries and its contribution to the development of society. He is the author of *Punched-card Systems and the Early Information Explosion* (Baltimore: John Hopkins University Press, 2009). He is currently studying computerization of air traffic control in Europe within the European Science Foundation (ESF) project The Emergence and Governance of Critical Transnational European Infrastructures.

J. Carles Maixé-Altés read both economics and history at the University of Barcelona, where he later received a doctorate in economic history (*cum laude*). His research interests include financial and banking history, and food trade. He was European Visiting Research Fellow at the University of Glasgow (2005) and Visiting Researcher at the University of Leicester

(2009). He is currently senior lecturer in economic history at the Department of Applied Economics, University of La Coruña.

His publications include *Comercio y banca en la Cataluña del siglo XVIII. La compañía Bensi & Merizano de Barcelona (1724–1750)* (A Coruña: Universidade de A Coruña, 1994); with E. Lindoso and M. Vilar, *El ahorro de los gallegos. Orígenes e historia de Caixa Galicia (1876–2002)* (A Coruña: Fundación Caixa Galicia, 2003); "Diversity in Banking Systems: France, Italy, and Spain (XIXth and XXth centuries)", in *Banking and Finance in the Mediterranean: A Historical Perspective*, ed. J. Consiglio, J.C. Martínez Oliva, and G. Tortella (Aldershot: Ashgate, forthcoming); as well as monographs in *Journal of International Money and Finance, Accounting, Business and Financial History, Journal of Management History, Revista de Historia Industrial, etc.*

Ian Martin is a lecturer at the Open University and a doctoral candidate at the Centre for the History of Science, Technology and Medicine, University of Manchester. His thesis is entitled "Centring the computer in the business of banking: Barclays bank and technological change, 1954–1974".

Joke Mooij studied Economic and Social History at the University of Groningen. She holds a PhD from Tilburg University and worked at the research department of *De Nederlandsche Bank* as a historian from 1988 to 2007. Since 2007, she has been company historian at Rabobank Nederland. In addition, she is a member of the Academic Advisory Council of the European Association for Banking and Financial History.

Her publications include "A History of International Financial Communications: The Netherlands since the 1850s", in *European Banking Overseas 19th and 20th Century*, ed. T. de Graaf et al. (Amsterdam: ABN AMRO Historical Archives, 2002); with H. Prast, "A Brief History of Institutional Design of Banking Supervision in the Netherlands", in *Banking Supervision at the Crossroads*, ed. T. Kuppens, H. Prast, and S. Wesseling (Cheltenham: Edgar Elgar, 2003). She has also published in *Financial History Review, Zeitschrift des Aachener Geschichtsvereins*, and *Journal of European Economic History*.

Juan Pablo Pardo-Guerra holds a PhD in Science and Technology Studies from the University of Edinburgh. He read physics at the Universidad Nacional Autonoma de Mexico (Mexico) and worked as a research assistant at El Colegio de Mexico. His research interests include the sociology of markets, the history of technology within the securities industry, and the dynamics of emerging technologies.

Martha Poon is completing dissertation work in the Science Studies Program at University of California, San Diego. Her research traces the history of the commercial credit scoring technology called a FICO score, innovated by the firm Fair, Isaac & Company Incorporated. She has been a visiting student at the CSI-ENSMP in Paris, as well as a visiting researcher at the Hagley Museum and Library in Wilmington, Delaware. She is currently located at the Center on Organizational Innovation-ISERP at Columbia University in New York. She has published in *The Sociological Review Monographs* and *Accounting, Organizations and Society.*

David Stearns received a doctorate from the University of Edinburgh in 2007. Since 2005 he has been a member of the Society for the History of Technology (SHOT).

He has worked as software developer at the Microsoft Corporation and chief software developer at Televisual Data Ltd. (Dundee, Scotland). He is currently an adjunct instructor of history at Seattle Pacific University and his forthcoming monograph on the history of Visa (1970–1984) will be published by Springer-Verlag.

Paul Thomes studied in Saarbrucken and Edinburgh. He received his doctorate in 1984, following his work on the history of the Prussian savings banks and a *Habilitation* in 1992, following his work on the economy of the early modern town. In 1993–1994 he was a department deputy at the Johann-Wolfgang-Goethe-University Frankfurt am Main. Since 1995, he has held the chair for economic and social history at RWTH Aachen University.

His major publications since 2000 include *1804–2004. 200 Jahre mitten in Europa. Die Geschichte der Industrie- und Handelskammer* (Aachen: Shaber, 2004); *Sparkassen und Banken im noerdlichen Rheinland 1789 bis 1913, in: Geschichtlicher Atlas der Rheinlande VII/16* (Bonn: Reiland, 2007); and *Da, wo Sie zu Hause sind. 150 Jahre Sparkasse Saarbruecken* (Saarbruecken Sparkasse Saarbruecken, 2008).

He is managerial editor of *Bankhistorisches Archiv. Banking and Finance in Historical Perspective*; *Scripta Mercaturae*; *grenzenlosLos*, Advisory Board of Revue belge d'histoire contemporain. He is a member of Gesellschaft fuer Sozial und Wirtschaftsgeschichte (board member), Institut fuer bankhistorische Forschung (board member), and Verein fuer Socialpolitik, Wirtschaftshistorischer Ausschuss.

Index

Printed in the United States
by Baker & Taylor Publisher Services